The Dialectics of Seeing

D0791761

The Dialectics of Seeing

Walter Benjamin and the Arcades Project

Susan Buck-Morss

The MIT Press   Cambridge, Massachusetts   London, England

Eighth, printing, 1999

First MIT Press paperback edition, 1991

© 1989 Susan Buck-Morss

All rights reserved. No part of this book may be reproduced in any form by any electronic or mechanical means (including photocopying, recording, or information storage and retrieval) without permission in writing from the publisher.

This book was set in Baskerville
by Asco Trade Typesetting Ltd., Hong Kong,
and printed and bound in the United States of America.

Library of Congress Cataloging-in-Publication Data

Buck-Morss, Susan.
  The dialectics of seeing: Walter Benjamin and the Arcades project/
Susan Buck-Morss.
    p. cm.—(Studies in contemporary German social thought)
  An English reconstruction and analysis of Benjamin's Passagen
-Werk.
  Bibliography: p.
  Includes index.
  ISBN 0-262-02268-0 (hardcover) 0-262-52164-4 (paperback)
  I. Benjamin, Walter, 1892–1940. Passagen-Werk. 2. Benjamin,
Walter, 1892–1940—Philosophy. 3. Benjamin, Walter, 1892–1940
—Political and social views. I. Benjamin, Walter, 1892–1940.
Passagen-Werk. English. 1989. II. Title. III. Series.
PT2603.E455P334   1989
944'.361081—dc19   89-30870
                                                     CIP

For Eric Siggia

Contents

Contents

Preface

This is an unorthodox undertaking. It is a picture book of philosophy, explicating the dialectics of seeing developed by Walter Benjamin, who took seriously the debris of mass culture as the source of philosophical truth. It draws its authority from a book that was never written, the *Passagen-Werk* (Arcades project), the unfinished, major project of Benjamin's mature years. Instead of a "work," he left us only a massive collection of notes on nineteenth-century industrial culture as it took form in Paris—and formed that city in turn. These notes consist of citations from a vast array of historical sources, which Benjamin filed with the barest minimum of commentary, and only the most general indications of how the fragments were eventually to have been arranged.

I have in the present study remained scrupulously close to the fragments of this never-written work. And yet it will be clear to anyone familiar with the *Passagen-Werk* that I have not reproduced it here but, rather, proceeded mimetically, extrapolating from it in order to illuminate the world that Benjamin experienced and described. I would be hard put to say whether this form of scholarship is a process of discovering the Arcades project, or inventing it. The reader is thus forewarned. What is given here is not an English-language summary of the original German and French manuscript. It is a different text, a story (of nineteenth-century Paris) told within a story (of Benjamin's own historical experience) with the goal of bringing to life the cognitive and political power of the *Passagen-Werk* that lies dormant within the layers of historical data of which it is composed.

But perhaps most of all, this is the story of the interpretive process itself. The meaning of Benjamin's commentary in the *Passagen-Werk* is cryptic. It provides the reader with few answers as to Benjamin's intent but many clues, and these point ineluctably beyond the text. Benjamin has simply not allowed us to write about his work as an isolated literary product. Rather (and this is no small part of its political power), the *Passagen-Werk* makes of us historical detectives even against our will, forcing us to become actively involved in the reconstruction of the work. It is only by acceding to the fact that his brilliant writing, which we are so predisposed to canonize, is really only a series of captions to the world outside the text, that we are able to make headway in penetrating the *Passagen-Werk*. He compels us to search for images of sociohistorical reality that are the key to unlocking the meaning of his commentary—just as that commentary is the key to their significance. But in the process, our attention has been redirected: Benjamin has surreptitiously left the spotlight, which now shines brightly on the sociohistorical phenomena themselves. Moreover (and this is the mark of his pedagogical success), he allows us the experience of feeling that we are discovering the political meaning of these phenomena on our own.

Benjamin described his work as a "Copernican revolution" in the practice of history writing. His aim was to destroy the mythic immediacy of the present, not by inserting it into a cultural continuum that affirms the present as its culmination, but by discovering that constellation of historical origins which has the power to explode history's "continuum." In the era of industrial culture, consciousness exists in a mythic, dream state, against which historical knowledge is the only antidote. But the particular kind of historical knowledge that is needed to free the present from myth is not easily uncovered. Discarded and forgotten, it lies buried within surviving culture, remaining invisible precisely because it was of so little use to those in power.

Benjamin's "Copernican revolution" completely strips "history" of its legitimating, ideological function. But if history is abandoned as a conceptual structure that deceptively transfigures the present, its cultural contents are redeemed as the source of critical knowledge that alone can place the present into question. Benjamin makes us aware that the transmission of culture (high and low), which is central to this rescue operation, is a political act of the highest import—not because culture in itself has the power to change the given, but because historical memory affects decisively the collective, political will for change. Indeed, it is its only nourishment.

Now, writing about the *Passagen-Werk* is exemplary of just the act of transmitting culture which Benjamin has problematized. This locates the present project in a highly charged conceptual space, one that will not tolerate too great a contradiction between form and content. And yet, I have found a certain degree of tension unavoidable. In form, this study is scholarly, adhering quite rigorously to the mandates of academic research, even as its content is a protest against academia's very understanding of culture. But I can see no politically justified reason for ceding to the latter a monopoly of philological rigor. Moreover, as the *Passagen-Werk* itself makes clear, the option of a short and popularly marketed summation of the *Passagen-Werk* would have in no way avoided the dangers of which Benjamin warned.

This book is long, and its argument is intricate. It demands effort on the part of the reader. Yet I have tried to ensure that such effort is not compounded by intellectual jargon that speaks only to those already initiated into the world of academic cults (among which the Benjamin "cult" now plays a leading role). The book requires no specialized disciplinary knowledge. It presupposes no particular philosophical background. It presumes only an openness to the proposition that the common, everyday objects of industrial culture have as much of value to teach us as that canon of cultural "treasures" which we have for so long been taught to revere.

I am grateful to the Andrew D. White Society for the Humanities of Cornell University for a fellowship that allowed me to begin this study of the *Passagen-Werk* in 1982–83. The *Deutsche Akademische Austauschdienst* generously provided support for research in Frankfurt am Main during the fall of 1984. Jürgen Habermas and Leo Löwenthal gave me encouragement when I needed it most. I have benefited immensely from discussions with friends in the United States, Germany, France, and the USSR: Hauke Brunkhorst, Jacques Derrida, Miriam Hansen, Axel Honneth, Claude Imbert, Martin Jay, Dmitri Khanin, Grant Kester, Burkhardt Lindner, Michael Löwy, Kirby Malone, Pierre Missac, Valery Podoroga, Gary Smith, Rolf Tiedemann, Heinz Wismann, and Irving Wohlfarth. Readings of the manuscript by Seyla Benhabib, Paul Breines, and Carol Halberstadt were enormously helpful, as was the research assistance of Leslie Gazaway, Dean Robinson, Schuyler Stevens, and Cynthia Witmann. Graduate students in a seminar on Benjamin in the spring of 1985 were inspirational: William Andriette, Paul Ford, Daniel Purdy, Kasian Tejapira, Jennifer Tiffany, Sharon Spitz, Michael Wilson, and Jiraporn Witayasakpan. The photography and art work of Michael Busch and Joan Sage are major contributions to this study, as is the camera work of Helen Kelley. Consultants and photographers who helped with the images include Ardai Baharmast, Grant Kester, Kirby Malone, Ro Malone, Danielle Morretti, Norma Moruzzi, Donna Squier, Leah Ulansey, and Rob Young. David Armstrong and Arline Blaker provided years of help in preparing the manuscript.

I thank Larry Cohen at The MIT Press for believing in the project. I appreciate his support.

A note on translations: Even when English translations of Benjamin are available, I have made my own, not always because I found the former to be lacking, but because in every case I have felt it necessary to make that judgment, and to benefit from the associations of meanings that come through more clearly in the original. Sometimes, however, the English translations are so artful that, out of respect for the talents of the translators, I have adhered strictly to their wording, and credited them by name.

Part I

Introduction

"We have," so says the illustrated guide to Paris from the year 1852, [providing] a complete picture of the city of the Seine and its environs, "repeatedly thought of the arcades as interior boulevards, like those they open onto. These passages, a new discovery of industrial luxury, are glass-covered, marble-walled walkways through entire blocks of buildings, the owners of which have joined together to engage in such a venture. Lining both sides of these walkways which receive their light from above are the most elegant of commodity shops, so that such an arcade is a city, a world in miniature."[1]

Comments Walter Benjamin: "This quotation is the *locus classicus* for the representation of the arcades [*Passagen*],"[2] which lent their name to his most daring intellectual project. The *Passagen-Werk* was to be a "materialist philosophy of history," constructed with "the utmost concreteness"[3] out of the historical material itself, the outdated remains of those nineteenth-century buildings, technologies, and commodities that were the precursors of his own era. As the "ur-phenomena" of modernity, they were to provide the material necessary for an interpretation of history's most recent configurations.

The Paris Passages built in the early nineteenth century were the origin of the modern commercial arcade. Surely these earliest, ur-shopping malls would seem a pitifully mundane site for philosophical inspiration. But it was precisely Benjamin's point to bridge the gap between everyday experience and traditional academic concerns, actually to achieve that phenomenological hermeneutics of the profane world which Heidegger only pretended.[4] Benjamin's goal was to take materialism so seriously that the his-

0.1 Passage Choiseul, Paris.

torical phenomena themselves were brought to speech. The project was to test "how 'concrete' one can be in connection with the history of philosophy."[5] Corsets, feather dusters, red and green-colored combs, old photographs, souvenir replicas of the Venus di Milo, collar buttons to shirts long since discarded—these battered historical survivors from the dawn of industrial culture that appeared together in the dying arcades as "a world of secret affinities"[6] *were* the philosophical ideas, as a constellation of concrete, historical referents. Moreover, as "political dynamite,"[7] such outdated products of mass culture were to provide a Marxist-revolutionary, political education for Benjamin's own generation of historical subjects, currently the victims of mass culture's more recent soporific effects. "[N]ever," wrote Benjamin to Gershom Scholem in the early stages of the project, "have I written with so much risk of failure."[8] "One will not be able to say of me that I have made things easy for myself."[9]

The Arcades "project" (as Benjamin most commonly referred to the *Passagen-Werk*),[10] was originally conceived as an essay of fifty pages.[11] But the "ever more puzzling, more intrusive face" of the project, "howling like some small beastie in my nights whenever I haven't let it drink from the most remote sources during the day,"[12] did not let its author off so easily. In order to bring it to the light of day—and "out of an all-too ostensible proximity to the Surrealist movement which could be fatal for me"[13]—Benjamin kept extending its ground and deepening its base, both spatially and temporally. Ultimately all of Paris was drawn in, from the heights of the Eiffel Tower to its nether world of catacombs and metros, and his research spanned more than a century of the city's most minute historical details.

Benjamin began the *Passagen-Werk* in 1927. Although there were interruptions, he worked on it intensively for thirteen years. The project was still unfinished in 1940 when, unsuccessful in his attempt to flee from France, he committed suicide. But from the originally planned, fifty-page essay there had grown an ensemble of material which, when published for the first time in 1982, numbered over a thousand pages. They consist of fragments of historical data gleaned primarily from the nineteenth- and twentieth-century sources Benjamin found in Berlin's Staatsbibliotek and Paris' Bibliothèque Nationale, and which he ordered chronologically in thirty-six files, or *Konvoluts*, each entitled with a key word or phrase. These fragments, embedded in Benjamin's commentary, comprise more than 900 pages. They are thematically only loosely arranged. To decipher their meaning we must rely on a series of notes (1927–29; 1934–35) that provide invaluable, if insufficient, evidence as to the overall conception that guided Benjamin's research, as well as the two "exposés" of the Arcades project (1935 and 1939) that describe briefly the contents of the intended chapters.

The posthumous publication of the *Passagen-Werk*, benefiting from the scrupulous editing of Rolf Tiedemann,[14] is an astoundingly rich and provocative collection of outlines, research notes, and fragmentary commentary. It demonstrates clearly that the Arcades project was the most significant undertaking of this very significant intellectual figure. But the *Passagen-Werk* itself does not exist—not even a first page, let alone a draft of the whole. This nonexistent text is the object of the present study.

Intellectual biographies have commonly spoken of Benjamin's thought in terms of three developmental, quasi-dialectical stages, describing the first (to 1924, when his friendship with Gershom Scholem was strongest) as metaphysical and theological, the second (when in Berlin during late Weimar he came under the influence of Bertolt Brecht) as Marxist and materialist, and the third (when in exile in Paris he was affiliated with the *Institut für Sozialforschung* and intellectually close to Theodor Adorno) as an attempt to sublate these two antithetical poles in an original synthesis. It was anticipated that the posthumous publication of the *Passagen-Werk* would be that synthesis, resolving the persistent ambiguities between the theological and materialist strands in his previously published works. The *Passagen-Werk* does indeed bring together all the sides of Benjamin's intellectual personality within one conception, forcing us to rethink his entire opus, including his early writings. It demonstrates, moreover, that he was not just a writer of brilliant but fragmentary aphorisms. The Arcades project develops a highly original philosophical method, one which might best be described as a dialectics of seeing.

Much of the secondary literature on Benjamin has been preoccupied with determining the influences (of Scholem, Brecht, or Adorno—or Bloch, Kracauer, even Heidegger) which were of most significance.[15] This study purposely avoids the convention of academic hermeneutics that defines the theories of one thinker in terms of the theories of another, as such a method ensures that the whole intellectual project becomes self-referential and idealist, hermetically sealed within precisely those musty corridors of academia from which Benjamin's work attempts to escape. It experiments with an alternative hermeneutic strategy more appropriate to his "dialectics of seeing," one that relies, rather, on the interpretive power of images that make conceptual points concretely, with reference to the world outside the text.

To the mind that would comprehend intellectual phenomena in terms of logical or chronological development wherein one thing leads to another, to use Benjamin's metaphor, "like the beads of a rosary,"[16] his work offers little satisfaction. It is grounded, rather, on philosophical intuitions sparked by cognitive experiences reaching as far back as childhood. These "develop" only in the sense that a photographic plate develops: time deepens definition and contrast, but the imprint of the image has been there from the start. In spite of the metamorphoses that his writing undergoes in style and form of expression, he held onto his philosophical intuitions tenaciously because, quite simply, he believed them to be true.

Where, then, to begin?

1

Temporal Origins

1

Origin [*Ursprung*], although a thoroughly historical category, nonetheless has nothing to do with beginnings [. . .]. The term origin does not mean the process of becoming of that which has emerged, but much more, that which emerges out of the process of becoming and disappearing. The origin stands in the flow of becoming as a whirlpool [. . .]; its rhythm is apparent only to a double insight.[1]

One can speak of the origin of the *Passagen-Werk* in the simple historical sense of the time and place it was conceived. But if "origin" is understood in Benjamin's own philosophical sense, as "that which emerges out of the process of becoming and disappearing," then the moment is arguably the summer of 1924, and the place is not Paris, but Italy. Benjamin had gone there alone, leaving his wife and six-year-old son in Berlin, in order to bring to paper his *Habilitationsschrift, Ursprung des deutschen Trauerspiels (The Origin of German Tragic Drama)*, with which he hoped to secure an academic position at the University of Frankfurt.

He stayed in Capri among Berlin friends, including Ernst Bloch. His marriage to Dora Pollak had for some time been in difficulty.[2] At thirty-two, he had not yet achieved economic independence from his parents, in whose Berlin household his own shaky finances still at times forced him to live. His father was an investor in innovative urban projects (including a department store and an ice-skating palace) with uneven success. Benjamin had a critical, indeed cynical evaluation of his parent's bourgeois existence, leading to "bitter arguments" with his father that "largely ruined" their relationship.[3] The chance for an academic position at Frankfurt was, he wrote to Gershom Scholem, his "last hope" for escaping "the increasingly gloomy atmosphere of the financial situation,"[4] made critical by Germany's astronomical inflation.[5]

As early as 1916, Benjamin had told Scholem that "he saw his future in a lectureship in philosophy," and the conception of his study on German *Trauerspiel* dates from this year.[6] Philosophical questions even then preoccupied Benjamin. But the canon of bourgeois philosophical texts in no way inspired his obedient respect. He made, Scholem recalls, "immoderate attacks on Kant," whose theory of experience he considered impoverished[7]; he was "repelled" by Hegel, whose "mental physiognomy" he called "that of an intellectual brute."[8] Nor did more recent philosophical debates capture his interest.[9] Shortly after he arrived in Italy, Benjamin attended an international congress for philosophy in celebration of the University of Naples' seventh centennial. It reinforced, he wrote to Scholem, his previous conviction (based not on Marxism, but on a more general criticism of culture) "that philosophers are the most superfluous, hence worst paid lackeys of the international bourgeoisie":

Nowhere did there appear to be a real concern with scholarly communication. As a result, the entire enterprise very soon fell into the hands of Cooks Tours, that provided the foreigners with countless "reduced-rate tours" in all directions through the countryside. On the second day I let the conference go its way and went to Vesuvius [. . .] and was yesterday in the splendid National Museum of Pompeii.[10]

Benjamin's choice in 1923 of Frankfurt as the place for his *Habilitation* was based less on hopes for intellectual collegiality[11] than on expediency. The Johann Wolfgang von Goethe Universität was new, liberal, and more open than most places for Jewish professors, and he had connections there. But one senses that in pursuing this possibility, Benjamin, more desperate than enthused, was going through the motions.[12] Granted, he enjoyed the isolated intensity of individual scholarship, and he had adopted many of the social formalities and private-familial living habits of the bourgeoisie in spite of himself. Moreover, given his idiosyncratic writing style and the academic nature of the topics he had thus far chosen to write about,[13] it was difficult to imagine him in anything but an academic profession. At issue was less the desirability than the *possibility* of traditional solutions. Benjamin believed that the bourgeois order was already undermined, and he clearly suspected that his life path was on quicksand. His mood is apparent in a short piece, later entitled "Imperial Panorama: A Tour of German Inflation," which was written while traveling in Germany in 1923.[14] It questions the viability of personal solutions of any kind, challenging attempts to claim for oneself a "special justification," given the "chaos" of the times, in which the phenomenon of bourgeois decline had become "stability itself"[15]:

The helpless fixation during the past decades on concepts of security and possession prevents the average German from perceiving the highly re- markable stabilities of an entirely new kind that underlie the present structure. Since the relative stability of the period before the war benefited him, he believed every condition that dispossessed him must, *eo ipso*, be regarded as unstable. But stable relations do not need to be pleasant rela- tions and earlier there were already millions for whom stabilized condi- tions amounted to stabilized wretchedness.[16]

The realm of private relations was not immune to the effects of inflation:

All more intimate personal relations are illuminated by the glare of an almost inhuman, piercing clarity in which they are scarcely able to sur- vive. Due to the fact that, on the one hand, money stands devastatingly in the center of all vital interests, yet on the other, precisely this is the barrier before which almost every human relationship breaks down, in both natu- ral and ethical relations, the sphere of unreflective trust, calmness, and health is increasingly disappearing.[17]

Benjamin gave this text to Gershom Scholem in the form of a scroll, on the occasion of the latter's emigration from Germany later that year. Referring to the almost Nietzschean pessimism hanging over the piece, Scholem recalled: "It was hard for me to understand what could keep a man who had written this in Germany,"[18] and he urged Benjamin to consider joining him in Palestine. Although Benjamin, sharing Scholem's interest in Judaic thought, was then comfortable expressing philosophy in theological terms,[19] and although he would later consider the proposal seriously, precisely in this year "in which the catastrophic development of inflation and the general breakdown of interpersonal relationships rendered the prospect of emigration acute for him," he "displayed an attitude of reserve toward Palestine [. . .]."[20]

Behind this reserve was Benjamin's awareness that his own creativity depended for its nourishment on the Europe that was disintegrating. What gave his philosophical intuitions a claim to truth was that they were embedded in his own historical experience, and addressed specifically to the generation that had shared them. That claim might indeed not survive a transplant to such radically different soil, nourished by a Zionism of which he was suspicious not only because of its nationalist particularism,[21] but because he saw in its "agricultural orientation"[22] an attempted escape, an artificial return to a preindustrial world. Contemporary historical reality was necessarily the philosopher's material, even if it now seemed to be leading him personally into a dead end.

2

These considerations determined Benjamin's state of mind in the summer of 1924, creating the specific constellation within which, without the author's yet being aware of it, the *Passagen-Werk* had its origins. There was a muse who presided over the moment. Like Ariadne, she promised to lead him out of the *cul de sac* that seemed to lie before him. But if her function befitted the antiquity of the Mediterranean world where they met, her means were the most modern: She was a Bolshevik from Latvia, active in postrevolutionary Soviet culture as an actress and director, and a member of the Communist Party since the Duma Revolution. In Benjamin's words, she was " 'an outstanding Communist,' " and " 'one of the most outstanding women I have ever met.' "[23] Her name was Asja Lacis. Beginning in June, Benjamin's letters to Scholem from Capri were full of "cryptic allusions," but Scholem was "able to put two and two together."[24] Benjamin was in love with her.

Asja Lacis has recalled in her memoirs their first meeting. She was in a shop to buy almonds and did not know the Italian word. Benjamin helped her by translating. He then came up to her on the piazza and asked if he could carry her packages, introducing himself with great bourgeois politeness. She recalled her first impression:

Eyeglasses that threw light like small spotlights, thick, dark hair, narrow nose, clumsy hands--the packages fell out of his hands. In brief, a solid intellectual, one from a well-to-do background. He accompanied me to the house, took his leave and asked if he might visit me [. . .].

He came back the very next day. I was in the kitchen (if this cubbyhole can be called a kitchen) and cooked spaghetti [. . .].

As we ate spaghetti, he said: "I have been noticing you for two weeks, how, in your white dresses, you and [your daughter] Daga who has such long legs, didn't walk across the piazza, but fluttered."[25]

Here is Benjamin's account to Scholem:

Right here much has happened [. . .] not the best for my work which it threatens to interrupt, perhaps also not the best for that bourgeois life-rhythm so indispensable for all work, but absolutely the best for a liberation of vitality and an intensive insight into the actuality of a radical Communism. I made the acquaintance of a Russian revolutionary from Riga [. . .].[26]

In retrospect, it might seem less surprising that Benjamin should have now experienced "an intensive insight into the actuality of a radical Communism" than the fact this had not happened sooner. Yet it was actually quite far from the anarcho-socialist politics of his earlier years in the *Jugendbewegung*, which rebelled against school and family rather than the economic system, and which called for social renewal as a generation rather than a class.[27] Benjamin had taken little political interest in the Bolshevik Revolution when it occurred,[28] even if he admired the conduct of left-wing German Communists during the war, particularly Karl Liebknecht's refusal to vote for war credits in the Reichstag.[29] He was bound to find intellectually barren and uninteresting the neo-Kantian, positivistic reception of Marxism that characterized the Social Democratic Party. And yet despite this, his persistent criticism of the bourgeois world in which he had been raised and which he now saw as in decline, touched close to the Marxist perception.[30]

Benjamin had always counted himself among the left-wing, indeed, radical intellectuals of his generation, but ever since his student days before the war, he had been skeptical of party politics, no matter what ilk. He wrote in 1913: "In the deepest sense, politics is choosing the lesser evil. Never does the Idea appear, always the Party."[31] Benjamin's resistance to active political participation had been a point of dispute with Ernst Bloch for as long as they had known each other, and Bloch, it will be remembered, was now with Benjamin on Capri. Given Benjamin's theological orientation in these early years, one might have expected he would have been sympathetic to Bloch's own Messianic interpretation of Marxism. But while he felt a kinship to elements of Bloch's thought, he could not accept the latter's totalizing fusion of empirical history and theological transcendence, Marx and the Apocalypse, and he read Bloch's *Geist der Utopie* (*Spirit of Utopia*) in 1919 with "impatience."[32]

The young Benjamin believed in the possibility of metaphysical knowledge of the objective world—"absolute" philosophical experience of truth as revelation[33]—and held that (against the basic tenet of idealism) it would not end up showing him his own reflection. He insisted that there was "'something perceptibly objective'" in history.[34] If he rejected from the start the Hegelian affirmation of history itself as meaningful,[35] he believed the meaning which lay within objects included their history most decisively.[36] Scholem reports that in 1916 Benjamin had on his desk

a Bavarian blue glazed tile, depicting a three-headed Christ; he told me that its enigmatic design fascinated him [. . .]. In the twenties he was apt to offer philosophical reflections as he brought forth a toy for his son [. . .]. In his room in Paris hung a tattoo artist's large pattern sheet [. . . of which he was] particularly proud.[37]

This quasi-magical cognitive attitude toward historical matter remained basic to Benjamin's understanding of materialism. Scholem recorded his "extreme formulation": "'A philosophy that does not include the possibility of soothsaying from coffee grounds and cannot explicate it cannot be a true philosophy.'"[38] As Bloch has commented, Benjamin proceeded "as if the world were language."[39] The objects were "mute." But their expressive (for Benjamin, "linguistic") potential became legible to the attentive philosopher who "named" them, translating this potential into the human language of words, and thereby bringing them to speech.[40] Marxism had no comparable theory of the language of objects. But what made Communism potentially more suited than theology for the task as Benjamin already understood it was that rather than turning its back on the realities of the present, Communism made precisely these its home, affirming the potential of present industrialism while criticizing its capitalist form, and thus grounding utopian thinking in actual historical conditions. Moreover, its universalism cut across the religious sectarianism of theology which, for all his appreciation of Judaism, Benjamin had never accepted.

In 1923 the redemptive moment in the otherwise profoundly gloomy piece, "Imperial Panorama: A Tour through German Inflation" was expressed theologically. Benjamin wrote that the sufferer of poverty and deprivation must "so discipline himself that his suffering becomes no longer the downhill road of hate, but the rising path of prayer."[41] This was the version Scholem received on the occasion of his emigration. When the piece was published in 1928, there had been a significant substitution: Now suffering is to become "no longer the downhill road of *grief*," but "the rising path of *revolt*"[42]—"minor revisions," states Scholem.[43] He is not totally wrong. Indeed, it is remarkable how little the structure of Benjamin's thought was altered in accommodating his "political radicalization."[44] But while Scholem means to demonstrate by this example the depth of Benjamin's commitment to (Judaic) theology, in fact it demonstrates how secondary for him was the theological formulation, compared to the philosophico-historical experience itself.[45] And, of course, the political implications of these "minor revisions" were profound.

Asja Lacis' work first raised for Benjamin the question: "What is the intelligentsia like in a country in which its employer is the proletariat? [. . .] What do intellectuals have to expect from a proletarian government?"[46] 1924 was the year of Lenin's death, when Soviet cultural life was still open to innovations. Lacis was part of the Communist Party's intellectual avant-garde, radical in aesthetic form as well as social content. In the year before their meeting she had worked with Brecht's Expressionist theater in Munich, and she would later become assistant to the "Agit-prop" director Erwin Piscator. Lacis saw her work as an integral part of the revolutionary transformation of society. As innovator of a proletarian children's theater, she designed a revolutionary pedagogy for children that was the antithesis of authoritarian indoctrination: Through their improvisational play on stage, children were to "teach and educate the attentive educators."[47] Such practices threw a critical light onto the musty halls of academia which Benjamin had been trying to convince himself to enter.

Work on the *Habilitationsschrift* was going slowly. In Capri he discussed it with Lacis, who recalled:

He was deep in work on *The Origin of German Tragic Drama*. When I learned from him that it had to do with an analysis of German Baroque tragedy of the seventeenth century, and that only a few specialists know this literature—these tragedies were never played—I made a face. Why busy oneself with dead literature? He was silent for a time, and then said: First I am bringing into the discipline of aesthetics a new terminology. In contemporary discussions of drama, the term tragedy and tragic drama are used indiscriminately, just as words. I show the fundamental difference between [them . . .]. The dramas of the Baroque express despair and contempt for the world—they are really sad plays.
[. . .]
Second, he said, his inquiry was not merely an academic piece of research; it had a direct connection to very actual problems of contemporary literature. He expressly emphasized that in his work he described Baroque plays in search of linguistic form as a phenomenon analogous to Expressionism. For that reason, so he said, I have handled the artistic problematic of allegory, emblem and ritual in such detail. Up to now the aestheticians have evaluated allegory as an art medium of second class. He wanted to prove that allegory was artistically a highly valued means, and more, it was a particular artistic form of understanding truth (*Wahrnehmen*).[48]

Despite Benjamin's defense (which, recounted by Lacis after the passing of half a century, is still one of the clearest summaries of the intent of his *Trauerspiel* study), her criticism hit its mark. Benjamin was having great difficulty writing the theoretical introduction to the piece, not only because of the distractions of being in love, but also because the "thematic restrictions" of the study were making it "awkward" for him to express his own thoughts.[49] Although he did complete a draft of the work by that fall, and was indeed quite pleased with the results[50] (which bear no trace of his new commitment to Communism), he began simultaneously to formulate a new writing project. It represented his response to what he called the "Communist signals" of that summer, which marked

[. . .] a turning point, awakening in me the will not, as before, to mask in an outmoded form the contemporary (*aktuell*) and political moments in my thinking, but to develop them, and to do this experimentally, in extreme form. Naturally this implies that what recedes is the literary exegesis of German literature [. . .].[51]

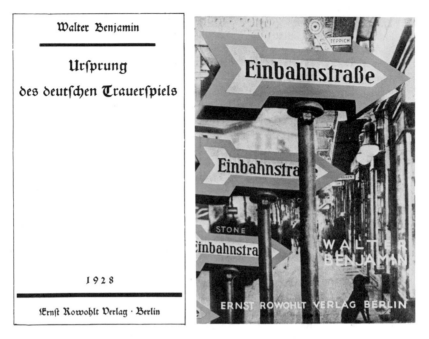

1.1 *The Origin of German Tragic Drama.*   **1.2** *One Way Street,* jacket design by Sasha Stone.

The new project, a "booklet for friends" of "my aphorisms, jokes, dreams,"[52] was written in short sections, many of which were published separately as fragments in daily newspapers. They appeared together in 1928 as *Einbahnstrasse (One Way Street)*, and included as possibly its earliest component the revised, politicized version of the 1923 fragment "Imperial Panorama: A Tour of German Inflation."

Work on this book of aphorisms not only overlapped the writing of his *Habilitationsschrift*, but undercut it. *One Way Street* describes the irretrievable passing of that world in which, with *The Origin of German Tragic Drama*, Benjamin was trying to make his mark. The methodological introduction of the *Trauerspiel* study, unabashedly abstract and esoteric, defines the form of the work as a "philosophical treatise."[53] The philosophical theory of "ideas" that it contains draws on the entire canon of traditional, academic philosophy, from Plato and Leibniz to Hermann Cohen and Max Scheler, and at the same time affirms "the topics of theology [. . .] without which truth cannot be thought."[54] Nothing could contrast more strongly than the opening section of *One Way Street*, which rejects the "pretentious, universal gesture of the book," denouncing as sterile any "literary activity [. . . that] takes place within a literary frame,"[55] and praises instead "leaflets, brochures, newspaper articles and placards" because only the "ready language" of these forms "shows itself capable of immediate effectiveness."[56] The opening section is named "Gas Station." It begins: "The construction of life at the moment lies far more in the power of facts than in convictions."[57] And it ends by stating that such convictions "are for the gigantic apparatus of social life what oil is for machines: you do not go up to a turbine and pour machine oil all over it. You spurt a bit of it in the hidden rivets and joints that you must know."[58] Between the *Trauerspiel* study and *One Way Street*, the author's understanding of his trade had changed from esoteric treatise writer to mechanical engineer.

3

In the *Trauerspiel* study, the abstractness of representation has the effect of sealing the reader within the text, that creates its own windowless world. As in the stuffy, upholstered bourgeois interiors of the nineteenth century, one is threatened with claustrophobia.[59] In contrast, the atmosphere of *One Way Street* has all the light, air, and permeability of the new architecture of Gropius or Corbusier. The outside world of gas stations, metros, traffic noises, and neon lights, which threatens to disrupt intellectual concentration, is incorporated into the text. These material substances rub against thought with a friction that generates cognitive sparks, illuminating the reader's own life–world. Gloomy descriptions of the decaying bourgeois order are juxtaposed with the most varied aphoristic observations: "In summer those who are fat attract attention, in winter, those who are thin."[60] "The Automobile Disease: [. . .] Its etiology: the secret wish to discover out of the general decline the quickest way to do oneself in."[61] "Genuine polemics takes a book in hand as lovingly as a cannibal prepares a baby."[62] "One complains about beggars in the South and forgets that their tenaciousness in front of one's nose is as justified as the obstinacy of the scholar before a difficult text."[63] All of these are assembled without regard for disparities of size and discontinuities in kind, like so many discrete pieces in a photomontage or a Cubist collage. In short, *One Way Street* represents an avant-garde, modernist aesthetics.[64]

But if the style of these two works is antithetical, the content of the old-fashioned work maintains a striking affinity to the new one. The *Trauerspiel* study attempts to "redeem" allegory theoretically. *One Way Street* does this practically, and transforms the meaning of redemption in the process. Not the allegorical object (tragic drama), but the allegorical practice is redeemed. In Baroque dramas, natural images—a dog, a stone, an old woman, a cypress tree—are emblematic representations of ideas.[65] In Benjamin's modernist fragments, images of the city and of commodities function similarly: a "filling station" (as we have seen) depicts the practical role of the intellectual. "Gloves" become the emblem for modern humanity's relation to its own animality.[66] Some titles hang like shop signs over their fragmentary contents ("Optician," "Stamp Shop," "Watches and Jewelry," "Dry Goods"); others are city commands for attention ("Caution, Steps!" "Begging and Loitering Forbidden!" "Post no Bills!" "Closed for Repairs!"), public warnings posted over what might otherwise be mistaken as private practices (writing, dreaming), while "Fire Alarm" is the warning sign over a discussion of revolutionary practice. *One Way Street* in no way mimics the stylized rhetoric and bombastic gestures of Baroque drama. It is not the desire to rehabilitate an arcane dramatic genre that motivates Benjamin,[67] but the desire to make allegory actual. The allegorical mode allows Benjamin to make visibly palpable the experience of a world in fragments, in which the passing of time means not progress but disintegration.

Parts of *One Way Street* are as sad and melancholy a commentary on the social state of things as any tragic drama, with cities in ruins,[68] social rituals empty,[69] the objects morbidly cold.[70] But there are others that recount moments of happiness—as a child, particularly, and as a lover—when, as fleeting instances of fulfillment, symbolic expression is demanded. If petrified nature and decaying objects provide the imagery adequate to allegory, the imagery of the symbol that would show fleeting matter in a redeeming light is (as the *Trauerspiel* study argued[71]) organic nature, active and live, and for that reason unalterably passing. On being in love:

1.3 Asja Lacis   **1.4** Dora Benjamin

Our feelings, dazzled, flutter like a flock of birds in the woman's radiance. And as birds seek protection in the leafy recesses of a tree, so our feelings take flight into the shaded wrinkles, the awkward gestures and invisible blemishes of the body we love, where they can lie low in safety.[72]

Recalling his own childhood experience of reading:

For a week you were wholly given up to the soft drift of the text that surrounded you as secretly, densely, and unceasingly as snowflakes. You entered it with limitless trust. The peacefulness of the book, that enticed you further and further! [. . . To the child] the hero's adventures can still be read in the swirl of letters like figures and messages in the drifting snowflakes. His breath is part of the air of the events narrated, and all the participants breathe with his life. He mingles with the characters far more closely than grown-ups do. He is unspeakably touched by the deeds, the words that are exchanged, and, when he gets up, is blanched over and over by the snow of his reading.[73]

Counterposed to the symbolic experience of reading, Benjamin describes the experience of writing in the mode of the allegorical: "The finished work is the deathmask of its conception."[74] Benjamin's point is that, whether it is expressed allegorically (as eternal passing) or symbolically (as fleeting eternity) temporality enters into every experience, not just abstractly as Heidegger would have it, as the "historicity" of Being, but concretely. That which is eternally true can thus only be captured in the transitory, material images of history itself. "[. . . T]ruth refuses (like a child or a woman who does not love us), facing the lens of writing while we crouch under the black cloth, to keep still and look amiable."[75]

Both *One Way Street* and *The Origin of German Tragic Drama* were published by Rowohlt in Berlin in January 1928. The dedication to *One Way Street*, like the title, expresses the irreversibility of history and the decisiveness of new events: "This street is named Asja Lacis Street after her who, like an engineer, cut it through the author."[76] But the dedication to *The Origin of German Tragic Drama* looks backwards and remembers:

Conceived in 1916. Written 1925.
Then, as now, dedicated to my wife.[77]

4

One year before these books were published, Benjamin formulated the earliest plans and notes for the *Passagen-Werk*. Observing that it contained the same "profane motifs" as *One Way Street* but in "fiendish intensification," he asserted that this project would close the "cycle of production" that had begun with *One Way Street*, just as the *Trauerspiel* study had completed the cycle on German literature.[78] Yet in the sense that we have just demonstrated, with the closing of the first "cycle," nothing essential to the theory of the *Trauerspiel* study had been left behind.[79] It has prompted us to look for the origins of the Arcades project at the historical moment when the two "cycles" overlapped, and to examine in some detail the two works that allegedly divide them. Applying Benjamin's definition of origins not to the literary genre of the tragic drama but to his own literary production, the *Passagen-Werk* emerged in the eddy between two antithetical movements, the disappearing, "outmoded form" of the *Trauerspiel* study and the bourgeois intellectual world which it represented on the one hand, and Benjamin's new avant-garde literary attitude and political commitment to Marxism that determined the "process of becoming" on the other. This was, as Scholem writes, "exactly in keeping with his true convictions, which at no time permitted him to write finis to an old way of thinking and to start a new one from a fresh Archimedean point."[80]

While surely in keeping with his character, Benjamin's position was philosophically ambiguous. The irreversibility of time and the consequence of inexorable decay that determines *One Way Street*—indeed, the concept of the temporality of truth generally—would seem to be in conflict with the *Trauerspiel* study's metaphysical understanding of philosophy as the representation of eternal ideas, as if "constellations" of truth were impervious to precisely that transitoriness which was supposed to be truth's most fundamental quality. Put another way: If the historical transiency of the physical world is its truth, how is *meta*-physical speculation about it possible? Benjamin's answer was at this time a visual image: "Methodological relationship between the metaphysical investigation and the historical one: a stocking turned inside out."[81] The issue is not thereby resolved, and it is a question to which we will need to return.[82]

Surely the influence of Asja Lacis on Benjamin was as decisive as it was irreversible. She recalled that it included a definitive rejection of immigration to Palestine.

Once [on Capri] he brought with him a text book of the Hebrew language and said he was learning Hebrew. His friend Scholem had promised a secure existence for him there. I was speechless, and then came a sharp exchange: The path of thinking, progressive persons in their right senses leads to Moscow, not to Palestine. That Walter Benjamin did not go to Palestine, I can say rightly was my doing.[83]

At the very least, Lacis was telescoping the course of events, as Benjamin was never closer to immigrating to Palestine than four years after this "sharp exchange" (and one year after his trip to Moscow).[84] Ultimately, it would be the *Passagen-Werk*, not "the path to Moscow," that kept him in Europe. But the "liberation of vitality" that he experienced as a philosopher, a writer, and a human being clearly was her doing,[85] and for anyone who has known the creative intensity of the erotic and the political as a double awakening, wherein work and passion are not separate corners of life but fused intensely into one, the decisive significance of their relationship will come as no surprise.

Yet Benjamin did not make any hasty changes in his life course. He returned to Berlin, to his wife Dora and their son.[86] And he persisted in his attempt to secure a teaching post in Frankfurt. By April 1925, Benjamin had finished revising the *Trauerspiel* study. He knew that it challenged not a few of the shibboleths of academic tradition, and that its theoretical originality was risky. The introduction, he admitted, was "an extravagant *hutzpa*—namely, no more nor less than the prolegomena to a theory of knowledge"[87]— but his attempt was apparently totally in earnest, even if in judging optimistically the chances of success, he was, as Lacis later said, "naive."[88] He submitted the work in May. His committee could not find it in themselves to accept it, not because it was daring, but because, as one member said, he was "'unable, despite repeated efforts, to get any understandable meaning out of it.'"[89] Benjamin was advised to withdraw his petition for the *Habilitation*, rather than suffer the embarrassment of rejection. He did this, reluctantly, in September. The following spring he composed a new "preface" addressed to the University at Frankfurt (but sent to Scholem). He counted this among his "most successful pieces."[90] It consisted of these lines:

I should like to tell, for a second time, the fairy tale of Sleeping Beauty.

She slept in her thorn bush. And then, after so and so many years, she awoke.

But not by the kiss of a fortunate prince.

The cook woke her up, as he gave the young cook a box in the ears that resounded through the castle, ringing from the pent-up energy of so many years.

A beautiful child sleeps behind the thorny hedge of the following pages.

Just don't let any prince of fortune decked out in the dazzling equipment of knowledge come near it. For in the bridal kiss, it will snap at him.

Much better that the author should awaken it, reserving for himself the role of head cook. For too long the box in the ears has been due, that with its shrill ring would pierce through the halls of knowledge.

Then, too, would this poor truth awaken, that has pricked itself on the outmoded spindle as, forbiddenly, it thought to weave itself into the rattletrap chambers of a professor's gown.[91]

5

Academia was "outmoded." The long-slumbering truth of metaphysics that Benjamin as author felt himself competent to "awaken" would have to appear otherwise than in the forbidden academic gown. Was it so preposterous to search in a shopping mall for more appropriate attire? Ernst Bloch remembered showing

Benjamin his commentary on *One Way Street*: "Here was—so I wrote—a store-opening of philosophy [. . .] with the newest spring models of metaphysics in the show-window," and Benjamin was visibly pleased,[92] perhaps because fashion expresses emblematically the essence of a metaphysics of transiency. As Benjamin wrote in the *Passagen-Werk*: "the eternal is in every case far more the ruffle on a dress than an idea."[93] But, to "turn the stocking inside out" and see the problem from the sociohistorical position, leaving the world of academia meant that Benjamin would subject his intellectual production to the conditions of the marketplace, where fashion showed its other true face, as a reified, fetishized commodity and as class ideology. As a freelance writer, he had access to the mass media of radio and newspapers. Was it possible, despite capitalist form, to subvert these cultural apparatuses from within? The effect of technology on both work and leisure in the modern metropolis had been to shatter experience into fragments, and journalistic style reflected that fragmentation. Could montage as the formal principle of the new technology be used to reconstruct an experiential world so that it provided a coherence of vision necessary for philosophical reflection? And more, could the metropolis of consumption, the high ground of bourgeois-capitalist culture, be transformed from a world of mystifying enchantment into one of both metaphysical and political illumination? To answer these questions was the point of the Arcades project. Benjamin had, indeed, not made things easy on himself.

In the late 1920s, during the years Benjamin was formulating the themes of the *Passagen-Werk*, he lived erratically, traveling extensively in Europe. He returned to Naples (via Spain) in September 1925. That November he visited Asja Lacis in Riga, where she was (illegally) directing Communist theater. In early 1926 he was back in Berlin; in the spring he moved to Paris, where he saw Ernst Bloch almost every evening, during "a half year of true symbiosis."[94] The autumn found him once again in Berlin; at the year's end he traveled to Moscow to see Lacis. The next spring and summer (April–October 1927) he returned to Paris. There he again saw Scholem (who was just beginning research into Sabbatianism as a Kabbalist movement), and found his "sometimes somewhat ostentatious self-assurance" hard to take[95]; yet he did not discourage Scholem's efforts to secure for him a permanent academic position in Jerusalem. The earliest notes for an "essay" on the Paris Arcades date from this summer. In November, Benjamin was back in Berlin. In the spring of 1928, he seriously considered going to Jerusalem. He separated from his wife Dora in the summer; their slow and painful divorce dragged on for a year. For two months that winter he lived with Asja Lacis, who had come to Berlin in November to work in the film department of the Soviet Trade Mission. It was through her that he became part of Berlin's leftist theater circle, and met and befriended Bertolt Brecht. In the autumn of 1929, he traveled with Lacis to Frankfurt. They spent several days in the nearby Taunus mountains at Königstein, in "unforgettable," conversations with Max Horkheimer, Theodor Adorno, and Gretel Karplus that marked a "historic" turning point in Benjamin's own philosophical approach, the "end of an epoch of careless, archaic, nature-biased philosophizing."[96] It was to this small group that Benjamin read his early notes to the *Passagen-Werk*, and the group enthusiastically heralded it as a model of what the new epoch of philosophizing would become.

In 1930 Benjamin spoke of beginning a "new life."[97] The historical moment could not have been less auspicious. The crisis in world capitalism brought severe unemployment to Germany, threatening his own economic position. The political crisis that brought the Nazis to power destroyed it decisively. In March 1933, urged by Gretel Karplus, he left Germany permanently. He moved to Paris, and took up the Arcades project again, this time with extensive historical research in the Bibliothèque Nationale. Except for extended visits with Brecht in Svendborg, Denmark (and with his son and former wife in San Remo), Benjamin stayed in Paris, convinced that the Arcades project could only be completed there. But when the city fell to Hitler in 1940, he had no choice but to leave. Aided in securing an American visa by the exiled Frankfurt *Institut für Sozialforschung*, he made plans to join Adorno, Horkheimer, and the other Institute members in New York, and named a text on which he was working "Central Park," in anticipation of asylum there. But when he encountered problems crossing the border into Spain, Benjamin took his own life with an overdose of morphine. His research notes, two exposés of the Arcades project, and several series of conceptual notes (including those read at Königstein), were left behind in Paris, and survived. It is these which, first published in 1982, constitute the *Passagen-Werk*.

2

Spatial Origins

One only knows a spot once one has experienced it in as many dimensions as possible. You have to have approached a place from all four cardinal points if you want to take it in, and what's more, you also have to have left it from all these points. Otherwise it will quite unexpectedly cross your path three or four times before you are prepared to discover it.[1]

Underlying Benjamin's transient existence during the late 1920s and 1930s is a structure that locates the *Passagen-Werk* geographically, and lends it a spatial order. Rather than consisting of a simple "path to Moscow," this order incorporates all four points on the compass (display A). To the West is Paris, the origin of bourgeois society in the political-revolutionary sense; to the East, Moscow in the same sense marks its end. To the South, Naples locates the Mediterranean origins, the myth-enshrouded childhood of Western civilization; to the North, Berlin locates the myth-enshrouded childhood of the author himself.

The Arcades project is conceptually situated at the null point of

Display A

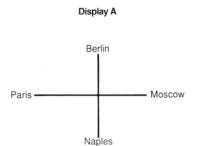

these two axes, the one indicating the advance of empirical history in terms of social and technological potential, the other defining history retrospectively as the ruins of an unfulfilled past. Not only schematically, but experientially, these four cities were decisive for the *Passagen-Werk*'s conception.

Naples

The *Passagen-Werk* would examine nineteenth-century neoclassicism as an ideological attempt to represent the unbroken pedigree of bourgeois civilization and the eternal verity of Western imperial domination. The historical disintegration visible in Italy's classical ruins challenged such mythical temporal claims, speaking instead of the transiency of empires. In 1924, Benjamin and Lacis toured these ruins.[2] But when they sat down to write an article together, it concerned a present-day process of decay. The article is a description of contemporary Naples, in which the central image of "porosity" (suggested by Lacis) captures the fact that the structuring boundaries of modern capitalism—between public and private, labor and leisure, personal and communal—have not yet been established: "Just as the living room reappears on the street [. . .] so the street migrates into the living room"[3]; "For sleeping and eating there is no prescribed hour, sometimes no place."[4] What Marxist theory conceptualizes as a transitional society appears here in images of spatial anarchy, social intermingling, and, above all, impermanence: "Building and activity interpenetrate [. . .]. Definition, imprint is avoided. No situation appears intended to last forever; no form claims to be 'so, and not otherwise.'"[5]

In the south of Italy, on the hollow and crumbling shell of the precapitalist order, modern social relations have been shakily, unevenly erected. Avoiding theoretical generalization, Benjamin presents this truth in the visual gesture of an anecdote:

In a bustling piazza a fat lady drops her fan. She looks about helplessly, too unshapely to pick it up herself. A cavalier appears and is prepared to perform this service for fifty lire. They negotiate and the lady receives her fan for ten.[6]

"Naples" speaks of the routinization of swindle and the professionalization of begging, expressions of the specifically capitalist form of Naples' underdevelopment, where "poverty and misery appear as contagious as they are pictured to be to children."[7] Benjamin and Lacis record the disorganization of the working class: "With the pawn shop and lotto, the state holds this proletariat in a vice: what it advances to them in one hand it takes back again with the other."[8] For this class, self-consciousness is less political than theatrical:

Even the most wretched person is sovereign in the double consciousness of playing a part in every corruption, every never-to-return image of Neapolitan street life, enjoying the leisure of their poverty, and following the grand panorama.[9]

Traditional life goes on, except now, as a tourist show, everything is done for money. Tours and replicas of the ruins of Pompeii are for sale[10]; natives perform the legendary eating of macaroni with their hands for tourists for a price.[11] Artists create their work in pastels on the street on which a few coins are tossed before feet erase it.[12] Cows are kept in five-story tenements.[13] Political events are turned into festivals.[14] One sees neither an ancient society nor a modern one, but an improvisatory culture released, and even nourished, by the city's rapid decay.

The essay "Naples" appeared in the *Frankfurter Zeitung* in 1926. It is to be compared with those articles that still comprise the "travel" section of Sunday newspapers. There is no lack of humor or entertainment. There is no explicit political message. Rather, hardly noticeable to the reader, an experiment is underway, how images, gathered by a person walking the streets of a city, can be interpreted against the grain of idealist literary style. The images are not subjective impressions, but objective expressions. The phenomena—buildings, human gestures, spatial arrangements— are "read" as a language in which a historically transient truth (and the truth of historical transiency) is expressed concretely, and the city's social formation becomes legible within perceived experience. This experiment would have central methodological import for the *Passagen-Werk*.

Moscow

At the turn of the year 1926–27, Benjamin traveled to Moscow. Shut out from conversation by his ignorance of the Russian language, he attempted to "see" the presence of the Revolution by the same kind of image analysis, the same sensory experience of temporality, that he and Lacis had employed in the essay on Naples. He explained his intent to Martin Buber, who had commissioned him to write an essay on "Moscow" for his journal *Die Kreatur*.

[...A]ll theory will be kept far from my presentation [...]. I want to present the city of Moscow at the present moment in such a way that "everything factual is already theory" [the citation is from Goethe], thereby refraining from all deductive abstraction, all prognosis, and even, within limits, all judgment [...].[15]

In the essay, the "concrete life-appearances" in Moscow that struck Benjamin most deeply are made to reveal "without theoretical excursus" their "internal position" in a political sense.[16] Like Naples, Moscow appears in transition, with elements of the village still playing "hide-and-seek"[17] with the city. But the transition is to socialism, so that the quality of transitoriness that in Naples lent to life the sense of theater, here places "each life, each day, each thought [...] on a laboratory table."[18] Whereas in Naples, transiency expressed the instability and precariousness of social outcomes left to fate, in Moscow the changing locations of offices and streetcar stops, and the incessant furniture rearrangements are self-conscious, underscoring society's "astonishing" experimentation, and an "unconditional readiness for mobilization."[19]

Nonetheless, Moscow's images are ambivalent. Begging exists only as a "corporation of the dying," having lost its "strongest base, society's bad conscience"[20]; but, simultaneously, the New Economic Policy (NEP) is creating a new monied class. If the Neapolitans sell their past to strangers, in Russia the proletarians themselves visit the museums, and feel at ease there.[21] Moscow's villagelike squares have not, as in Europe, been "profaned and destroyed" by monuments.[22] And yet icons of Lenin are sold as tourist replicas of the Revolution which, like religion before it, is in danger of becoming reified and dominating the people who created it.[23] The ambivalence of these images is evidence that it makes a difference which class rules—but that the future is not thereby guaranteed.[24]

Remarkable is Benjamin's sense of where the critical moment for the success of the Revolution lies. It is not in the realm of the production quotas, but in the juncture between political power and consumer power. Whereas under capitalism, "the market value of all power can be calculated" in terms of money, in Russia, by holding the NEP men apart from the Party, the Soviet state has "severed" the "convertibility of money into power."[25] This "one indispensable condition" will determine the Revolution's success:

[. . .] that never (as one day happened even to the Church) should a black market of power be opened. Should the European correlation of power and money penetrate Russia, too, then perhaps not the country, perhaps not even the Party, but Communism in Russia would be lost. People here have not yet developed European consumer concepts and consumer needs. The reasons for this are above all economic. Yet it is possible that in addition an astute Party stratagem is involved: to equal the level of consumption in Western Europe, the trial by fire of the Bolshevik-bureaucracy, at a freely chosen moment, steeled and with the absolute certainty of victory.[26]

Soviet society was undergoing "the conversion of the revolutionary effort into a technological effort," concerned most pressingly not with social change, but with "electrification, canal construction, the building of factories."[27] At the same time, and this is why Benjamin considers the Party's attitude toward mass consumption so crucial, the point of the revolution is social, not economic. Increasing the level of production is merely a means to the end of a society beyond scarcity that can fulfill not only material but aesthetic and communal needs. The vibrancy of collective fantasy is a crucial indicator of the healthy development of these needs. Limited to an analysis of nonlinguistic expressions, Benjamin finds this collective fantasy in an unofficial form of popular culture, namely, the non-essentials for sale from unlicensed vendors in the temporary stalls and markets that scatter color on the snow-covered city streets: paper fish, picture books, lacquered boxes, Christmas ornaments, personal photographs, confectionery delights, and more: "Shoe polish and writing materials, handkerchiefs, dolls' sleighs, swings for children, ladies' underwear, stuffed birds, clothes hangers [. . .]"[28]

Commodities here as elsewhere (like religious symbols in an earlier era) store the fantasy energy for social transformation in reified form. But the exigencies of socialist accumulation demand that this energy be displaced onto production, while consumption is indefinitely postponed. Moreover, the unofficial culture of Moscow's street markets, even as it expresses collective fantasy, does so largely in preindustrial form. Hence the new significance of artists, who are socially useful precisely as experimenters who discover the human and cultural potential within the new technology. Hence also the dilemma of the Party. Economic revolution is the prerequisite of the cultural revolution which is its goal, but in struggling to achieve the former the latter is neglected, or even repressed. In the Soviet Union, as economic planning takes precedence, official culture itself becomes reactionary.

It is now apparent in Russia that European values are being popularized in just the distorted, desolating form for which ultimately they have imperialism to thank. The second academic theater—a state-supported institute—is presenting a performance of the *Oresteia* in which a dusty Greek antiquity struts about the stage with as much phoniness as in a German court theater.[29]

Avant-garde experimentation is no longer encouraged:

Controversies regarding form still played a not inconsiderable role at the time of the civil war. Now they have fallen silent. And today the doctrine is official that subject matter, not form, decides the revolutionary or counter-revolutionary attitude [*Haltung*] of the work. Such doctrines cut the ground from under the feet of the literary producers [. . . T]he intellectual is above all a functionary, working in the departments of censorship, justice, finance, and, if he survives ruin, participating in the action—which, however, in Russia means power. He is a member of the ruling class.[30]

For two months (December 6–February 1), Benjamin observed Soviet cultural life, living in a Moscow hotel, his pension subsidized by the Soviet state.[31] He had come to Russia with the thought of commitment, to Asja Lacis and the Communist Party.[32] As his personal diary of the trip testifies,[33] both anticipations were disappointed. The artists and intellectuals with whom Benjamin came in contact were members of the left-cultural opposition who felt themselves caught in a double-bind, as commitment to the Party of revolution increasingly entailed the repression of what they saw as the intelligentsia's revolutionary work. One had, frustratingly, more freedom to develop the new technological forms in bourgeois centers (Berlin, Paris) that co-opted the results. The alternatives were power without freedom, or freedom without power. The potential of intellectuals to contribute to the creation of a truly socialist culture demanded both, and nowhere did they exist together. In his diary, Benjamin outlined the dilemma:

Within the Party: the enormous advantage of being able to project your own thoughts into something like a preestablished field of force. The admissibility of remaining outside the Party is in the final analysis determined by the question of whether or not one can adopt a marginal position to one's own tangible objective advantage without thereby going over to the side of the bourgeoisie or adversely affecting one's own work. [. . .] Whether or not my illegal incognito among bourgeois authors makes any sense. And whether, for the sake of my work, I should avoid certain extremes of "materialism" or seek to work out my disagreements with them within the Party.[34]

Although recognizing that not joining might be a mistake, Benjamin still felt himself drawn to an independent position "as a left-wing outsider"; he wondered whether such a position could be consolidated economically, "which would continue to grant me the possibility of producing extensively in what has so far been my sphere of work."[35]

Benjamin is reporting here a conversation he had, not with Lacis, but with Bernhard Reich, an Austrian dramatist who as a Communist had immigrated to Russia, but was now critical of the Party's cultural line.[36] Reich was not only Benjamin's source of entry into Soviet intellectual circles; he was romantically involved with Lacis, whom he married in later life. For most of Benjamin's stay (until she moved into Reich's apartment), Lacis was in a sanitorium, convalescing from a "nervous breakdown,"[37] and although she could leave in the daytime to be with Benjamin, their time alone together was limited. None of the three—Lacis, Reich, Benjamin—were monogamous in their relationships.[38] Yet the emotional painfulness of Benjamin's situation haunts his diary, even if his laconic account of events stops short of full explanations. Early in his visit, Benjamin told Lacis that he wanted to have a child with her.[39] But he held back, at times more than she. Their meetings lacked ease. They quarreled explosively, expressed affection tentatively. Benjamin communicated his emotions through the mediation of his writings; Lacis asserted her independence through political disagreements. Their affair remained suspended in a force field, as if a resolution of tension would be as compromising in the personal realm as in the political one.

Benjamin's interpretations of literary texts have been described critically as only allegories for his own lived experiences.[40] The matter may well be the reverse, that Benjamin perceived his own

life emblematically, as an allegory for social reality, and sensed
keenly that no individual could live a resolved or affirmative existence in a social world that was neither. The reader of Benjamin's
Moscow diary feels impatience (as one can discern Lacis did then).
Why was there not more of Jack Reed in this man's character; why
could he not commit himself in love and in politics? His last days in
Moscow were preoccupied with buying Russian toys for his collection. His last meeting with Asja was as indecisive as all the earlier
ones. His last words in the diary are these: "At first she seemed to
turn around as she walked away, then I lost sight of her. Holding
my large suitcase on my knees, I rode through the twilit streets to
the station in tears."[41] Was his impotence childish, or wise? Or was
it both?

Paris

At the beginning of his stay in Moscow, Benjamin wrote to Jula
Cohn: "[. . .V]arious circumstances make it likely that from now
on I will contribute substantial articles to Russian journals from
abroad, and it is possible that I might do considerable work for the
[*Great Soviet*] *Encyclopedia*."[42] He in fact completed one article for
the *Encyclopedia*, an entry on Goethe.[43] It is a clearly written, highly
original interpretation of the impact of class on the production, reception, and historical transmission of Goethe's work. But (ironically repeating the judgmental values of bourgeois academics) the
Soviet editorial board considered it too unorthodox, and ultimately
rejected it.[44] As Benjamin wrote to Hofmannsthal in June 1927:
"[. . .] I was able to observe [in Moscow] for myself just how
opportunistically it [the editorial board] vacillated between their
Marxist program of knowledge and their desire to gain some sort of
European prestige."[45]

Benjamin was writing from Paris, during an extended stay which
resulted in the earliest notes for the Arcades project. In part, they
were written collaboratively with Franz Hessel, Benjamin's Berlin
editor, also living in Paris, with whom he had been working for
several years on a translation of Proust's *Remembrance of Things
Past*.[46] In part, they were Benjamin's own notes, which soon began
to take on much larger proportions than the originally planned article. The latter notes particularly show the influence of Paris' most

avant-garde literary movement: Surrealism.[47] Benjamin recalled that the conception for the *Passagen-Werk* was inspired by reading Louis Aragon's Surrealist novel, *Le Paysan de Paris*, in which the Paris arcades figure centrally:

[. . .E]venings in bed I could not read more than a few words of it before my heartbeat got so strong I had to put the book down [. . .]. And in fact the first notes of the *Passagen* come from this time. Then came the Berlin years, in which the best part of my friendship with [Franz] Hessel was nourished by the *Passagen*-project in frequent conversations. From that time came the subtitle: A dialectical Fairy Scene.[48]

Benjamin's early notes[49] are fragments of commentary in which the great majority of the project's themes are stated in abbreviated fashion. They are assembled in no particular order: Arcades, fashion, boredom, kitsch, souvenirs, wax figures, gaslight, panoramas, iron construction, photography, prostitution, *Jugendstil*, flâneur, collector, gambling, streets, casings, department stores, metros, railroads, street signs, perspective, mirrors, catacombs, interiors, weather, world expositions, gateways, architecture, hashish, Marx, Haussmann, Saint-Simon, Grandville, Wiertz, Redon, Sue, Baudelaire, Proust. Central methodological concepts are also present in the notes: dream image, dream house, dreaming collective, ur-history, now-of-recognition, dialectical image.

The list itself suggests the Surrealists' fascination with urban phenomena, which they experienced both as something objective and as something dreamt. In 1927 Benjamin began to write an essay on Surrealism (published in 1929). At a time when the Communist Party was critical of the avant-garde,[50] this essay expresses Benjamin's enthusiasm for the "radical concept of freedom"[51] to which the Surrealists gave voice, and for their "profane illumination"[52] of the material world. They presented the "surrealist" face of Paris, "the center of this world of things and the most dreamed-of object,"[53] in images which had the psychic force of memory traces in the unconscious.[54] André Breton's novel *Nadja* (1928), Benjamin notes, is a book more about Paris than about the elusive heroine named in the title.[55] Breton includes photographs of Paris empty of people that mark the narrated events as if transient experience could be made present within the material space of cafés and streetcorners known to the reader. Louis Aragon's novel, *Le Paysan de Paris*, describes in detail one arcade, the Passage de l'Opera, just before this material space itself disappeared, torn down to build the Boulevard Haussmann. In both books the ephemeral quality of the material world is charged with meaning. The early *Passagen-Werk* notes speak of a "crossroads" in "the development of thinking" where, in regard to "the new gaze at the historical world," a decision must be made concerning "its reactionary or revolutionary evaluation. In this sense, the same thing is at work in Surrealism and Heidegger."[56]

At the same time, Benjamin's essay also criticizes the nihilistic anarchism of Surrealism, the lack of a constructive, dictatorial, and disciplined side to its thinking that could "bind revolt to the revolution."[57] The Surrealists recognized reality as a dream; the *Passagen-Werk* was to evoke history in order to awaken its readers from it. Hence the title for the Arcades project in this early stage: "a dialectical Fairy Scene." Benjamin was intending to tell the story of Sleeping Beauty once again.[58]

Berlin

From autumn 1928 to spring 1933, Benjamin spent most of his time in Berlin. In these last years of the Weimar Republic, he managed to eke out a living, working in his own "little writing factory,"[59] and he achieved considerable success.[60] He was a regular contributor (1926–29) to the Berlin literary journal *Literarische Welt*, which published his articles "almost weekly,"[61] while his contributions (1930–33) to the *Frankfurter Zeitung* averaged fifteen articles per year. Using the format of the book review, he turned these *feuilletons* into a forum for a politicized discussion of the literary writer's social situation.[62]

Even more innovative was Benjamin's work in the new mass medium of radio. In the years from 1927–33, radio stations in Frankfurt and Berlin broadcast eighty-four programs written and delivered by Benjamin.[63] These included a regular program for Berlin youth that drew on the common experience of the city, much as the novels of Aragon and Breton had drawn on their readers' common experience of Paris, as the context as well as the content of the story. But these programs were not fiction, nor was their style surreal. While entertaining and often humorous, they had a pedagogic purpose, to teach their young audiences to read both the urban landscape and the literary texts generated within it as expressions of social history. The politically critical stance of these shows is explicit. For example, at the close of a program entitled "The Bastille, the Old French State Prison," we are told: "All these things show how much the Bastille has been a tool of power, how little a means of justice."[64] But the programs are totally free of an authoritarian voice. Rather, the didactic message emerges effortlessly and disarmingly out of historical anecdotes, adventure stories, and biographies of literary figures. As storyteller, Benjamin seems to be in complicity with children—and also with the lower classes for whom education has traditionally been a lesson in intellectual humiliation. He comments in a program about Theodor Hosemann, a nineteenth-century lithographic illustrator of children's books:

Now, one would have thought that, out of pride, the Berlin populace would not have been able to let this artist alone, who portrayed their city in every small detail. But that was not at all the case. [. . .] The entire art of Hosemann seemed to them a bit common, not refined or learned enough. Right then they were troubling their heads over such aesthetic questions as: whether it is finer to paint historical pictures, great battles, and scenes of parliaments and inaugurations of kings, or so-called genre paintings [. . .] scenes from daily life, for example the portly monk who raises his wine glass, letting the sun shine through the wine and smiling contentedly, or a girl reading a love-letter, surprised by her father in the background, who looks in through a crack in the door [. . .]. But thank goodness there were others. The common people [das Volk] and the children. It was precisely for them that Hosemann labored.[65]

These programs affirm the intrinsically progressive, antielitist potential of radio as a medium of communication, capable of establishing a new form of folk culture.[66] They show the influence of Lacis' work with proletarian children's theater in their antiauthoritarian approach to political education. And they bear strongly the impact of his friendship with Brecht in their use of entertainment forms for didactic content.[67]

Together with Brecht, Benjamin planned a journal named *Krise und Kultur* (*Crisis and Culture*) which, without Party affiliation, was to serve as

[. . .] an organ in which experts from the bourgeois camp [he named Giedion, Kracauer, Korsch, Lukács, Marcuse, Musil, Piscator, Reich, Adorno, and others] should try to present the crisis in science and art

[. . .] with the purpose of demonstrating to the bourgeois intelligentsia that the methods of dialectical materialism are dictated by their own necessities [. . .]. The journal should serve as propaganda for dialectical materialism *through its application to questions that the bourgeois intelligentsia is compelled to acknowledge as their own.*[68]

Benjamin had indeed taken up the role of the "left-wing outsider" that he had contemplated in Moscow as a tempting alternative to Party membership.[69] He wrote to Scholem during a short visit to Paris in January 1930 that his goal was "to be considered as the best critic of [contemporary] German literature," which entailed "recreating" the genre of literary reviews.[70] Yet the conditions of cultural crisis that allowed Benjamin, however tenuously, to sustain himself as an outsider, allowed criticism from the Right to flourish as well. Benjamin's efforts had been to convince bourgeois intellectuals that their own objective interests compelled them to the side of the proletariat. Meanwhile, the proletariat was itself shifting sides.[71]

The Nazi slogan, "*Deutschland Erwache!*" ("Germany, Awaken!") urged something very different from Benjamin's conception, not awakening from recent history, but recapturing the past in a pseudo-historical sense, as myth. Hitler used the mass medium of radio to foster a political culture antithetical to that for which Benjamin was working. Fascism reversed the avant-garde practice of putting reality onto the stage, staging not only political spectacles but historical events, and thereby making "reality" itself theater. Moreover, this totalitarian inversion of the Left-cultural program was triumphant in terms of political success, as the Left was not. For Benjamin, who understood "self-reflection" not in the psychological, but the "historico-philosophical" sense,[72] these developments were experienced as a personal crisis. Against the backdrop of fascism, the pedagogic plan of the *Passagen-Werk*, a presentation of history that would *de*mythify the present, had become all the more urgent. He wrote to Scholem in 1930 that the Arcades project was still "the theater of all my struggles and all my ideas," necessitating, for a "firm scaffolding, a more serious theoretical grounding, "nothing less than a study of certain aspects of Hegel as well as certain parts of *Capital.*"[73] Benjamin was realizing how much work, and therefore time, the project would entail. For the left-wing intellectual "outsider," however, time was running out.

In the summer of 1931 and again in 1932,[74] Benjamin contemplated suicide. Asja Lacis had returned to Moscow in 1930; that same year his mother died; his divorce was final. If he claimed to be at peace with his subsequent loneliness—whether in his Berlin apartment with its two-thousand volume library or in a primitive summer house in Ibizza—he was weary of the financial "struggle for existence,"[75] which became increasingly arduous with fascism's rising strength. He wrote to Scholem in July 1932, of "success in the small things but failure in the large ones," among which he counted, centrally, the *"Paris Passagen."*[76] By 1933, even the "small things" could find no publisher, due to a sense of "terror regarding every stance or method of expression that does not conform totally to the official [fascist] one."[77] The political atmosphere in Berlin had grown stifling, allowing one "scarcely to breathe."[78] In January 1933, Benjamin broadcast his last radio program for youth. It was the story of an actual event, the flood on the Mississippi in 1927, an apparently "natural" disaster that was in fact caused by the state. In an attempt to save the port city of New Orleans, the United States government assumed emergency, dictatorial power and ordered the destruction of dams protecting miles of shore upstream, an act that led to an unanticipated degree of devastation of this agricultural region. Benjamin tells his young listeners the story of two brothers, farmers in Natchez, whose entire means of production were thereby destroyed, and who, stranded, climbed to their rooftop to escape the flood waters. As the river rose, one brother did not wait for death, but jumped into the water: "'Farewell, Louis! You see, it has taken too long. [...] I've had enough.'"[79] But the other, holding on until seen and rescued by a passing boat, lived to tell the story. The brothers personified two sides of Benjamin's own reaction to economic annihilation. In April 1931 he had described himself as "[...] a shipwrecked person adrift on the wreck, having climbed to the top of the mast which is already torn apart. But he has the chance from there to give a signal for his rescue."[80]

For seven years, until the next flood, it was the survivor in Benjamin's character who won out.

Arcades

The arcades that in the nineteenth century housed the first consumer dream worlds appeared in the twentieth as commodity graveyards, containing the refuse of a discarded past. The power of the arcades to evoke history for people of Benjamin's era was captured by Franz Hessel in his 1929 book, *Spazieren in Berlin* (*A Walk in Berlin*), which describes Berlin's *Kaisergalerie* (modeled after the Paris arcades):

I cannot enter it without a damp chill coming over me, without the fear that I might never find an exit. I am hardly past the shoeshine and newspaper stands under the lofty arches of the entrance, and I feel a mild confusion. A window promises me dancing daily and that Meyer without whom no party would be complete. But where is the entrance? Next to the ladies' hairdresser there is another display: stamps and those curiously named tools of the collector: adhesive pockets with guaranteed acid-free rubber, a perforation gauge made of celluloid. "Be sensible! Wear wool!" demands the next window of me [. . .]. I [. . .] almost stumbled over the peep shows, where one poor schoolboy stands, his school bag under his arm, wretched, immersed in the "scene in the Bedroom." [. . .]

I linger over [. . .] Knipp-Knapp cufflinks, which are certainly the best, and over the Diana air rifles, truly an honor to the goddess of the hunt. I shrink back before grinning skulls, the fierce liqueur glasses of a white bone cocktail set. The clowning face of a jockey, a handmade wooden nutcracker graces the end of the musical toilet paper holder [. . .].

The whole center of the arcade is empty. I rush quickly to the exit; I feel ghostly, hidden crowds of people from days gone by, who hug the walls with lustful glances at the tawdry jewelry, the clothing, the pictures [. . .]. At the exit, at the windows of the great travel agency, I breathe more easily; the street, freedom, the present![81]

The way the past confronted one in these neglected arcades as freely associated, long-forgotten images, was an external physical experience that paralleled the internal, mental experience of "involuntary memory" described in Proust's *Remembrance of Things Past*, which together Hessel and Benjamin had translated. In 1932, just after Benjamin had contemplated suicide, he wrote down fragmentary reminiscences of his own childhood in Berlin. These texts[82] occupy a middle position between Proust's personal memories and the collective history Benjamin intended to evoke in the Arcades project. Sparked by rooms in which he had lived, Proust's memories remain personal, locked in the private world of the bourgeois interior. Benjamin was concerned, rather, with how public space, the city of Berlin, had entered into his unconscious and, for all his protected, bourgeois upbringing, held sway over his imagination. Benjamin's recollections are of covered markets, desolate schoolrooms, rides to the railroad station, shopping excursions, skating rinks, student meetinghouses, brothel rooms, cafés, and, as a young child, the mythically charged *Tiergarten* with its stone lions, labyrinthine hedge, and Hercules Bridge. Associated with these public spaces, memories of his earliest class awareness and sexual awareness become part of a common, sociohistorical past; nothing pleased Benjamin more than Scholem's response that there were times reading them when he was able to come across his own childhood.[83]

Writing these reminiscences marked Benjamin's leavetaking of any homeland, and was in fact an explicit attempt to immunize himself against homesickness.[84] When he took up the Arcades project again in Paris in 1934, it had a "new face,"[85] more sociological, more scientific than the early notes he and Hessel had made, and was, of course, more remote from his own personal history than were the texts on Berlin. Yet he retained the notion that the Arcades project would present collective history as Proust had presented his own—not "life as it was," nor even life remembered, but life as it has been "forgotten."[86] Like dream images, urban objects, relics of the last century, were hieroglyphic clues to a forgotten past. Benjamin's goal was to interpret for his own generation these dream fetishes in which, in fossilized form, history's traces had survived. He wrote: "[. . . W]hat Proust experienced in the phenomenon of remembrance as an individual, we have to experience in regard to fashion."[87] And:

As Proust begins his life story with awakening, so must every work of history begin with awakening; indeed, it actually must be concerned with nothing else. This work is concerned with awakening from the nineteenth century.[88]

The covered shopping arcades of the nineteenth century were Benjamin's central image because they were the precise material replica of the internal consciousness, or rather, the *un*conscious of the dreaming collective. All of the errors of bourgeois consciousness could be found there (commodity fetishism, reification, the world as "inwardness"), as well as (in fashion, prostitution, gambling) all of its utopian dreams. Moreover, the arcades were the first international style of modern architecture, hence part of the lived experience of a worldwide, metropolitan generation. By the end of the

2.1 Galleria Principe, Naples.

nineteenth century, arcades had become the hallmark of a "modern" metropolis (as well as of Western imperial domination), and had been imitated throughout the world, from Cleveland to Istanbul, from Glasgow to Johannesburg, from Buenos Aires to Melbourne. And as Benjamin was well aware, they could be found in each of the cities that had become points of his intellectual compass: Naples, Moscow, Paris, Berlin.

2.2   GUM, Moscow.

2.3 Passage Choiseul, Paris.

2.4 Kaisergalerie, Berlin.

Part II

Introduction

1

We are ready to enter the *Passagen* material itself. The reader will protest that it is high time, suspecting the lengthy introduction has been a delaying tactic in order to avoid plunging into the real substance of the work. The reason for the delay has been the need to establish as a context both the personal and social history in which the project is embedded. This need is not *pro forma*. The *Passagen-Werk* is a double text. Ostensibly a social and cultural history of Paris in the nineteenth century, it is in fact intended to provide a political education for Benjamin's own generation. It is an "ur-history," a history of the *origins* of that present historical moment which, while remaining largely invisible, is the determining motivation for Benjamin's interest in the past. And although this second level will not be treated thematically until Part III, it is important for the reader to be aware of the nature of Benjamin's historical experiences from the start.

Now, it must not be forgotten that there is no *Passagen-Werk*. We are in a real sense confronting a void. The phenomenon to which the title applies, volume V of the *Gesammelte Schriften*, provides abundant traces of an intended work without being one. Yet in sheer quantity, this volume constitutes a sixth of Benjamin's intellectual production, and its fragments of research and commentary bear on that set of concerns that guided all of his mature thinking and writing. The documents published as the *Passagen-Werk* comprise no totality. Their coherence is in relation to the rest of Benjamin's work, from which they can be only artificially demarcated. Indeed, the *Passagen-Werk* material contributed directly to these other writings, even as the latter not infrequently affords us the clearest explanation as to the meaning of its fragmentary material. Display B is a chronological table that shows this interrelationship. The list of related essays is not exhaustive. (Ideas for countless minor pieces—reviews of contemporary literature, film, photography—were bor-

Display B

	Passagen-Werk		Related Works
		1923	Baudelaire translations "The Task of the Translator"
		1924	"Naples"
		1925	Proust translations
		1926	
	"Passages"	1927	"Moscow"
	"Paris Passages I" (A° series)	1928	One Way Street
Stage I	"Paris Passages II" (a° series)		The Origin of German Tragic Drama
	"The Ring of Saturn, or Something on Iron Construction"	1929	"Surrealism" "On the Image of Proust"
		1930	
			Hashish experiments
		1931	"Karl Kraus" "A Short History of Photography"
		1932	"Berlin Chronicle" "Berlin Childhood in 1900"
		1933	"On the Mimetic Faculty"
	Konvolut Stage I	1934	"The Author as Producer" "Kafka"
	Notes for 1935 exposé		
	1935 exposé	1935	"The Artwork in the Age of Technical Reproduction" (published 1936)
Stage II	Konvolut Stage II	1936	"The Storyteller"
		1937	"Edward Fuchs, Collector and Historian"
	Konvolut Stage III	1938	"The Paris of the Second Empire in Baudelaire" ("Central Park")
Stage III	1939 exposé	1939	"On Some Motifs in Baudelaire"
		1940	Theses "On the Concept of History"

rowed at times whole cloth from the *Passagen-Werk.*) But they represent Benjamin's major articles during the late twenties and thirties, and they are related to the *Passagen* complex as the visible tip of the iceberg of his intellectual activity.[1]

As the display indicates, it is possible to distinguish three stages of the Arcades project. Stage I (1926–29) resulted in (a) the short text, "Passages,"[2] which is "the only fully formulated and interconnected text" from the very early period of collaboration with Franz Hessel[3]; (b) fragmentary notes from 1927–29, organized by the editor as "Paris Passages I" (A° series) and the conceptually more developed "Paris Passages II (a° series), which articulate the motifs (e.g., boredom, dust, fashion, the nineteenth century as Hell), historical figures (Grandville, Fourier, Baudelaire, etc.), social types (whore, collector, gambler, flâneur), and cultural objects (particularly the arcades and their contents) that interested Benjamin for philosophico-historical reasons; and finally, (c) the short piece "Saturn's Rings, or Something on Iron Construction," the only "finished" pages of text.[4] Benjamin's original conception, a politicized version of Sleeping Beauty as a fairy tale of "awakening," retold along Marxist lines, was intended to "set free the huge powers of history that are asleep within the 'once upon a time' of classical historical narration."[5]

When Benjamin resumed work on the Arcades project in exile in 1934, he abandoned the title of "A Dialectical Fairy Scene" because it was "impermissibly poetic."[6] During 1934, he initiated Stage II by writing a series of twenty-two conceptual notes which, while not really breaking from the earliest conception, gave to it "new and intervening sociological perspectives."[7] He referred to the "strongly changed aspects" of the project,[8] and wrote that it was now "less a galvanization of the past than anticipatory of a more humane future."[9] These new notes resulted in the 1935 exposé of the project written for the Institute for Social Research,[10] with the new title: "Paris—The Capital of the Nineteenth Century." The shift that took place in 1934–35 involved a more self-conscious and deliberate attempt to ground the project in Marxist terms.[11] Benjamin wrote that the concept of "the fetish character of commodities" now stood "at the center."[12]

Stage III of the project (1937–40) was dominated by Benjamin's work on a book about the poet Charles Baudelaire, also commis-

sioned by the Institute. The latter received a version of the middle
section of the book in 1938, and rejected it; a rewritten section was
accepted in 1939. Both these versions drew so thoroughly from the
Passagen-Werk notes and commentary that it has been recently
argued the planned Baudelaire book supersedes the *Passagen-Werk*
completely.[13] Yet Benjamin continued to add to the other *Konvoluts*
right through to 1940, and he composed a new, modified French
version of the *Passagen-Werk* exposé in 1939.

It was during the second stage that Benjamin began his elaborate filing system. Working daily in Paris' Bibliothèque Nationale,
he read extensively in nineteenth-century sources,[14] directed by the
motifs of the early notes. The consequent amassing of annotated
research notes necessitated for purely practical reasons a fundamental reorganization. He set up a filing system wherein the early motifs became key words under which the relevant historical
documentation was assembled. These files are the *Konvoluts*. By
December 1934, Benjamin had copied many of the early notes into
this new key word system,[15] arranging them along with subsequent
research and commentary by means of a rigorous numbering code
(A1, 1...; A1a, 1...; A1, 2...etc.) His entries ultimately numbered in the thousands. Because the numbering is generally chronological, and because Benjamin on two occasions had the *Konvolut*
material photocopied, we can distinguish three periods of *Konvolut*
entries: early (before June 1935); middle (before December 1937);
and late (to May 1940).[16] A list of the key words of Benjamin's
filing system follows[17]:

Konvolut Title	Time Period of the Entries		
	early	middle	late
A. Arcades, Novelty shops, salesmen	A1–A5a	A6–A10a	A11–A13
B. Fashion	B1–B4a	B5–B7a	B9*–B10a
C. Ancient Paris, Catacombs, Demolitions, Ruin of Paris	C1–C3a	C4–C7a	C8–C9a
D. Boredom, Eternal Recurrence	D1–D2a	D3–D4a	D6*–D10a
E. Haussmannization, Barricade Fighting	E1–E6a	E7–E10a	E11–E14a
F. Iron Construction	F1–F4a	F5–F7a	F8–F8a

Konvolut Title	Time Period of the Entries		
	early	middle	late
G. Methods of Display, Advertising, Grandville	G1–G8a	G9–G14a	G15–G16a
H. The Collector	H1–H2a	H3–H3a	H4–H5
I. The Interior, Trace	I1–I4a	I5–I5a	I6–I8
J. Baudelaire	—	—	J1–J92a
K. Dream City and Dream House, Dreams of the Future, Anthropological Nihilism, Jung	K1–K3a	K4–K4a	K5–K9a
L. Dream House, Museum, Fountain Hall	L1–L2a	L3–L4a	L5–L5a
M. The Flâneur	M1–M5a	M6–M13a	M14–M21a
N. Epistemology, Theory of Progress	N1–N3a	N4–N7a	N8–N20
O. Prostitution, Gambling	O1–O6a	O7–O10a	O11–O14
P. The Streets of Paris	P1–P2a	P3–P4a	P5
Q. Panorama	Q1–Q2a	Q3–Q3a	Q4–Q4a
R. Mirror	R1–R2a	—	R3
S. Painting, *Jugendstil*, Newness	S1–S4a	S5–S6a	S7–S11
T. Forms of Lighting	T1–T2a	T3–T3a	T4–T5
U. Saint-Simon, Railroads	U1–U9a	U10–U16a	U17–U18
V. Conspiracies, *Compagnonnage*	V1–V3a	V4–V8a	V9–V10
W. Fourier	W1–W6a	W7–W16a	W17–W18
X. Marx	—	X1–X2a	X3–X13a
Y. Photography	Y1–Y4a	Y5–Y8a	Y9–Y11
Z. Doll, Automaton	—	—	**
a. Social Movement	a1–a6a	a7–a19a	a20–a23
b. Daumier	—	b1–b1a	b2
c.			
d. Literary History, Hugo	d1–d1a	d2–d14a	d15–d19
e.			
f.			
g. Stock Market, Economic History	g1–g1a	g2–g3a	g4
h.			

Konvolut Title	Time Period of the Entries		
	early	middle	late
i. Technologies of Reproduction, Lithography	—	—	i1–i2
k. The Commune	k1–k1a	k2–k3a	k4
l. The Seine, oldest Paris	—	l1–l1a	l2–l2a
m. Idleness	—	—	m1–m5
n.			
o.			
p. Anthropological Materialism, History of Sects	—	p1–p3a	p4–p6
q.			
r. *Ecole polytechnique*	—	r1–r3a	r4–r4a
s.			
t.			
u.			
v.			
w.			

2

In the fall of 1934, Benjamin wrote to Horkheimer: "The clear construction of a book stands before my eyes,"[18] and he reiterated to Adorno in the spring that he now had a "major plan" for the "'Passages.'"[19] On May 20, he informed Scholem it was the first plan that "approximated—from afar" that of a book[20]; the same day he wrote Brecht that for this "book," he needed to inform himself about "a number of things" through his research.[21] The 1935 exposé described six "provisional chapter divisions"[22] for the project, each of which brought together a historical figure[23] with a historical phenomenon:

   I. Fourier or the Arcades

  II. Daguerre or the Dioramas

 III. Grandville or the World Expositions

 IV. Louis Philippe or the Interior

V. Baudelaire or the Streets of Paris

VI. Haussmann or the Barricades

It would seem logical to presume that the 1935 exposé provides the closest approximation to the "clear construction" of the book that by then Benjamin had in his mind's eye.[24] But in fact this exposé was a very incomplete rendering of the material already assembled. Not only does it leave out important conceptions from the early notes, as Adorno critically observed[25]; it neglects significant aspects of the notes of 1934 that develop these early themes still further. What holds the 1935 exposé together is the central problematic of the effect of industrial production on traditional cultural forms. It connects directly to the 1936 essay, "The Work of Art in the Age of its Technical Reproduction" by revealing "the hidden structural character of present-day art."[26] The exposé's central concern, the effects of industrialization on art and their implications for *present* cultural practice, acted like a magnet on the *Konvolut* fragments—at the same time disturbing their position in earlier constellations suggested by his original notes, that in fact pulled them in quite different directions. The 1935 exposé *could* have been the *Passagen-Werk* had Benjamin been willing to discard these previous constellations—and not to construct new ones. He seems to have been not at all disposed to do either.

With the relentless tenacity of the collector (that nineteenth-century figure whose social physiognomy he described in the *Passagen-Werk* so perceptively), Benjamin refused to let go of any of his concerns that had the power to charge the material. Instead he superimposed them, with the result that the project's fragments are bewilderingly overdetermined. Moreover, the conceptions double back on each other, so that chronological divisions in no way correspond to thematic ones. For example: The file on "Marx" (*Konvolut* X) was not begun until Stage II of the documentation. But the "theory of Marx" is referred to in the early entry "O°, 67." And although evidence of real study of *Capital* does not appear until the second stage, an early note ("Q°, 4") gives the page reference in the rare, first edition of *Capital* to the crucial passage on the fetish character of commodities.[27] The cosmology of Blanqui which represents the most significant addition of material in the 1939 exposé in fact repeats the theme of the nineteenth century as Hell that, lamented by Adorno for its absence in the 1935 exposé, played such a prominent role in the 1927–29 notes. While the title "A Dialectical Fairy Scene" was dropped after Stage I, the motifs of "dream world" and "dream image," and the understanding of dialectics as "awakening" from a dream were not given up.[28] The Baudelaire *Konvolut* was not developed until Stage III. Yet Stage I anticipates the "very important" theme of "Baudelairean allegory"[29] that becomes central to the Baudelaire "book" of this last stage. Moreover, this "book" not only returns to the earliest notes, but reaches back even earlier to the *Trauerspiel* study, passages of which are cited directly in fragments added to the *Konvoluts* during Stage III, while the conception of empathy (*Einfühlung*) that is central to Benjamin's much-admired theory of experience in the second Baudelaire essay of 1939, marks the return of an idea expressed in the earliest notes that had, in the meantime, been neglected.[30]

Every attempt to capture the *Passagen-Werk* within one narrative frame must lead to failure. The fragments plunge the interpreter into an abyss of meanings, threatening her or him with an epistemological despair that rivals the melancholy of the Baroque allegoricists. (I admit to not a few moments in the past seven years when yielding to such despair—or, alternatively, reveling in the semiotic free fall, under the banner of that postmodernism which already claims Benjamin as its own—seemed a delicious temptation.) Yet as I shall argue, what saves the project from arbitrariness is Benjamin's *political* concern that provided the overriding orientation for every constellation. Indeed, if the attempt to interpret this massive assembly of research material is justified, it is due not to any intrinsic value in adding to the hagiography that has come to surround Benjamin's name, but to the fact that this overriding concern is still very much our own.

Although the arrangement of *Passagen-Werk* material in the chapters that follow is admittedly arbitrary, the focus of the interpretation is not. To say that the *Passagen-Werk* has no necessary narrative structure so that the fragments can be grouped freely, is not at all to suggest that it has no conceptual structure, as if the meaning of the work were itself totally up to the capriciousness of the reader. As Benjamin said, a presentation of confusion need not be the same as a confused presentation.[31] And although the fact will not be heard gladly by many of those who presently cite Benjamin in support of their own epistemological arbitrariness—which they claim is liberating and democratic, but which, when totally without principle, is literally tyrannical—the Arcades project makes it abundantly clear that Benjamin considered such capriciousness of meaning as a historically particular hallmark of the modern era, one that needed to be critically understood, not blindly affirmed. Moreover, aesthetics and literary theory were not to take the place of philosophy, but, rather, to relinquish their traditional subject matter to philosophical interpretation.

3

Benjamin described the *Passagen-Werk* as a project in *Geschichtsphilosophie*. Translated, the term is imprecise. The German language allows for a montage of two concepts (*Geschichts/Philosophie*; *Natur/Geschichte*) without stipulating the semantic nature of their connection, but in this case English is more fastidious. If *Geschichtsphilosophie* is translated (as is usually the case) "philosophy of history," the implication is that history develops in a philosophically meaningful way, manifesting a teleological plan or goal. If it is translated "historical philosophy," the implication is that philosophy develops in a historically relative fashion, as the expression of an evolving *Zeitgeist*. Both ideas miss Benjamin's point, which was to construct, not a philosophy *of* history, but philosophy *out* of history, or (this amounts to the same thing) to reconstruct historical material as philosophy—indeed, "philosophical history"[32] might be a less misleading nomenclature.

In the *Passagen-Werk* Benjamin was committed to a graphic, concrete representation of truth, in which historical images made visible the philosophical ideas. In them, history cut through the core of truth without providing a totalizing frame. Benjamin understood these ideas as "discontinuous."[33] As a result, the same conceptual elements appear in several images, in such varying configurations that their meanings cannot be fixed in the abstract. Similarly, the images themselves cannot be strung together into a coherent, noncontradictory picture of the whole. A historical construction of philosophy that is simultaneously (dialectically) a philosophical reconstruction of history, one in which philosophy's ideational elements are expressed as changing meanings within historical images that themselves are discontinuous—such a project is not best discussed in generalities. It needs to be shown.

The next four chapters are an attempt to demonstrate what is at stake in the conception. Each deals with the same three concepts—myth, nature, and history—as they enter into four distinct theoretical constellations, and focuses thereby on a specific, conceptual center of gravity of the *Passagen-Werk* (of which the number is multiple, but not unlimited). These "conceptual centers," implicit in the *Konvolut* entries, have here been made explicit, in order to present Benjamin's detailed historical research within a conceptual frame that makes the philosophical significance of this research apparent. Chapter 3, "Natural History," deals with the conception of the Arcades project as an ur-history of the nineteenth century. It explains how Benjamin viewed the world of industrial objects as fossils, as the trace of living history that can be read from the surfaces of the surviving objects, and it introduces the significance of visual "concreteness" in Benjamin's methodology of dialectical images in a discussion of his conception of ur-phenomena.

Chapter 4, "Mythic History," deals with Benjamin's critique of progress. The first part of the chapter is descriptive, summarizing the copious research with which Benjamin documented how the phantasmagoria of progress became embedded within nineteenth-century discourse by focusing on material that would not be treated systematically by social historians until our generation.[34] Yet such an archaeology of knowledge was only part of the task of Benjamin's "philosophical history." The second half of chapter 4 describes how Benjamin attempted to construct a counter-discourse by unearthing buried markers that expose "progress" as the fetishization of modern temporality, which is an endless repetition of the "new" as the "always-the-same." The rebus in which *this* temporality appears is fashion.

In chapter 5, Benjamin's controversial idea of wish images in the collective unconscious is examined with some philological detail, and discussed in the context of his theory of the superstructure as a dialectic between utopian imagination and the new technological potential. It examines his philosophico-political understanding of modern culture, revolving around the polar concepts of modernity and antiquity, organic nature and the new nature produced by industry, and suggests criteria for distinguishing authentic from pseudo-"sublations" of these polarities, which allow us to identify as progressive those cultural forms that do not repeat the old, but *redeem* it. Chapter 6 focuses on Benjamin's analysis of modern allegory as it is expressed in the poetry of Baudelaire. Benjamin treated Baudelaire's poetry as a social object, not a literary one. The result is a startling modification of his early theory of allegory as presented in the *Trauerspiel* study, one that reveals the absolutely new conditions under which this literary form had been reanimated. It tells us more about the nature of commodity society, captured in the image of the ruin, than about either Baudelaire's aesthetic intention or the continuity of literary forms.

In a very rough way, the chapters are chronological: The conception of an ur-history of the nineteenth century and of historical objects as ur-phenomena goes back to the early notes and the first stage of *Konvolut* entries. Similarly, except for the material on Blanqui, the motifs of chapter 4 (Hell, dust, gambling, fashion) are part of what Adorno referred to as the "glorious first draft" of the Arcades project which Benjamin read at Königstein in 1929. The problematic discussed in chapter 5 corresponds to that which forms the structure of the 1935 exposé (and the 1936 Artwork essay), while chapter 6 draws heavily from *Konvolut* J on Baudelaire which was not begun until Stage III of the project (late 1937). Yet this chronological order is in no way meant to suggest a developmental one. The documents give us every reason to take Benjamin at his word, that with the 1935 exposé nothing of the early draft was given up[35]; nor was it ever abandoned. The three "stages" represent, not a sequence, but an overlay of material and an overlapping of concerns.

As Adorno wrote after working through the Arcades documents in the summer of 1948, if reconstructing the *Passagen-Werk* "were possible at all, then only Benjamin himself could have done it."[36] The arrangement made here does not pretend to be such a reconstruction. Nor, for all its length, does it exhaust the extraordinarily rich fund of material in the thirty-six *Konvoluts*. Its purpose is pedagogic. As a conceptual arrangement of Benjamin's research into the history of Paris in the nineteenth century, it begins with simpler ideas and builds on them, in order to show that underlying these fragmentary pieces of data and minute historical details, there is a coherent and persistent philosophical design.

3

Natural History: Fossil

1

[. . . Benjamin had,] as no one else, the ability to regard historical things, manifestations of the objectified spirit, "culture," as if they were nature [. . .]. His entire thought could be characterized as "natural-historical" [*naturgeschichtliches*]. The petrified, frozen, or obsolete inventory of cultural fragments spoke to him [. . .] as fossils or plants in the herbarium to the collector.[1]

Within the concept of history, time indicates social change and the uniqueness and irreversibility of human events. Traditionally, it has taken on meaning in opposition to "nature," in which time is change only in the sense of cyclical repetition. Charles Darwin's theory of evolution undermined this binary, however, by arguing that nature itself had a unique, nonrepetitive, historical course. In the late nineteenth century, Social Darwinists applied the terms of Darwin's natural history to discussions of "social evolution." Originally, Darwin's theory had a critical impulse, involving an understanding of history in scientific, empirical terms that challenged theological myth and Biblical dogma. But within Social Darwinism, that critical impulse was lost. The idea of social "evolution" in effect glorified the blind, empirical course of human history. It gave ideological support to the social status quo by claiming that competitive capitalism expressed true human "nature," that imperialist rivalries were the healthy result of an inevitable struggle for survival, and that the ruling "races" were justified as the dominators on the basis of "natural" superiority. Within this pseudoscientific discourse, the claim of social injustice became a logical impossibility.

Social Darwinism was based on an inherent contradiction, one which had been exposed by more than one critic in Benjamin's time. Dolf Sternberger (whom Benjamin knew in Frankfurt before 1933)[2] argued in his 1938 book, *Panorama: Views of the Nineteenth Century*, that the "endless panorama" of social evolution made barely perceptible the battlefield left behind by "natural selection":

[. . . C]ivilization [. . .] stoutly keeps corroborating with extinction and extermination as if indeed civilization were not itself; if the "civilized races" have in fact gained the upper hand, they are for this very reason more savage than the savages. This paradox lies concealed in Darwin's theory of transitions.[3]

In 1932 Theodor [Wiesengrund-] Adorno, as newly appointed professor at Frankfurt University, gave a lecture that called for a "reorientation of the philosophy of history [*Geschichtsphilosophie*]."[4] Entitled "The Idea of Natural History," it turned the paradox inherent in this term into a dialectical argument. The speech shows the influence of his talks with Benjamin in 1929 at Königstein when the Arcades plan was discussed, and it makes direct reference to the *Trauerspiel* study that had been the reason for Benjamin's rejection by Frankfurt University several years earlier. Arguing against the philosophical synthesis of nature and history in Heidegger's premise that "historicity" (*Geschichtlichkeit*) is the "nature" of Being, Adorno employed nature and history as dialectically opposed concepts, each of which provided a criticism of the other, and of the reality each was supposed to identify.[5] In such an analysis

[. . .] the moments of nature and history do not disappear into each other, but break simultaneously out of each other and cross each other in such a way that what is natural emerges as a sign for history, and history, where it appears most historical, appears as a sign for nature.[6]

Benjamin expressed the same idea in an early *Passagen-Werk* note that lays down as "the axiom of the way to avoid mythic thinking": "No historical category without natural substance; no natural substance without its historical filter."[7] The method relies on juxtaposing binary pairs of linguistic signs from the language code (here history/nature), and, in the process of applying these signs to material referents, crossing the switches. The critical power of this maneuver depends on both the code, wherein meaning arises from binaries of signifier/signifieds independent of the referents, and the referents, the materially existing objects, which do not submit to language signs meekly, but have the semantic strength to set the signs into question.

That a critical, dialectical "idea" of natural history can also be expressed in an image was demonstrated several years later by John Heartfield, who developed the new technique of photomontage. His image, entitled "German Natural History" (figure 3.1), appeared on the August 1934, cover of *Arbeiter Illustrierte Zeitschrift* (the *Workers' Illustrated Journal*) as a direct political attack against Hitler's Reich by criticizing its "evolution" out of the Weimar Republic.

Heartfield was a member of the Berlin Marxist circle of Brecht, Lacis, Reinhardt, and Piscator. In the late Weimar period, he designed theater sets for them that incorporated photographs, placing the new technologies of image-reproduction "consciously [. . .] in the service of political agitation."[8] He was quite close to Brecht, and Benjamin knew both him and his work.[9] Intriguing for Benjamin in Heartfield's work must have been the use of allegorical forms of representation in combination with the most modern techniques of photographic montage.

Like most of Heartfield's images, the poster, "Deutsche Naturgeschichte," is a modern-day emblem,[10] using the conventions of *inscriptio* (title) and *subscriptio* (caption) to make the image function as a form of moral and political instruction. German "natural history" is represented allegorically in the three biological stages of development of the Death's Head Moth, a progression of metamorphoses that suggests a causal link between the Weimar Republic and fascism (Ebert was the first chancellor of Weimar, Hindenberg its last president, who in turn approved Hitler as chancellor). At the same time, this progression (on a dying tree branch) is seen as retrogression, and "development" applies only to increasing clarity as to the nature of the beast: the visible mark of the skull, or death's head, in its final Hitlerian form. I have chosen to discuss this particular poster, not to stress Heartfield's influence on Benjamin, but to make a didactic point. (It might have been made instead, for example, with Kafka's story, "Metamorphosis," in which the human hero turns into an insect, an allegorical image

3.1 "German Natural History," photomontage by John Heartfield, 1934.

in which the evolutionary process from animal to man is similarly inverted.) Yet Benjamin was evidently struck by this particular photomontage (well after he had conceived of similar motifs for the *Passagen-Werk*). In 1936, the year after a major Heartfield exposition in Paris,[11] the identical image appears in his correspondence, in a critical comment on bourgeois intellectual development since Fichte: "'The revolutionary spirit of the German bourgeoisie has been transforming itself into the chrysalis from which the Death's Head Moth of National Socialism later crawled.'"[12]

Heartfield tells us in the caption to "German Natural History" that "metamorphosis" has three meanings: one from the discourse of nature (the insect's stages), one from that of history (Ebert-Hindenberg-Hitler), and one (listed first) from the discourse of myth: "In mythology: the metamorphosis of human beings into trees, animals, stones." It is this meaning which both explains the representation and provides a critical judgment of the referent. Heartfield presents the natural evolution of German political history in the mythical form of a metamorphosis of humans into nature, in order to make the critical point that the belief in evolutionary progress as social history's natural course *is* a myth, in the fully negative sense of illusion, error, ideology. Heartfield, a Communist, was not attacking the capitalist class' affirmation of Social Darwinism to justify its own dominance, but, rather, the affirmation by Social Democrats of the idea of historical progress, which had lulled them into a false sense of security regarding the adequacy of Weimar parliamentarianism for socialist politics.[13]

Note that the ideological fusion of nature and history when reproduced by Heartfield through an allegorical use of photomontage allows the gap between sign and referent to remain visible, thus enabling him to represent their identity in the form of a critique. Benjamin had worked similarly in *One Way Street*, constructing a montage of verbal rather than photographic images that, instead of confounding nature and history into one, relied on the semantic gap between these terms to identify critically the objective essence of Weimar's economic inflation and the bourgeoisie's social decline. In "Imperial Panorama":

A curious paradox: people have only the narrowest private interests in mind when they act, yet in their behavior they are more than ever deter-

3.2 "Voice from the Swamp: 'Three thousand years of strict inbreeding demonstrate the superiority of my race,'" photomontage by John Heartfield, 1936.

mined by the instincts of the mass. And, more than ever, mass instincts have grown mad and hostile to life. Where the dim instincts of the animal—as numerous stories relate—finds a way of escaping from an approaching yet still-invisible danger, here society, wherein people have only their own lowly well-being in mind, falls victim to even the most nearby danger with brutelike dullness, but without the dim knowledge of animals, as a blind mass [. . .]. Thus in this society the picture of imbecility is complete: uncertainty, indeed, perversion of the instincts vital for life, and helplessness, indeed, decay of the intellect. This is the state of mind of the entire German bourgeoisie.[14]

Against the animalistic yet self-destructive behavior of the bourgeoisie—who were demonstrating all the signs of a vanishing species—Benjamin opposed the constructive potential of the new industrial era: "Humans as a species reached the end of their development tens of thousands of years ago; but humanity as a species is just at its beginning"[15]—so radical a break with the "natural" state of things was the social *promise* of technology, the beginning of a truly human history. Marx had argued similarly that until the new potential of industrialism was realized, all history was only "prehistory," dominated by the "natural laws" of capitalism that resulted in a repetitive cycle of inflation, depression, and unemployment. So long as people were held under the power of these blind forces, the promise of a universal human history could not come into its own.[16]

Extreme optimism concerning the promise of the "new" nature of technology, and total pessimism concerning the course of history, which without proletarian revolution would never leave the stage of prehistory—this orientation characterizes all stages of the Arcades project. The montage of nature and history with which Benjamin had already experimented in *One Way Street* was developed in it as an expression of the prehistoric state of present history, but with this difference. The *Passagen-Werk* treats the historical *origins* of the present: Natural history becomes ur-history. Its goal is not only to polemicize against the still-barbaric level of the modern age, but, raising polemics to historico-philosophic theory, to disclose the essence of the "new nature" as even more transient, more fleeting than the old. Natural history as ur-history meant bourgeois prehistory as prehistoric. This was a central image in the *Passagen-Werk*.

The short half-life of technologies and commodities, the rapid turnover in style and fashion, was experienced in high capitalism as extreme temporal attenuation. For those living in the 1920s, the novelties of even one's parents' youth—gaslight instead of neon signs, buns and bustles instead of bobbed hair and bathing suits— belonged to a distant past. Those early bourgeois artifacts which managed to survive in the aging arcades where, "for the first time, the most recent past becomes distant,"[17] were the archaic residues, the petrified ur-forms of the present.

When as children we were given those great collected editions, *The Cosmos and Humanity, New Universe*, or *The Earth*, would our gaze not fall first of all on the colored [illustrations] of petrified landscapes or the "lakes and glaciers of the first ice age"? Such an idealized panorama of a scarcely past ur-epoch opens up when we gaze into the Passages that have spread into every city. Here is housed the last dinosaur of Europe, the consumer.[18]

A later formulation specifies:

Just as there are places in the stones of the Miocene or Eocene Age that bear the impression of huge monsters out of these geological epochs, so today the Passages lie in the great cities like caves containing fossils of an ur-animal presumed extinct: The consumers from the preimperial epoch of capitalism, the last dinosaurs of Europe.[19]

The pre-1850 consumers are "ur-animals" not because *consumption* has disappeared, but because it no longer exists in its early capital- ist form. By the twentieth century the original arcades had failed financially, because their small specialty shops of luxury goods were unable to compete with huge new department stores that sold mass-produced commodities at a pace rapid enough to compensate for falling rates of profit. It is for this reason that Benjamin calls the early bourgeois consumers "the last dinosaurs of Europe," grown extinct due to the "natural" evolution of that industrial capitalism which the bourgeoisie itself unleashed. In the dying arcades, the early industrial commodities have created an antedeluvian land- scape, an "ur-landscape of consumption,"[20] bearing witness to the "decline of an economic epoch" which the "dreaming collective" mistakes for "the decline of the world itself."[21] Like the caves of an archaeological site, they contain the last century's fashions *in situ*:

In the window displays of beauty salons are the last women with long hair. They have rich, undulating hair masses with a "permanent wave" — fossilized hair curls.[22]

Leftover commodities "grow on the walls" of these deserted caves like scar tissue, "ancient, wild flora which, blocked off from the "sap" of consumer traffic, "entwine with each other in the most irregular fashion."[23] Faded wall posters contain "the first drops of a rain of letters that today pours down without let-up day and night on the city and is greeted like the Egyptian plague. . . ."[24] The light filters through their dingy glass roofs as into an aquarium of primitive sea life.[25] Shop signs hang in them like zoo signs, "recording not so much the habitat as the origin and species of captured animals."[26] Already in the nineteenth century, the interiors of bourgeois dwellings were "a kind of casing," in which the bourgeois individual as a "collector" of objects was embedded with all his appurtenances, "attending to his traces as nature attends to dead fauna embedded in granite."[27] The physiognomy of Paris, which has been shaped by social forces, is compared by Benjamin to a geological formation that has the attraction of a volcanic landscape:

As a social formation, Paris is a counterimage to that which Vesuvius is as a geographic one: A threatening, dangerous mass, an ever-active June of the Revolution. But just as the slopes of Vesuvius, thanks to the layers of lava covering them, have become a paradisiacal orchard, so here, out of the lava of the Revolution, there bloom art, fashion, and festive existence as nowhere else.[28]

As is obvious particularly in the last quotation, the new nature that comprises the Parisian landscape has its "alluring as well as threatening face."[29] Similarly, the fossilized commodity remains are not merely "failed material."[30] As traces of prior life, they are historical clues, with an objective meaning that separates Benjamin's "idea" of natural history from the simpler, more polemical form of Heartfield's montage. Benjamin perceived historical nature as an expression of truth's essential transitoriness in its contradictory extremes—as extinction and death on the one hand, and as creative potential and the possibility for change on the other.

Not only nature, but all the categories in Benjamin's theoretical constructions have more than one meaning and value, making it possible for them to enter into various conceptual constellations. Adorno, in his speech on "Natural History," showed the influence of Benjamin when he spoke of a "logical structure" different from that of traditional philosophy, where concepts like nature and history, myth and transiency had been distinguished from one another by "invariants" in their meaning. Instead, "they come together around a concrete historical facticity, one that opens itself up in connection with their moments, in its one-time-only uniqueness."[31] The point of difference between Adorno and Benjamin, which eventually became a source of conflict,[32] was that Benjamin believed such philosophico-historical constellations could be represented by a dialectical image rather than by dialectical argumentation.

The conception of "dialectical image" is overdetermined in Benjamin's thought. It has a logic as rich in philosophical implications as the Hegelian dialectic, and, indeed, the unfolding of its complexities is a task of each and every chapter of this study. In the present context it refers to the use of archaic images to identify what is historically new about the "nature" of commodities. The principle of construction is that of montage, whereby the image's ideational elements remain unreconciled, rather than fusing into one "harmonizing perspective."[33] For Benjamin, the technique of montage had "special, perhaps even total rights" as a progressive form because it "interrupts the context into which it is inserted" and thus "counteracts illusion"[34] and he intended it to be the principle governing the construction of the *Passagen-Werk*: "This work must develop to the highest point the art of citing without citation marks. Its theory connects most closely with that of montage."[35]

There is, of course, another use of montage that creates illusion by fusing the elements so artfully that all evidence of incompatibility and contradiction, indeed, all evidence of artifice, is eliminated—as in the falsified photographic document, as old as photography itself (figure 3.3). This was the principle as well of the "panoramas," those artificially constructed, lifelike replicas of scenes from history and nature—everything from battlefields to alpine vistas—that were favorite attractions in the nineteenth century, and they provided a keyword for the *Passagen-Werk*.[36] "Panorama," was "plagiarized"[37] from Benjamin by Sternberger as the title for his book. It contained a critique of the popularization of Darwin's theory as a "panorama of evolution" (figure 3.4) that makes history look like a "natural progression" from ape to man, so that "the eye and the mind's eye can slide unhindered, up and down, back and forth, across the pictures as they themselves 'evolve'."[38]

Not the medium of representation, not merely the concreteness of the image or the montage form is crucial, but whether the construc-

3.3 Falsified photograph of violence against the clergy by the Paris Communards, photomontage by E. Appert, 1871.

tion makes visible the gap between sign and referent, or fuses them in a deceptive totality so that the caption merely duplicates the semiotic content of the image instead of setting it into question.[39] When historical referents are called "natural" in uncritical affirmation, identifying the empirical course of their development as progress, the result is myth; when prehistoric nature is evoked in the act of naming the historically modern, the effect is to demythify. But Benjamin's aim was not merely to criticize "natural history" as ideology; it was to show how, within the right configuration, the ideational elements of nature and history could reveal the truth of modern reality, its transitoriness as well as its primitive stage.

It was crucial to Benjamin's theory that for the purposes of philosophical understanding there was no absolute, categorical distinction between technology and nature—Ludwig Klages was "reactionary" to suggest otherwise.[40] Technology was of course socially and historically produced, which is why Georg Lukács termed it "second nature," in order to criticize the presumption that the world in its given form was "natural" in the ontological sense. In the *Passagen-Werk*, Lukács' concept of "second nature" does not play a role, however, although Benjamin was familiar with

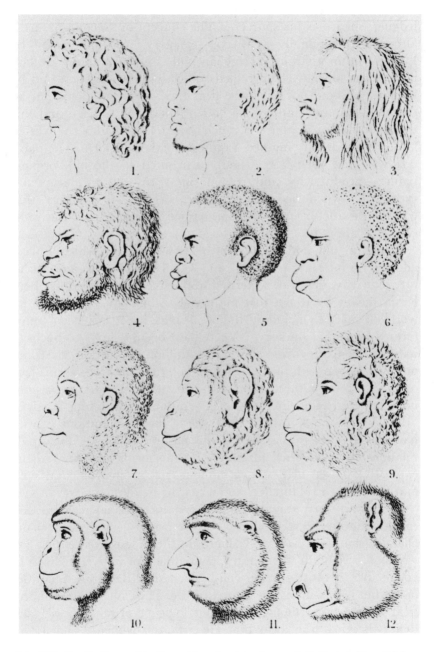

3.4 "The Family Group of the Katarrhinen," artist unknown, in E. Heckel, *Die natürliche Schöpfungsgeschichte*, 1902.

the latter's writings (and although Adorno used this term, acknowledging Lukács as his source.)[41] The concept of "second nature," although intentionally a Marxist category, was understood by Lukács within a strongly Hegelian philosophical frame.[42] Second nature was alienated and reified subjectivity, a world created by humans who did not recognize it as their own. For Benjamin, in contrast, material nature was "other" than the subject, and this remained true no matter how much human labor had been invested in it. Yet modernity marked a radical break in its form. The paradox was that predicates usually attributed to the old, organic nature—productivity and transitoriness as well as decay and extinction—when used to describe the *in*organic "new nature" that was the product of industrialism, named precisely what was radically new about it.

Benjamin did not use the term "new nature," which I have adopted for interpretive clarity, and which strikes me as more accurate than, say, the Marxist term "productive forces," because Benjamin meant by it not just industrial technology but the entire world of matter (including human beings) as it has been transformed by that technology.[43] There have been, then, two epochs of nature. The first evolved slowly over millions of years; the second, our own, began with the industrial revolution, and changes its face daily. This new nature, its powers still unknown, can appear ominous and terrifying to the first generations confronting it, given "the very primitive form of the ideas of these generations"[44] who have yet to learn to master, not this nature itself, but humanity's relationship to it. Such mastery demands being receptive to the expressive power of matter, a mimetic, not an instrumental skill; and it is the central intellectual task of the modern era.

In this still early stage of industrial nature it is no accident that early modernity feels an affinity for the primitive and the archaic: Classical antiquity was a "fashion" in the nineteenth century (as we shall see[45]); in Benjamin's own time "primitivism" was in vogue. But it must also be emphasized that Benjamin identifies only what is new in history as prehistoric. The conception is dialectical. There is no biological or ontological "primitiveness" that defies historical transformation. He criticized explicitly such a contention: "The archaic form of prehistory which has been evoked in every era, and most recently by Jung, is the one that makes illusory appearance in history all the more blinding by assigning to it nature as a home."[46]

2

In the mid-thirties, Benjamin decided to include actual images in the *Passagen-Werk*. He wrote to Gretel Karplus: "This is in fact new: As a part of my study I am taking notes on important and rare image material. The book—this much I have known for some time—can be furnished with the most important illustrative documents [. . .]."[47] From May to September 1935, and again in January 1936, he worked in the archives of the *Cabinet des estampes* in the Bibliothèque Nationale. If such research in iconographic documentation was "still rare" among historians,[48] it was unheard of among philosophers. Benjamin had copies made of relevant illustrations which he found there, keeping them in his Paris apartment as "a kind of album."[49]

The album appears to have been lost.[50] It makes little difference, however, for Benjamin's philosophical conception whether the "images" of the nineteenth century which he found for the project were pictorially or verbally represented. Whichever form they took, such images were the concrete, "small, particular moments" in which the "total historical event" was to be discovered,[51] the "perceptible ur-phenomenon [*Urphänomen*][52] in which the origins of the present could be found. Benjamin has borrowed the term urphenomenon from Goethe's writings on the morphology of nature. Goethe observed that whereas in the science of physics or chemistry the object of knowledge was a cognitive abstraction constituted by the subject, in biological science it was perceived immediately, in the act of "irreducible observation."[53] The objective laws and regularities of living organisms were graphically visible in their structural forms. Goethe believed the archetypal ur-forms of these structures revealed the essence of biological life, and moreover, that they existed empirically, as one plant or animal among others, providing concrete materializations of the Platonic ideas. In 1918, Benjamin wrote that what Goethe called ur-phenomona were not symbols in the sense of poetic analogies, but, rather, "ideal symbols" in which the ideal essences of which Plato spoke appeared in sensual forms.[54] Georg Simmel in his 1913 study of Goethe described the concept in detail:

The ur-phenomenon—the emergence of colors out of light and darkness, the rhythmic ebb and flow of earth's gravitation, the source of climatic change, the development of the plant organism out of the leaf-shape, the type of vertebrates—is the purest, most typical case of a relation, combination, or development of natural existence; in this respect, it is on the one hand, something other than the commonplace phenomenon, which tends to show this fundamental form in muddied mixtures and diffractions. And yet on the other hand, it is still precisely something that appears, perhaps given only as an intellectual spectacle, but at times actually "exhibited somewhere naked before the eyes of the attentive observer" [Goethe].[55]

Simmel points out the philosophical significance of this conception:

We normally imagine the general law of objects as positioned somehow outside of the thing: partly objective, [. . .] independent of the accident of its material realization in time and space, partly subjective, [. . .] exclusively a matter of thought and not present to our sensual energies that can perceive only the particular, never the general. The concept of the ur-phenomenon wants to overcome this separation: It is none other than the timeless law within a temporal observation; it is the general that reveals itself immediately in a particular form. Because such a thing exists, he [Goethe] can say: "The highest thing would be to grasp that everything factual is already theory. The blue of the sky reveals to us the fundamental law of chromatics. One would never search for anything behind the phenomena; they themselves are the theory."[56]

Simmel notes that this "genial synthesis"[57] of essence and appearance produces "a very remarkable shift in the problem of knowledge":

Whereas as a rule every form of Realism proceeds from *theoretical knowledge* as prior and immediate, attributing to it the ability to grasp objective being, copy it, and express it faithfully, here the point of emanation is actually appropriated by the object. The merging together between it and thoughts-in-knowledge is not an epistemological fact, but a metaphysical one.[58]

I have cited Simmel's discussion at length because Benjamin was directly influenced by it. As an after note to the *Trauerspiel* study, he wrote the following comment, which he later added to the *Passagen-Werk* material:

In studying Simmel's presentation of Goethe's concept of truth, {particularly his excellent elucidation of the ur-phenomenon}, it became very clear to me that my concept of origins in the *Trauerspiel* book is a strict and compelling transfer of this fundamental concept of Goethe out of the realm of nature and into that of history.[59]

When Benjamin spoke of the transient historical objects of the nineteenth century as ur-phenomena, he meant that they exhibit visibly—and metaphysically as an "authentic synthesis"[60]—their developmental, conceptual essence. The *Passagen-Werk* deals with economic facts that are not abstract causal factors, but ur-phenomena,

...] which they only become after they let develop out of themselves [...]—unfold would be a better word—the series of concrete historical forms of the arcades, just as the leaf lets unfold out of itself the abundant variety of the empirical plant world.[61]

A concrete, factual representation of those historical images in which capitalist-industrial economic forms could be seen in a purer, embryonic stage was to be the stuff and substance of the work. From the early notes: "Formula: construction out of facts. Construction within the complete elimination of theory. What only Goethe in his morphological writings attempted."[62]

It was because of Benjamin's belief that metaphysical essences were immediately visible within the facts that Adorno was wary of the notion of "dialectical images." He took literally Benjamin's contention: "Method of this work: literary montage. I have nothing to say, only to show,"[63] and presumed that a completed *Passagen-Werk* would have consisted of nothing more than a "shocklike montage of the material."[64] Adorno wrote to Horkheimer in May 1949:

At the beginning of last year I finally received the Arcades material hidden in the Bibliothèque Nationale. During last summer I worked through the material in the most detailed fashion, and some problems then arose [...]. The most significant is the extraordinary restraint in the formulation of theoretical thoughts in comparison with the enormous treasure of excerpts. This is explained in part by the (for me, already problematic) idea which is formulated explicitly in one place, of the work as pure "montage," that is, created from a juxtaposition of quotations so that the theory springs out of it without having to be inserted as interpretation.[65]

Adorno's understanding of Benjamin's use of montage is not the only possible one. Rolf Tiedemann, editor of the *Passagen-Werk*, reports:

In later statements Adorno took the montage idea even more literally, and insisted that Benjamin had nothing more in mind than mounting one quotation next to another. In his many discussions with Adorno, the editor was, however, unable to convince himself that literary montage as perceived by Benjamin as a method was identical to a simple montage of quotations. [. . .] In place of mediating theory, the form of commentary was to have appeared, which he defined as "interpretation out of the particulars" [N2, 1]; interpretation and commentary are, however, not imaginable in any other way than as representation. [. . .] The quotations are instead the material that Benjamin's representation was to employ.[66]

The evidence points in favor of Tiedemann's reading. Crucial is Benjamin's understanding of "montage" as a form which, if already visible in the early arcades, in the kaleidoscopic, fortuitous juxtaposition of shop signs and window displays (figure 3.5), was raised by technology during the course of the century to the level of a conscious principle of construction. The kaleidoscope was itself an invention of the nineteenth century.[67] But it was preceded by the Chinese Puzzle (figure 3.6) which, because its juxtaposed elements were not randomly arranged but cohered around a central idea, was the true ur-phenomenon of the principle of montage as a *constructive* principle.[68]

The technical potential of this new principle came to fruition at the end of the century with the building of the Eiffel Tower (figure 3.7), the earliest architectural form of the principle of montage:

Here the power of visual plasticity is silenced in favor of an extraordinary tension of intellectual energy which the energy of the inorganic material brings to extremely small, extremely effective forms, binding them with one another in the most effective fashion [. . .] Every one of the 12,000 metal pieces is determined precisely to the millimeter, [as is] every one of the 2½ million rivets [. . .][69]

It is in this same sense that we should understand Benjamin's own plan for the *Passagen-Werk*:

[. . .] to erect the large constructions out of the smallest architectural segments that have been sharply and cuttingly manufactured. Indeed, to discover the crystal of the total event in the analysis of the small, particular moments. This means breaking with vulgar historical naturalism. To grasp the construction of history as such. In the structure of commentary [*Kommentarstruktur*].[70]

3 Natural History: Fossil

3.5 Interior, Passage du Grand Cerf, Paris (top).

3.6 "Chinese Puzzle, or: The Latest Craze," nineteenth century (bottom).

3.7   Exterior detail, Eiffel Tower, built by Gustav Eiffel, 1889.

In the *Passagen-Werk*, each of these "small, particular moments" was to be identified as an ur-form of the present. Benjamin's commentary, in which those facts were embedded, provided the rivets that allowed the fragments to cohere as the philosophical representation of history as a "total event."

The language of technology was new for Benjamin, but not the conception. In his early (1918) note on Goethe's theory of ur-phenomena as Platonic "ideal symbols," he cautioned against understanding such symbols as themselves the "palace of philosophy"; rather, the task of the philosopher was "to fill up the walls of the palace to the point where the images appear to be the walls."[71] In fragmentary images the essences appear concretely, but it is the philosophical construction that, even if invisible, gives support and coherence to the whole. When Benjamin praised montage as progressive because it "interrupts the context into which it is inserted," he was referring to its destructive, critical dimension (the only one that Adorno's observations recognize). But the task of the Arcades project was to implement as well the constructive dimension of montage, as the only form in which modern philosophy could be erected.

4

Mythic History: Fetish

1

Within myth, the passage of time takes the form of predetermination. The course of events is said to be predestined by the gods, written in the stars, spoken by oracles, or inscribed in sacred texts. Strictly speaking, myth and history are incompatible. The former dictates that because human beings are powerless to interfere in the workings of fate, nothing truly new can happen, while the concept of history implies the possibility of human influence upon events, and with it, the moral and political responsibility of people as conscious agents to shape their own destiny.

Myths give answers to why the world is as it is when an empirical cause and effect cannot be seen, or when it cannot be remembered. Although they satisfy the desire felt by human beings for a meaning-filled world, it is at the high price of turning that world back upon them as inescapable fate. Mythic time is, clearly, not limited to a particular discourse. Science as well as theology, rationalism as well as superstition can claim that events are inexorably determined. Nor are mythic explanations limited to a particular epoch. They have their (Western) source in classical antiquity and Biblical narrative. But they reappear in the most recent cosmological speculations, for example, the interpretation of nuclear holocaust as the fulfillment of Biblical prophecy—a devilish attempt, from the critical perspective of "history," to throw the responsibility onto God for the terrifying situation that human beings have themselves created.

Interpretations of nuclear war as divinely preordained deny the possibility of human control, and thus the possibility of history itself. But science can encourage a blind faith in technological "progress" that may be even more likely than theological fatalism to bring about the mythic Armageddon. In both cases, the political point is that when temporality is conceived under the mythic sign of predetermination, people are convinced that the present course of events cannot be resisted.

The *Passagen-Werk* is fundamentally concerned with debunking mythic theories of history whatever form their scenarios may take—inevitable catastrophe no less than continuous improvement. But Benjamin was most persistent in his attack against the myth of automatic historical progress. In his lifetime, at the very brink of the nuclear age and the twilight of technological innocence, this myth was still largely unshaken, and Benjamin considered it to be the greatest political danger. Whereas earlier interpreters have seen his pessimism regarding the course of history as a late characteristic of his thinking, coming as a response to the Nazi-Soviet Non-Aggression Pact or the impending war, the *Passagen-Werk* makes it clear that it was his long-standing (if intensifying) concern.[1] The earliest notes describe the project's aim: "to drive out any trace of 'development' from the image of history"[2]; to overcome "the ideology of progress . . . in all its aspects."[3] A pre–1935 entry elaborates:

It can be considered one of the methodological objectives of this work to demonstrate a historical materialism within which the idea of progress has been annihilated. Precisely on this point historical materialism has every reason to distinguish itself sharply from bourgeois mental habits. Its basic principle is not progress, but actualization.[4]

It is thus no surprise that when Benjamin deals directly with Darwinian theories of social evolution in the *Passagen-Werk*, it is to attack the premise of progressive development. He criticizes the "doctrine of natural selection" because "[. . .] it popularized the notion that progress was automatic. Moreover, it promoted the extension of the concept of progress to the entire realm of human activity."[5] Benjamin's own ideational constellation of "natural history," in contrast, presumes no happy outcome, and indeed, no necessary social outcome at all.

There is nothing natural about history's progression. But (on this Benjamin insisted) nature does progress historically. The new nature of industry and technology represents real progress at the level of the means of production—while at the level of the relations of production, class exploitation remains unchanged. Here again, it is the conflation of nature and history that leads to error: Whereas social evolution is a myth when it identifies history's barbarism as natural, when industrial progress is taken as the point of departure, the mythic error consists of mistaking advances in nature for advances in history itself.

Benjamin's late (1940) text, *Über den Begriff der Geschichte* (known as the Theses on History), argues that the equation of technological with historical progress had led the German working class to set the wrong political goals:

It regarded technological development as the direction of those waters through which it thought itself to be moving. From there it was but a step to the illusion that factory work, which was a characteristic of technical progress, was itself a political accomplishment . . . [bypassing] the question of how . . . [the factory's] products were to benefit the workers while still not being at their disposal. It acknowledges only progress in the mastery of nature, not the retrogression of society.[6]

Originally, the idea of progress was the standard by which Enlightenment thinkers judged history and found it lacking.[7] It is only when "progress becomes the signature of the course of history *in its totality*" that this concept is identified with "uncritical assumptions of actuality rather than with a critical position of questioning."[8] Benjamin searches out the origins of this mistaken identity. In quite conventional neo-Marxist terms, he claims that the concept of progress forfeited its critical power when "the bourgeoisie conquered its power positions in the nineteenth century."[9] But quite unconventionally, he attempts to document this claim visually, in terms of the physical transformation of the city of Paris.

2

In the eighteenth century the bourgeois Enlightenment challenged the theological position that the heavenly and earthly cities were contradictory extremes, one full of sin and suffering, the other a place of redemption and eternal bliss. It called on human beings to use their own, God-given reason to create the "heavenly" city here and now, and as an earthly paradise, material happiness was to be a basic component of its construction. The industrial revolution seemed to make possible this practical realization of paradise. In the nineteenth century, capital cities throughout Europe, and ultimately throughout the world, were dramatically transformed into glittering showcases, displaying the promise of the new industry and technology for a heaven-on-earth—and no city glittered more brilliantly than Paris. Thomas Appleton, a Bostonian whose life spanned the nineteenth century, caught both the old and new conception in a sentence: "'good Americans, when they die, go to Paris.'"[10] So legendary[11] was the "concrete imagery of broad, tree-lined boulevards, the shops, cafes, and theatres, the good food and wine of this earthly city" that it "might easily eclipse a nebulous vision of celestial pearly gates and golden stairs."[12]

Urban brilliance and luxury were not new in history, but secular, public access to them was. The splendor of the modern city could be experienced by everyone who strolled its boulevards and parks, or visited its department stores, museums, art galleries, and national monuments. Paris, a "looking-glass city,"[13] dazzled the crowd, but at the same time deceived it. The City of Light, it erased night's darkness—first with gas lanterns, then with electricity, then neon lights—in the space of a century.[14] The City of Mirrors—in which the crowd itself became a spectacle—it reflected the image of people as consumers rather than producers, keeping the class relations of production virtually invisible on the looking glass' other side. Benjamin described the spectacle of Paris as a "phantasmagoria" —a magic-lantern show of optical illusions, rapidly changing size and blending into one another. Marx had used the term "phantasmagoria" to refer to the deceptive appearances of commodities as "fetishes" in the marketplace. The *Passagen-Werk* entries cite the relevant passages from *Capital* on the fetish character of commodities, describing how exchange value obfuscates the source of the value of commodities in productive labor.[15] But for Benjamin, whose point of departure was a philosophy of historical experience rather than an economic analysis of capital, the key to the new urban phantasmagoria was not so much the commodity-in-the-market as the commodity-on-display, where exchange value no less than use value lost practical meaning, and purely representational value came to the fore. Everything desirable, from sex to social status, could be transformed into commodities as fetishes-on-display that held the crowd enthralled even when personal possession was far beyond their reach. Indeed, an unattainably high price tag only enhanced a commodity's symbolic value. Moreover, when newness became a fetish, history itself became a manifestation of the commodity form.

3

Panoramas (figure 4.1) were a common attraction in the arcades, providing sweeping views that unrolled before the spectators, giving them the illusion of moving through the world at an accelerated rate. The experience corresponded to that of moving along a street of commodity display windows. What follows in this section is a "panoramic" tour of the ur-forms of the phantasmagoria of progress which Benjamin unearthed in his research. Not only does this allow us to cover a good deal of *Passagen-Werk* ground in a short space. By replicating the principle of panoramic representation, it

4.1 Viewers at a Panorama.

provides a sense of that construction of history which Benjamin's own, dialectically constructed images were designed to interrupt.

Arcades

The arcades were "the original temple of commodity capitalism"[16]: "Arcades—they beamed out onto the Paris of the Second Empire like fairy grottoes."[17] Constructed like a church in the shape of a cross (in order, pragmatically, to connect with all four surrounding streets), these privately owned, publicly traversed passages displayed commodities in window showcases like icons in niches. The very profane pleasure houses found there tempted passersby with gastronomical perfections, intoxicating drinks, wealth without labor at the roulette wheel, gaiety in the vaudeville theaters, and, in the first-floor galleries, transports of sexual pleasure sold by a heavenly host of fashionably dressed ladies of the night: "The windows in the upper floor of the Passages are galleries in which angels are nesting; they are called swallows."[18]

Angela
one flight up on the right[19]

During the Second Empire of Napoleon III, the urban phantasmagoria burst out of the narrow confines of the original arcades, disseminating throughout Paris, where commodity displays achieved ever grander, ever more pretentious forms. The Passages "are the precursors of the department stores."[20] The phantasmagoria of display reached its apogee in the international expositions.

World Expositions

The first world exposition was held in London in 1851. Its famous Crystal Palace was constructed out of the same iron and glass that originally had been used in the Passages, but more daringly, in monumental proportions.[21] Entire trees were covered over by the one-hundred-twelve-foot roof. Industrial products were displayed like artworks, vying with ornamental gardens, statues, and fountains for the public's attention. The exposition was described by contemporaries as "'incomparably fairylike.'"[22] The Crystal Palace blended together old nature and new nature—palms as well

4.2 Crystal Palace, London, 1851.

as pumps and pistons—in a fantasy world that entered the imagination of an entire generation of Europeans. In 1900, Julius Lessing wrote:

I remember from my own childhood years how the news of the Crystal Palace reached over into Germany, how, in remote provincial towns, pictures of it were hung on the walls of bourgeois rooms. All that we imagined from old fairy tales of princesses in a glass casket, of queens and elves who lived in crystal houses, seemed to us to be embodied in it [...].[23]

While not the place of the first international exposition, Paris was host to some of the grandest. Its earliest[24] took place in 1855 under a "'monstrous glass roof,'"[25] and "'all Europe was on the move to view the wares'."[26] The structure built for the next Paris fair in 1867 was compared to the Colosseum: "'It looked as if there were before you a monument built on another planet, Jupiter or Saturn, in a taste we do not know, and in colors to which our eyes are not yet accustomed.'"[27] Subsequent fairs in 1889 and 1900 left permanent traces on the city landscape: the Grand Palais, Trocadero, and Paris' hallmark, the Eiffel Tower.[28] The expositions' displays were compared by Sigfried Giedion to *Gesamtkunstwerke*[29] (total works of art). The reason was precisely their phantasmagoric quality, a blend of machine technologies and art galleries, military cannons and fashion costumes, business and pleasure, synthesized into one dazzling visual experience.

The international fairs were the origins of the "pleasure industry [*Vergnugungsindustrie*]," which

[...] refined and multiplied the varieties of reactive behavior of the masses. It thereby prepares the masses for adapting to advertisements. The connection between the advertising industry and world expositions is thus well-founded.[30]

At the fairs the crowds were conditioned to the principle of advertisements: "Look, but don't touch,"[31] and taught to derive pleasure from the spectacle alone.

Wide spans of glass windows originated in the arcades, as did window shopping as the activity of the flâneur. But here display was not a financial end in itself. The shops full of "novelties" and the pleasure establishments depended on a public clientele of the well-to-do. At world's fairs, in contrast, the commerce in commodities was not more significant than their phantasmagoric function as "folk festivals" of capitalism[32] whereby mass entertainment itself became big business.[33] There were eighty thousand exhibitors at Paris' 1855 fair.[34] In 1867, the fair's fifteen million visitors[35] included four hundred thousand French workers to whom free tickets had been distributed, while foreign workers were housed at French government expense.[36] Proletarians were encouraged by the authorities to make the "pilgrimage" to these shrines of industry, to view on display the wonders that their own class had produced but could not afford to own, or to marvel at machines that would displace them.[37]

Phantasmagoria of Politics

The *Passagen-Werk* is fundamentally concerned with the effect of the fairs on workers and working-class organization: Three different workers' delegations were sent to London in 1851: "None of them accomplished anything of significance. Two were official [sent by the French and Paris governments]; the private one came with subsidizing from the press [. . .]. The workers had no influence on putting these delegations together."[38]

It has been claimed that the world expositions were the birthplace of the International Workingman's Association, because they provided the opportunity for workers from different nations to meet and discuss common interests.[39] But despite the initial fears of those in power,[40] the fairs proved to have quite the contrary effect. A phantasmagoria of politics had its source in the world expositions no less than a phantasmagoria of merchandise, wherein industry and technology were presented as mythic powers capable of producing out of themselves a future world of peace, class harmony, and abundance. The message of the world exhibitions as fairylands was the promise of social progress for the masses without revolution. Indeed, the fairs denied the very existence of class antagonisms.[41] Even when workers were permitted to elect their own delegation to them,[42] any potentially revolutionary consequences of such a proletarian assembly was co-opted. Benjamin cites David Riazanov, Soviet editor of the complete works of Marx and Engels (in which Marx's early writings first appeared):

"The interests of industry . . . were placed in the foreground, and the necessity of an understanding between the workers and industrialists was heavily emphasized as the only means whereby the bad situation of the workers could be improved . . . We cannot consider . . . this congregation as the birthplace of the IWA [International Workingman's Association]. This is a legend . . . ."[43]

The Russian Marxist George Plekhanov believed that world expositions could teach a very different lesson. Writing after the 1889 Parisian Exposition that, significantly, celebrated the centennial of the French Revolution, he expressed optimism as to its progressive effect:

[. . . "I]t was as if the French bourgeoisie had been out to prove intentionally to the proletariat, before its very eyes, the economic possibility and necessity of a social revolution. The world exposition gave this class an excellent idea of the previously unheard of levels of development of the means of production that have been attained by all civilized countries, and that have far transcended the wildest fantasies of utopians of the past century . . . This same exposition demonstrated further that the modern development of productive powers, given the anarchy presently reigning in production, must necessarily lead to industrial crises that are evermore intensive and thus evermore destructive in their effects on the workings of the world economy."[44]

Such a view was more wishful thinking than fact, as the historical logic of world expositions was the reverse: The wider the gap between progress in developing the means of production and "anarchy" (crisis and unemployment) in the world economy, the more these capitalist folk festivals were needed to perpetrate the myth of automatic historical progress in order to prevent the proletariat from deriving just such a revolutionary lesson.

National Progress on Display

In the late nineteenth century, the world expositions thus took on an additional meaning. Not only did they provide a utopian fairyland that evoked the wonder of the masses. Each successive exposition was called upon to give visible "proof" of historical progress toward the realization of these utopian goals, by being more monumental, more spectacular than the last (figure 4.3[45]). The original exposition was purely a business venture, committed to

4.3 Paris Exposition, 1900, photo by Emile Zola.

A Profound Faith in the Future

Whatever the magnificence of past expositions, they must of necessity be eclipsed by the new expositions that mark the path open to humanity, and summarize its successive conquests.

This is what makes for the success of these periodic festivals of industry; it is the principal reason for the powerful attraction that they exercise on the masses. The expositions are not only days of leisure and gaiety in the midst of the toils of the people. They appear, at long intervals, as the summits from which we measure the course we have travelled. Mankind goes out from them comforted, full of courage and animated with profound faith in the future. This faith, once the exclusive possession of a few noble spirits of the last century today gains ground more and more; it is the common religion of modern times, a fertile cult, in which the universal expositions take place as majestic and useful ceremonies; as necessary demonstrations for the existence of a nation that is industrious and animated by an irresistible need for expansion; as enterprises that prove themselves less by the material benefits of all kinds that flow from them, than by the powerful impetus they give to the human spirit.

[The 1900 exposition. . .] will be the end of a century of stupendous soaring of science and the economy; it will also be the threshold of an era, the grandeur of which experts and philosophers are prophesizing, and the reality of which, without doubt, will surpass the dreams of our imagination.

laissez-faire principles of trade. But by 1900, governments had got-
ten involved to the point where they were hardly distinguishable
from entrepreneurs themselves.[46] As part of the new imperialism,
"national" pavilions promoted national grandeur, transforming
patriotism itself into a commodity-on-display. And the state became a customer: World fairs claimed to promote world peace,
while displaying for government purchase the latest weapons of
war.[47]

Urbanism

The role of the state in constructing the modern phantasmagoria
was not limited to world fairs. Benjamin deals centrally with the
new urbanism financed by the state, which was contemporaneous
with the fairs,[48] and which in Paris was the obsessive occupation of
Napoleon III's minister, Baron Haussmann.[49] The phantasmagoric illusions fostered by this "artist of demolition"[50] figured heavily
in the mythic imagery of historical progress, and functioned as a
monument to the state's role in achieving it. As a classic example of
reification, urban "renewal" projects attempted to create social
utopia by changing the arrangement of buildings and streets—
objects in space—while leaving social relationships intact. Under
Haussmann, schools and hospitals were built, and air and light
were brought into the city,[51] but class antagonisms were thereby
covered up, not eliminated.

Haussmann's slum "clearance" simply broke up working-class
neighborhoods and moved the eyesores and health hazards of
poverty out of central Paris and into the suburbs.[52] His system of
public parks and "pleasure grounds" provided the illusion of social
equality,[53] while behind the scenes his building projects initiated a
boom of real estate speculation whereby the government expanded
the private coffers of capitalists with public funds.[54] Railways penetrated to the heart of Paris, and railroad stations took over the function of city gates.[55] The demolition of Paris occurred on a massive
scale, as destructive to the old Paris as any invading army might
have been.[56] The urban "perspectives"[57] which Haussmann
created from wide boulevards, lined with uniform building facades
that seemed to stretch to infinity and punctuated by national
monuments, were intended to give the fragmented city an appear-

ance of coherence. In fact the plan, based on a politics of imperial centralization, was a totalitarian aesthetics, in that it caused "'the repression of every individualistic part, every autonomous development'" of the city,[58] creating an artificial city where the Parisian [. . .] no longer feels at home.'"[59]

As with the world fairs, the *Passagen-Werk*'s concern is with the political effects of urbanism in undermining the revolutionary potential of the working class:

The true goal of Haussmann's works was the securing of the city against civil war [. . .]. The width of the avenues was to prohibit the erection [of street barricades], and new streets were to provide the shortest routes between the barracks and the working-class sections. Contemporaries christened the undertaking "strategic beautification."[60]

Haussmann's "strategic beautification" is the ur-form of the culture of modern statism.

Progress Deified

In 1855, the year of the first Paris Exposition, Victor Hugo, "'the man of the nineteenth century as Voltaire had been man of the eighteenth','"[61] announced: "'Progress is the footstep of God himself'."[62] Progress became a religion in the nineteenth century, world expositions its holy shrines, commodities its cult objects, and Haussmann's "new" Paris its Vatican City. The Saint-Simonians were the self-proclaimed, secular priests of this new religion, writing poems of praise to industry's advances, and distributing their tracts by the millions (18,000,000 printed pages between 1830 and 1832).[63] In these mass-produced, low-cost publications, the great entreprenurial enterprises, including world expositions, received their sanctification. They imbued railroad construction with a sense of mission. Benjamin cited the Saint-Simonian Michel Chevalier:

"One can compare the zeal and enthusiasm which civilized nations today give to the construction of railroads with that which occurred some centuries ago with the erection of churches . . . Indeed, it can be demonstrated that the word religion comes from *religare* [to bind together] . . . , the railroads have more affinity than one would have thought with the spirit of religion. There has never existed an instrument with so much power for . . . uniting peoples separated from one another."[64]

Such "uniting" of peoples contributed to the illusion that industrialism on its own was capable of eliminating class divisions, achieving the common brother- and sisterhood that had traditionally been religion's goal. Indeed, the most decisive political characteristic of Saint-Simon's theory was his conception of workers and capitalists united in a single "industrial class,"[65] and he considered entrepreneurs exploited "because they paid interest."[66] Benjamin observed: "The Saint-Simonians had only very limited sympathies for democracy"[67]; according to them: "All social antagonisms dissolve in the fairy tale that *progrés* is the prospect of the very near future."[68]

Bigger is Better

Railroads were the referent, and progress the sign, as spatial movement became so wedded to the concept of historical movement that these could no longer be distinguished. But speed was not the only metaphor that took on a mythic identity with progress. Under conditions of competitive capitalism, pure numbers, abundance, excess, monumental size, and expansion entered into this semantic constellation, and became "progress'" very effective advertisement:

"Thus not long ago the [store] called 'Chaussée d'Antin' announced its new inventory by the meter [. . .]. In all, about eleven million meters of manufactured goods. The *Tintamarre* observed, after it recommended the 'Chaussée d'Antin' to its readers as 'the number one fashion house in the world' and also the most 'solid,' that 'the entire French railroad' consisted altogether of not even ten thousand kilometers. This *one* store could therefore cover all the railways of France like a tent with its materials, 'which in the summer heat would actually be quite pleasant.' Three or four similar establishments published similar measures of length, so that with the materials taken altogether, not only Paris . . . but the entire department of the Seine could be placed under a great weather-protecting roof, 'which once again, would be very pleasant in rainy weather' [. . .].

"One hears: 'The Ville de Paris, the largest store in the capital,' 'the Villes de France, the largest store in the Empire,' 'The "Chaussée d'Antin," the largest store in Europe,' 'The Coin de Rue, the largest store in the world.' In the world! Then none larger on the whole earth; that must be the limit. Oh, no! 'The Magazins du Louvre' still haven't been considered, and these have the title, 'the largest stores in the Universe.'"[69]

Elephantism permeated fantasies of state power as well:

"If one had to define in a word the new spirit that was going to preside over the transformation of Paris, one would call it 'megalomania.' The Emperor and his prefect [Haussmann] wished to make of Paris the capital not only of France, but of the world."[70]

"Paris will become the world, and the universe will be Paris [. . .]. Paris will climb to the clouds, scale the heavens of the heavens, make districts for itself out of the planets and the stars."[71]

Cosmic proportions, monumental solidarity, and panoramic perspectives were the characteristics of the new urban phantasmagoria. All of its aspects—railroad stations, museums, wintergardens, sport palaces, department stores, exhibition halls, boulevards—dwarfed the original arcades and eclipsed them. These once magical "fairy grottoes" that had spawned the phantasmagoria went into eclipse: Their narrowness appeared stifling, their perspectives claustrophobic, their gaslight too dim.

4

Where in the new does the boundary run between reality and appearance?[72]

How could this phantasmagoria be seen through? How could the mythic metaphors of progress that had permeated public discourse be unmasked and exposed as the mystification of mass consciousness, particularly when the big-city glitter of modernity seemed to offer material proof of progress before one's very eyes? Searching the historical records for counterevidence, Benjamin used all the scholarly imagination at his disposal to discover within them counterimages that rubbed harshly against the grain of the semantics of progress, with its unmediated identification of technological change with social betterment, and its imagery of the inevitable coming of a heaven-on-earth. Where Marx himself had fallen under the spell of the discourse of progress, identifying revolutions as the "locomotives of world history," Benjamin countered: "Perhaps it is totally different. Perhaps revolutions are the reaching of humanity traveling in this train for the emergency brake."[73] Where the megalomania of monumental proportions, of "bigger is better," equated both capitalist and imperialist expansion with the progressive course of history, Benjamin sought out the small, discarded objects, the outdated buildings and fashions which, precisely as the "trash" of history, were evidence of its unprecedented material destruction. And where the Saint-Simonians appropriated the discourse of religion that still had powerful semantic force in order to lend history legitimacy, Benjamin reversed the direction of this discourse from a vindication of the forward course of history to a radical critique of history when viewed with a backward gaze.

Consider the prize-winning design to remodel the Porte Maillot (figure 4.4). The contest (advertised as a *concours d'idées* unlikely to lead to actual construction) was sponsored by the city of Paris in 1931. The dramatic focus of the winning composition (by Bigot) was a gigantic winged sculpture, an "angel of victory" celebrating the history of French military triumphs, to be erected at the Rond Point de la Défense. A classical figure, she faces the future with calm confidence. Her monumental grandeur dwarfs the crowd that feels its insignificance as a consequence, its childlike dependence on forces greater than itself, given the cosmic scale of world events and the destinies of nations. What could be more unlike this monument

4.4 Statue of Victory, proposed for the Rond Point de la Defense, Bigot, 1931.

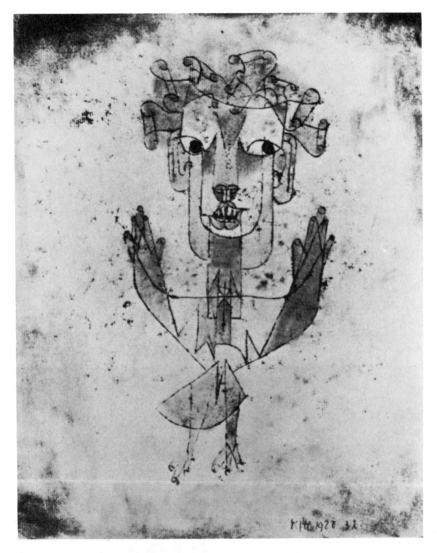

4.5 "Angelus Novus," Paul Klee, 1920.

to mythic progress than Paul Klee's painting, "Angelus Novus" (figure 4.5), in which Benjamin found the "Angel of History" personified, and which in relation to the viewer retains human proportions? But it is the caption that produces the critical force of this image:

There is a picture by Klee called "Angelus Novus." An angel is presented in it who looks as if he were about to move away from something at which he is staring. His eyes are wide open, mouth agape, wings spread. The angel of history must look like that. His face is turned toward the past. Where a chain of events appears to *us*, *he* sees one single catastrophe which relentlessly piles wreckage upon wreckage, and hurls them before his feet. [. . .]. The storm [from Paradise] drives him irresistibly into the future to which his back is turned, while the pile of debris before him grows toward the sky. That which we call progress is this storm.[74]

A construction of history that looks backward, rather than forward, at the destruction of material nature as it *has actually taken place*, provides dialectical contrast to the futurist myth of historical progress (which can only be sustained by forgetting what has happened).

Dust

The phantasmagoric understanding of modernity as a chain of events that leads with unbroken, historical continuity to the realization of social utopia, a "heaven" of class harmony and material abundance—this conceptual constellation blocked revolutionary consciousness like an astrological force. Benjamin focuses on small, overlooked motifs in the historical sources that explode it. Where the myth imagined the force of machines as a power driving history forward, Benjamin provides material evidence that history has not budged. Indeed, history stands so still, it gathers dust. The historical documents attest to it. In 1859:

Return from the *Courses de la Marche*: "The dust has surpassed all expectations. The elegant people back from the *Marche* are practically buried under it, just as at Pompeii; and they have to be disinterred, if not with pickaxes, then at least with a brush."[75]

Dust settles over Paris, stirs, and settles again.[76] It drifts into the Passages and collects in their corners[77]; it catches in the velvet drapes and upholstery of bourgeois parlors[78]; it clings to the historical wax figures in the Musée Gravin.[79] The fashionable trains on women's dresses sweep through dust.[80] "Under Louis-Philippe dust even spreads itself over the revolutions."[81]

Fragility

If history has not budged, this does not make Paris more secure. On the contrary, behind the illusion of permanence that the monumental facades of Haussmann's Paris sought to establish, the city is fragile. Indeed, the remarkable thing is that "'Paris still exists.'"[82] The ability to capture this fragility is what Benjamin appreciated in Charles Meyron's ink sketches of Paris, composed on the eve of Haussmann's catastrophic demolitions. The latter's "modernization" of Paris obliterated history by wiping out its traces. Meyron's scenes, in contrast, captured the essentially fleeting character of modern history, and commemorated the suffering of the living by recording its traces:

A criterion for whether a city is modern: the absence of memorials ("New York is a city without memorials"—Döblin). Meyron made modern memorials out of tenement houses.[83]

Transiency *without* progress, a relentless pursuit of "novelty" that brings about nothing new in history—in making visible the outlines of *this* temporality, Benjamin provides the direct counterimage to an approaching heaven-on-earth: "Modernity, the time of Hell."[84] The image of Hell is the dialectical antithesis of the nineteenth century's depictions of modern reality as a Golden Age, and provides its radical critique. A note to the 1935 exposé gives this "dialectical schema":

Hell—Golden Age. Keywords for Hell: Boredom, Gambling, Pauperism. A canon of this dialectic: Fashion. The Golden Age as catastrophe.[85]

Benjamin was not suggesting that the myth of progress be replaced by a conservative or nihilistic view that hellish repetition is the essence of history in its entirety. (He criticized the belief in "eternal recurrence" as itself "ur-historical, mythical thinking."[86]) On the contrary, the deadly repetitiveness of time that is part of the archaic, mythic imagery of Hell describes what is truly modern and novel about commodity society. Conversely, novelty is not lacking in the archaic: "The punishments of hell are in every case the newest that exists in this realm."[87] The image of modernity as the time of Hell

[. . .] deals not with the fact that "always the same thing" happens (*a forteriori* this is not about eternal recurrence) but the fact that on the face of that oversized head called earth precisely what is newest doesn't change; that this "newest" in all its pieces keeps remaining the same. It constitutes the eternity of Hell and its sadistic craving for innovation. To determine the totality of features in which this "modernity" imprints itself would mean to represent Hell.[88]

Fashion

In the image of Hell as a configuration of repetition, novelty, and death, Benjamin opened up to philosophical understanding the phenomenon of fashion that is specific to capitalist modernity.[89] A "metaphysics of fashion" was planned for the *Passagen-Werk*,[90] and the early notes describe along what lines it was to be conceived. Not only is fashion the modern "measure of time"[91]; it embodies the changed relationship between subject and object that results from the "new" nature of commodity production. In fashion, the phantasmagoria of commodities presses closest to the skin.

Now clothing is quite literally at the borderline between subject and object, the individual and the cosmos. Its positioning surely accounts for its emblematic significance throughout history. In the Middle Ages, the "proper" attire was that which bore the imprint of the social order: Cosmetics were a reflection of a divinely ordered cosmos, and a sign of one's position within it.[92] Of course, class position was then as static as the nature in which human beings saw their own lives reflected: Accident of birth determined one's social situation; the latter, in turn, determined one's probabilities of death. At a time when such historical mediations of biology were accepted as fate, styles in clothing reinforced the social hierarchy by reiterating it. Against this background, the positive moment of modern fashion stands out clearly. Its constant striving for "novelty," for separation from the given, identifies generational cohorts, whose dress symbolizes an end to the dependency and natural determinacy of childhood, and entry into their own collective role as historical actors. Interpreted affirmatively, modern fashion is irreverent toward tradition, celebratory of youth rather than social class, and thus emblematic of social change. The *Passagen-Werk* tells us that "fashion" spread to the lower classes in the nineteenth century. 1844: "'cotton cloth replaces brocades, satins . . . and soon, thanks to the revolutionary spirit [of 1789], the attire of the lower classes becomes more comfortable and more attractive to see.'"[93] A "'plebian character'" of attire itself became fashionable.[94] For women specifically, changes in fashion were a visible indicator of new social freedom. Benjamin cites this 1873 text:

"The triumph of the bourgeoisie modifies female attire. Dress and hair style become wider . . . the shoulders are broadened by mutton sleeves [. . . I]t wasn't long before hoops came back into fashion and bouffant skirts were made. Thus attired, women appeared destined for a sedentary life inside the family, because their mode of dress had nothing that gave the idea of movement or appeared to favor it. This turned about totally with the arrival of the Second Empire. The bonds of the family loosened, an ever-growing luxury corrupted morals [. . .]. Dress for the woman thus changed from head to foot . . . The hoop was drawn back and brought together in an accentuated bustle. Everything possible was developed to prevent the woman from sitting; everything that made it difficult for her to walk was eliminated. She wore her hair and dressed as if to be seen from the side. Indeed, the profile is the silhouette of a person . . . who passes by, who escapes us."[95]

At some times Benjamin describes fashions as predictive of historical change,[96] but at others (increasingly in the 1930s) he reads fashion for an explanation as to why it has not.[97] In the 1935 exposé Benjamin remarks: "Fashion prescribed the ritual by which the fetish commodity wished to be worshiped."[98] That ritual could not have been more distinct from those tradition-bound rites of holidays and seasonal celebrations by which the "old" nature had been revered, marking the recurrent life cycles of organic nature. The spring rites of fashion celebrated novelty rather than recurrence; they required, not remembrance, but obliviousness to even the most recent past. In the Hades of Greek and Roman mythology, the river Lethe caused those who drank of its waters to forget their former life. The effect on collective historical memory of satisfying the thirst for novelty through fashion was not otherwise.[99] "Fashions are the medicament that is to compensate for the fateful effects of forgetting, on a collective scale."[100]

Reified in commodities, the utopian promise of fashion's transitoriness undergoes a dialectical reversal: The living, human capacity for change and infinite variation becomes alienated, and is affirmed only as a quality of the inorganic object. In contrast, the ideal for human subjects (urged into rigorous conformity to fashion's dictates)[101] becomes the biological rigor mortis of eternal youth. It is for this that the commodity is worshiped—in a ritual that is, of course, destined to fail. Valéry speaks of the "'absurd superstition of the new.'"[102] Benjamin makes us *see* it, in revealing the logic of modernity as "the time of Hell":

How, namely, this time doesn't want to know death, also how fashion mocks death, how the acceleration of traffic, the tempo of communicating information whereby newspaper editions supersede each other, aim precisely at the elimination of all sudden endings, and how death as an incision is connected with all straight courses of divine time.[103]

Sterility

Woman is the central figure in Benjamin's "metaphysics of fashion," not only because Paris was the capital of specifically female fashions,[104] but because women's fecundity personifies the creativity of the old nature, the transiency of which has its source in life rather than death. Women's productivity, organic in contrast to the mechanical productivity of nineteenth-century industrialism, appears threatening to capitalist society, as Malthus argued at the beginning of the century, and as aesthetic style represented at its end: "The high point of a technical arrangement of the world lies in the liquidation of fecundity. The ideal beauty of *Jugendstil* is represented by the frigid woman. *Jugendstil* sees in every woman not Helena but Olympia."[105] But if woman's fecundity threatens commodity society, the cult of the new threatens her in turn. Death and decay, no longer simply a part of organic life, are thrown up at the woman as a special punishment or fate. Her "'continuous effort to be beautiful'"[106] is reminiscent of the repetitive punishment of Hell. "'From the weakness of women's social position'"[107] arises the extraordinary appeal to her of fashion. Being "'everyone's contemporary'"[108] means never growing old; always being "newsworthy"—"that is the most passionate and most secret satis-

4.6 "Fashionable people represented in public by their accoutrements"—Grandville, 1844.

faction which fashion gives to women."[109] But fashion does not change the social reality that transformed women's biological potency into a weakness in the first place,[110] and sees even the living flower as "an emblem of sin."[111] With the smallest variations,[112] fashion covers up reality. Like Haussmann's urban renewal, it rearranges the given, merely symbolizing historical change, rather than ushering it in.

In the process of displacing nature's transiency onto commodities, the life force of sexuality is displaced there as well. For what is it that is desired? No longer the human being: Sex appeal emanates from the clothes that one wears (figure 4.6[113]). Humanity is what you hang your hat on.

In a macabre inversion of the utopian dream of a reconciliation between humanity and nature, fashion "'invents an artificial humanity.'"[114] Clothes mimic organic nature (sleeves resemble penguin wings[115]; fruit and flowers appear as hair ornaments[116]; fishbones decorate hats, and feathers appear not only here, but on evening pumps, and umbrellas[117]), whereas the living, human body mimics the inorganic world (skin strives through cosmetics to attain the color of rose taffeta[118]; crinoline skirts turn women into "triangles" or "X's,"[119] or "'walking bells'").[120]

Death

Birth, writes Benjamin, is a "natural" condition, death is a "social" one.[121] Fashion is the "transcendence" [*Aufhebung*] of the former as a new source of newness; it "transcends" the latter by making the inorganic commodity itself the object of human desire.[122] Fashion is the medium that "lures [sex] ever deeper into the inorganic world"—the "realm of dead things."[123] It is "the dialectical switching station between woman and commodity— desire and dead body."[124] With its power to direct libidinal desire onto inorganic nature, fashion connects commodity fetishism with that sexual fetishism characteristic of modern eroticism, which "lowers the barriers between the organic and inorganic world."[125] Just as the much-admired mannequin has detachable parts,[126] so fashion encourages the fetishistic fragmentation of the living body.[127] The modern woman who allies herself with fashion's newness in a struggle against natural decay represses her own productive power, mimics the mannequin,[128] and enters history as a dead object, a "gaily decked-out corpse."[129] Fashion "prostitutes the living body to the inorganic world,"[130] at the moment when prostitutes themselves begin to rely on the commodity appeal of fashionable dress, selling their living bodies as a thing.[131]

For fashion was never anything but the parody of the gaily decked-out corpse, the provocation of death through the woman, and (in between noisy, canned slogans) the bitter, whispered *tête-à-tête* with decay. That is fashion. For this reason she changes so rapidly, teasing death, already becoming something else again, something new, as death looks about for her in order to strike her down. She has given him tit for tat for a hundred years. Now finally she is ready to leave the field. But on the shore of a new Lethe that rolls its asphalt stream through the arcades, he sets up the armature of prostitutes as trophy.[132]

Aging prostitutes who collect in the arcades along with the other outdated objects of desire are clues to the truths of fashion that, turning the body into a sexual commodity, knows to escape from death only by mimicking it.

Chthonic Paris

In the representation of Hell as the essence of modern society, the *Passagen-Werk* examines, literally, the underground of Paris, its systems of subterranean passageways. The catacombs: In the Middle Ages, for a price, you could be taken down into them and shown "the devil in his hellish majesty," during the French Revolution clandestine news of impending revolt passed through them undetected, and "still today, one can pay two francs for an entry ticket to visit this most nightlike Paris, which is so much cheaper and less dangerous than the world above."[133] The old stone quarries: It is better not to wander in them without a guide " 'if one doesn't want to be marooned and die of hunger.' "[134] The cave at Chatelet: prisoners were held in this " 'tomb of Hell' " before being sent to the galleys.[135] The underground passages beneath the forts of Paris, " 'so extensive they could hold half the population of Paris,' "[136] were used to imprison the insurrectionists of June 1848.[137] The Paris sewers: Haussmann's engineering successes with the city's water system led to the comment that he was " 'more inspired by the gods of the netherworld than those on high.' "[138] And finally, Paris' most modern underworld, which evokes for Benjamin the most ancient:

The metro, where evenings the lights glow red [. . .] shows the way down into the Hades of names: Combat, Elysée, Georges V, Etienne Marcel, Solferino, Invalides, Vaugirard have thrown off the tasteful chain of streets and squares, and, here in the lightning-pierced, whistle-pierced darkness, have become misshapened sewer gods, catacomb fairies. This labyrinth conceals in its innards not just one, but dozens of blind, rushing bulls, into whose jaws not once a year one Theban virgin, but every morning thousands of anemic young cleaning women and still sleepy salesmen are forced to hurl themselves.[139]

As part of the "mythological typology" of Paris,[140] the arcades enter into this underworld constellation not in their original fairyland form, but as they exist ghostlike, in the present. The "compact darkness" that at night seems to leap out of the Passages at passersby, causing them to hurry away in fear, are like "the places one was shown in ancient Greece that descended into Hades"; their "history, condition and dispersal" become this century's key to the past, to the "underworld into which Paris sank."[141]

Recurrence

Modernity's mythic temporality reanimates as contemporary social types the archaic figures of Hades, whose punishments are echoed in the repetitiveness of modern existence:

The essence of mythic occurrence is recurrence. In it is inscribed as a hidden figure the futility that stands written in the stars for several heroes of the underworld (Tantalus, Sisyphus, or the Danaides).[142]

For the "heroes" of mass society, the experience of futility is not different. (We have already seen how fashion metes out this punishment.) The nineteenth-century phantasmagoria depicted cashiers in the café windows as fairy goddesses; Benjamin compares them instead to the Danaides, punished in Hades by having to draw water through a sieve and pour it into broken cisterns.[143] There is "a particular structure of fate that can be recognized only in money; and a particular structure of money that is recognized only in fate."[144] This fate pursues those who themselves pursue happiness, and hope that money will buy it: The modern Tantalus is the eternal seeker of love from a streetwalker or any passerby, like the modern gambler[145] playing his lucky number at the roulette wheel whose eye "falls compulsively, like the ivory ball, into the red or black slot":

Does he not transform the arcades into a Casino, a gambling hall where he places the red, blue, and yellow chips of emotion on women, on a face that appears suddenly—will it return his gaze?—on a silent mouth—will it speak to him? That which looks out at the gambler from every number on the green cloth—happiness—here winks to him out of every woman's body, as the chimera of sexuality: as his type.[146]

Sin

In Benjamin's images, Hell names reality directly,[147] and the sin of the living is their own punishment. This sin has its source, not in desire itself (—"only ignorant idealism can believe that sensual desire, no matter of what sort, could designate the theological concept of sin"[148]—), but in desire's superstitious (mythic) surrender to fate. This occurs in fashion, when active, sensual desire is surrendered to objects and perverted into the passive desire for new sensations.[149] Similarly:

In the gambler and the prostitute it is superstition which supplies the representations of fate, filling all desire-filled intercourse with fate-inquisitiveness and fate-lasciviousness, and itself lowering desire to its throne.[150]

In the early notes, in explicitly theological language, Benjamin describes an alternative "life with God" that is connected to desire by the name: "The name itself is the cry of naked desire. This holy, sober, fate-less in-itself, the name, knows no greater opponent than fate [. . .].[151] Benjamin is citing himself here in a different context, drawing on his own earlier writings on language, in which the idea of the "name" refers to the God-granted, cognitive power of humans, among all natural creatures, to translate Being into language, that is, to reveal its meaning: Adam, as the first philosopher, named the creatures of Paradise.[152] It is just this power—and moral responsibility as divine creatures—that humans, sinfully, throw away when they allow themselves to *be* named by a mythic fate and bow down before it. In its political form, this sin is fascism:

Lodged in fate is the [fascist] concept of "total experience" that is deadly by nature. War is unsurpassed in prefiguring it (—"The fact that I was born a German, it is for this that I die").[153]

Boredom

Monotony is nourished by the new.[154]

Hellishly repetitive time—eternal waiting punctuated by a "discontinuous" sequence of "interruptions"[155]—constitutes the particularly modern form of boredom, that in Paris already in the 1840s, "began to be experienced as epidemic."[156] "'France is bored,'" announced Lamartine in 1839.[157] Haussmann's remodeling did not help matters: "'These great streets, these great quays, these great buildings, these great sewers, their physiognomy badly copied or badly imagined, [. . .] exhale boredom.'"[158] Benjamin comments: "The more that life is regulated administratively, the more people must learn waiting. Games of chance have the great attraction of making people free from waiting."[159] Endless waiting thus makes the finality of fate seem appealing. Boredom, however, is not escaped easily. It threatens the gambler, the drug user, the flâneur, and the dandy who appear to choose their fate freely[160] no less than the externally compelled workers at their machines who cannot.[161] Benjamin calls boredom an "index of participation in the collective sleep."[162] But it is a sleep in which class differences are crucial. If history, far from progressing with the pace of technology, is stuck like a broken record in the present structure of social relations, it is because the workers cannot afford to stop working, any more than the class that lives off this labor can afford to let history go forward. "We are bored when we do not know what we are waiting for."[163] The upper classes do not know, and do not wish to know, that the objective source of boredom is because history is languishing—and the moment of their own overthrow is delayed. They are addicted to boredom,[164] as they are to remaining asleep. The average man— and the poet[165]—blames boredom on the weather.[166] But for the working class, industrial labor shatters the illusion that nature rather than society is to blame. Benjamin characterizes "factory work as the economic substructure of the ideological boredom of the upper classes" for whom boredom is merely fashionable, citing Engels (1844) on the condition of the working class in England:

"The gloomy routine of an endless agony of work, in which the identical mechanical process is undergone again and again, is like the task of Sisyphus: The burden of work, like rocks, falls back repeatedly upon the exhausted workers."[167]

Benjamin distinguishes politically between different social types in terms of their attitude toward boredom: the gambler just killing time,[168] the flâneur who "charges time with power like a battery," and "finally, a third type: he charges time and gives its power out again in changed form:—in that of expectation."[169] It is surely the revolutionary whom Benjamin here intends, for whom "boredom is the threshold of great deeds."[170] But the truly infernal horror of modern time is that revolution itself can become its victim, condemned to repeat itself, and condemned to fail: 1789, 1830, 1848, 1871—Four "revolutions" in the name of universal democracy and justice, each ushering in a consolidation of the same particular interests and particular class control; all but the first, temporary interruptions, which left the social relations of class fundamentally unassailed.

5

Imprisoned at the Fort du Taureau during the Paris Commune, Auguste Blanqui, now an old man and a veteran of all three of the century's revolutions, wrote a book of cosmological speculations[171] that included images of history so close to the *Passagen-Werk*'s presentation of modernity as Hell that when Benjamin stumbled upon this little-known text at the end of 1937,[172] he could not help but see it as documentary substantiation of his own work. The crucial difference between their positions was that Blanqui, while identifying the phantasmagoria as infernal rather than heavenly, did not see as a consequence the inadequacy of the anarchist politics of putschism that had been his own lifelong position. Instead, he made the mistake of absolutizing the Hell of commodity society, describing it with complementary monumentality.[173] Blanqui projected not progress, but catastrophe onto the whole universe:

The cosmic view that Blanqui outlines in [this last written book], taking his data from the mechanistic natural sciences of bourgeois society, is an infernal one—and at the same time complementary to that society which B{lanqui} was forced to acknowledge as victor over himself at the end of his life. What is truly upsetting is that there is no irony whatsoever in this description. It is an unrestrained submission, but at the same time the most terrible accusation against a society that throws this image of the cosmos as its projection onto the heavens.[174]

Blanqui's vision is one in which "'one chooses by chance or by choice, no difference; one does not escape from fate'."[175] There is no escape, because human existence undergoes precisely the same process of duplicating reproduction that characterizes the mass-produced commodity:

". . . [A person's] existence divides in two, a planet for each one, until it bifurcates a second, a third time, to thousands of times [. . .] ten thousand different editions."[176]

On all the planets, throughout the universe:

"The same monotony, the same immobility on alien stars. The universe repeats itself without end, and stays in its place, pawing the ground."[177]

The punishments of ancient Hades could not have been more unendurable than Blanqui's description of the present history of the living:

"That which I write in this moment in a cell of the prison of the Fort du Taureau I have written and I will continue to write for eternity, at a table, with a pen, in clothes, in circumstances that are absolutely similar. It is the same for everyone. One after another, each of these planets sinks into the flames of renewal, reviving and then falling again, the monotonous flowing of an hourglass that turns itself around and empties itself eternally. The new is always old, and the old continuously new. [. . .] The number of our doubles is infinite in time and space. [. . .] These doubles are flesh and bone, indeed, pants and jacket, crinoline and chignon. They are not at all phantoms. They are the present eternalized. Here, however is a great flaw: there exists no progress. Alas! No, they are vulgar re-editions, redundant reproductions."[178]

Benjamin credits Blanqui for seeing through the phantasmagoria of progress, but he did not see its source. It is the "accelerated progression of economic crises" that keeps history cyclical.[179] The Hell that he finds in reality is reflected in his theory directly rather than dialectically, that is, rather than mediated by the very idea of historical progress that has been put into question. Instead: "The thought of eternal recurrence makes a mass article out of historical occurrence itself."[180] For Blanqui as for Nietzsche,[181] the historical determinants (and therefore limits) of this phantasmagoria are not recognized. The spell of eternal recurrence catches them in its "magic circle."[182] In the second (1939) version of the *Passagen-Werk* exposé, Benjamin's new introduction ends with the following passage:

The phantasmagoria of culture itself ultimately finds expression in Haussmann's transformation of Paris. The fact that the glitter with which the society of commodity production thereby surrounds itself and its illusory sense of security are, however, not a reliable shelter is restored to memory by the collapse of the Second Empire and the Paris Commune. In the same epoch, the most feared opponent of this society, Blanqui, revealed to it the terrifying traits of this phantasmagoria in his last book. In this text, humanity figures as condemned. Everything new that it might hope for will unveil itself as nothing but a reality which has always been there. It will be just as incapable of furnishing a liberating solution as a new fashion is of renewing society. Blanqui's cosmic speculation teaches that humanity will be prey to the anxiety of myth for so long as the phantasmagoria has a place in it.[183]

6

Definition of the "modern as the new in connection with that which has always already been there."[184]

The sensation of the newest, the most modern, is in fact just as much a dream form of events as the eternal return of the same.[185]

In the two image spheres just considered—natural history as prehistoric and modernity as Hell—the nineteenth-century origins of the most recent historical phenomena, when named as reincarnations of the most archaic, open themselves up to critical understanding. Both images contain the same conceptual elements—history and nature, myth and transitoriness—but in configurations so different that their meanings pull in opposite directions. If after a century the original arcades appear prehistoric, it is because of the extremely rapid changes which industrial technology has wrought upon the urban landscape. But the experience of time brought about by this rapid change has been precisely the opposite: hellish repetition. Both images criticize a mythical assumption as to the nature of history. One is the assumption that rapid change is historical progress; the other is the conclusion that the modern is *no* progress:

What is most particular to dialectical experience is that it dissipates the illusory appearance of the always-the-same, indeed, even of simple repetition in history. Authentic political experience is absolutely free of this illusion.[186]

The essence of modernity cannot be defined abstractly without falling into logical contradiction. But abstract logic is merely the self-referential reflection of reason and expresses no substantive truth. In contrast, as "names" of modernity, both the "new" and the "archaic" are necessary to express the dialectical truth of this particular historical constellation in its contradictory extremes

Belief in progress, in endless perfectibility (—an unending moral task—) and the conception of eternal recurrence are complementary. They are ineluctable antinomies, in the face of which the dialectical conception of historical time needs to be developed. Against this dialectical conception, eternal recurrence emerges as precisely that "flat rationalism" of which the belief in progress is accused, and this latter belongs to the mythical mode of thinking just as much as does the conception of eternal recurrence.[187]

The kind of historical change that would leave myth behind—because the new nature really had brought about a new society—has not yet occurred. And this confronts us with an even greater paradox, one that demonstrates decisively that the conceptual elements are not invariants. Because such a radical historical change has never existed before in history, it can only find expression *as* myth. It follows that, condemned in one configuration, myth is to be redeemed in another.

5

Mythic Nature: Wish Image

1

The arcades as dream- and wish-image of the collective.[1]

Benjamin was struck by an incontestable, empirical fact: Consistently, when modern innovations appeared in modern history, they took the form of historical restitutions. New forms "cited" the old ones out of context. Thus: "There is an attempt to master the new experiences of the city in the frame of the old ones of traditional nature."[2] And: "[The nineteenth century develops] a thirst for the past."[3]

It was "insane that the French fashions of the Revolution and Napoleon I's Empire mimicked the [ancient] Greek proportions with modern cut and sewn clothing."[4]

The *Passagen-Werk* material is full of evidence of this fusion of old and new. Fashion continuously drew on the past: "[W]ith the Munich Exposition of 1875, the German Renaissance became fashionable."[5] Mechanical looms in Europe mimicked handwoven shawls from the Orient, while the first women's "sportswear" (designed in the 1890s for bicycle riding) "strove [with its tight-fitting waists and rococo skirts] for the conventional ideal-image of elegance."[6] When Baudelaire searched for the words to describe the specifically modern struggles of the urban poet, he revived the "archaic image of the fencer."[7] When social utopians conceived of new, communal societies, it was as a restitution of small-scale agricultural production. Fourier's phalansterie, a highly complex, machinelike social organization conceivable only within a modern context,[8] was to produce "the land of Cockaigne, the ur-old wish symbol of leisure and plenty [. . .]."[9]

Nowhere was the restorative impulse more evident than in the forms taken by the new technologies themselves, which imitated precisely the old forms they were destined to overcome. Early photography mimicked painting.[10] The first railroad cars were designed like stage coaches, and the first electric light bulbs were shaped like gas flames.[11] Newly processed iron was used for ornament rather than structural supports, shaped into leaves, or made to resemble wood.[12] Industrially produced utensils were decorated to resemble flowers, fauna, seashells, and Greek and Renaissance antiques.[13] "Wild Salome" appeared in a *Jugendstil* poster for cigarettes.[14] The newly invented bicycle was named by a poet "the Horse of the Apocalypse."[15] And the earliest form of air travel was celebrated by a staging of Uranus' rise from the earth:

The balloon driver Poitevin, underwritten by great publicity, undertook in his gondola [during the Second Republic] an ascension of Uranus with maidens dressed up as mythological figures.[16]

In the field of architecture, the wrought iron and steel that was first developed for railroads[17] would ultimately be combined with glass for the construction of modern skyscrapers.[18] But the Passages, the first constructions of iron and glass, instead resembled Christian churches,[19] while the first department stores with their immense glassed-in roofs "seemed to have been modeled after Oriental bazaars."[20] Benjamin speaks of iron and glass "come too early"[21]: "In the middle of the last century no one yet had an inkling of how to build with iron and glass."[22] An early entry in the *Passagen-Werk* notes: "Transportation in the stage of myth. Industry in the stage of myth. (Railroad stations and early factories)."[23] The 1935 exposé elaborates: "[Early nineteenth-century] architects mimic the pillars of Pompeiian columns; factories mimic private villas, as later the first railroad stations are modeled on chalets."[24] "'One simply transferred the way of building with wood onto iron'."[25]

Under the archaic masks of classical myth (figure 5.1) and traditional nature (figure 5.2), the inherent potential of the "new nature"—machines, iron shaped by new processes, technologies and industrial materials of every sort—remained unrecognized, unconscious. At the same time, these masks express the desire to

5.1 Poseidon adorns a fountain worked by an invisible steam engine, Crystal Palace Exposition, London, 1851.

5 Mythic Nature: Wish Image

5.2 Fountain of iron in the shape of dolphins, shells, and aquatic plants, Crystal Palace Exposition, London, 1851.

"return" to a mythic time when human beings were reconciled with the natural world.

Benjamin writes: "Fashion, like architecture, [. . .] stands in the darkness of the lived moment [*im Dunkel des gelebten Augenblicks*]."[26] He has taken this phrase from Ernst Bloch. It is central to Bloch's social utopian philosophy, describing the mystical "*nunc stans*," the momentary, fleeting experience of fulfillment dimly anticipatory of a reality that is "not-yet." According to Benjamin, if the "not-yet" of the new nature is expressed in archaic symbols rather than in new forms commensurate with it, then this condition of modern consciousness has its parallel in the inadequacies of development in the economic base. He is most explicit in a passage from the *Passagen-Werk* exposé. It begins with a quotation from Jules Michelet: "Every epoch dreams the one that follows it." Benjamin comments:

To the form of the new means of production which in the beginning is still dominated by the old one (Marx), there correspond in the collective consciousness images in which the new is intermingled with the old. These images are wish images, and in them the collective attempts to transcend as well as to illumine the incompleteness of the social order of production. There also emerges in these wish images a positive striving to set themselves off from the outdated—that means, however, the most recent past. These tendencies turn the image fantasy, that maintains its impulse from the new, back to the ur-past. In the dream in which every epoch sees in images the epoch that follows, the latter appears wedded to elements of ur-history, that is, of a classless society. Its experiences, which have their storage place in the unconscious of the collective, produce, in their interpenetration with the new, the utopia that has left its trace behind in a thousand configurations of life from permanent buildings to ephemeral fashions.[27]

The real possibility of a classless society in the "epoch to follow" the present one, revitalizes past images as expressions of the ancient wish for social utopia in dream form. But a dream image is not yet a dialectical image, and desire is not yet knowledge. Wishes and dreams are psychological categories which for Benjamin have no immediate status as philosophical truth. Parting company with the romanticism of Ernst Bloch (who in turn criticized Benjamin's "surrealist philosophizing" for its lack of subjectivity[28]), Benjamin was reluctant to rest revolutionary hope directly on imagination's capacity to anticipate the not-yet-existing. Even as wish image, utopian imagination needed to be interpreted through the material objects in which it found expression, for (as Bloch knew) it was upon the transforming mediation of matter that the hope of utopia ultimately depended: technology's capacity to create the not-yet-known.

2

The text on collective wish images cited above makes theoretical assertions rather than arguments, and they are by no means self-evident. It may be helpful to consider the passage more closely, this time in an earlier version of the exposé that is significantly different in wording and somewhat less elliptical:

To the form of the new means of production that in the beginning is still dominated by the old one (Marx), there correspond in the societal super-structure wish images in which the new is intermingled with the old in fantastic ways.[29]

Now, Marx argued that when the new means of production comes into being, its socialist potential is fettered by still-existing capital-ist relations—hence the inadequacy of development of the econo-mic base. But as an entry in *Konvolut* F, "Iron Construction," makes clear, Benjamin believed these fetters must be understood in terms of the collective imagination, as inadequacies of form as well as of social relations—and that he understood Marx to have meant this as well. Benjamin cites *Capital*:

"Just how much in the beginning the old form of the means of production dominated the new forms is demonstrated . . . perhaps more strikingly than anywhere by an experimental locomotive that was tested before the discovery of today's locomotives, which had in fact two feet that it raised up alternatingly, like a horse. Only after further development of mechan-ics and the accumulation of practical experience does the form become totally determined by the mechanistic principle and thereby completely emancipated from the traditional physical form of the work-instrument that bursts forth into a machine."[30]

Benjamin comments on Marx's observation: "Just what forms, now lying concealed within machines, will be determining for our epoch we are only beginning to surmise."[31] Here is the "new nature"[32] still in its mythic stage. Technology, not yet "emanci-pated," is held back by conventional imagination that sees the new only as a continuation of the old which has just now become obsolete. Benjamin notes: "The conservative tendency in Parisian life: As late as 1867 an entrepreneur conceived of a plan to have five hundred sedan chairs circulating in Paris."[33]

Now Benjamin tells us that this formal inadequacy of the new nature is not synonymous with (but only "corresponds" to) "wish images" which, far from restraining the new within the given forms, reach back to a more distant past in order to *break from* conventional forms. The early version of the exposé continues:

This intermingling owes its fantastic character above all to the fact that in the course of social development, the old never sets itself off sharply from the new; rather, the latter, striving to set itself apart from the recently outmoded, renews archaic, ur-temporal elements. The utopian images that accompany the emergence of the new always concurrently reach back to the ur-past. In the dream in which every epoch sees in images before its eyes the one that follows it, the images appear wedded to elements of ur-history.[34]

It is necessary to make a distinction: In nature, the new is mythic, because its potential is not yet realized; in consciousness, the old is mythic, because its desires never were fulfilled. Paradoxically, collective imagination mobilizes its powers for a revolutionary break from the recent past by evoking a cultural memory reservoir of myths and utopian symbols from a more distant ur-past. The "collective wish images" are nothing else but this. Sparked by the new, from which they "maintain their impulse,"[35] they envision its revolutionary potential by conjuring up archaic images of the collective "wish" for social utopia. Utopian imagination thus cuts across the continuum of technology's historical development as the possibility of revolutionary rupture (display C). This means that each of the "corresponding" elements—mythic nature and mythic consciousness—works to liberate the other *from* myth. "Wish images" emerge at the point where they intersect.

Benjamin is not maintaining that the contents of past myths provide a blueprint for the future. To believe that they could is purely utopian. Nowhere in his writings do the ur-images have a status other than that of dream symbol. They provide the motivation for future emancipation, which will not be literally a restoration of the past, but will be based on new forms that "we are only beginning to surmise." "Every epoch dreams the one that follows it"—as the *dream* form of the future, not its reality. The representations of the

5 Mythic Nature: Wish Image

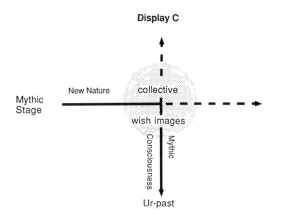

collective unconscious are not revolutionary on their own, but only when dialectically mediated by the material, "new" nature, the as-yet unimagined forms of which alone have the potential to actualize the collective dream. The images are thus less pre-visions of postre-volutionary society than the necessary pro-visions for radical social practice. Hence Benjamin's theory of revolution as "innervation": Wish images "innervate" the "technical organ of the collective," supplying it with nerve stimulation that prompts revolutionary action—"like the child who learns [the practical task of] grasping by trying [impossibly] to catch the moon in its hands."[36]

By attaching themselves as surface ornamentation to the industrial and technological forms which have just come into existence, collective wish images imbue the merely new with radical political meaning, inscribing visibly on the products of the new means of production an ur-image of the desired social *ends* of their development. In short, even as they mask the new, these archaic images provide a symbolic representation of what the human, social meaning of technological change is all about. Thus it is of the utmost political significance that Victor Hugo saw in mass reproduction the historically real, objective form of Christ's miraculous division of bread to feed the multitudes: "The multiplication of readers is the multiplication of bread. The day when Christ discovered this symbol, he foresaw the printing works."[37] Similarly, it is crucial that Fourier's early nineteenth-century utopia, in which fish swim in rivers of lemonade and sharks help humans hunt for fish,[38] "filled the ur-old wish symbol of leisure and plenty [. . .] with new life,"[39] and that utopian socialists generally resurrected images of an originary Golden Age:

"Yes, when the entire world, from Paris to China, O divine Saint-Simon, will come to embrace your doctrine, then must the Golden Age return in all its brilliance, the rivers will flow with tea and chocolate; sheep fully roasted will gambol on the plain, and pike cooked in butter will navigate the Seine; steamed spinach will spring from the ground with a border of croutons. The trees will bear stewed apples; and grain will grow in bales ready to harvest; it will snow wine, it will rain chickens, and ducks will drop from the sky with a garnish of turnips."[40]

Such visions are proof of the "too early" stage[41] of both technology and imagination. Their fantastic forms are "the most authentic witness" of "just how caught in a dream technological production was in its beginnings."[42] At the same time, however, they tell us that utopian desires have been attached to the new nature from the start. Insofar as their image traces have been lost in history, it is politically necessary to redeem them.[43] When Benjamin states that these images "pertain" to a "classless society," it is because the fairy-tale quality of the wish for happiness that they express presupposes an end to material scarcity and exploitative labor that form the structural core of societies based on class domination. The early version of the exposé passage concludes:

It is not because of being consciously garbled by the ideology of the ruling class that the reflections of the substructure within the superstructure are inadequate, but because the new, in order to shape itself visually, always connects its elements with those pertaining to a classless society. The collective unconscious has more of a share in it than the consciousness of the collective. Out of it come the images of utopia that have left their traces behind them in a thousand configurations of life from buildings to fashions.[44]

In the beginning of an era, there is an intuitive, "too-early" apprehension of the future. The residues of past cultural creations bear witness to it. But if the anticipatory wish symbols that leave their traces on these creations have remained "unconscious," this is another way of saying the collective is not even aware that it is dreaming—with the inevitable result that symbol turns into fetish, and technology, the means for realizing human dreams, is mistaken for their actualization. Commodity fetishes and dream fetishes become indistinguishable. When processed food appears on the shelf

5.3 "Human Happiness—food for the asking—in the Fourierist utopia"—Grandville, 1844.

as if it had dropped from a Saint-Simonian sky, commodities begin their "'theological capers,' "[45] the wish images become a phantasmagoria, and dream turns into delusion. When mass media are seen as themselves the democratization of culture, distributed as miraculously as Christ's multiplying food, they too become fetishes.

The tremendous power of the new technology has remained in the hands of the ruling class that wields it as a force of domination, while privately appropriating the wealth it produces. In this context, dream symbols are the fetishized desires that advertise commodities. And the collective goes on sleeping. But should it awaken, the utopian symbols can be redeemed as a manifestation of truth. Essential to this truth is its transitoriness. The wish symbols, signposts in a period of transition, can inspire the refunctioning of the new nature so that it satisfies material needs and desires that are the source of the dream in the first place. Wish images do not liberate humanity directly. But they are vital to the process.

3

"It is easy to understand that every great . . . 'interest,' when it first steps upon the world stage, extends in 'idea' or 'imagination' far beyond its real limits, and mistakes itself for the interest of humanity in general. This illusion forms that which Fourier calls the tone of every historical epoch."[46]

The technological capacity to produce must be mediated by the utopian capacity to dream—and vice versa. Was Benjamin presuming an autonomy of the imagination incompatible with historical materialism? Adorno thought so. He would not have considered the transiency of collective wish symbols sufficient cause for their redemption. Ultimately he saw no distinction between these dream images and conventional consciousness in that both were produced within the distorting context of class society. It was precisely the exposé passage on wish images considered above that so troubled him.[47] It seemed to eternalize in a most ahistorical way the contents of the collective psyche. Adorno appears to have understood Benjamin as affirming literally Michelet's idea that every age dreams its successor, as if dream images were dialectical images pure and simple, and he protested:

[. . . I]f the dialectical image is nothing but the mode in which the fetish character is conceived within collective consciousness, then indeed the Saint-Simonian conception of the commodity world might be brought to light, but not its reverse side, namely the dialectical image of the nineteenth century as Hell.[48]

The image of Hell, central to the "glorious first draft" of the Arcades project, appeared to Adorno to have been repressed in the exposé. The remaining idea of "wish images" was, he claimed, "undialectical," implying an "immanent," almost "developmental" relationship to a utopian future.[49] Against this Adorno insisted: "The fetish character of the commodity is not a fact of consciousness, but dialectic in the eminent sense that it produces consciousness."[50] And he urged: "The concept of the commodity as a fetish must be documented, as is surely your intent, by the man who discovered it"[51]—that is, by Marx himself.

Benjamin's response (via Gretel Karplus) was to agree with "almost all" of Adorno's reflections, but to claim that his conception in the exposé was not different. He had not given up the theme of Hell that figured so essentially in the early notes; rather, these notes and the exposé represented "the thesis and antithesis of the work."[52] That Adorno remained unconvinced, given the exposé's elusive wording, is not surprising. Yet the *Passagen-Werk* material substantiates Benjamin's claims. Throughout it, images of the nineteenth century as Hell figure prominently (as we have seen[53]). Benjamin *had* worked through the relevant passages of *Capital* on commodity fetishism.[54] Where the exposé spoke of the new as "intermingled with the old," Adorno said that he missed the inverse argument, that "the newest, as mere appearance and phantasmagoria, is itself the oldest."[55] But Benjamin's still-central conception of "natural history" made precisely this point.[56] Their disagreement was in fact limited to their evaluation of the collective's utopian desire (and hence the degree to which mass culture could be redeemed). Benjamin affirmed this desire as a transitory moment in a process of cultural transition. Adorno dismissed it as irredeemably ideological. In denying the autonomy of collective desire, he clearly believed his position to be the more rigorous from a dialectical materialist standpoint. Yet the argument lies close at hand that on this issue Benjamin was in fact in accord with Marx's own perceptions. In several texts, most explicitly in the *18th Brumaire of*

Louis Bonaparte, it was Marx who, well before Benjamin, observed the crucial role played by images that conjured up the symbols and myths of antiquity at times of radical historical rupture. Marx wrote:

And just when [human beings] seem engaged in revolutionizing themselves and objects, in creating something that has never existed before, precisely in such epochs of revolutionary crisis they anxiously conjure up to their service the spirits of the past and borrow from them names, battle slogans and costumes in order to present the new scene of world history in this time-honored disguise and this borrowed language. Thus Luther wore the mask of the Apostle Paul, the revolution of 1789 to 1814 draped itself alternately as the Roman Republic and the Roman Empire [. . .].[57]

Marx goes on to criticize the bourgeois "revolutionaries" of 1848, whose citings of the past were no more than parodic *re*-citings in a farcical attempt to repeat the Revolution of 1789. He attributes the nineteenth-century predilection for ancient Rome to the bourgeoisie's need for "self deception," in order to "hide from themselves" the class limitations of the "content of their struggles."[58] At the same time, Marx recognizes that such historical masks are capable not only of concealing, but also of glorifying the very newness of the present historical drama, and that this can serve a progressive purpose *so long as the masking is temporary*:

Thus at another stage of development, a century earlier, Cromwell and the English people borrowed the language, passions and illusions of the Old Testament for their bourgeois revolution. When the real goal was reached, when the bourgeois transformation of English society was accomplished, Locke displaced Habakkuk.

The awakening of the dead in the case of this revolution served to glorify new struggles rather than parody old ones, to amplify the present task in the imagination, not to take flight from achieving it in reality, to rediscover the spirit of revolution, not to make its ghost walk about again.[59]

Marx warns that "the social revolution of the nineteenth century cannot create its poetry out of the past, but only from the future."[60] Yet he does not assume that the new "poetry" will be produced *ex nihilo* by the working class as soon as bourgeois ideological hegemony is overthrown. He compares the process to learning a new language:

It is like the beginner [who . . .] always translates back into the mother tongue, but appropriates the spirit of the new language and becomes capable of producing freely within it only by moving about in it without re-calling the old [. . .].[61]

Surely Benjamin means nothing else when, in considering the in-adequacies of collective consciousness vis-à-vis the new technology, he asks:

When and how will the worlds of form that have arisen in mechanics, in film, machine construction and the new physics, and that have over-powered us without our being aware of it, make what is natural in them clear to us? When will the condition of society be reached in which these forms or those that have arisen from them open themselves up to us as natural forms?[62]

So close is Benjamin to Marx's own formulation that the fact these passages are *missing* from the *Passagen-Werk* material must come as a surprise. Benjamin includes other passages from *18th Brumaire*,[63] while leaving this discussion (which occurs at the very beginning of Marx's text) unacknowledged. That the omission was accidental is unlikely. Rather, it suggests Benjamin realized that although his arguments paralleled those of Marx, they did not coincide. Marx was concerned with the moment of political revolution; Benjamin was concerned with the transition to socialism that comes after it.

In *18th Brumaire*, Marx wrote that socialist society "cannot begin itself until it has shed all superstition in regard to the past," and has "let the dead bury the dead."[64] But he left unexplained just how this shedding of the past was to be achieved. The result is a gap in Marx's theory which, whether or not he intended it to be, has been bridged by an implicit faith in historical progress, eco-nomically determined, as if once socialist production relations were established, industrial-technological production would itself gener-ate the socialist imagination capable of producing a brand new cul-ture. Benjamin's trip to Moscow had convinced him that seizing political power and nationalizing the economy, while the precondi-tions for socialist transformation, were not its guarantee, and that so long as the Soviet government repressed cultural innovation, the political revolution itself was in danger of being lost.[65] If his 1935 exposé put forth the notion that socialist culture would need to be constructed out of the embryonic, still-inadequate forms that preexisted in captialism, it was in the Artwork essay composed the same year that Benjamin articulated a full-blown theory of the superstructure[66]: Whereas Marx had discovered in the capitalist economic base not only the creation of conditions which would lead to increasing exploitation of the proletariat but also those "that would make it possible to abolish capitalism itself," Benjamin argued that within the superstructure there was a separate (and relatively autonomous) dialectical process, "no less noticeable [...] than in the economy," but proceeding "far more slowly."[67] It is *this* dialectic that makes possible the transition to a socialist society.[68] It plays itself out between the collective imagination and the productive potential of the new nature that human beings have brought into being, but do not yet consciously comprehend. Moreover, this dialectic has developed *not* by "burying" the dead past, but by revitalizing it. For if future history is not determined and thus its forms are still unknown, if consciousness cannot transcend the horizons of its sociohistorical context, then where else *but* to the dead past can imagination turn in order to conceptualize a world that is "not-yet"? Moreover, such a move itself satisfies a utopian wish: the desire (manifested in the religious myth of awakening the dead) "to make [past] suffering into something incomplete,"[69] to make good an unfulfilled past that has been irretrievably lost.

The socialist transformation of the superstructure, which begins within capitalism under the impact of industrial technology, includes redeeming the past, in a process that is tenuous, undetermined, and largely unconscious. As a result of the distortions of capitalist social relations, the progressive and retrogressive moments of this process are not easily discerned. One of the tasks that Benjamin believed to be his own in the *Passagen-Werk* was to make both tendencies of the process visible retrospectively. He traces their origins to the forcefield between art and technology, which in the nineteenth century became falsely perceived as oppositional camps, with the result that even attempts to reconcile them produced reactionary cultural forms.

4

The relationship between art and technology is a central theme in the *Passagen-Werk*. The 1935 exposé presents this relationship in a programmatic way,[70] outlining specifically the impact in the nineteenth century of photography on art, engineering on architecture, and mass journalism on literary production.[71] The result is an original contribution to Marxist theory,[72] suggesting not merely the ground for a materialist aesthetics and sociology of art (although both are implied). It identifies a structural transformation in the relationship of consciousness to reality—specifically, fantasy to productive forces—that has general theoretical significance, and that is capable of informing every sort of critical cultural practice. It could be said that for Benjamin progressive cultural practice entails bringing both technology and imagination out of their mythic dream states, through making conscious the collective's desire for social utopia, and the potential of the new nature to achieve it by translating that desire into the "new language" of its material forms. Benjamin writes that in the nineteenth century, the development of the technical forces of production "emancipated the creative forms (*Gestaltungsformen*) from art, just as in the sixteenth century the sciences liberated themselves from philosophy."[73] This is quite an extraordinary claim. It implies that, just as reason ("the sciences"), once having become secularized ("liberated from philosophy"), became free to be applied instrumentally to processes of social production, so imagination, inspired by "the creative forms" of technology and diverted from purely aesthetic goals (that is, "emancipated from art"), can be applied to the task of constructing a new basis for collective social life.

Previously, bourgeois art had appropriated the imaginative discovery of new forms as its own terrain, defined by the very fact of its separation from social reality. Following Adorno, one can argue that this separation was beneficial, sustaining a power of imagination that, because it was able to resist the given state of things, was the source of the utopian impulse intrinsic to bourgeois art. On one level, Benjamin surely would not disagree. Yet he would insist that the "autonomy of art" becomes a hollow phrase in light of the tremendous creativity of industrial production which itself constantly revolutionizes reality's material forms. In an argument absolutely dependent on Marxist theoretical claims (yet without precedent in Marx's own theory of the cultural superstructure[74]), Benjamin was suggesting that the objective (and progressive) tendency of industrialism is to fuse art and technology, fantasy and function, meaningful symbol and useful tool, and that this fusion is, indeed, the very essence of socialist culture.

It is important to emphasize that Benjamin understood the synthesis of technology and art as a structural tendency, not synonymous with history's actual course. In fact the nineteenth century witnessed an institutionalization of the split between technology and art to a degree previously unknown in history. This split was strikingly manifested in the establishment (in 1794) of *l'Ecole polytechnique* as separate from, and moreover in rivalry with, *l'Ecole des beaux arts*. The former trained builders and "engineers"[75] for the construction of industrial edifices, naval ships and military fortifications.[76] The latter trained artists and "decorators,"[77] whose work was valued precisely because it refused to subject aesthetic imagination to functional purposes.[78] In this split, architecture fell to *l'Ecole des beaux arts*, a fact that "'worked to its detriment.'"[79] Previously, architecture had included the science of engineering.[80] Of all the arts, it had been "[. . .] the earliest to grow away from the concept of art, or better said, [. . .] it least tolerated the view that it was "art," a view which the nineteenth century forced upon the products of intellectual activity to a degree previously unimagined, yet with no more justification than before."[81]

The architectural style of the Paris arcades was emblematic of the warring tendencies of engineering and "art." Demanding the skills of both, it was recognized by neither *Ecole* as an object worthy of instruction.[82] On the one hand, the continuous glass roofs that became their hallmark in the 1820s were technologically advanced skylighting constructions; on the other, the interior "walls" of their shop galleries were the most derivative ornamental facades, replete with neoclassical columns, arches, and pediments that were the epitome of architectural "good taste." As dialectical images, the arcades thus had a "hermaphroditic position,"[83] fusing the two tendencies which elsewhere developed in total, and hostile, isolation.

It was the engineers who, together with workers, gave shape to the "new" nature of industrial forms: railroads,[84] machines,[85] and bridges. Benjamin cites Sigfried Giedion: "'It should be noted that the marvelous aspects which the new construction out of iron afforded the cities [. . .] for a long time were accessible to workers and engineers exclusively.'"[86] Sharing Giedion's enthusiasm for

5.4   Pont Transbordeur, Marseilles, built 1905.

these "marvelous aspects," Benjamin contrasts the "ornamental style" of the architects (which he connects with "boredom"[87]) to Giedion's "excellent examples" of bridge scaffolding. Referring to Giedion's photograph of the Pont Transbordeur in Marseilles (figure 5.4), he writes the word: "Marxism. For who else but engineers and proletarians at that time took the steps that alone revealed fully that which was new and decisive about these constructions, the feeling of space?"[88]

Throughout the nineteenth century, the "fine art" of architecture defensively held itself back from engineering innovations: "'Those whose aesthetic conscience was particularly sensitive hurled out from the altar of art curse after curse upon the building engineers.'"[89] The accepted nineteenth-century architectural "style" remained oriented toward the preindustrial past, and the most respected style was neoclassicism. "'In the nineteenth century ancient Greek architecture again bloomed in its old purity'" —at least so it appeared to what Benjamin called the "vulgar consciousness" of the time.[90] When iron *was* used for scaffolding, it was given a "stone covering"[91] so that it was visible only from the

5.5   Main Reading Room, Bibliothèque Nationale, built by Henri Labrouste, 1868 (top).

5.6   Avenue de l'Opera, late nineteenth century (bottom).

interior (figure 5.5), or used only for decorative effect. "'Henri Labrouste, artist of restrained and austere talents, inaugurated successfully the ornamental use of iron in the construction of the Bibliothèque Sainte-Genevieve [1850s] and the Bibliothèque Nationale [1860s].'"[92] On exterior facades (figure 5.6), iron was used in continuous balconies as surface design in direct contradiction to the new potential for verticality, illustrating "the tendency, again and again in the nineteenth century, to ennoble technical exigencies with artistic aims."[93]

"The sensitivities of [architects] demanded that the ever-stronger horizontal tendency of the house...come to expression...And they found the means in connection with the traditional iron balcony. They introduced it on one or two floors over the whole width of the front [. . .]. When house appeared next to house, these balcony gratings fused into one another and strengthened the impression of a street wall [. . .]."[94]

Iron, known to humankind since prehistory, was rapidly transformed from "'cast iron to wrought iron to ingot steel,'" demonstrating its "'unlimited possibilities.'"[95] Exclaimed Benjamin: "Iron as revolutionary building material!"[96] But architects, still trained in the tradition of Alberti, brought to any "artificial" form of iron "'a certain mistrust precisely because it was not immediately present in nature.'"[97] Moreover, they polemicized against the mathematics of static physics that was the essential tool of engineers, claiming mathematics was "'powerless to assure the solidarity of buildings.'"[98]

Ostracized from the dictates of "good taste," engineering submitted to the dictates of practical use.[99] "'The source of all architecture out of iron and glass in the contemporary sense is the greenhouse.'"[100] Such "houses for plants" were the model for Paxton's plan of the Crystal Palace (executed by engineers rather than architects).[101] Subsequent exposition halls imitated Paxton's design, as metaphorical "hothouses" for the new machinery.[102] It was in buildings for the new mass culture that the principle of iron and glass construction proliferated, at first "'under the banner of purely utilitarian buildings'": "iron halls" were built as warehouses, workshops, and factories,[103] covered marketplaces (*Les Halles*) and railroad stations (*Garde de l'Est*). As practical, protective shelters for a mass public, iron halls well suited the "'need for unbroken space,'"[104] because of the expanse such construction allowed. Ben-

5.7 Camera by Bourguin in the shape of a truncated pyramid, flanked by bronze dragons that serve only to make the apparatus heavier and more ornate, Paris, ca. 1844

jamin noted that these buildings were connected with transitoriness in both the spatial sense (as railroad stations, places of transit) and the temporal one (as galleries for world expositions, typically torn down after they closed).

Spared the self-conscious mediation of "art," such structures settled into the collective imagination in an unconscious form, as buildings for use rather than contemplation—at least for a time. Ultimately, iron and glass construction, having bowed to the challenge of architectural style, itself became one, and began (predictably) to think of emulating the past:

"By 1878, it was believed that salvation could be found in iron architecture: Its vertical aspiration [. . .] the preference for over-filled spaces and the lightness of the visible skeleton fanned hopes in the birth of a style that would revive the essence of Gothic genius [. . .]."[105]

The 1889 Paris Exposition was heralded as the "'triumph of iron.'"[106] Built for it was the Gallery of Machines (dismantled in 1910 "'out of artistic sadism'"[107]) and the Eiffel Tower, the latter an "incomparable" monument to the new "heroic age of technology,"[108] which survived after the close of the fair because of

5 Mythic Nature: Wish Image

5.8 Photograph of the Ingres Gallery of Painting, Exposition Universelle, Paris, 1855

its utility as a tower for wireless transmission.[109] Assembled by riveting together sectional iron pieces, the Eiffel Tower, for all its lacelike effects, employed the same principle of construction as railroad tracks, and anticipated skyscrapers directly.[110] "Modernism" in architecture had arrived. The Eiffel Tower was an enormous popular success; but still the "artists" protested:

"We come, writers, painters, sculptors, architects . . . in the name of French art and history that are both threatened, to protest against the erection in the very heart of our capital of the needless and monstrous Eiffel Tower . . . overwhelming with its barbarous mass Notre Dame, the Sainte-Chapelle, the Tour Saint-Jacques, all our monuments humiliated, all our architectural works diminished."[111]

5

The invention of photography, with its exact rendering of nature, enabled technology to overtake artists at their own task, and undermined the uniqueness, the one-time-only "aura" of the masterpiece by allowing for the mass reproduction of images.

The first international exposition at which photography was exhibited was held in 1855 in Paris.[112] The invention of photography was prefigured in the 1820s by the dioramas, those glassed-in, three-dimensional scenes of figures in a realistic setting which, "by means of technical artifice," attempted "a perfect imitation of nature," including the temporal movement of changing daylight, sunsets, or a rising moon.[113] The dioramas mimicked reality so successfully that the painter David urged his students to make studies of nature from them.[114] Dioramas (and subsequent cosmoramas, pleoramas, panoramas, and diaphanoramas,[115] as well as wax-figure cabinets)[116] were the "too early" precursors of photography[117] and film[118] just as the arcades (in which they were frequently found) were too early anticipations of modern architecture. "Just as architecture begins to outgrow art with iron construction, so painting does the same through the panoramas."[119]

Benjamin appreciated the lithographer A. J. Wiertz, whose early essay on photography "ascribes to it the philosophical enlightenment of painting [. . .] in a political sense": images become intellectually reflective and thereby "agitational."[120] Wiertz wrote: "'Do not think that daguerreotype kills art. No, it kills the work of patience; it renders homage to the work of thought,'" and he carried this principle over into his own work, believing that ultimately photography and art would work together.[121]

With photography, the artist's attempt to replicate nature was made scientific.[122] It extended the human sense of sight in a way commensurate with Marx's idea in the 1844, "Economic and Philosophic Manuscripts" that the human senses in their "'true, anthropological [i.e., social] nature'" are "'nature as it comes to be through industry,'"[123] even if such nature, due to "'private property,'" now exists only in "'alienated form.'"[124] That the "'human eye'" perceives differently than the "'crude, nonhuman eye'"[125] is demonstrated by photography, presenting to our vision new discoveries about nature, and not merely beautiful images. François Arago, speaking in the 1850s on the place of photography in the history of technology, "prophesizes its scientific application— whereupon the artists [predictably missing the point] begin to debate its artistic value."[126]

Photography secularized the image by bringing it up close. On the photography exhibit of the 1855 Paris Exposition:

"The public crowded into the exhibitions, standing before countless portraits of famous and celebrated personalities, and one can imagine what it
meant in that epoch that one could see the famed personages of the
theatre, the podium, in short of public life, at whom until now one had
only been able to gaze in wonder from a distance."[127]

From the start, photography was part of popular culture. Pioneers
like Nadar expanded its subject matter, taking a hundred expo-
sures of Paris' catacombs and sewers,[128] and including all social
classes and ranks in his portraiture.[129] The photographic method
encouraged the practice of amateurs, so that the line between artist
and public began to blur. Arago reported to the Chamber in 1851
on the effects of the invention:

"'[. . . T]he opticians' shops were besieged; there were not enough lenses,
not enough dark rooms to satisfy the zeal of so many eager amateurs. The
sun sinking on the horizon was followed with a gaze of regret, taking with
it the raw material of the experiment. But on the following day you could
see great numbers of experimenters at their windows in the first hours of
daylight, striving with every kind of nervous precaution to induce onto the
prepared plaques images of the nearby dormer window, or the view of a
population of chimneys.'"[130]

Photography democratized the reception of visual images by bringing even art masterpieces to a mass audience.[131] Benjamin believed
this democratization of production and reception as well as the
non-"auratic," scientific approach to objects were tendencies intrinsic to the medium,[132] and he considered them progressive.[133]
Because photography intruded so decisively upon the image preserve of painters, it inevitably challenged and changed the way the
latter went about their work. Arago wrote:

"Whoever has just once in his life covered his skin with the magic cloak of
photography and peered into the camera in order to see there those
wonderful miniature reproductions of natural images must have been
. . . struck by the question of what, indeed, will our modern painting come
to once photography has succeeded in fixing colors just as permanently as
it now does forms."[134]

Defenders of artists insisted that it was "impossible for a human
countenance to be captured by machine."[135] Yet portraits were
precisely the genre most vulnerable to the encroachments of photography, even if they changed what such portraits recorded: "What
makes the first photographs so incomparable is perhaps this: that

they represent the first image of the encounter of machine and human being."[136] Artists asserted the superiority of their trade, but their unconscious response was an acknowledgment of vulnerability. "Apparent symptom of a radical displacement [*Verschiebung*]: painting must put up with being judged by the standard of photography."[137] Artists began to move in directions in which photography could not (yet) compete:

The paintings of Delacroix avoid competition with photography not only by their power of color but—there was then no action photography—by the stormy movement of their subjects. Thus it was possible for him to be kindly disposed toward photography.[138]

And subsequently: "As Impressionism gives way to Cubism, painting has created a domain into which photography at the outset cannot follow."[139]

Thus painters attempted to defend themselves against the new technology. They thereby missed the real threat to their cultural creativity, the effects of the capitalist market. Already in the early arcades, the window arrangements of commodities "displayed art in service of the salesman."[140] In the course of his research, Benjamin found a lithograph depicting the beginning of art as advertising:

[. . .] a painter who makes his way forward with two yard-long, narrow planks, on each of which he has painted several garnishings and arrangements of meat products. Title: "Misery and the arts." "Dedicated to Monsieur the Butcher." Caption: "The man of art within the impediments of his trade."[141]

Another showed the proletarianization of artistic production in terms of worker exploitation:

Lithograph: A poor devil looks on sadly as a young man signs the picture that the former has painted. Title: "The artist and the amateur of the nineteenth century." Caption: "It is by me, seeing that I sign it."[142]

Due to the distorting effects of capitalist social relations, the mass culture in which art and technology converged did so to the detriment of both. On the side of art, production methods began to resemble those of any commodity: Needing to compete with photography, artists were forced to speed up production, mimic mechanized reproduction by hand, and turn out "individual" portraits with a rapidity that rendered only what was typical about the sub-

5 Mythic Nature: Wish Image

5.9 Studio photograph of Walter Benjamin and his brother George as "Alpinists," ca. 1900.

ject, while the new style of "genre paintings" was based on the concept of repeatability. On the side of photography (which in portraiture clearly had the competitive edge[143]) the limitless reproduction of images extended the sphere of market society "enormously," which in turn encouraged "modish variations of camera techniques" in order to increase sales.[144] Moreover, the retrogressive canons of artistic style induced photographers to be more "painterly" in their images (figure 5.9), placing subjects before "picturesque," backdrops, utilizing props, and retouching and otherwise "embellishing" the image in the name of aesthetic standards.[145]

6

Nowhere were the distorting effects of capitalism clearer than in the realm of literary production. Here the threat to traditional art

5.10   "Literature being reeled off and sold in chunks"—Grandville, 1844.

forms came from the technology of rapid printing,[146] and from the journalistic style that emerged as the consequence of the mushrooming of mass newspapers. In "The Author as Producer" (1934),[147] Benjamin describes the potential effects of new literary technologies making it clear that he considers them progressive in the political sense because they tend to create a democratic forum for information and lower the boundary between literary producer and audience[148]; and because they destroy the old notion of individual artistic genius and completed, self-contained "works," replacing the concept of the "masterpiece" with a political notion of writing as "intervention" which has an "organizing function."[149] The writer's most important strategic task is less to fill the new literary forms with revolutionary content than to develop the revolutionary potential of the forms themselves. So long as the mass press "still belongs to capital," however, this task is riddled with "insoluble antinomies."[150] "The newspaper is the scene of this literary confusion."[151] Capitalist journalism commodifies writing, treating it as a product to be consumed by a passive audience. In a context where the traditional standards of "literature" are stubbornly clung to, the result is a "decline of writing," a "debasement of the word."[152] But in the "unselective" assembling of readers and facts, and by needing to cater to the "smoldering impatience" of the readers who, "excluded, believe that they have the right to speak out in their own interests,"[153] a "dialectical moment is concealed: The decline of writing in the bourgeois press proves to be the source of its regeneration under socialism."[154] Benjamin defines the situation of the socialist press (equating it with the actually existing press in the Soviet Union) as one in which the worker, as "expert," becomes literate in an active sense. He or she "gains access to authorship," the qualifications for which thus become "public property"; "living conditions" themselves become "literature," while the latter loses relevance as a purely aesthetic form.[155]

The *Passagen-Werk* material gives evidence from the early years of industrial capitalism of both positive and negative poles of this dialectic as they appear, fully entangled, in the historical phenomena themselves. Benjamin is particularly concerned with the transformation of literary works into commodities,[156] and the effects of capitalist relations on the production process. He finds prototypical the production innovations of the dramatist Eugène Scribe:

"While he made fun of the great industrialists and men of money, he learned from them the secret of their success. It did not escape his sharp eye that all wealth in essence rests on the art of having others work for us and thus, a pathbreaking genius, he transferred the fundamental principle of the division of labor from the workshops of fashion tailors, cabinet-makers, and steel-spring factories, into studios for the dramatic artist, who before this reform, with one head and one pen, still only earned the proletarian salary of an isolated worker."[157]

But regardless of salary, the writers within these studio workshops were "proletarian" now in the literal sense of the word, as they had lost control over the production apparatus. And if salaries of worker-writers rose, Scribe's wealth as the owner of their labor power grew exponentially:

Scribe chose the material, he ordered the plot in its broad outlines, indicated the special effects and brilliant exits, and his apprentices set dialogue or small verses thereto. If they made progress, then naming their name in the title (next to that of the firm) was their adequate payment, until the best of them became independent and produced works with their own hand, perhaps also attaching new helpers to themselves. Thus, and with the protection of the French publishing laws, Scribe became a millionaire several times over.[158]

Alexandre Dumas, similarly, was less a novelist than the owner of a "factory of novels"[159] in which other writers mass produced "his" works. Dumas boasted of producing four hundred novels and thirty-five dramas in twenty years, in a process that "'permitted 8,160 persons to earn a livelihood.'"[160]

"Who knows the titles of all the books M. Dumas has signed his name to? Does he know them himself? If he doesn't keep a double register with debits and credits, he has no doubt forgotten...more than one of those children for whom he is the legal father or natural father, or godfather. The productions of these last months have not been less than thirty volumes."[161]

Before mid-century, newspapers were still too expensive to allow for mass readership.

Because of the rareness of newspapers, one read them in groups at the cafés. Otherwise they could be obtained only by subscription, which cost 80 francs per year. In 1824 the twelve most widely distributed newspapers had altogether about 56,000 subscriptions. Indeed, the liberals as well as the royalists were interested in keeping the lower classes away from newspapers.[162]

In 1828, journals were first brought within the grasp of the lower classes, a potentially democratic change[163] that was, however, made possible by precisely that force which began to transform news information into a commodity: paid advertising. At first it was literature itself that was advertised, in the form of unsolicited literary reviews.[164] The next step was to generalize the principle:

The thought of using a newspaper insert to advertise not only books but industrial products, was that of a certain Dr. Veron, who did so well in this way with his *pâte de Regnauld*, a cold medicine, that on an investment of 17,000 francs he received a return of 100,000.[165]

Along with advertising inserts and single issue sales, the editor Emile de Giradin introduced the "feuilleton," a special section in mass newspapers for literature and reviews in which novels appeared serially prior to their publication as books.[166] This format, along with the literary periodicals and reviews that proliferated by mid-century,[167] had significant repercussions on literary form, resulting in essay treatments, short stories, or serial novels. Under capitalist relations, style adapted to the exigencies of the medium: "There were feuilleton honoraria of up to 2 francs per line. Many authors wrote just dialogue as much as possible, in order to make money on the partially empty lines."[168]

The new mass readership drew authors into national politics as well.[169] Benjamin searches out the origins of this phenomenon, unique in our own era, whereby cultural producers, as popular entertainers, became mass politicians (Lamartine, Chateaubriand, Sue, Hugo), not always (or indeed not usually) with the most enlightened results. The philosophical idealism[170] entrenched in bourgeois literature carried over into political positions. Balzac "'deplored the downfall of the Bourbons, which signified to him the loss of the arts,'"[171] and advocated peasant "socialism" along the lines of a reestablished feudalism.[172] Chateaubriand made the political stance of "'vague sadness'" a fashion.[173] Lamartine exhorted patriotism over socialism,[174] employing his poetic rhetoric for nationalist glorification "'as if he had made it his job,'" so one contemporary criticized him, "'to prove the truth of Plato's statement that poets should be thrown out of the Republic [. . .].'"[175]

Those authors first in a position to speak to the masses did not speak *for* the masses,[176] at least not in a way that would make it possible for them to understand their objective historical situation, because as writers, they did not understand their own. Victor Hugo, whose fiction documented accurately the suffering of the urban poor,[177] is exemplary. Although in November 1848, Hugo cast his vote against General Cavignac's repression of the workers' June revolt,[178] he subsequently voted "'consistently with the right',"[179] and gave his "enthusiastic endorsement" to Louis Napoleon as presidential candidate,[180] hoping (in vain) to become the latter's Minister of Education.[181] Equating words themselves with revolution,[182] Hugo exemplified the new significance of literature for political propaganda as an aspect of the phantasmagoria of mass politics. His unreliable political judgment was not unique among writers. Balzac, an opponent of the breakup of landed estates, saw no other cure for petty-bourgeois hoarding than the contradictory position of turning them into small landholders.[183] Alexandre Dumas was offered money by the government in 1846 to go to Algiers and write a book that would spread among his five million French readers "'a taste for colonization.'"[184] Lamartine, moved to provide the masses with the rhetoric of "'a single idea,' 'a conviction'" around which they could rally,[185] placed his literary skills at the services of the state. The cognitive strength of these writers was limited to describing social appearances, not uncovering the social tendencies that underlay them, and that were affecting their own conditions of production so deeply.

One has only to regard the format of a nineteenth-century newspaper (figure 5.11), in which the feuilleton occupied the bottom quarter of the front page, to see, literally, how thin was the line between political fact and literary fiction. News stories were literary constructions; feuilleton novelists used news stories as content. The tendency of mass media is to render the distinction between art and politics meaningless. Benjamin was vitally concerned with what happens when the two realms merge, as he believed they were bound to, due to the "[. . .] massive melting-down process of literary forms, a process in which many of the oppositions in which we have been accustomed to think may lose their relevance."[186] At issue is not whether the line is crossed, but how. Benjamin sees two possibilities: Either (as was the case with Lamartine, Hugo, etc.), the new technologies of literary reproduction are used by writers as the means for a rhetorical representation of reality that slips into

5.11   Front page of *Le Petit Journal*, September 24, 1869.

political propaganda,[187] or, by focusing on these new technological forms themselves, writers begin to illuminate both their emancipatory potential, and the political realities that presently distort their effects. The choice is between swaying the public or educating it, between political manipulation or technical awareness. The latter politicizes not so much through an elaboration of the deficiencies in the present social order as through demonstrating that this order constrains the means that already exist to rectify them.[188]

But in the nineteenth century, artists and writers generally did not understand the positive potential of the new technologies for cultural production any more clearly than they did the dangers of using these technologies to aestheticize mass politics. Balzac pronounced newspapers as " " "deadly to the existence of modern writers." " "[189] Gautier (like Balzac, a monarchist) praised Charles I's suppression of the press, claiming that it " " "rendered a great service to the arts and to civilization" " ":

" 'Newspapers are of the species of courtiers or horse dealers who interpose themselves between the artists and the public, between the king and the people . . . their perpetual barking . . . hurls such mistrust . . . into the mind that . . . royalty and poetry, the two grandest things in the world, become impossible.' "[190]

Architects, as we have seen, distrusted mathematics. But engineers were no more clairvoyant, coming only "slowly" to "new methods of fabrication."[191] And if artists preached "art for art's sake," and, scorning the new technology, insisted: " 'A drama is not a railroad,' "[192] it was also true "that the very Arago who reported the famous positive evaluation of [photography], reported in the same year [. . .] a negative evaluation of the railroad construction planned by the government."[193] (" 'Among other arguments, the difference in temperature at the entrance and exits to the tunnels would, it was said, lead to fatal heat and chills.' "[194]) But was the "progressive" alternative simply to make an art object of railroads themselves?

Theatre du Luxembourg, 30 December 1837: "A locomotive with 'several elegant wagons' appears on the stage."[195]

7

The images of nineteenth-century architecture *and* engineering, painting *and* photography, literature *and* journalism were a tangle of both anticipatory and fettering elements. It was not surprising that in the darkness of the lived moment, neither artist nor technician was able to differentiate clearly between the two. Granted, technology was inherently progressive, promising socialist forms of living and culture; but so long as its development was appropriated for the purposes of capitalism and the state, it produced only reified dream images of that promise, a phantasmagoria of the "new nature." Similarly, even if the industrial reproduction of artistic and literary forms was inherently democratic, so long as, under commodity production, culture was produced as manipulation rather than enlightenment, fostering passive consumption rather than active collaboration, the democratic potential of mass culture remained unrealized.

Neither technician nor artist was to be affirmed unequivocally. Both, lacking control over the means of production,[196] submitted to the demands of the market and thereby helped to perpetuate the nonidentity between social utility and capitalist profitability. As producers of strategic beautification or of patriotic oration, both served the interests of political reaction.[197] Both were caught up in the dream-state of technology. At the same time, both managed to express progressive elements in their work in spite of it. Benjamin concludes: "The attempt to draw out a systematic confrontation between art and photography must fail"; rather, as was the case in other areas of cultural production, it could best be understood as "a moment in the confrontation between art and technology which history has produced"[198]—but which "history" would not automatically resolve: The *Ecole des beaux arts* and *Ecole polytechnique* were not the thesis and antithesis of a historical process. The rivalry between them was a symptom of that process, not itself the dialectical working out of its contradictions. Technology was a challenge to art; forces of production were in contradiction with relations of production. But these two facts could not be neatly superimposed so that the terms of the former lined up unequivocally on the sides of progress and reaction.

Moreover, given the present mode of production, all "syntheses" between art and technology were premature. Within Benjamin's intellectual landscape, they belonged to the anticipatory realm of dreams. The sheltering arcades were the first modern architecture for the public. But they were also the first consumer "dream houses," placed at the service of commodity worship. In the nineteenth century, when the tempo of technological transformations threatened to outstrip the capacity of art to adapt itself to them, advertising became the means of reestablishing a link between technology's forces and social desires: "The advertisement is the cunning with which the dream imposed itself upon industry."[199] At the same time, the development of advertising was symptomatic of the transformation of information into propaganda, so that in commercial art fantasy only "prepares" itself to become socially "practical" in a positive sense.[200] Similarly, before photography can obtain a "revolutionary use-value," the photographer must "rescue" the image from "the fashions of commerce," with the proper caption.[201] In the feuilleton, writers find their rightful place as communicators to a mass audience and as commentators on everyday life, but the commercial genres of their literature—physiognomies of the crowd, panoramas of the boulevard, the reveries of the flâneur—transform reality into an object that can be consumed passively, pleasurably, and directly in its dream form,[202] rather than "refunctioning" the communication apparatus into a tool that will make it possible to wake up from the dream. Given the ambivalence of the phenomena, those artworks that eschewed the new social pressures and espoused the doctrine of *l'art pour l'art* were as much to be redeemed as, for different reasons, the tendency of tacking aesthetic "masks" onto the new forms. The latter were warning signs that fantasy's new social usefulness did not make its utopian aspect superfluous. In short, the liquidation of traditional art would remain premature, so long as its utopian promise was left unrealized.

If the situation had been simple, if art and technology *had* been the opposing poles of a historical dialectic within the superstructure, then there would have been nothing easier than their "synthesis." The new culture would emerge as a process of aestheticizing technology, or conversely, of proclaiming technology as art. Both these forms were attempted in the early twentieth century, the first by *Jugendstil*, which strove to renew art from the "form-treasures of technology"[203] and to "stylize" them "ornamentally"[204] as natural symbols; the second by Futurism which, pronouncing technology beautiful, wished to raise it to an art form in itself. Benjamin criticizes them on the same grounds: "The reactionary attempt to release technologically determined forms from their functional contexts and to reify them as natural constants—i.e., to stylize them—occurred similarly in *Jugendstil* and later in Futurism."[205]

Despite Adorno's reservations, Benjamin's theory of mass culture did provide criteria for a critique of cultural production under capitalism. But it also identified how in spite of these conditions, socialist imagination could come—indeed, was coming into being. The cultural transformation which Benjamin was investigating is not to be thought of simply as a new aesthetic style. It involves giving up the ingrained habit of thinking in terms of the subjective fantasy of art versus the objective material forms of reality. The dialectic which was "no less visible" in the superstructure than in the substructure would transform the very way these two societal components were related. The binary of substructure and superstructure would itself be drawn into the "melting-down process."[206]

8

Recall that the collective fantasy released at the beginning of the new era of industrialism reaches back to an ur-past. In the temporal dimension, images of the ancient, mythic origins of Western civilization become prominent (one manifestation of which is neoclassicism). Materially, the technologically produced "new" nature appears in the fantastic form of the old, organic nature. The *Passagen-Werk* gives repeated documentation of how the modernity that was emerging in the nineteenth century evoked both of these realms, in what might seem to be a collective expression of nostalgia for the past and the outmoded. But Benjamin leads us to understand a different motivation. On the one hand, it is an "attempt to master the new experiences of the city" and of technology "in the frame of the old, traditional ones of nature"[207] and of myth. On the other hand, it is the distorted form of the dream "wish," which is not to redeem the past, but to redeem the desire for utopia to which humanity has persistently given expression. This utopia is none other than the communist goal stated by Marx in the 1844 "Economic and Philosophic Manuscripts"[208]: the harmonious reconciliation of subject and object through the humanization of nature and the naturalization of humanity, and it is in fact an ur-historical motif in both Biblical and classical myth. Greek antiquity, no heaven-on-earth in reality, achieved such a reconciliation symbolically in its cultural forms. To replicate these forms, however, as if some "truth" were eternally present within them, denies the historical particularly which is essential to all truth. Rather, the ur-utopian themes are to be rediscovered not merely symbolically, as aesthetic ornamentation, but actually, in matter's most modern configurations.

It is with the new, technological nature that human beings must be reconciled. This is the goal of socialist culture, and the meaning of Benjamin's question, already cited:

When and how will the worlds of form that have arisen in mechanics, in film, machine construction and the new physics, and that have overpowered us without our being aware of it, make what is natural in them clear to us? When will the condition of society be reached in which these forms or those that have arisen from them open themselves up to us as natural forms?[209]

The paradox is that precisely by giving up nostalgic mimicking of the past and paying strict attention to the new nature, the ur-images are reanimated. Such is the logic of historical images, in which collective wish images are negated, surpassed, and at the same time dialectically redeemed. This logic does not form a discursive system in a Hegelian sense. The moment of sublation reveals itself visually, in an instantaneous flash[210] wherein the old is illuminated precisely at the moment of its disappearance. This *fleeting* image of truth "is not a process of exposure which destroys the secret, but a revelation which does it justice."[211]

9

Can such a cognitive experience (which, literally, *e-ducates* our imagination, leading it out of its still mythic stage) be illustrated in the context of the present discussion? By way of conclusion, here are two such attempts, demonstrating both the moment of critical negation in the dialectics of seeing that exposes the ideology of

bourgeois culture, and the moment of redemption, as a fleeting revelation of truth. The first illustration, constructed out of extremes
of archaic and modern, makes visible the difference between the
repetition of the past and its redemption. In the second, the new
nature flashes together with the old in an anticipatory image of
humanity and nature reconciled.

Archaic/Modern

Not only architectural tastes were dominated by neoclassical aesthetics in the nineteenth century. Bourgeois theater enthusiastically
restaged the ancient Greek tragedies, defining "classics" as those
works, the truth of which was untouched by historical passing. In
the genre of caricature (more receptive to the new technologies of
lithographic reproduction due to its lower status as an art form) the
artist Honoré Daumier produced images of his own class[212] which,
in making the bourgeois subject their object, lent to his visual representations "'a sort of philosophical operation.'"[213] His humor
provided the critical distance necessary to recognize the pretentions
of the bourgeois cloak of antiquity.[214] Daumier showed neoclassicism to be not the recurrence of an eternally valid form, but a
peculiarly bourgeois style of historical distortion. He depicted
the bourgeoisie *depicting* antiquity, in a way that articulated the
former's transiency, not the latter's permanence (figures 5.12 and
5.13). Baudelaire suggested as the motto for a book by Daumier on
ancient history: "Who will deliver us from the Greeks and the
Romans?"—and he recognized in this artist a fellow modernist
because of it. He wrote:

"Daumier swoops down brutally on antiquity and mythology and spits on
it. And the impassioned Achilles, the prudent Ulysses, the wise Penelope,
and that great ninny Telemachus, and beautiful Helen who loses Troy,
and steaming Sappho, patron of hysterics, and ultimately everyone, has
been shown to us in a comic ugliness that recalls those old carcasses
of actors of the classic theater who take a pinch of snuff behind the
scenes."[215]

Daumier's images provide the critical negation of bourgeois classicism. But it is to the "dramatic laboratory" of Brecht's epic theater,
the most technically experimental of contemporary dramatic forms,

5.12 "Bernice, Titus, and Antiochus," Honore Daumier, from *Le Charivari*, 1839 (top).

5.13 "The Maidens of Penelope," Honoré Daumier, from the cycle *Ulysses*, 1852 (bottom).

that we must look for a reanimation of the *scientific* power of classical theater—as Benjamin's defense of Brecht makes clear:

[Brecht...] goes back, in a new way, to the theater's greatest and most
ancient opportunity: the opportunity to expose the present. In the center
of his experiments is man. The man of today; a reduced man therefore, a
man kept on ice in a cold world. But since he is the only one we have, it is
in our interest to know him. He is subjected to tests and observations.
[...] Constructing out of the smallest elements of human behavior that
which in Aristotelian drama is called "action"—this is the purpose of epic
theater.[216]

Similarly, in technological structures, classical form returns, a fact
of which Le Corbusier, a founder of architectural modernism, was
aware. Benjamin clearly affirmed the new architecture as the (historically *transient*) form adequate to the period of transition. He
wrote: "In the first third of the last century no one yet had an
inkling of how one must build with glass and iron. The problem has
long since been resolved by hangars and silos."[217] As if to illustrate
this point, the plates that accompanied a 1923 edition of Le Corbusier's collected articles included photographs of hangars and silos.
Moreover, they juxtaposed such modern forms to the buildings of
antiquity, in order to demonstrate how architects of the contemporary era, rather than imitating antiquity intentionally, take their
lead from the engineers who, unwittingly, have discovered its forms
anew (figures 5.14–5.17). Benjamin asks rhetorically: "Do not all
great triumphs in the area of form come into existence [...] as
technological discoveries?"[218]

Old Nature/New Nature

The earliest *Passagen-Werk* notes state that the work of Grandville is
to be "compared with the phenomenology of Hegel."[219] In fact this
graphic artist (whom Surrealists as well as silent filmmakers recognized as their precursor) made visible the "ambivalence between
the utopian and cynical element"[220] in the bourgeois idealist
attempt to subsume nature under its own, subjective categories.
His images depict nature as pure subjectivity in its most specific,
bourgeois-historical form, that is, as commodity. A contemporary
of Marx, Grandville's "cosmology of fashion" portrays nature
decked out in the latest styles as so many "specialty items."[221]

5.14 and 5.15 Contemporary grain elevators (Le Corbusier).

5 Mythic Nature: Wish Image

5.16 and 5.17 Details of the Parthenon (Le Corbusier).

5.18 "Flowers and fruit rejoice in the coming of spring"—Grandville, 1844.

5 Mythic Nature: Wish Image

5.19 "Venus as an evening star"—Grandville, 1844 (top).

5.20 "An interplanetary bridge; Saturn's ring is an iron balcony"—Grandville, 1844 (bottom).

5.21 "A dog walking his man"—Grandville, 1844.

Grandville "brings well to expression what Marx calls the 'theological capers' of commodities,"[222] and, pursuing commodity fetishism "to its extremes, reveals its nature."[223] In his work the image of humanity reconciled with nature is given a cynical twist: Nature imitates humanity's fetishized forms as "so many parodies by nature on the history of humanity."[224] "Grandville's fantasies transfer commodity-character onto the universe. They modernize it."[225] Comets, planets,[226] flowers, the moon and evening star are animated, only to receive the "human" attribute of being transformed into a commodity (figures 5.18–5.20).[227] But in depicting the "battle between fashion and nature,"[228] Grandville allows nature to gain the upper hand (figure 5.21). An active, rebellious nature takes its revenge on the humans who would fetishize it as a commodity (figure 5.22).

The myth of human omnipotence, the belief that human artifice can dominate nature and recreate the world in its image, is central to the ideology of modern domination. Benjamin names this fantasy (which is believed with deadly seriousness by whose who wield technology's power over others): "childish."[229] Grandville depicts it, when, "God knows, not gently," he stamps human characteristics onto nature, practicing that "graphic sadism" which would

5 Mythic Nature: Wish Image

5.22 "Fish fishing for people, using various desirable items as bait"—Grandville, 1844.

5.23 "The marine life collection, showing that underwater plants and animals are based on forms invented by man—fans, wigs, combs, brushes, etc."—Grandville, 1844.

5 Mythic Nature: Wish Image

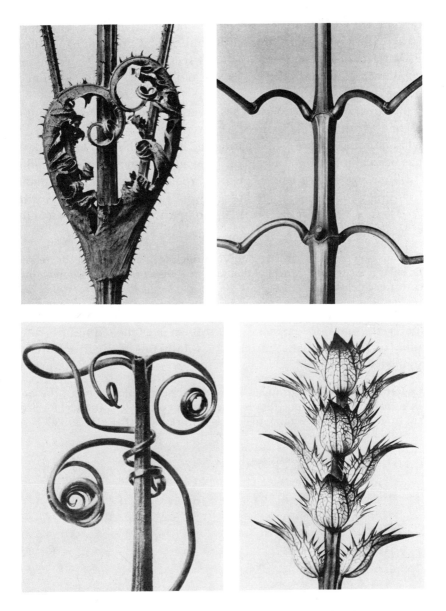

5.24, 5.25, 5.26, 5.27 Photographs of plants as ur-forms of art, Karl Blossfeldt, 1928.

become the "fundamental principle" of the advertising image.[230] Grandville's caricatures mimic the hubris of a humanity so puffed up with its new achievements that it sees itself as the source of all creation and brutally imagines the old nature totally subsumed under *its* forms (figure 5.23).

But this cognitive experience is inverted when the new technique of photographic enlargement (figures 5.24-5.27) shows us with what cunning nature, anticipating the forms of human technology, has been allied with us all along! Photography thereby takes us like "Liliputians" into a land of gigantic and "fraternal" organic plant forms,[231] wrote Benjamin in his review of Karl Blossfeldt's *Urformen der Kunst* (*Ur-forms of Art*) in 1928. Comparing Blossfeldt to Grandville, Benjamin commented:

Is it not remarkable that here another principle of advertising, the gigantic enlargement of the world of plants is now seen to heal the wounds that caricature delivered to it?"[232]

Here is a use of technology not to dominate nature but to take off the "veil" that our "laziness" has thrown over the old nature, and allow us to see in plant existence "a totally unexpected treasure of analogies and forms."[233]

Ur-forms of art—yes, granted. Still, what else can these be but the ur-forms of nature?—Forms, that is, that were never merely a model for art, but from the very beginning, ur-forms at work in all that is creative?[234]

6

Historical Nature: Ruin

1

Transitoriness is the key to Benjamin's affirmation of the mythic element in cultural objects, redeeming the wish-images attached to the transitional, "too-early" ur-forms of modern technology as momentary anticipations of utopia. But in the process of commodification, wish image congeals into fetish; the mythic lays claim to eternity. "Petrified nature" (*erstarrte Natur*) characterizes those commodities that comprise the modern phantasmagoria which in turn freezes the history of humanity as if enchanted under a magic spell.[1] But this fetishized nature, too, is transitory. The other side of mass culture's hellish repetition of "the new" is the mortification of matter which is fashionable no longer. The gods grow out of date, their idols disintegrate, their cult places—the arcades themselves—decay. Benjamin notes that the first electric street-lighting (1857) "extinguished the irreproachable luminosity in these passages, which were suddenly harder to find [. . .]."[2] He interprets Zola's novel *Thérèse Raquin*, written a decade later, as an account of "the death of the Paris arcades, the process of decay of an architectural style."[3] Because these decaying structures no longer hold sway over the collective imagination, it is possible to recognize them as the illusory dream images they always were. Precisely the fact that their original aura has disintegrated makes them invaluable didactically:

To cite an observation of Aragon that constitutes the hub of the problem: That the Passages are what they are here for us [*für uns*], is due to the fact that they in themselves [*an sich*] are no longer.[4]

We have come around full circle, and are once again under the sign of "Natural History," in which history appears concretely as the mortification of the world of things. Let us review: As a montage (and expressed far more concretely in the German language which itself builds words by montage), the idea of "natural history" (*Naturgeschichte*) provides critical images of modern history as prehistoric—merely natural, not yet history in the truly human sense. This was the point of Benjamin's viewing the nineteenth century as the distant ice age of industrialism. But in the image of the fossil, Benjamin captures as well the process of natural decay that marks the survival of past history within the present, expressing with palpable clarity what the discarded fetish becomes, so hollowed out of life that only the imprint of the material shell remains.

It was Adorno who provided the intellectual mapping of Benjamin's approach. In "The Idea of Natural History" (1932), he pointed out that Lukács conveyed a similar meaning with the concept of "second nature": "this alienated, reified, dead world" of fixed aesthetic forms and hollow literary conventions, from which the "inmost soul has been extracted."[5] Both Benjamin and Lukács demonstrated that "the petrified life within nature is merely what history has developed into."[6] But Lukács, relying on Hegel's philosophical legacy, was led ultimately to a totalizing conception of metaphysical transcendence, whereas Benjamin, schooled in the very different tradition of the Baroque allegorical poets, remained focused on the fragmentary, transitory object. Adorno maintained that in revealing the significance of Baroque allegory for the philosophy of history, Benjamin accomplished "something essentially different" from Lukács[7]: He brought the idea of history "out of infinite distance into infinite proximity"[8]:

If Lukács lets the historical, as that which has been, transform itself back into [frozen] nature, then here is the other side of the phenomenon: Nature itself is presented as transitory nature, as history.[9]

Now it must be emphasized that Adorno's appreciation here of Benjamin's *Trauerspiel* study was based on its (unintended) contribution to a materialist—and, indeed, Marxist—conception of history. And if we wish to understand how this conception in turn contributed to the *Passagen-Werk*, we, too, will need to consider this early study, before returning to the nineteenth century and to Benjamin's analysis of its own allegorical poet, Charles Baudelaire.

We can begin by recalling that central to the Baroque vision of nature as the allegorical representation of history is the emblem,[10] a montage of visual image and linguistic sign, out of which is read, like a picture puzzle, what things "mean." Of course, in the representation of the commodity fetish as fossil, Benjamin himself created such an emblem: Under the sign of history, the image of petrified nature is the cipher of what history has become. The allegorical poets read a similar meaning into the emblem of the human skull, the skeletal residue with its empty stare that was once an animated, human face (figure 6.1).

History, in everything it displays that was from the beginning untimely, sorrowful, unsuccessful, expresses itself in a face—no, in a skull. [. . . I]t articulates as a riddle, the nature not only of human existence pure and simple, but of the biological historicity of an individual in this, the figure of its greatest natural decay.[11]

The emblem of the skull can be read in two ways. It is human spirit petrified; but it is also nature in decay, the transformation of the corpse into a skeleton that will turn into dust. Similarly, in the concept of *Naturgeschichte*, if hollowed-out nature (the fossil) is the emblem of "petrified history," then nature too has a history, so that historical transiency (the ruin) is the emblem of nature in decay. In seventeenth-century Europe, when the religious polity was in shatters due to protracted war, the Baroque allegoricists contemplated the skull as an image of the vanity of human existence and the transitoriness of earthly power. The ruin was similarly emblematic of the futility, the "transitory splendor"[12] of human civilization, out of which history was read as "a process of relentless disintegration [. . .]."[13] In these "riddle figures" of historically transient nature, Benjamin locates

[. . .] the core of the allegorical way of seeing, and the Baroque secular exposition of history as the suffering of the world; it is meaningful only in periods of decline. The greater the meaning, the greater the subjection to death, because death digs out most deeply the jagged line of demarcation between physical nature and meaning.[14]

An emblem by Florentius Schoonovius (figure 6.2) expresses this idea. The *subscriptio* (caption) reads:

MAIOR AD-
ÆQUATUS.

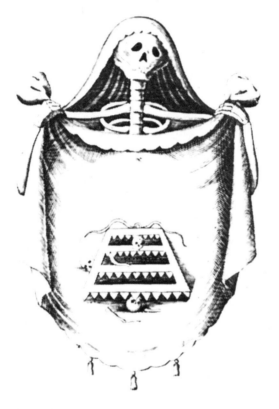

Quos diverſa parit SORS, MORS *inamabilis æquat,*
Et pede metitur TE *PARI cæca pari.*
At major virtus majori funere donat.
MAIOR ADÆQUATOS *ſic* PARIS *inter erit.*

6.1 Baroque emblem with the common motif of a human skull, signifying the equalizing power of death.

Vivitur ingenio.

EMBLEMA XXIX

Regna cadunt, urbes pereunt, nec quæ fuit olim
Roma manet, præter nomen inane, nihil.
Sola tamen rerum, doctis quæsita libellis,
Effugiunt structos Fama decusque rogos.

6.2 "Vivitur Ingenio," emblem by Florentius Schoonhovius, ca. 1618.

Rulers fall, cities perish, nothing of
What Rome once was remains.
The past is empty, nothing.
Only those things of learning and
Books that give fame and respect
Escape the funeral pyre created
By time and death.[15]

The meaning of this emblem corresponds closely to a Baroque text cited by Benjamin:

"Considering that the pyramids, pillars, and statues of all kinds of material become damaged with time or destroyed by violence or simply decay . . . that indeed whole cities have sunk, disappeared, and are covered over by water, that in contrast writings and books are immune from such destruction, for if any should disappear or be destroyed in one country or place, one can easily find them again in countless other places, then to speak of human experience, nothing is more enduring and immortal than books."[16]

In preparing the 1935 exposé, Benjamin made a short notation: "fetish and skull."[17] More generally, throughout the *Passagen-Werk* material, the image of the "ruin," as an emblem not only of the transitoriness and fragility[18] of capitalist culture, but also its destructiveness,[19] is pronounced. And just as the Baroque dramatists saw in the ruin not only the "highly meaningful fragment,"[20] but also the objective determinate for their own poetic construction, the elements of which were never unified into a seamless whole,[21] so Benjamin employed the most modern method of montage in order to construct out of the decaying fragments of nineteenth-century culture images that made visible the "jagged line of demarcation between physical nature and meaning."

It was the Baroque poets who demonstrated to Benjamin that the "failed material" of his own historical era could be "elevated to the position of allegory."[22] What made this so valuable for a dialectical presentation of modernity was that allegory and myth were "antithetical."[23] Indeed, allegory was the "antidote" to myth, and precisely this was "to be demonstrated" in the *Passagen-Werk*.[24] Yet the Baroque, Christian conclusion that because the world of material referents crumbles it is ultimately not real—"nothing," while the truth of written texts is immortal because these mental products survive the material destructiveness of history, was a position that for both philosophical and political reasons Benjamin felt compelled to reject.

2

Allegory is in the realm of thought what ruins are in the realm of things.[25]

The image realm of classical antiquity was as central to Benjamin's discussion of *Trauerspiel* as it was to the Arcades project. Antiquity's mythological cosmology anthropomorphized the forces of (old) nature as gods in human form, signifying a continuity between natural, human, and divine realms. This pagan pantheon was destroyed by later history in the very material sense: The great sculpted figures of the gods, the pillars of their temples, survived physically only in fragments. While architecture bore visibly the marks and wounds of the history of human violence,[26] the ancient gods were banished as "heathen" by a triumphant Christianity, leaving behind a nature hollowed out of the divine spirit with which they had once animated it. The new religion, in contrast, believed in the mortification of the flesh and a guilt-laden nature.[27] The pantheon of ancient gods, "disconnected from the life contexts out of which they sprang,"[28] became "dead figures," standing arbitrarily for the philosophical ideas they had once embodied as living symbols: "The deadness of the figures and the abstraction of the concepts are therefore the precondition for the allegorical metamorphosis of the pantheon into a world of magical creature-concepts."[29]

Connected as they were with paganism generally, and with corporality and sexuality in particular, these ancient deities endured within the religiously charged atmosphere of the Baroque only in debased form.[30] They survived as demons, as astrological signs, as the faces of Tarot cards, and they were applied to a moral purpose as personifications of the passions.[31] Venus/Aphrodite, for example, once the natural symbol that raised human eros to the level of divine love, lived on as "Dame World," the profane, allegorical emblem of earthly passion. Whereas originally her nakedness transfigured the erotic in accord with the "'purer nature of the gods that was embodied in the pantheon,'"[32] in a Christian context she appeared dressed in contemporary fashion; or, her nakedness was interpreted as a moral allegory that "the sin of lust cannot be

Temporality of the Symbol: Fleeting Eternity

6.3 Statue of Venus/Aphrodite, divine symbol of love in the transitory form of natural beauty, Hellenistic.

6 Historical Nature: Ruin

Temporality of Allegory: Eternal Fleetingness

6.4 Vanitas: Three stages of Life, allegorical representation of the transitoriness of earthly beauty, Hans Balding Grien (student of Dürer), 1510.

concealed."[33] Similarly, Cupid survived in the art of Giotto only
"'as a demon of wantonness with a bat's wings and claws'"; and
the mythological "faun, centaur, siren, and harpie" continued to
exist "as allegorical figures in the circle of Christian Hell.[34] The
surviving "marble and bronze sculptures of antiquity still retained
for the Baroque and even the Renaissance something of the horror
with which Augustine had recognized in them 'the bodies of the
gods, as it were.'"[35]

Forfeiture of divinity and transformation into the demonic were
the price these deities had to pay for survival in the Christian
era. Allegorical interpretation became "their only conceivable
salvation"[36] Without it, "in an unsuitable, indeed, hostile environ-
ment [...] the world of the ancient gods would have had to die
out, and it is precisely allegory that rescued it."[37]

Relevant here, and significant as well for the Arcades project, is
Benjamin's distinction in the *Trauerspiel* study between symbol and
allegory. It will be remembered that he rejected as "untenable" the
established canon (which rested on Goethe's formulation) that the
difference between symbol and allegory hinged on how idea and
concept related the particular to the general.[38] Not the distinction
between idea and concept was decisive, but the "category of
time."[39] In allegory, history appears as nature in decay or ruins
and the temporal mode is one of retrospective contemplation; but
time enters the symbol as an instanteous present—"the mystical
Nu"[40]—in which the empirical and the transcendent appear
momentarily fused within a fleeting, natural form.[41] Organic nature that is "fluid and changing"[42] is the stuff of symbol (figure
6.3), whereas in allegory (figure 6.4), time finds expression in nature mortified, not "in bud and bloom, but in the overripeness and
decay of her creations."[43]

The *Trauerspiel* study argued that allegory was in no way inferior
to the symbol. Allegory was not merely a "playful illustrative technique," but, like speech or writing, a "form of expression,"[44] one
which the objective world imposed upon the subject as a cognitive
imperative, rather than the artist's choosing it arbitrarily as an aesthetic device. Certain experiences (and thus certain epochs) were
allegorical,[45] not certain poets. In the Middle Ages, the ruins of a
conquered, pagan antiquity made "[...] knowledge of the impermanence of things [...] inescapable, derived from observation,
just as several centuries later, at the time of the Thirty Years War,

6 Historical Nature: Ruin

6.5 Hill of Skulls, anonymous, German, 1917.

the same knowledge stared European humanity in the face."[46] Of significance was the fact that "in the seventeenth century the word *Trauerspiel* was applied in the same way to both dramas and historical events."[47] At the moment Benjamin was writing, European humanity again looked the ruins of war in the face, and knowledge of history as a desolate "place of skulls"[48] (*Schädelstätte*) was once more inescapable (figure 6.5).

When Benjamin conceived of the Arcades project, there is no doubt that he was self-consciously reviving allegorical techniques. Dialectical images are a modern form of emblematics. But whereas the Baroque dramas were melancholy reflections on the inevitability of decay and disintegration, in the *Passagen-Werk* the devaluation of (new) nature and its status as ruin becomes instructive politically. The debris of industrial culture teaches us not the necessity of submitting to historical catastrophe, but the fragility of the social order that tells us this catastrophe is necessary. The crumbling of the monuments that were built to signify the immortality of civilization becomes proof, rather, of its transiency. And the fleetingness of temporal power does not cause sadness; it informs political practice. The importance of such practice was the reason for Benjamin's own critical distance from Baroque allegory, already implicit in the *Trauerspiel* book, but from a political position of radical pacifism rather than revolutionary socialism. The reader will need to bear with this digression into the esoteric realm of the *Trauerspiel* a bit longer. Because Benjamin's criticism of Baroque allegory remained crucial to the Arcades project, and because its philosophical implications are fundamental to our discussion both here and in later chapters,[49] it is necessary to outline his argument clearly before proceeding.

3

Deadening of affects [. . .] distance from the surrounding world [. . .] alienation from one's own body [. . . these things become] symptom[s] of depersonalization as an intense degree of sadness [. . .] in which the most insignificant thing, because a natural and creative connection to it is lacking, appears as a chiffre of an enigmatic wisdom in an incomparably fruitful connection. In accord with this, in the background of Albrecht Dürer's "*Melancholia*" [figure 6.6], the utensils of everyday life lie on the ground unused, as objects of contemplation. This engraving anticipates the Baroque in many ways.[50]

6 Historical Nature: Ruin

6.6 "Melancholia. I," woodcut, Albrecht Dürer, sixteenth century.

Benjamin's analysis of Baroque tragic drama was philosophical rather than literary. He argued that "modern allegory" (which began in the Renaissance) became caught in a philosophical antinomy. Rooted in scholarly attempts to decipher Egyptian hieroglyphs, which were believed to be God's writing in natural images rather than a phonetic language, it presumed on the one hand that the thing pictured really was the thing meant: being (*Seiendes*) *was* meaning—"The hieroglyphs, therefore, as the replicas of divine ideas!"[51] Such a language of images implied there was nothing arbitrary in the connection between sign and referent. Natural images promised to disclose the universal language through which God communicated the meaning of His creations to human beings.[52] Not only Egyptian hieroglyphs, but also Greek myths and Christian symbols were looked to for deciphering the divine meaning of the material world.[53]

On the other hand, by the seventeenth century, due to the plurality of pagan and Christian cosmologies that had been amassed in history and preserved in those authoritative texts in which truth was believed to reside, natural phenomena were overdetermined, laden with a multiplicity of meanings: "For every idea that comes to mind, the moment of expression coincides with a veritable eruption of images, embodied in the mass of metaphors that lie littered chaotically about."[54] The impulse for systematic completion of knowledge came up against a semiotic arbitrariness intensified by "'the dogmatic power of the meanings handed down from the ancients, so that one and the same object can be an image just as easily of a virtue as a vice, and eventually can signify everything.'"[55] The apparent arbitrariness of meanings had the effect of compelling allegoricists to choose a variant that represented intended meanings of their own—thus allegory became a correspondingly abitrary aesthetic device, in direct contradiction to the philosophical claim on which it was grounded. Benjamin insists that since "within a purely aesthetic approach, paradox must have the last word," one must, as the allegoricists did, move to the "higher realm of theology" in order to achieve a resolution to this dilemma.[56] Within Baroque theological discourse, the fact that nature could only be "read uncertainly by the allegoricists"[57] was explained by the theological "guilt" of nature after the Fall from Paradise.[58] Christianity concentrated the "multiplicity" of pagan

elements within this natural world into "one theologically rigorously defined Antichrist" in "the form of Satan," in whom "the
material and the demonic" were "knotted inextricably together."[59]
Satanic laughter, the "sneering laughter of Hell" that "overshoots
language,"[60] is connected with that superfluity of meanings of objects which is a sign of nature's fallen state. "The allegorical sig-
nifier is prevented by guilt from finding its meaning fulfilled in
itself."[61] Satan rules over the abyss of hollowed-out matter of which
history is composed, and it is he who "as initiator, leads man to a
knowledge that lies at the foundation of punishable conduct."[62]

The allegoricists heaped emblematic images one on top of
another, as if the sheer quantity of meanings could compensate for
their arbitrariness and lack of coherence.[63] The result is that nature, far from an organic whole, appears in arbitrary arrangement,
as a lifeless, fragmentary, untidy clutter of emblems.[64] The coherence of language is similarly "shattered."[65] Meanings are not only
multiple, they are "above all" antithetical[66]: The crown means a
cypress wreath, the harp an executioner's axe.[67] Allegoricists, like
alchemists, hold dominion over an infinite transformation of meanings, in contrast to the one, true word of God.[68] As knowledge of the
material world, theirs is a knowledge of "evil," the contradictions
and arbitrariness of which are experienced as a descent into Hell. It
is theological revelation that arrests this fall.

Just as those who plummet downward turn somersaults in their fall, so the
allegorical intention would fall from emblem to emblem into the dizziness
of its bottomless depths, were it not that, in precisely the most extreme
among them, it had to make such an about turn that all its evil, arrogance,
and godlessness appears as nothing but self-delusion.[69]

Knowledge of evil—Satan himself—as self-delusion. This is the
Baroque theological resolution to the paradoxical meanings of
objective matter. It involves a dialectical move to a metalevel, at
which the contradictory meanings of emblems themselves become
an emblem, the sign of *their* opposite: the eternity of the one, true
Spirit. If the earthly realm is known only in antitheses, then truth
emerges as the antithesis of all this. As the "place of skulls," Golgatha represents the forsakenness of nature by picturing its transitoriness. But in Christianity this emblem is transfigured: Natural
death is understood as itself only transitory, passing over into eternal life.

The inconsolable confusion of the place of skulls [*Schädelstätte*] that can be read as the schema of allegorical figures out of a thousand engravings and descriptions of the time is not solely emblematic of the wasteland of human existence. Transitoriness is not only signified, not only represented allegorically, but is itself a sign, presented as allegory: the allegory of Resurrection.[70]

Hence: "Ultimately, in the signs of death of the Baroque—if only in the redemptive return of its great arc—the allegorical outlook makes an about turn."[71] Benjamin cites the drama of Lohenstein: "'Yea, when the Highest comes to reap the graveyard harvest/ Then will I, a death-skull, become an angel's face.'"[72] Here, at a stroke, the dizzying descent is reversed, the nightmarish evil of Satan disappears: "It is in God's world that the allegoricist awakens."[73]

Benjamin's stated purpose in the *Trauerspiel* study is not so much to evaluate this Christian resolution as to demonstrate that in Baroque allegory, such theological thinking is primary, hence the inadequacy of a purely literary interpretation of tragic drama. The closing pages of the *Trauerspiel* book are largely limited to a description of the theological solution to allegory's antinomy. Yet there are unmistakable clues as to Benjamin's own position, which must be read not as an affirmation but as a fundamental critique, one which had political as well as philosophical implications. The outline of this critique might remain unnoticed by the naive reader, but given the context of Benjamin's other writings,[74] it is legible, even if its presentation is indirect. If the critique had been made explicit, it might be summarized as follows.

The Baroque poets saw in transitory nature an allegory for human history, in which the latter appeared, not as a divine plan or chain of events on a "road to salvation,"[75] but as death, ruin, catastrophe; and it was this essentially philosophical attitude that gave allegory a claim beyond mere aesthetic device. The forsakenness of nature, understood as a theological truth, was the source of the melancholy of the allegoricists: "The steadfastness which expresses itself in the intention of mourning is born out of loyalty to the world of things."[76] But it is a world of "dead objects," a realm of "infinite hopelessness."[77] In it, political action is judged as mere arbitrary intrigue.[78] Now at the crucial point—and this follows necessarily from the melancholic's politics of contemplation rather than intervention—allegory deserts both history and nature and (like the whole tradition of idealist philosophy that comes after it), takes refuge in the spirit. All hope is reserved for a hereafter that is "emptied of everything that contains even the imperceptible breath of the world."[79] When Baroque allegory attempts to rescue a devalued nature by making its very devaluing meaningful as the sign of its opposite, redemption, then loyalty turns into betrayal:

Evil as such—exists only in allegory, is nothing other than allegory, and means something other than it is. It means in fact precisely the nonexistence of what it presents. The absolute vices, as exemplified by tyrants and intriguers are allegories. They are not real [. . .].[80]

Evil disappears, but at what a cost! In order to remain true to God, the German allegoricists abandon both nature and politics: "[Their . . .] intention ultimately does not remain loyal [treu] to the spectacle of the skeleton, but, treacherously [treulos] leaps over to the Resurrection."[81] This "treacherous" leap from the mournful spectacle of history as a "sad drama" to the miracle of resurrection, done in the name of allegory, is in a philosophical sense its negation. "Allegory loses everything that was most its own."[82] Benjamin quotes from a text of 1652: "'Weeping, we scattered seed on the fallow ground, and sadly we went away'"[83]; he comments: "Allegory goes away empty-handed."[84] When the allegoricists, claiming that the fragments of failed nature are really an allegory of spiritual redemption as their opposite, a redemption guaranteed only by the Word, when they declare evil as "self-delusion" and material nature as "not real," then, for all practical purposes allegory becomes indistinguishable from myth. Benjamin criticizes the attempt to get away from the arbitrary subjectivity of allegory, as itself pure subjectivity: It "sweeps away" the entire objective world as a "phantasmagoria," and the subject is "left entirely on its own."[85]

In short, Benjamin criticizes Baroque allegory for its idealism. As Tiedemann has written: "From the time of the Trauerspiel book, the program of Benjamin's philosophy is the anti-idealist construction of the intelligible world."[86] It is this program that binds the Trauerspiel study to the Passagen-Werk. In 1931, Benjamin recognized the former study as "already dialectical," and if it was "certainly not materialist" in a Marxist sense, still it bore a "mediated" relationship to dialectical materialism.[87] When Benjamin was working on the 1935 exposé to the *Passagen-Werk*, he wrote to Adorno:

[. . . M]uch more clearly than in any previous stage of the plan (in a manner that indeed surprises me), the analogies of this book with the Baroque book come to light. You must allow me to see in this state of affairs an especially meaningful confirmation of the remelting process which has led the entire mass of thoughts originally set in motion by metaphysics to an aggregate condition in which the world of dialectical images is secured against all the objections provoked by metaphysics.[88]

This "remelting process" was in fact Adorno's and Benjamin's shared project, one that they had begun in 1929 during their "unforgettable conversations at Königstein,"[89] when Benjamin first discussed his *Passagen*-project and read some of the early notes. One of these notes reads: "Parallels between this work and the *Trauerspiel* book: Both have the same theme: Theology of Hell. Allegory, advertisement, Types: martyr, tyrant—whore, speculator."[90] As I have argued elsewhere, the Königstein discussion had a momentous impact on Adorno.[91] The *Passagen*-project was perceived at the time by both of them as a Marxist refunctioning of the philosophical method of the *Trauerspiel* book, making it "safe," as Benjamin said—if not from metaphysics,[92] then from "the objections provoked by metaphysics," by tying its truth claims totally to the material world. Adorno joined enthusiastically in this attempt, not only teaching the *Trauerspiel* study in his seminar as a young philosophy professor at the university in Frankfurt am Main (the place that had rejected this book as Benjamin's *Habilitationsschrift*[93]) but putting a dialectical, materialist version of its method into practice in a critical interpretation of Kierkegaard[94] which aimed at nothing less than the philosophical liquidation of idealism. This is not the place to describe again the specifics of Adorno's argument.[95] It can be noted, however, that the publication of the *Passagen-Werk* provides additional proof as to the closeness of their collaboration on this general project. Not only does the "bourgeois interior" play a crucial role in both the Kierkegaard study and the *Passagen-Werk*[96] as a "dialectical image" in which the reality of industrial capitalism is manifested visibly.[97] Within the *Passagen-Werk*'s important *Konvolut* on epistemology, Benjamin makes the strikingly dialogical gesture of citing—not passages from the *Trauerspiel* study directly—

but Adorno's recontextualized citings of these passages in the Kierkegaard book.[98]

We have already seen how Adorno, in his 1932 speech ("The Idea of Natural History"), praised Benjamin's analysis of allegory in the *Trauerspiel* book in connection with Lukács' theory of second nature as "hollowed-out" literary conventions. The next step (one which, as they both knew, Lukács himself took in *History and Class Consciousness*), was to identify this "hollowing-out" process with the commodity form of objects, and hence with the capitalist mode of production. Such an argument figures importantly in Adorno's study of Kierkegaard. But in the *Passagen-Werk* it is absolutely central, explaining the key position of Baudelaire as the writer who brought the mute, "new" nature of urban industrialism to speech, and providing the means for deciphering the historico-philosophical truth of this very bourgeois poet.

4

What I have in mind is to show Baudelaire as he lies embedded in the nineteenth century. The imprint that he has left behind upon it must stand out as clearly and untouched as that of a stone which, having rested in a site for a decade, one day rolls from its place.[99]

"All the visible universe is nothing but a shop of images and signs."—Charles Baudelaire[100]

Baudelaire's book of poems, *Les Fleurs du mal* (*Flowers of Evil*), condemned as an offense to public morals when it appeared in 1857, manifested a radically new aesthetic sensibility that drew its breath from the "decadent" sense experience of the modern city. At the same time, these poems were concerned with the premodern, Christian problem of sin and evil, expressed in an allegorical form that had been out of literary fashion since the time of the Baroque. While the new aesthetic sensibility influenced practicing poets who came after him, it was Baudelaire's return to premodern, ethico-religious themes that preoccupied his interpreters.[101] The latter were quick to compare him with Dante, whose Catholic beliefs and allegorical forms he shared.[102] They considered (as did the poet himself) that Baudelaire's unique and genial contribution was to sustain allegory, "'one of the most ancient and natural forms'"[103] in order to express the universal, human problem of evil within the changed context of modern life, thus guaranteeing the continuity of literary tradition despite the disruptive shocks of modern experience.

For Benjamin, on the contrary, the fusion of past and present in Baudelaire's work was highly problematic, precisely because of the *dis*continuity of experience to which his new aesthetic sensibility bore witness.[104] He saw as the central question: "How is it possible that an attitude which at least in appearance is as out of keeping with its time as that of the allegoricists, takes pride of place in [*Les Fleurs du mal*,] the poetic work of the century?"[105] And because Benjamin considered that neither the poet's biographical particularities nor "universal" human concerns had explanatory power, the answer to this question was by no means self-evident.

Benjamin had argued in the *Trauerspiel* study that Baroque allegory was the mode of perception peculiar to a time of social disruption and protracted war, when human suffering and material ruin were the stuff and substance of historical experience—hence the return of allegory in his own era as a response to the horrifying destructiveness of World War I. But the historical experience that gave birth to *Les Fleurs du mal* was not comparable. Paris in the mid-nineteenth century, in which time and place Baudelaire's poems were written, was at the bursting point of unprecedented material abundance. It was the era of the first department stores, Haussmann's boulevards, international expositions—a world about which Balzac wrote as early as 1846: "'The grand poem of the exhibition of goods sings its verses of color from *la Madeleine* to the gate of Saint-Denis.'"[106] To be sure, the bloody June days in the 1848 Revolution provided a very different image. But this moment of political violence was not the content of Baudelaire's poems.[107] Rather, it was precisely the splendor of the newly constructed urban phantasmagoria with its promise of change-as-progress that elicited in him the most prototypically melancholic allegorical response.

"It is very important that the modern is not only an epoch for Baudelaire, but an energy, by the strength of which it relates immediately to antiquity"[108]—and in the allegorical mode. In Baudelaire's poem, "The Swan," the poet is traversing the newly rebuilt Place du Carrousel when his memory is suddenly flooded with the image of Andromache, wife of Hector, who was left a widow with the destruction of Troy. Superimposed on images of modern Paris, this ancient figure takes on allegorical meaning:

> Andromache, I think of you!
> . . .
> The old Paris is gone (the face of a city
> Changes more quickly, alas! than the mortal heart)
> . . .
> Paris changes, but nothing of my melancholy
> Gives way. New palaces, scaffolding, blocks,
> Old suburbs, everything for me becomes allegory,
> While my dear memories are heavier than rocks.[109]

Why is it that Baudelaire confronts the new "just as the seventeenth-century allegoricists confronted antiquity"?[110] Why does the most modern face of Paris remind him of a city already in ruins? What is it about the absolutely new experience of modernity that makes its objects correspond to the allegorical form in which the pagan figures survived in the Baroque, so hollowed out of their original meaning that they become allegorical signs, this time of the poet's own melancholy memories? Benjamin's answer is intrepid.[111] Citing the *Trauerspiel* passage that traces the particular character of allegorical perception to the way the gods of antiquity survived as natural forms in a Christian era that condemned nature, he writes:

For Baudelaire one comes closer to the facts if one reverses the formula. The allegorical experience was original for him; one can say that he appropriated from antiquity, and from the Christian era as well, only what was needed in order to set this original experience—which had a *sui generis* substrate—into motion in his poetry.[112]

Now Benjamin makes the claim that if in Baroque allegory the debasement of nature had its source in Christianity's confrontation with pagan antiquity, in the nineteenth century the debasement of the "new" nature has its source in the production process itself: "The devaluation of the world of objects within allegory is outdone within the world of objects itself by the commodity."[113] Benjamin cites Marx: "'If one considers the concept of value, then the actual object is regarded only as a sign; it counts not as itself, but as what it is worth.'"[114] Commodities relate to their value in the marketplace just as arbitrarily as things relate to their meanings within

6.7 Store Window, Avenue des Gobelins, photograph by Eugène Atget, Paris, 1925.

Baroque emblematics. "The emblems return as commodities."[115] Their abstract and arbitrary meaning is their price (figure 6.7). Again, Benjamin appeals to Marx:

"With its price tag the commodity enters the market. If its substantive quality and individuality create the incentive to buy, for the social evaluation of its worth this is totally unimportant. The commodity has become an abstraction. Once it has escaped from the hand of its producers and is freed from its real particularity, it has ceased to be a product controlled by human beings. It has taken on a 'phantom-like objectivity,' and leads its own life. 'A commodity appears at first glance a self-sufficient, trivial thing. Its analysis shows that it is a bewildering thing, full of metaphysical subtleties and theological capers.'"[116]

Benjamin comments:

The "metaphysical subtleties" in which, according to Marx, [the commodities] indulge, are above all those of fixing their price. How the price of the commodity is arrived at can never be totally foreseen, not in the course of its production, nor later when it finds itself in the market. But just this is what happens with the object in its allegorical existence. The meaning which the melancholy of the allegoricist consigns to it is not one that was expected. But once it contains such meaning, then the latter can at any time be removed in favor of any other. The fashions of meanings [in Baroque allegory] changed almost as rapidly as the prices of commodities change. The meaning of the commodity is indeed: Price; as commodity it has no other. Thus the allegoricist with the commodity is in his element.[117]

In the nineteenth century, allegory did not become a style as it had in the Baroque: "As an allegoricist, Baudelaire was isolated."[118] But when he gave allegorical form to the modern, he expressed what the objects of his world had truly become—even if this was not his conscious intent,[119] and even if he had no understanding of the objective origins of their allegorical status. "The possible establishment of proof that his poetry transcribes reveries experienced under hashish in no way invalidates this interpretation."[120]

But if the social value (hence the meaning) of commodities is their price, this does not prevent them from being appropriated by consumers as wish images within the emblem books of their private dreamworld. For this to occur, estrangement of the commodities from their initial meaning as use-values produced by human labor is in fact the prerequisite. It is, after all, the nature of the allegorical object that once the initial hollowing out of meaning has occurred and a new signification has been arbitrarily inserted into it, this meaning "can at any time be removed in favor of any other." Adorno described the process this way: "'[...T]he alienated objects become hollowed out and draw in meanings as ciphers. Subjectivity takes control of them by loading them with intentions of wish and anxiety'"[121]—and Benjamin added: "To these thoughts it should be noted that in the nineteenth century the number of 'hollowed-out objects' increases in a mass and tempo previously unknown."[122] Baudelaire's allegorical representations were antithetical to the mythic form of the objects as wish images. He showed, not the commodities filled with private dreams, but private dreams as hollowed out as the commodities. And if his poetic representation of the new nature did not concern literally its price, he was drawn to the allegorical attitude precisely because of the ephemeral value which was the mark of the commodity on display. The poem, "The Confession," reveals:

> That it is a sad trade to be a lovely woman,
> That it is the banal labor
> Of a dancer who entertains, manic, cold, and fainting
> With her mechanical smile.
>
> That to try to build on hearts is a foolish thing;
> That all things crack—love and beauty—
> Until Oblivion throws them in his sack
> Voiding them to eternity![123]

Baudelaire's poetry ripped apart the harmonizing pretensions of the mythic phantasmagoria that was just then congealing around the commodities: "'The century surrounding him that otherwise seems to be flourishing and manifold, assumes the terrible appearance of a desert.'"[124] Benjamin notes in this context: "The allegory of Baudelaire—in contrast to the Baroque—has the mark of rage."[125] The destructiveness of his use of allegory was intentional: "Baudelairean allegory bears traces of violence, which was necessary in order to rip away the harmonious facade of the world that surrounded him."[126] The images disclosed behind this facade became emblems of his own inner life. To them he wrote his poems as captions.

"If Baudelaire did not fall into the abyss of myth that constantly accompanied his path, it was thanks to the genius of allegory."[127]

As exemplary of Baudelaire's use of "allegory against myth,"[128] Benjamin names "Morning Twilight," a poem that expresses "the sobbing aloud of the person waking up, represented in the stuff and substance of the city."[129] He notes a "key passage" where "the morning wind drives out the clouds of myth. The view of the people and how they [themselves] promote these clouds is laid free"[130]— in the poem: "The air is full of the shiver of things escaping,/And the man is weary of writing, the woman of love."[131] But Baudelaire's use of force against myth is limited to tearing away the phantasmagoria by means of his images of the city's exhausted inhabitants—prostitutes in dull sleep, poor women waking to the cold, dying people in hospital beds, night revellers staggering home. It combines with inaction.

The description nowhere has in view getting its hands on the object; its task is solely to blanket the shivering of one who feels himself ripped anew out of the protection of sleep.[132]

The mood of the poem's last lines is one of resignation:

Dawn, shivering in her rose and green attire,
Makes her slow way along the deserted Seine
While melancholy Paris, old laborer,
Rubs his eyes, and gathers up his tools.[133]

Indicative of Baudelaire's "rage" against the city's phantasmagoria is his rejection of those elements of nineteenth-century style that contributed most centrally to the "harmonious facade" of Paris in the Second Empire: on the one hand, the attempt to represent the new nature in the organic forms of the old, and on the other, the ahistorical use of the forms of classical antiquity. With regard to the former, in contrast to contemporary poets like Hugo who were fond of describing the metropolis and its undulating crowds with images of the ocean,[134] in Baudelaire, organic nature is itself mechanized (the "flowers" of Evil makes the city its topic[135]; the human body assumes industrial forms[136]). With regard to the latter, that neoclassicism which saw antiquity as a sign of eternal verity rather than material transiency filled Baudelaire with contempt. His invective against the idealized representation of pagan themes, writes Benjamin, "reminds one of the medieval clerics. Chubby-cheeked cupid receives his special hatred [. . .]."[137] The reference is to

Baudelaire's "vehement invective against Cupid—*à propos* of a critique of the neo-Greek school"[138]:

"And yet are we not very weary of seeing paint and marble squandered on behalf of this elderly scamp [...]? [...] his hair is thickly curled like a coachman's wig; his fat wobbling cheeks press against his nostrils and his eyes; it is doubtless the elegiac sighs of the universe which distend his flesh, or perhaps I should rather call it his meat, for it is stuffed, tubular and blown out like a bag of lard hanging on a butcher's hook; on his mountainous back is attached a pair of butterfly's wings."[139]

The figure of Cupid was, of course, intended to have quite the opposite effect. Icon of commercialized love, it appeared everywhere in the nineteenth century from salon paintings to the edible creations of confectioners. Benjamin refers to the "tension between emblem and advertising image."[140] Within advertising, a new, dissimulating aura is injected into the commodity, easing its passage into the dream world of the private consumer. In contrast, the allegorical intention points backward in time, as if puzzling to remember an original meaning that has been lost.

[... T]he purpose of the advertisement is to blur over the commodity character of things. Allegory struggles against this deceptive transfiguring of the commodity-world by disfiguring it. The commodity tries to look itself in the face.[141]

Advertising images attempt to "humanize" products in order to deny their commodity character; consumers continue this effort when they provide cases and covers for their possessions, sentimentally providing them a "home."[142] In contrast, Baudelaire sought, "in a heroic way,"[143] to present the commodity itself in human form. As the antithesis of Cupid on a candy box, he "celebrates [the commodity's] becoming human in the whore."[144]

The prostitute is the ur-form of the wage laborer, selling herself in order to survive.[145] Prostitution is indeed an objective emblem of capitalism, a hieroglyph of the true nature of social reality in the sense that the Egyptian hieroglyphs were viewed by the Renaissance[146]—and in Marx's sense as well: "'Value transforms ... every product of labor into a social hieroglyph. People then try to decode the meaning of the hieroglyph in order to get behind the secret of their own social product [...].'"[147] The image of the whore reveals this secret like a rebus. Whereas every trace of the wage laborer who produced the commodity is extinguished when it is torn out of context by its exhibition on display,[148] in the prostitute, both moments remain visible. As a dialectical image, she "synthesizes"[149] the form of the commodity and its content: She is "commodity and seller in one."[150]

Baudelaire makes modern, metropolitan prostitution "one of the main objects of his poetry."[151] Not only is the whore the subject matter of his lyrical expression; she is the model for his own activity. The "prostitution of the poet," Baudelaire believed, was "an unavoidable necessity."[152] He wrote in an early poem (addressed to a streetwalker): "'I who sell my thoughts and wish to be an author.'"[153] In the cycle, *Spleen and Ideal*: "'The Venal Muse' shows how intensely Baudelaire at times saw in literary publication a kind of prostitution"[154]:

> Like a choir boy, you swing a censer
> To earn your evening bread,
> Singing *Te Deums* in which you don't believe,
>
> Or, starving acrobat, you display for sale
> Your charms and smile, soaked with unseen tears,
> To cheer the spleen of the vulgar herd.[155]

5

As with all nineteenth-century cultural producers, the poet's livelihood depended on the new, mass marketplace in order to sell his poems, a fact of which Baudelaire was well aware,[156] even as he resisted it and paid the financial consequences.[157] Benjamin wrote: "Baudelaire knew how things really stood for the literary man: As flâneur, he goes to the marketplace, supposedly to take a look at it, but already in reality to find a buyer."[158]

It was in fact during his flânerie that Baudelaire composed his poems. At times he did not own a work table.[159] He made aimless wandering through the city streets itself a method of productive labor. In "The Sun":

> I walk alone, practicing my fantastic fencing
> Sniffing at every risk-filled corner for a rhyme
> Stumbling over words like cobblestones
> Colliding at times with lines I dreamed of long ago.[160]

The city of Paris is not often described in Baudelaire's poems; rather, it is the "scene of their action" (*Schauplatz*),[161] the necessary setting for imagistic renderings of those moments of existence that Baudelaire did not so much experience as endure, or "suffer" (*leiden*).[162] They entered his memory as a disconnected sequence of optical displays.[163] Paris, however familiar,[164] gave him no sense of belonging. Its crowds were his refuge[165]; its streets the rooms where he worked. Yet although he was born there: "No one felt less at home in Paris than Baudelaire."[166] The poet wrote: " 'What are the dangers of the forest and prairies next to the daily shocks and conflicts of civilization?' "[167] Parrying these shocks only served to isolate the individual more fully.[168] The world in which Baudelaire had become "a native," did "not thereby grow any more friendly."[169] "The allegorical intention is alien to *every* intimacy with things. To touch them is to violate them. Where it reigns, even habits cannot be established."[170]

Benjamin writes: "A Hell rages in the soul of the commodity [. . .]."[171] Precisely the Baroque vision of Hell returns here: a guilty and abandoned nature that can no longer "find its meaning fulfilled in itself," plunged into an abyss of arbitrary, transitory meanings, pursued by the "allegorical intention" that, in its desire for knowledge, falls "from emblem to emblem" into "the bottomless depths."[172] It is the realm in which the devil reigns supreme. The vision of the abyss haunted Baudelaire: "For a long time ... it seems that I have had a dream that I am tumbling across the void and a crowd of idols made of wood, iron, gold and silver fall with me, follow me in my fall, pounding and shattering my head and loins."[173]

In "The Irremediable," Paris' nighttime streets become an "emblem catalogue"[174] of Hell:

Someone condemned, descending without light,
At the edge of an abyss . . .
. . .
Where viscous monsters lie waiting
Their large and phosphorous eyes
Making the dark night darker still.[175]

As flâneur, Baudelaire "empathized himself into the soul of the commodity."[176] His empathy sprang from a mimetic capacity which itself paralleled the commodity's capacity to take on various meanings. It went so far as to affect his personal appearance: "On the physiognomy of Baudelaire as that of a mime: Courbet [who was painting the poet's portrait] reported that he looked different every day."[177] Baudelaire was "his own impresario,"[178] displaying himself in different identities—now flâneur, now whore; now ragpicker,[179] now dandy. He "played the role of a poet [. . .] before a society that already no longer needed real ones"[180]; he wrote of "bracing his nerves to play a hero's part."[181] Not the least of his roles was as the Devil himself, complete with the satanic gesture: "'the sneering laughter of Hell.'"[182] Benjamin comments: "Precisely this laughter is [. . .] peculiar to Baudelaire [. . .]."[183] "His contemporaries often referred to something about his way of laughing that gave one a fright."[184] In his poetry:

Am I not a false chord
In the divine symphony,
Thanks to voracious Irony
Who jolts and gnaws at me?[185]

In empathizing with the commodity, Baudelaire assumed its guilt as his own: "[W]hen Baudelaire depicts depravity and vice, he always includes himself. He doesn't know the gesture of the satirist."[186] Note that this "depravity" is not physical desire but its insatiability,[187] not sexual pleasure but its futureless repetition,[188] not the display of sexual beauty but its fetishistic fragmentation,[189] and the rapidity with which organic life is discarded as useless.[190] In short, it is not material nature itself, but the qualities that it assumes in its commodity form. The poem, "The Destruction," provides an allegorical representation of these qualities:

Ceaselessly, the devil agitates my ribs
Surrounding me like an impalpable vapor
I swallow, and sense him burning in my lungs,
Filling them with endless, guilty desire.
. . .
He throws in my eyes, bewildered and deluded,
Soiled garments, opened wounds,
And the bloody implements of destruction.[191]

Benjamin writes:

The "bloody implements" [*appareil sanglant*], the display of which is thrust upon the poet by the devil, is allegory's courtyard: the strewn implements with which allegory has so disfigured and mauled the material world that only fragments remain as the object of its contemplation.[192]

Rather than seeing sexuality as the instrument of destruction in this poem, Benjamin claims it is the poet's "allegorical intention" that violates the scene of pleasure, ripping apart the myth of sexual love, the illusory promise of happiness that reigns supreme in commodity society. The poem, "A Martyr," "rich in connections by its positioning immediately after 'The Destruction,'"[193] is a tableau, literally a *nature morte*: It depicts a decapitated woman in her bloodstained bed, murdered by her "lover"; a rose and gold stocking "remains on her leg like a souvenir"; her head "rests like a renonculous upon the nighttable."[194] Benjamin comments: "The allegorical intention has done its work on this martyr: She is smashed to pieces."[195]

Baudelaire experienced the commodity—the allegorical object— "from the inside,"[196] which is to say that his experiences were themselves commodities. "The allegories [in Baudelaire's poems] stand for what the commodity has made out of the experiences that people in this century have."[197] It affects the most basic biological drives:

"In the end, we have, [. . .] haughty priests of the Lyre,
. . .
Drunk without thirst; eaten without desire."[198]

It affects, above all, libidinal desire, severing the sexual instinct of pleasure (*Sexus*) from the life instinct of procreation (*Eros*). Benjamin comments on Baudelaire's description of lovers "tired out by their labors":

With the Saint-Simonians, industrial labor appears in the light of the sex act; the idea of joy in work is conceived according to the image of the desire to procreate. Two decades later the relationship has reversed: The sex act itself stands under the sign of that joylessness which crushes the industrial worker.[199]

It is in the form of self-alienation, the "hollowing out of inner life"[200] which is "euphemistically called 'lived experience' (*Erlebnis*)"[201] that the commodity form finds expression in Baudelaire's poetry.

The unique significance of Baudelaire consists in his having been the first and most unswerving to have made the self-estranged person *dingfest* in the double sense of the term [i.e., apprehended it, and taken it into custody].[202]

Experience is "withered,"[203] a series of "souvenirs." "The 'souvenir' [*Andenken*] is the schema of the transformation of the commodity into a collector's item."[204] In Baudelaire's poetry, the experiences of his own inner life are subject to this same fate. Benjamin explains:

The souvenir is the complement of the *Erlebnis*. In it is deposited the increasing self-alienation of the person who inventories his[/her] past as dead possessions. Allegory left the field of the exterior world in the nineteenth century in order to settle in the inner one.[205]

Baudelaire, "incomparable as a ponderer,"[206] inventoried the moments of his past life as a clutter of discarded possessions, trying to remember their meaning, trying to find their "correspondences."[207] In "Spleen II," this is made explicit:

I have more memories than if I had lived a thousand years.
A chest of drawers littered with balance sheets,
With verses, love letters, romantic songs, law suits,
With a thick plait of hair wrapped up in some receipts,
Hides fewer secrets than my own sad brain.
It is a pyramid, an immense cave
Full of more corpses than a common grave.
—I am a cemetery abhorred by the moon,
Where, like remorse, long earthworms crawl and gnaw
Incessantly at the dead most dear to me.
I am an old boudoir with faded roses
And tangled heaps of clothes now out of date [. . .].[208]

Benjamin's point is that these discarded objects are not a metaphor for Baudelaire's emptiness, but its source.[209]

He notes: "To establish: That Jeanne Duval was Baudelaire's first love."[210] If Jeanne Duval, the prostitute who became the poet's mistress, was indeed his first love, then the experience of the commodity stood at the very origin of his mature desire. In the poems written for her, she appears reified, motionless, inorganic—and therefore lasting. Benjamin notes:

Fetish:
"Her polished eyes are made of charming jewels
And in her strange, symbolic nature where
Inviolate angel mingles with ancient sphinx,

Where all is gold, steel, light and diamonds
There shines forever, like a useless star,
The cold majesty of the sterile woman."[211]

And again: "O jet-eyed statue, great angel with brazen face!"[212]

Such imagery reveals sexual pleasure as "totally incompatible with comfortableness [*Gemütlichkeit*]."[213] Baudelaire's long affair with Jeanne Duval was his most intimate human relationship. But with his "profound protest against the organic,"[214] his desire for her merges with necrophilia. He describes her: "'Blind and deaf machine, fertile in cruelties,'" and Benjamin comments: Here "sadistic fantasy tends toward mechanical constructions."[215] On "You whom I worship" (to Jeanne Duval) Benjamin writes: "nowhere more clearly than in this poem is sex played off against eros."[216] The last verse:

I advance the attack and climb in assault,
Like a chorus of worms going after a corpse,
I cherish you, O, implacable, cruel beast!
Right through to the coldness which pleases me best![217]

6

Prostitution, the oldest profession, takes on totally new qualities in the modern metropolis:

Prostitution opens up the possibility of a mythical communication with the masses. The emergence of the masses is, however, simultaneous with that of mass production. At the same time prostitution seems to contain the possibility of surviving in a living space in which the objects of our most intimate use are increasingly mass articles. In the prostitution of large cities the woman herself becomes a mass article. It is this totally new signature of big-city life that gives real meaning to Baudelaire's reception of the [ancient] doctrine of original sin.[218]

The modern prostitute is a mass article in the "precise sense," due to the fashions and makeup that camouflage her "individual expression," and package her as an identifiable type: "later this is underscored by the uniformed girls in the review."[219] Benjamin notes:

That it was this aspect of the prostitute which was decisive for Baudelaire is indicated not the least by the fact that in his many evocations of the whore, the bordello never provides the backdrop, although the street often does.[220]

The mass-produced article had its own allure.[221] Benjamin observes: "With the new manufacturing processes that leads to imitations, an illusory appearance [*Schein*] settles into the commodity."[222] Baudelaire was not immune to its intoxication. He wrote: "'The pleasure of being within the crowd is a mysterious expression of the delight [*jouissance*] of the multiplication of numbers.'"[223] But in Baudelaire's "strategically positioned"[224] poem, "The Seven Old Men," this pleasurable appearance of the crowd is ripped away: The poem, claims Benjamin, exposes the human physiognomy of mass production. It takes the form of an "anxiety-filled phantasmagoria," a "seven-times repeated apparition of a repulsive-looking old man."[225]

> He was not bent, but broken, and his spine
> Formed such a sharp right angle with his leg
> That his walking stick, perfecting his demeanor
> Gave him the contour and the clumsy gait
> Of some lame animal [. . .].
>
> His likeness followed: beard, eye, back, cane, tatters,
> Spawned from the same Hell; no trait distinguished
> His centenarian twin, and both these baroque specters
> Marched with the same tread toward an unknown goal.
>
> To what infamous plot was I exposed,
> Or what evil luck humiliated me thus?
> For seven times, as I counted minute to minute
> This sinister old fellow multiplied![226]

The "broken" old man, for all his repulsive eccentricities, is as much a repetitious "type" of the industrial city as the woman-as-commodity (figure 6.8), and Benjamin makes the direct association: "'The Seven Old Men' [. . .] Review girls."[227] Both express the "dialectic of commodity production in high capitalism"[228]: the shock of the new, and its incessant repetition.

6.8 "Tiller Girls," Berlin, Weimar Period.

Explaining why the mass article is a source generally of anxiety, Benjamin writes:

The individual represented thus [as in "The Seven Old Men"] in his multiplication as always-the-same testifies to the anxiety of the city dweller that, despite having set into motion his most eccentric peculiarities, he will not be able to break the magic circle of the type.[229]

And he writes specifically of Baudelaire:

Baudelaire's eccentric peculiarities were a mask under which, one may say out of shame, he tried to hide the supra-individual necessity of his form of life, and to a certain degree his life course as well.[230]

Baudelaire's bohemian eccentricities were as much economic necessities[231] as gestures of nonconformism. In the new conditions of the marketplace, poetic "originality" was no less the victim of the loss of "aura" than were the mass articles of industrial production. Benjamin claims that Baudelaire's previously neglected fragment, "Loss of a Halo," is of a significance that "cannot be overestimated," because it in fact acknowledges this changed status of poetic genius, bringing out "the threat to aura through the experience of shock."[232] In this fragment Baudelaire relates a story of losing his halo on the muddy street pavement. So as not to risk breaking his neck in the "moving chaos" of the traffic, he leaves it there, amused that "some bad poet" might pick it up and "adorn himself with it."[233] Benjamin writes: "The loss of halo concerns the poet first of all. He is forced to exhibit his own person in the marketplace"[234]—whereas "the exhibition of aura" from now on becomes "an affair of fifth-rank poets."[235]

The lack of aura in Baudelaire's poetry has an objective source: "The mass article stood before Baudelaire's eyes as model."[236] His poetry bears witness that not even the stars were spared its impact: As "the rebus image of the commodity," stars are "the always-again-the-same in great masses."[237]

Benjamin considers it exemplary of the "renunciation of the magic of distance" and the "extinction of illusory appearances" in Baudelaire's poetry that in his skies, "the stars recede."[238] Listing the "main passages about stars in Baudelaire," Benjamin notes that they most frequently concern their absence ("dark night"; "night without stars," etc.).[239] He refers to "Evening Twilight,"[240] in which starlight is no match for the city's illumination:

[. . . U]nhealthy demons in the atmosphere
Awaken as sluggishly as businessmen,
Banging shutters and porch roofs in their flight.
And through the lamplight trembling with the wind,
Prostitution ignites, blazing in the street.[241]

Characteristic of aura, besides its "unique phenomenon of distance,"[242] was the sense that "the gaze is returned."[243] Precisely this is denied by Baudelaire's images:

"I know of eyes more melancholy,
. . .
Emptier and deeper than yourselves, O Skies!"[244]

And again:

"Your eyes, illuminated like shop windows,
. . .
Insolently make use of borrowed power."[245]

The poet "has become addicted to those blank eyes which do not return his glance, and submits without illusions to their sway."[246]

"In the economy of the psyche, the mass article appears as an obsessive idea."[247] Benjamin notes "the attraction that a few small numbers of basic situations exercised on Baudelaire [. . . .] He seems to have stood under the obsession of turning back to every one of his main motifs at least once."[248] It is this, claims Benjamin, not "some ingenious ordering of the poems, let alone any secret key,"[249] that determines the structure of *Les fleurs du mal*. The source of this repetition "lies in the strict exclusion of every lyrical theme that did not bear the stamp of Baudelaire's own, suffering-filled experience."[250] Moreover, Baudelaire turned this inner psychological characteristic into a market advantage. In his attempt to compete in the literary marketplace, where poetry was an especially vulnerable commodity,[251] he had to distinguish his own work from that of other poets.[252] "He wanted to create a *poncif* [stereotype; cliché]. Lemaitre assured him that he had succeeded."[253]

Baudelaire—through his deep experience of the nature of the commodity—was able, or forced, to acknowledge the market as an objective authority [. . .]. He was perhaps the first to have conceived of an originality that was market-oriented, and that precisely by that fact was more original at the time than any other (to create a *poncif*). This creation included a certain intolerance. Baudelaire wanted to make room for his poems, and with this goal in mind, to repress [. . .] the competition.[254]

Baudelaire's obsession, his "specialty"[255] (indeed, his trademark[256]), was the " 'sensation of the new.' "[257] Benjamin speaks of "the inestimable value for Baudelaire of *nouveauté*. The new cannot be interpreted, or compared. It becomes the ultimate retrenchment of art."[258] Making novelty "the highest value" was the strategy of *l'art pour l'art*, the aesthetic position Baudelaire adopted in 1852. As nonconformism, it was in "rebellion against the surrender of art to the market."[259] Ironically, however, this "last line of resistance of art" converged with the commodity form that threatened it: Novelty is "the quintessence of false consciousness, the tireless agent of which is fashion."[260] It is the "appearance of the new [that] is reflected like one mirror in another in the appearance of the always-the-same."[261] The same dialectic of temporality lies concealed in Baudelaire's own sensibility.

Baudelaire "did not know nostalgia."[262] At the same time, he renounced progress:

It is very significant that "the new" in Baudelaire in no way makes a contribution to progress. [. . .] It is above all the "belief in progress" that he persecutes with hate, as a heresy, a false doctrine, not merely a simple error.[263]

The object of Baudelaire's destructive attack against the phantasmagoria of his age thus included the "harmonious facade" of continuous historical progress. In its place, expressed in his poems is (in Proust's words) " 'a strange sectioning of time,' "[264] shock-like segments of "empty time,"[265] each of which is like a " 'warning signal.' "[266] His "spleen places a century between the present moment and the one that has just been lived."[267]

Without continuity, without a belief in the future, Baudelaire's " 'passion for travel, for the unknown, the new' " becomes a " 'preference for what is reminiscent of death.' "[268] "The last poem of the *Fleurs du mal*: ("Le Voyage")—"O Death, old captain, it is time! Lift the anchor!' The last journey of the flâneur Death. Its goal: Novelty."[269] Indeed: "For people as they are today, there is only one radical novelty—and that is always the same: Death."[270] "To one filled with spleen, it is the entombed person who is the transcendental subject of history."[271]

Benjamin wanted to demonstrate "with every possible emphasis" that Baudelaire's perception of modern temporality was not unique, that "the idea of eternal recurrence pushes its way into the world of Baudelaire, Blanqui, and Nietzsche at approximately the same moment."[272] Thus: "The stars that Baudelaire banished from his world are precisely those which in Blanqui became the scene of eternal recurrence"[273] and which, as an "allegory of the cosmos,"[274] "make a mass article out of history itself."[275] These three figures of the era of high capitalism not only share a lack of illusion; they have in common an inadequacy of political response. In the case of Nietzsche, nihilism, and the dictum: "There will be nothing new"[276] for Blanqui, putschism and ultimately cosmological despair[277]; for Baudelaire, the "impotent rage of someone fighting against the wind and rain."[278] Having no political understanding beyond that which, as with Blanqui, led to conspiratorial politics, Baudelaire's ultimate position is one in which rage turns into resignation:

> "As for me, I shall be quite satisfied to leave
> A world where action is never sister of the dream."[279]

7

The key to Baudelaire's political position is the image of "petrified unrest," ("*erstarrte Unruhe*") constant disquiet which "knows no development": "Petrified unrest is also the formula for the image of Baudelaire's own life [. . .]."[280] In the Baroque era, when allegorical perception was similarly tied to an understanding of political action as conspiracy (the court intriguer[281]), "the image of petrified unrest" was provided by "'the desolate confusion of the place of skulls'"[282] But *sui generis* to the experience of capitalism, the hollowness that the Baroque had found in outer nature now invades the inner world. Thus: "Baroque allegory sees the corpse only from the outside. Baudelaire sees it also from the inside."[283] This means that he experienced the death of the soul in the still-living body, and read material history as a world already "sinking into rigor mortis."[284] It means that for Baudelaire, "Strindberg's thought" is binding: "Hell is not something that lies ahead for us, but *this life here*."[285]

The difference helps explain Baudelaire's reactions in the following incident. Impressed by a sixteenth-century woodcut reproduced in Hyacinthe Langlois' book on the history of the dance of death (figure 6.9), Baudelaire instructed Bracquemond in 1858 to draw a frontispiece for the second edition of *Les fleurs du mal*, using this woodcut as a model.

[Baudelaire's] instructions: "A skeleton that forms a tree with the legs and ribs forming the trunk, the arms outstretched in a cross sprouting leaves and buds, and sheltering several rows of poisonous plants in small pots spaced apart as in a greenhouse."[286]

Bracquemond's design (figure 6.10), although quite true to the model's main image, displeased Baudelaire greatly. Benjamin writes:

Bracquemond evidently raised difficulties, and mistook the intention of the poet in that he concealed the pelvis of the skeleton with flowers and didn't treat the arms like tree branches. Moreover, according to Baudelaire, the artist does not know what a skeleton like a tree should look like and also doesn't have an eye for how vices are to be represented as flowers.[287]

"In the end a portrait of the poet by Bracquemond was substituted" and the project was abandoned.[288] It was taken up again, however, by Félicien Rops in 1866, as the design for the frontispiece of Baudelaire's *Epaves*. Baudelaire considered the new version (figure 6.11) a success, and accepted it.

"To interrupt the course of the world—that was the deepest will of Baudelaire,"[289] and in this sense he went beyond the passive melancholy of the Baroque allegoricists. "The allegory of Baudelaire bears—in opposition to the Baroque—the traces of anger needed to break into this world and lay its harmonious structures in ruins."[290] But if Baudelaire succeeded in this, and if in his refusal of the Christian solution of spiritual resurrection he remained more faithful to the new nature than the Baroque allegoricists had to the old,[291] he knew no recourse but to "hold onto the ruins."[292]

The destructive impulse of Baudelaire is nowhere interested in getting rid of that which declines. That comes to expression in allegory, and it is this which constitutes its regressive tendency. On the other hand, however, precisely in its destructive fervor, allegory is concerned with the banishment of the illusory appearance that proceeds out of every "given order,"

6.9 Sixteenth-century woodcut, chosen by Baudelaire as model for the frontispiece of *Les Fleurs du mal*, 2nd edition.

6.10 Plan for frontispiece of *Les Fleurs du mal*, Bracquemond, 1859–60, rejected by Baudelaire.

6.11   Frontispiece of Baudelaire's *Epaves*, design by Félicien Rops, 1866.

be it of art or of life, as if from the transfiguring order of the totality or the organic, making it appear bearable. And that is the progressive tendency of allegory.[293]

In the Arcades project Benjamin himself practiced allegory against myth. But he was aware of its "regressive tendency." The *Passagen-Werk* was to avoid not only the "betrayal of nature" involved in the spiritual transcendence of the Baroque Christian allegoricists, but also that political resignation of Baudelaire and his contemporaries which ultimately ontologizes the emptiness of the historical experience of the commodity, the new as the always-the-same. It needed to demonstrate that far more violence than Baudelaire's "allegorical intention" was required in order to redeem the material world.

The course of history as it is represented in the concept of catastrophe has in fact no more claim on the thinking man than the kaleidoscope in the hand of a child which collapses everything ordered into new order with every turn. The justness of this image is well founded. The concepts of the rulers have always been the mirror thanks to which the image of an "order" was established.—The kaleidoscope must be smashed.[294]

Part III

Introduction

1

Konvolut "J" of the *Passagen-Werk*, entitled "Baudelaire," is the bulkiest by far of the *Konvoluts*, accounting for over 20 percent of the project's collected material. Begun in the late 1920s,[1] it ultimately took on a life of its own. In 1937 Benjamin conceived of a separate book on Baudelaire, which he planned "to develop as a miniature model" of the *Passagen-Werk*.[2] The project received the financial support of the Institute for Social Research, and Benjamin completed the middle section of the study in fall 1938. This section was the now infamous, three-part essay, "The Paris of the Second Empire in Baudelaire," which Adorno, speaking for the Institute, vehemently criticized. It was the montagelike juxtaposition of images and commentary (the very touchstone of Benjamin's conception) that Adorno considered so unsuccessful. He claimed the "astonished presentation of simple facts" lacked theoretical (dialectical) mediation.[3] Asked to rewrite the essay, Benjamin chose to revise its middle section only ("The Flâneur"), under the title, "On Some Motifs in Baudelaire." This very much altered, and indeed more "theoretical" version—the middle of the middle of the "book"—was accepted enthusiastically by the Institute in 1939. Now that the *Passagen-Werk* material has been published, its massive assembly of facts makes it appear indisputable that the form of the first highly criticized Baudelaire essay was indeed more of a "miniature model" of what the Arcades project would have become. All the more devastating, then, was Adorno's fundamental disapproval of the originality of construction which Benjamin had labored to develop.

The case for the model-like nature of the first Baudelaire essay is in fact strengthened by the recent discovery of papers that Benjamin entrusted to George Bataille, and that now form part of the Bataille Estate in the archive of the Bibliothèque Nationale.[4] Among these papers is a folder which contains a detailed, preliminary plan for the Baudelaire book. In long lists under headings that were to correspond to themes ("Allegory," "Ennui," "the Prostitute," "Literary Market," "the Commodity," "Eternal Recurrence," etc.) Benjamin marshaled *Passagen-Werk* fragments by their identifying letters and numbers, ransacking *Konvolut* J, and noting material from other of the project's diverse crannies as well. These lists are a rough ordering, intended as an intermediate phase in the structuring of the Baudelaire "book."[5] When he went through them again in the summer of 1938, as he was actually constructing the first Baudelaire essay, he narrowed down their number (roughly by half) and ordered them into a three-part schema. He then worked further on the schema of the second part, arranging the entries in an order that matches quite exactly the finished essay, "The Paris of the Second Empire of Baudelaire" (while no such schema exists in the folder for the second Baudelaire essay[6]). This first essay is in fact constructed with so little theoretical mortar between the *Passagen-Werk* fragments that the essay stands like a dry wall, and Adorno rightly identified the (to him, lamentable) principle of montage that governed the form of the whole.

The original speculation that the papers in Bataille's archive contained the plans for a completed *Passagen-Werk* has been disappointed.[7] But just how significant the Baudelaire project had become in Benjamin's labors is a question that still causes considerable dispute. In their exhaustive report on the archive papers,[8] Michael Espagne and Michael Werner make the strong case that Benjamin intended the Baudelaire study to supplant the "failed"[9] *Passagen-Werk* altogether. They base their argument on the fact that such a significant proportion of the *Passagen-Werk* material found its way into the Baudelaire notes. Yet the vast majority of this material comes from "J," while the other thirty-five *Konvoluts* are represented (if at all) by relatively few examples. Furthermore, historical figures such as Fourier, Grandville, and Haussmann, who figure as

207

importantly as Baudelaire in the 1935 *and* 1939 exposés, are virtually unrepresented. Moreover, Espagne and Werner cannot answer why, if the Arcades project had been abandoned, Benjamin continued between 1937 and 1940 to add material to all thirty-six of the *Konvoluts*, not just to "J," or, indeed, what compelling *intellectual* motive he would have had for abandoning the greater project,[10] referring instead to the "historical situation" in general, and Benjamin's economic plight in particular.[11] They lead one to assume that the Baudelaire essay was unique as a raid on the *Passagen-Werk* entries, whereas in fact there was little Benjamin wrote after 1927 that did not relate directly to (and even "steal" from) the Arcades project, sometimes appropriating the same quotation or idea in different (con)texts, for very different signifying purposes. The *Passagen-Werk* files were the working lexicon of Benjamin's research and ideas, or more accurately, his historical warehouse of documentary parts and supporting theoretical armatures, out of which during the thirties he constructed the wide range of his literary-philosophical works.[12]

All of this the papers in the Bataille Archive make clear. They provide, however, simply no evidence that Benjamin himself ever considered the *Passagen-Werk* a "failed" project, or that the Baudelaire study had come to replace it. Nor do other available documents suggest it. Instead Benjamin was explicit concerning the relationship between the two, writing in August 1938 (just as he was finishing the first Baudelaire essay): "This book is not identical to the 'Paris Passages.' Yet it harbors not only a considerable portion of the informational material collected under the sign of the latter, but also a number of its more philosophical contents."[13] His letter to Horkheimer the following month that accompanied the finished essay is even more explicit[14]:

As you know, the Baudelaire [*sic.*] was originally planned as a chapter of the "Passages," specifically, as the next to the last. Thus it was not something I could write before formulating the work in progress, nor would it be understandable without this prior formulation. I kept stalling on the idea that the Baudelaire could be published in the [Institute's] journal, if not as a chapter of the Passages, then at least as an extensive essay of maximum scope. Only in the course of this summer did I recognize that a Baudelaire essay of more modest size, but one which did not deny its responsibility to the Arcades project, could come into being only as part of a Baudelaire book. Enclosed you are receiving, to speak precisely, three such essays—namely the three component pieces that together are relatively self-contained, and that comprise the second part of the Baudelaire book. This book is to lay down decisive philosophical elements of the "Passages" project, hopefully in definitive formulation. If, besides the original outline, there was a subject matter that bid the optimal chances for laying down the conception of the "Passages," then it was Baudelaire. For this reason, the orientation of substantive as well as constructive elements essential to the "Passages" evolve out of the subject matter itself.[15]

If we take Benjamin at his word, not only was the *Passagen-Werk* still a going concern; it was his major concern, subsuming the Baudelaire book under it, rather than vice versa.[16] In other words, in the midst of pressure from the Institute to deliver a "Baudelaire book," Benjamin kept working on the "Passages" under a new alias.

Given that the planned Baudelaire book was first conceived as a chapter of the larger work, would it not be reasonable to assume that all of the "chapters," so condensed and abbreviated in both exposé descriptions, would ultimately have been extended to the point where each could, and indeed should, stand on its own?[17] Benjamin foresaw this possibility in at least[18] two cases: "I would see the development that the Baudelaire chapter is in the process of undergoing reserved for two chapters of the 'Passages,' the ones on Grandville and on Haussmann."[19]

The possibility that, in order to give himself space to develop the historical significance of what was now over a decade of research, Benjamin would have dissolved the "Passages" into a series of works, all of which were within the same theoretical armature, does not indicate a "failed" *Passagen-Werk*, but, on the contrary, one that had succeeded only too well.

2

In his letter to Horkheimer accompanying the first Baudelaire essay, Benjamin wrote that this essay was "self-sufficient" only in the formal sense, for it "did not make visible the philosophical foundation of the *entire* book, and ought not to."[20] This would occur only in the book's concluding section.[21] He described his plan for the book's three parts in the dialectical schema of "thesis," "antithesis," and "synthesis": "In this construction, the first part presents the problematic: Baudelaire as allegoricist." The second part (the essay he was sending) "turns its back on the aesthetic theory question of the first part and undertakes a socially critical interpretation of the poet," one that points out "the limits to his achievement." This section "is the precondition for the Marxist interpretation, which, however, it does not by itself accomplish." Not until the third section, "to be called: The Commodity as Poetic Object," would the Marxist interpretation come into its own.[22] From the 1938 document "Central Park," in which Benjamin developed theoretical motifs for the Baudelaire study, we know the specific question that he wished to "keep for the [book's] conclusion":

How is it possible that an attitude which at least in appearance is as out of keeping with its time as that of the allegoricist, takes pride of place in [*Les Fleurs de mal*,] the poetic work of the century?[23]

The reader will recognize the quotation. It is precisely the question, Benjamin's answer to which we have just considered in chapter 6.[24] Were we justified in conflating the arguments of the *Passagen-Werk* and the Baudelaire "book" at that point? Benjamin gives us every reason to answer yes—without implying that the *Passagen* project had been given up. He wrote to Horkheimer in 1938 of an "autonomous group of motifs" of the Baudelaire book's third part in which "the fundamental theme of the old 'Arcades project,' the new and always-the-same," will first "come into play."[25] And he continued in a letter to Adorno the following week: "The substance of the third part is to demonstrate the conspicuous convergence of its basic thoughts with [those of] the Arcades plan."[26]

In line with their thesis of a "failed" *Passagen-Werk*, Espagne and Werner argue that Benjamin's work on the Baudelaire "book," subsequently reflected in the substantive changes of the 1939 exposé (—which also included the addition of a new introduction and conclusion based on the texts of Blanqui,[27] as well as "extensive changes" in "Fourier" and "Louis Philippe,"[28]—) represented a fundamental shift in the philosophical conception of the project, leading to internal contradictions so serious that they threatened to undermine the entire edifice. They refer specifically to the contradiction between the "continuous phenomenology of the commodity form" and the "discontinuity implied by the dialectical image."[29]

The crucial point is that this ambivalence was not *new*. It had its source in the tension between the historical and metaphysical poles of interpretation that haunted the Arcades project from the start (reminding us of his even earlier note for the *Trauerspiel* study: "methodological relationship between the metaphysical investigation and the historical one: a stocking turned inside out"[30]). As problematic as this theoretical frame may have been,[31] it did not suddenly become so in 1938.

The "dialectical image" has as many levels of logic as the Hegelian concept. It is a way of seeing that crystallizes antithetical elements by providing the axes for their alignment. Benjamin's conception is essentially static[32] (even as the truth which the dialectical image illuminates is historically fleeting). He charts philosophical ideas visually within an unreconciled and transitory field of oppositions that can perhaps best be pictured in terms of coordinates of contradictory terms, the "synthesis" of which is not a movement toward resolution, but the point at which their axes intersect. In fact, it is precisely as crossing axes that the terms continuity/discontinuity—the simultaneity of which so troubles Espagne and Werner—appear in the very early *Passagen* notes in connection with the dialectical "optics" of modernity as both ancient and new: They are to be understood as the "fundamental coordinates" of the modern world.[33]

3

Let us take a moment to develop this notion that Benjamin thought in coordinates. His unfolding of concepts in their "extremes" can be visualized as antithetical polarities of axes that cross each other, revealing a "dialectical image" at the null point, with its contradictory "moments" as axial fields. Against the skepticism of Espagne and Werner, we will go so far as to suggest that a pattern of coordinates functions as the invisible structure of the *Passagen-Werk*'s historical research, enabling the project's seemingly disparate, conceptual elements to cohere. The axes of these coordinates can be designated with the familiar Hegelian polarities: consciousness and reality. If the termini are to be antithetical extremes, we might name those on the axis of reality, petrified nature/transitory nature, while in the case of consciousness, the termini would be dream/waking. At the null point where the coordinates intersect, we can

Display D

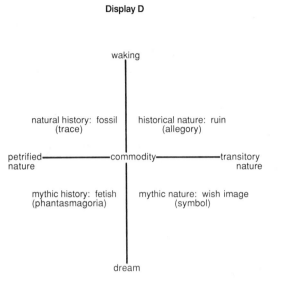

place that "dialectical image" which, by 1935, stood at the "mid-point"[34] of the project: the commodity. Each field of the coordinates can then be said to describe one aspect of the physiognomic appearance of the commodity, showing its contradictory "faces": fetish and fossil; wish image and ruin. In the positioning of the fields, those under the sign of transitoriness would need to be affirmed. Display D represents this invisible, inner structure of the *Passagen-Werk*.

Here the *fossil* names the commodity in the discourse of ur-history, as the visible remains of the "ur-phenomena." Even after his early, metaphoric ur-landscape of consumer dinosaurs and modern ice ages recedes, Benjamin sustains the physiognomy of the fossil in the idea of the "trace" (*Spur*),[35] the imprint of objects particularly visible in the plush of bourgeois interiors or the velvet lining of their casings (—here ur-history turns into a detective story, with the historical "trace" as clue). The *fetish* is the keyword of the commodity as mythic phantasmagoria, the arrested form of history. It corresponds to the reified form of new nature, condemned to the modern Hell of the new as the always-the-same. But this fetishized phantasmagoria is also the form in which the human, socialist potential of industrial nature lies frozen, awaiting the collective political action that could awaken it. The *wish image* is the transitory, dream form of that potential. In it, archaic meanings return in anticipation of the "dialectic" of awakening. The *ruin*, created intentionally in Baudelaire's allegorical poetry, is the form in which the wish images of the past century appear, as rubble, in the present. But it refers also to the loosened building blocks (both semantic and material) out of which a new order can be constructed. Note that the figures of the collector, the ragpicker,[36] and the detective wander through the fields of the fossil and ruin, while the fields of action of the prostitute, the gambler, and the flâneur are those of wish images, and of the fetish as their phantasmagoric form. Haussmann builds the new phantasmagoria; Grandville represents it critically. Fourier's fantasies are wish images, anticipations of the future expressed as dream symbols; Baudelaire's images are ruins, failed material expressed as allegorical objects.

4

As the reader may have guessed, this image of coordinates underlies the presentation of the *Passagen-Werk*'s historical material in the preceding four chapters. As a heuristic schema, it was adopted because it allowed the dense and multiple elements of the Arcades project to be treated with continuity and coherence without doing violence to the antithetical polarity of "discontinuity." Nowhere do these coordinates actually appear in the *Passagen-Werk*. Such a structure is virtual, not explicit. Yet the sources tell us repeatedly that from his early years, Benjamin was at home with coordinates as a way of thinking. Scholem reports that he typically spoke of his new thoughts as a "system of coordinates."[37] The *Trauerspiel* study describes the idea of *Trauerspiel* as the "unique crossing of nature and history," the "point of indifference" of which was "transiency"; and it speaks generally of "ideas" as developing out of polar extremes that delineate a "conceptual field" in which the elements can be ordered. But the earliest and most striking reference to coordinates is in Benjamin's 1919 dissertation, "The Concept of Art Criticism in German Romanticism," which explicitly justifies seeing such orderings even if they were not consciously intended. In response to the criticism that the Romantics did not think systematically, Benjamin wrote that it "could be proven beyond all doubt that their thinking was determined by systematic tendencies and connections":

[. . .] or, to express it in the most exact and unassailable form, that [their thinking] lets itself be *related* to systematic thought processes, that it in fact allows itself to be brought into a correctly chosen system of coordinates, whether or not the Romantics have fully provided this system themselves.[38]

Granted, in Benjamin's published works, we have only one example of an "idea" worked out explicitly as a system of coordinates,[39] and it is a peripheral, insignificant one at that. It is found in the notes to the second Baudelaire essay, describing, not the armature of the essay in its entirety, but the conceptual positioning of a single motif, "idleness," as one field within the general idea of physical activity (display E)[40]:

Display E

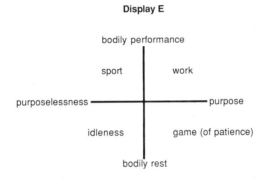

Granted, too, that coordinates exhaust neither the concept of "dialectical images" nor Benjamin's visual schemata for thinking.[41] There is no reason to claim for the system of coordinates in display D anything more than the heuristic value which first prompted its construction, that is, that it makes coherent in one perceptual grasp the whole span of the *Passagen* material assembled between 1927 and 1940—and the fact that Benjamin himself encouraged the discovery of such "systematic tendencies" even when not explicitly stated by the author—at least, so it seemed to *this* author when she adopted it as a conceptual frame. It thus came as a surprise to find (quite wondrously, just where Espagne and Werner had been looking[42]) an oblique and yet explicit confirmation of what before had intuitively seemed accurate. Benjamin's Paris manuscripts in the Bataille Archive include a note (display F) to the Baudelaire "book"—the "miniature model," please remember, for the

Display F

The schemata of coordinates have, in the optimal case, 11 concepts: 4 for the termini of the axes, four for the fields, two for the axes, one for the point of intersection.

The three parts of the work have a thesis, antithesis and synthesis to present.

The man who goes the length of the path of passion of male sexuality, comes through his sacred value to be a poet. The poet to whom no social mission can be imparted, makes the market and the commodity his objects.

Death, or the corpse, will form the middle of the crossing axes for the schematism of the first part. In the corresponding position in the third part will stand the commodity as the social reality which underlies that of the domination of the principle of death in this poetry.

Arcades project—that contains the following verbal description: "The schemata of coordinates have, in the optimal case, 11 concepts: 4 for the termini of the axes, four for the fields, two for the axes, one for the point of intersection."[43] And more: For "the schematism" of the book's "third part" (that, please recall, was to demonstrate its "conspicuous convergence" with the thoughts of the Arcades project), there was to stand at the "middle of the crossing axes," that image which since 1934 had stood at the "midpoint" of the Arcades project: "the commodity."

5

Such conceptual plotting is not truly meaningful, however, until we consider the second temporal level of the *Passagen-Werk*: Benjamin's own historical era. The whole elaborate structure of the *Passagen-Werk* must be seen within the temporal axis that connects the nineteenth century to Benjamin's "present," the dimension which, by transforming emblematic representation into philosophy of history and historical image into political education, provides dialectical images with their explosive charge. To reconstruct this historical axis is the point of the next three chapters.

7

Is This Philosophy?

1

How this work was written: rung by rung, in whatever way chance offered a narrow foothold, and always like someone who climbs up dangerous heights, and cannot allow himself to look about for a moment, lest he become dizzy (but also to save the full power of the panorama that opens up to him for the end).[1]

In 1935 Adorno wrote Benjamin that he would like to see the Arcades project "not as a historico-sociological investigation," but as "*prima philosophia* in your particular sense":

I view the Arcades project as not only the center of your philosophy, but the decisive standard of what can be articulated philosophically today; as *chef d'oeuvre*, nothing else, and so decisive in every way—including personally, that is, in terms of success—that I would view as catastrophic and absolutely incorrigible any lessening of the inner promise of this work, and any sacrifice of your own categories thereby.[2]

Not only must Brecht's influence be avoided.[3] Theoretical "concessions" to the *Institut für Sozialforschung* would be similarly "a misfortune,"[4] and Adorno warned Benjamin that financial support from the Institute, while acceptable for other articles, should be avoided in this case.[5]

The following week Gretel Karplus wrote from Berlin, echoing Adorno's concerns:

And now what lies most on my heart: the Arcades project. I recall the conversation that we had in Denmark last September, and I am very perplexed, as I simply do not know which of your plans you are now implementing. It astonishes me that Fritz [Pollock of the Institute] is championing the notes [i.e., the exposé to the project that Benjamin had just agreed with Pollock to compose]; are you thinking, then, of a work for the *Zeitschrift* [the Institute's journal]? I would see in this an enormous danger: the frame is surely nothing but narrow in comparison, and you could never write that for which your true friends have been waiting for years, the great philosophical work [. . .].[6]

These letters are revealing, not only for the reservations both express concerning the adequacy of the Institute's "critical theory" as an intellectual context for Benjamin's work, but also for the tremendously high expectations Benjamin's friends had for the Arcades project. In fact, Benjamin could not afford to do without the Institute's backing. If it were to fund him only for additional articles, work on the *Passagen* would be held back.[7] Moreover, Benjamin believed the exposé, while written at the invitation of the Institute, made "concessions to no side, and if I know anything about it at all, it is that no school will be in a hurry to claim it."[8] That the Institute might attempt to put intellectual constraints on the project he considered less a danger than the possibility it would lack financing altogether. As to expectations that the Arcades study would produce a philosophical masterpiece, Benjamin's own evaluation was based on the rather less heroic criterion of its political positioning. The 1935 exposé, while avoiding "orthodox Marxism," took "a solid position" within "the Marxist discussion" to which, as philosophy, it contributed:

Because in fact the philosophy of a work is not so much bound to its terminology as to its position, I believe this is indeed the exposé of the "great philosophical work" about which Felizitas [G. Karplus] speaks, even if for me this designation is not the most urgent one. What concerns me above all, as you know, is the "Ur-history of the 19th Century."[9]

2

This "Ur-history of the 19th Century" was, then, intended as a philosophical construction. In the fragmentary notes assembled in *Konvolut* N (many of which would find their way into the Theses on History),[10] Benjamin described his method, which, it must be said, strained the traditional conceptions of both history and philosophy to the breaking point. It broke radically with the philosophical canon by searching for truth in the "garbage heap"[11] of modern history, the "rags, the trash,"[12] the ruins of commodity production, that were thoroughly tainted with the philosophically debased qualities of empirical specificity, shifting meanings, and, above all, transiency:

A final abandonment of the concept of "timeless truth" is in order.[13] "The truth will not run away from us" [. . .]. Herewith is expressed the concept of truth from which these representations decisively break.[14]

As a reconstruction of the past, Benjamin's method ran roughshod over von Ranke's sacrosanct principle of showing the matter "'as it actually was'": Such history had been "the strongest narcotic of the [nineteenth] century."[15] Benjamin had not the least concern for the conventions of empathic "'appreciation.'"[16] Instead his objective was to "rescue"[17] the historical objects by ripping them out of the developmental histories—of law, religion, art, etc.[18]—into which fictional and falsifying narratives they had been inserted in the process of their transmission. Ur-history was thoroughly political knowledge, nothing less than a revolutionary Marxist pedagogy. Yet as Marxism, its theoretical armature was equally unorthodox.[19] If in the process of working on the Arcades project Benjamin came to refer to himself as a "historical materialist," he was well aware that he was filling this nomenclature with very new meaning.

Crucial—and also most difficult—would be the "construction" of the work. He wrote to Gretel Karplus that in the 1935 exposé "the constructive moment" was still lacking:

I'll leave undecided whether this is to be sought in the direction that you two [she and Adorno] suggest. But this much is certain: The constructive moment for this book means that which the philosopher's stone means in alchemy. There is otherwise only one thing that can be said about it for now: that it will have to sum up in a new, concise, and very simple manner the contrast between where this book stands and the tradition of historical research up to now. How? That remains to be seen.[20]

Benjamin was at least convinced of one thing: what was needed was a visual, not a linear logic: The concepts were to be imagistically constructed,[21] according to the cognitive principles of montage.[22] Nineteenth-century objects were to be made visible as the origin of the present,[23] at the same time that every assumption of progress was to be scrupulously rejected[24]: "In order for a piece of the past to be touched by present actuality, there must exist no continuity between them."[25] Benjamin noted: "'Construction' presupposes 'destruction.'"[26] Historical objects are first constituted by being "blasted" out of the historical continuum.[27] They have a "monadological structure," into which "all the forces and interests of history enter on a reduced scale."[28] "Truth [. . .] is bound to a temporal nucleus which is lodged in both the known and the knower."[29] In a tension-filled constellation with the present,[30] this "temporal nucleus" becomes politically charged, polarized dialectically," as "a force field, in which the conflict between its fore- and after-history plays itself out."[31]

As fore-history, the objects are prototypes, ur-phenomena that can be recognized as precursors of the present, no matter how distant or estranged they now appear. Benjamin implies that if the fore-history of an object reveals its possibility (including its utopian potential), its after-history is that which, as an object of natural history, it has in fact become. Both are legible within the "monadological structure" of the historical object that has been "blasted free" of history's continuum.[32] In the traces left by the object's after-history, the conditions of its decay and the manner of its cultural transmission, the utopian images of past objects can be read in the present as truth. It is the forceful confrontation of the fore- and after-life of the object that makes it "actual" in the political sense—as "presence of mind" (*Geistesgegenwart*)[33]—and it is not progress but "actualization" in which ur-history culminates.[34] "Thus, as a flashing image, in the now of recognition [*im Jetzt der Erkennbarkeit*], the past is to be held fast."[35] Benjamin was counting on the shock of this recognition to jolt the dreaming collective into a political "awakening."[36] The presentation of the historical object within a charged force field of past and present, which produces political electricity in a "lightning flash"[37] of truth, is the "dialectical image." Unlike Hegel's logic, it is "dialectics at a standstill"[38]:

Where thought comes to a standstill in a constellation saturated with tensions, there appears the dialectical image. It is the caesura in the movement of thought. Its positioning, of course, is in no way arbitrary. In a word, it is to be sought at the point where the tension between the dialectical oppositions is the greatest. The dialectical image [. . .] is identical to the historical object; it justifies blasting the latter out of the continuum of history's course.[39]

Benjamin summarizes: "Re: the basic theory of historical materialism":

1) The historical object is that for which the act of knowledge is carried
out as its "rescue." 2) History decomposes into images, not into narratives. 3) Wherever a dialectical process is effected, we are dealing with a
monad. 4) The materialist representation of history entails an immanent
critique of the concept of progress. 5) Historical materialism supports its
procedure on the foundation of experience, common sense, presence of
mind, and the dialectic.[40]

"Common sense" (*gesunder Menschenverstand*) was not a simple, self-
evident matter of reading meaning out of empirically given surfaces, specifically because the cognitive experience provided by the
dialectical image was one of historical time as well as (or by means
of) extension in space. "Presence of mind" (*Geistesgegenwart*) referred to the actuality of past objects within a present context that
gave them a meaning they did not have originally. "The dialectic"
allowed the superimposition of fleeting images, present and past,
that made both suddenly come alive in terms of revolutionary
meaning. To describe the experience of "revolutionary historical
consciousness," Benjamin cites Baudelaire's account of temporal
experience under the influence of hashish: "'Although [the night]
must have seemed long to me . . . it nonetheless seemed that it had
lasted only several seconds or, more, that it had not become part of
eternity."[41]

As an immediate, quasi-mystical apprehension, the dialectical
image was intuitive. As a philosophical "construction," it was not.
Benjamin's laborious and detailed study of past texts, his careful
inventory of the fragmentary parts he gleaned from them, and the
planned use of these in deliberately constructed "constellations"
were all sober, self-reflective procedures, which, he believed, were
necessary in order to make visible a picture of truth that the fictions
of conventional history writing covered over. This debunking of
fictions was in the spirit of the Enlightenment:

The entire ground must for once be reclaimed for reason, and cleared of
the underbrush of delusion and myth. This is to be accomplished here for
the nineteenth century.[42]

But it was enlightenment in an era when, under the weight of its
own products, society had sunk into a twilight zone of dream and

myth. Benjamin's description of critical reason differs markedly from that which had been articulated in the Enlightenment's sunnier days:

> To reclaim those areas where formerly only delusion has grown. To forge ahead with the whetted axe of reason, looking neither left nor right, so as not fall to fall victim to the horror beckoning from the depths of the primeval forest [*Urwald*].[43]

3

> The provocative assertion that an essay on the Paris arcades has more philosophy in it than observations on the Being of beings strikes closer to the meaning of Benjamin's work than the search for that skeleton of concepts which remains identical to itself, and which he relegated to the junkroom.[44]

All of Benjamin's comments cited above in section 2 regarding the method of the *Passagen-Werk* can be found in *Konvolut* N ("On Epistemology, Theory of Progress"). This *Konvolut* was surely intended to provide the substance for the epistemological essay that Benjamin planned as "a separate chapter, either at the end or the beginning" of the work, which, was to function like the "epistemologico-critical prologue" of the *Trauerspiel* study, in the sense that it would be "put to the test in the material" that comprised the book as a whole.[45] The methodological deliberations in *Konvolut* N are intensely vivid. They are not for that reason easily comprehended.

How was this method to be "put to the test" on the historical material that Benjamin had compiled? How are we to understand the "dialectical image" as a form of philosophical representation? Was "dust" such an image? fashion? the prostitute? expositions? commodities? the arcades themselves? Yes, surely[46]—not, however, as these referents are empirically given, nor even as they are critically interpreted as emblematic of commodity society, but as they are dialectically "constructed," as "historical objects," politically charged monads, "blasted " out of history's continuum and made "actual" in the present. This construction of historical objects clearly involved the mediation of the author's imagination. The cognitive experience of history, no less than that of the empir-

how can they be either given that they purport to say nothing?

ical world, required the active intervention of the thinking subject. And yet Benjamin insisted, in accordance with the method of literary montage: "I have nothing to say, only to show."[47] Here, in what appear to be paradoxical extremes in Benjamin's method, is the source of a dilemma in interpretation. Are dialectical images too subjective in their formulation? Or, are they not subjective enough?

After the initial, politically charged reception that greeted the first volumes of Benjamin's complete works in the early 1970s, he has quite rapidly gained respectability within universities, the institutional guardians of the cultural heritage, where he has been inserted into the developmental histories of the disciplines and bent to fit existing course progressions. Recent academic discussions of Benjamin have been dominated by aestheticians and literary and cultural critics, with the result that, if today he is considered as a philosopher at all, then in the poetic tradition of German Romanticism (the subjective idealism of which he attacked[48]) or as the precursor of such recent, postsubjective currents of thought as deconstruction and postmodernism (characterized not infrequently by an anthropological nihilism which he criticized vehemently[49]). The failure of both appropriations to do the matter justice is due to the fact that Benjamin, while a "literary" writer, was not, in the traditional sense of the term, a literary thinker.[50] He interpreted literature as objective, not subjective expression. He criticized the stress on "taste" in *l'art pour l'art* and "the chosen word" in *Jugendstil* as a reflection of the new consumerism,[51] and analyzed "the problem of a literature without an object" in Mallarmé's theory of *poesie pur* as an expression of the distancing of the poet from the affairs of his own class, a problem "rerecorded" in Mallarmé's poems in the motifs of "the blank, the absence, the silence, the void," which, far from saying nothing,

[. . . allow] us to read the fact that the poet no longer takes it upon himself to represent the goals pursued by the class to which he belongs. Establishing his production on this fundamental renunciation of all the manifest experiences of his class brings with it specific and significant difficulties. They make the poetry esoteric. Baudelaire's works are not esoteric.[52]

Such commentaries on texts are identifiably Marxist, just as his commentaries on reality are admittedly poetic. Yet to read Benjamin as a writer of allegorical "literature," or even as a "Marxist" literary critic, is a sure way to ensnare oneself in theoretical paradoxes that not even dialectical subtleties can resolve. In order to plot out this problem (—and it is a serious one intellectually—) we will consider two extremes of interpreting Benjamin as a literary thinker. They will allow us to show that if Benjamin threw the traditonal language of Western metaphysics into the junkroom, it was to rescue the metaphysical experience of the objective world, not to see philosophy dissolve into the play of language itself.

Exemplary of one interpretive extreme is the critique that Hans Robert Jauss, professor of literary criticism and romance philology, levies against Benjamin. Commenting on the latter's interpretation of Baudelaire's poem, "Parisian Dream," Jauss argues that Benjamin's description of this poem as a "'fantasy of the forces of production having been shut down'" (when the poem represents neither workers nor factories directly[53]) is itself an example of "the method of allegoresis," without which, he adds, "an interpretation of the literary superstructure from the conditions of the economic infrastructure is seldom to be had."[54] Now if we view Benjamin's interpretation of the socioeconomic origins of the allegorical in Baudelaire as itself an allegory, then we would seem to be ontologically in a vicious circle (the "reality" of which the poem [says Benjamin] is an allegory, is an allegorical reading [says Jauss] of the poem), and epistemologically in an infinite regress (is the poem allegorical, or the interpetation, or the interpretation of this interpretation...?). None of this bothers Jauss, it should be noted, because in his "opinion," a Marxist interpretation of the superstructure, even if it is unavoidably "allegorical," is "legitimate hermeneutically," so long, that is, as "it recognizes its subjective heuristics and therefore its partiality, and consequently no longer makes the dogmatic claim of having achieved the true and—now finally—'objective' reading."[55] (Of course, just the claim to objectivity is what a Marxist interpretation cannot abandon.) Watered down by Jauss' liberal pluralism, Benjamin's interpretation of Baudelaire becomes just another way of doing literary criticism, one among many hermeneutic strategies, subjective and partial— and affirmed for these qualities.

Jauss is aware that Benjamin himself believes the allegorical in Baudelaire's poetry has an objective source: the social reality of commodity production which finds expression within it. However, "this attempt to justify a materialist genesis for Baudelaire's recourse to allegory" leads to insights that do not "measure up" to Benjamin's insights elsewhere.[56] At least, Jauss reiterates, this is his "opinion,"[57] to which he is entitled. But he violates his own insistence as to the subjectivity of interpretations when he presumes as fact, not opinion, that Baudelaire's poetry was part of an inner aesthetic development (based on the relationship between literary production and its critical reception) along a historical continuum that moves from mimesis to allegoresis, an interpretive act that in turn claims "objectivity" for a developmental historical continuum within literature. In fact this continuum reveals more about the transmission of literature than about Baudelaire's poetry.[58] The criticism of Paul de Man is to the point, and deserves to be cited at length. De Man writes:

For [Jauss' student, Karlheinz] Stierle, following Jauss who himself followed [Hugo] Friedrich, it goes without saying that the crisis of the self and of representation in lyric poetry of the nineteenth and twentieth centuries should be interpreted as a gradual process. Baudelaire continues trends implicitly present in Diderot; Mallarmé (as he himself stated) felt he had to begin where Baudelaire had ended; Rimbaud takes an even further step in opening up the experimentation of the surrealists—in short, the modernity of poetry occurs as a continuous historical movement. This reconciliation of modernity with history in a common genetic process is highly satisfying, because it allows one to be both origin and offspring at the same time. The son understands the father and takes his work a step further, becoming in turn the father [. . .]. Such a reconciliation of memory with action is the dream of all historians. In the field of literary studies, the documented modernism of Hans Robert Jauss and his group, who seem to have no qualms about dating the origins of modernism with historical accuracy, is a good contemporary example of this dream. In their case, it rests on the assumption that the movement of lyric poetry away from representation is a historical process that dates back to Baudelaire [,] as well as being the very movement of modernity.[59]

De Man, of course, is implying that Jauss' historical continuum is itself allegoresis, one that expresses the desire for a father-to-son inheritance.[60] Ironically, in the context of Jauss' continuous historical movement, Benjamin's "allegorical" method is suddenly no longer just another subjectively relative mode of interpretation, but rather, that movement's culmination!

If, from Baudelaire to Benjamin, allegory's line of descent is presumed to be direct, then the history of modern literature becomes
the saga of allegory's triumph over mimetic representation. De
Man notes as a consequence: "the assumed correspondence between meaning and object is put into question. From this point on,
the very presence of any outward object can become superfluous";
it leads Jauss to characterize allegorical style "[...] as 'beauté
inutile,' the absence of any reference to an exterior reality of which
it would be the sign. The 'disappearance of the object' has become
the main theme."[61] Assuming de Man's description of Jauss'
conceptual frame is correct, "from this point on," discussions of
Benjamin's thinking within it are distortions. For Benjamin was concerned with the *rescue* of historical objects, not their disappearance.
One begins to question whether the literary concept of "allegory"
is adequate for describing what dialectical images are all about.

The relation of Benjamin to modernism and allegory is also discussed by the literary theorist Peter Bürger, but it is handled quite
differently. A student of Surrealism, Bürger sees the avant-garde
movement as representing a crisis within art and a radical rupture
from earlier bourgeois aesthetics, and Benjamin stands on the contemporary side of this great divide. Eschewing developmental history, Bürger draws on Benjamin's own understanding of literary
traditions as *dis*continuous, a convergence of the long-past with the
most modern, so that insights into the nature of allegory that have
not been achieved until the modern era can be fruitful when applied
retroactively, leaping over centuries of literary "development" that
intervene. Hence, "[...] it was Benjamin's experience in dealing
with works of the avant-garde that made possible both the development of the category [of allegory] and its application to the Baroque, not the other way around."[62] The montage-like construction
that Benjamin found significant in allegory as an expressive form
reflected the contemporary experience of modern art. Burger cites
the *Trauerspiel* study,[63] and comments:

The allegorist pulls one element out of the totality of the life context, iso-
lating it, depriving it of its function. Allegory is therefore essentially fragment [...]. The allegorist joins the isolated fragments of reality and
thereby creates meaning. This is posited meaning; it does not derive from
the original context of the fragments.[64]

Bürger maintains that, far from leaving the world of objective matter behind, the allegorical form of avant-guarde montage brings reality into the artwork, destroying both art's separate status and its appearance of totality. This attack on art "as an institution,"[65] in fact makes the historical fiction of culture's self-contained development (*pace* Jauss) impossible to sustain: "The insertion of reality fragments into the work of art fundamentally transforms that work. [. . . The parts] are no longer signs pointing to reality, they *are* reality."[66] For Bürger, the crucial significance of this movement is political: "a new type of engaged art becomes possible."[67]

Of course, art as a form of political or moral instruction is hardly new, and allegory has long been used as the medium of its expression. But prebourgeois art, tied as it was to religion and ritual, made no claim to be "autonomous" from the "praxis of life," so that the allegorical representation of "reality fragments" did not have the same effect as an *institutional* challenge. It is specifically within the bourgeois era that such representation functions in a revolutionary way, because its very form involves the direct intervention of that reality from which art had thought itself insulated. Art is drawn into politics, and this is true no matter what the artist's conscious political intent. For it is not the content of the work, but its effect on "the institution within which the work functions"[68] that determines the political effects of avant-garde art. Furthermore, the avant-garde's shattering of the boundary between representation and reality means that the political impact of the modern artwork can remain undogmatic, independent of an overarching political position. It allows for a reception of empirical testing by the audience:

In the avant-gardiste [*sic.*] work, the individual sign does not refer primarily to the work as a whole but to reality. The recipient is free to respond to the individual sign as an important statement concerning the praxis of life, or as political instruction. This has momentous consequences for the place of engagement within the work. Where the work is no longer conceived as organic totality, the individual political motif is no longer subordinate to the work as a whole but can be effective in isolation.[69]

Yet Bürger recognizes that despite the revolutionary form of the avant-garde, it has proved inadequate as political praxis. The avant-garde movement has challenged, but failed to destroy the established institution[70]; rather, it has been co-opted by it. Brecht, whom Bürger considers "the most important materialist writer of our time," was more realistic (than the Surrealists, for example), because he used the avant-garde principle of montage for the more limited purpose of "refunctioning" culture as an institution.[71] It is this institution, Bürger maintains, that "determines the measure of political effect avant-garde works can have, and that [. . .] in bourgeois society continues to [define art as . . .] a realm that is distinct from the praxis of life."[72] Bürger concludes that the contradiction between the avant-garde's bringing reality into art, and the bourgeois institution's keeping art separate from reality cannot be resolved within bourgeois society, and this leads him to a position of cultural pessimism similar to that of Adorno.

Whether Benjamin's recourse to the constructive principle of montage puts him in the company of the aesthetic avant-garde depends on whether his work[73] can be categorized as "aesthetics" at all. But what Bürger's discussion allows us to point out is that, fundamental to the avant-garde, and evident in montage as its formal principle, is an oscillation between the intrusion of objective "reality" into the artwork, and the subjective control over the meanings of these real objects that this technique allows. The fact that in montage, as in allegory generally, "the parts have more autonomy as signs,"[74] can have two antithetical results, and this becomes the source of an epistemological instability. On the one hand, it allows the literary producer to manipulate meanings, with the result that art's "engagement" becomes indistinguishable from political propaganda (a charge that can be levied against Marxists in general and Brecht in particular). On the other hand, it may lead the artist to view the haphazard juxtaposition of "found" objects (the Surrealists' "*objets trouvés*") as magically endowed with "meaning " on their own, as a result of what Bürger calls an "ideological [. . .] interpretation of the category of chance" that is "tantamount to resignation on the part of the bourgeois individual."[75] In the first case, epistemology appears indeed to be confronted, due to the arbitrariness of the referent, with "the disappearance of the object"; in the second, "the disappearance of the subject" seems to be the issue. If both are gone, one is left only with language and its textual traces—in fact the epistemological ground of that contemporary position held by certain structuralists, deconstructionists, and postmodernists who have claimed Benjamin as their precursor. Is the claim justified?

4

It was Adorno who first pointed out these tendencies in Benjamin's epistemology, but they evoked from him criticism rather than praise. He was concerned when he discovered in Benjamin's work any sacrifice of objective reflection for the sake of political correctness, any attempt to affirm the working class that transformed theory into propaganda—evidence, he suspected, of the deleterious influence of Brecht.[76] And he was just as alarmed by the opposite tendency, the Surrealist-inspired, "wide-eyed presentation of mere facts" that had caused the first Baudelaire essay to settle "on the crossroads between magic and positivism," as Adorno wrote to Benjamin, with the warning: "This spot is bewitched."[77]

But Benjamin would have known full well where he stood. With the dialectical image, he had consciously placed himself in close proximity not only to the Surrealists, but to the Baroque emblemists as well. The *Passagen-Werk*'s pictorial representations of ideas are undeniably modeled after those emblem books of the seventeenth century, which had widespread appeal as perhaps the first genre of mass publication. The gambler and the flâneur in the Arcades project personify the empty time of modernity; the whore is an image of the commodity form; decorative mirrors and bourgeois interiors are emblematic of bourgeois subjectivism; dust and wax figures are signs of history's motionlessness; mechanical dolls are emblematic of workers' existence under industrialism; the store cashier is perceived "as living image, as allegory of the cashbox."[78]

Now Benjamin was surely aware that his earlier criticism of the Baroque emblemists had a direct bearing on his own work. The lasting importance of the *Trauerspiel* study was that it provided him with a thoroughly analyzed reference point for charting his later philosophical course. The *Passagen-Werk* is indebted to Baroque allegory, no less for its differences than its affinities.

We have already discussed the main lines of Benjamin's argument in the *Trauerspiel* study,[79] which we may recall, is a philosophical, not a literary analysis. As a literary device, allegory has been used since ancient times to convey an author's own meanings or intentions in an indirect manner. But within philosophy, allegory has another status as the mode in which not the subject, but the

objective world expresses meaning. The German Baroque dramatists understood each of nature's elements as full of signification,
that humans only needed to interpret in order to uncover truth. But
the fact that each element could be translated in a multiplicity of
paradoxical ways so that ultimately any object could stand for anything else, implied referential arbitrariness, which seemed to negate
the very claim of a "meaningful" nature. As we have seen, Benjamin praised the Baroque dramatists for recognizing that this
paradox demanded a "theological" (thus philosophical) solution,
not an aesthetic one. But he criticized the *particular* theological
frame which they employed, because in the dialectical leap from the
hill of skulls to the resurrection of the spirit, they "treacherously"
(*treulos*) abandoned to the devil the very sorrow-filled nature,
the very physical suffering that had been their original concern.[80]
The Baroque concept of Christian redemption stood opposed to
both nature and history, as an event that belonged, not to this
world, but to the purely spiritual realm of subjective inwardness.
Was another resolution possible? The *Trauerspiel* book does not
tell us explicitly, but Benjamin knew that there was.

"I continue to find it very strange," wrote Scholem in his
reminiscences, "that around 1930 Benjamin told at least two men
(Max Rychner and Theodor Adorno) that only someone familiar
with the Kabbalah could understand the introduction to his book
on tragic drama [. . .]."[81] This was the more remarkable, he continued, as Benjamin never discussed the connection with him, who
alone would have understood it. But in dedicating a copy of the
book for Scholem, Benjamin wrote: "'To Gerhard Scholem,
donated to the Ultima Thule of his Kabbalist library'—as if this
work indeed somehow belonged in a kabbalistic library."[82]
Scholem asks:

[. . . W]as he indulging in a game of hide-and-seek with me? Did he succumb to the temptation to indulge in some showing off, or did he want to
shroud the reproach of incomprehensibility, which few pages of his *oeuvre*
would suggest more than this introduction, by referring to something even
more incomprehensible (which is how the Kabbalah must have seemed to
them [Rychner and Adorno])? I do not know.[83]

It was evident to Scholem that Benjamin's theory of language in
the *Trauerspiel* introduction was indebted to ideas from Kabbalist
theory.[84] It argues that not Plato, but Adam was "the father of

philosophy."[85] Benjamin writes that the language of Adam as the name giver of God's creations, "is so far removed from play or arbitrariness that, quite the contrary, it confirms the paradisiacal condition as such [. . .]."[86] This discourse is the model for which philosophy must strive: "philosophical contemplation" reinstates the "original perception of the words."[87]

Remember Benjamin's statement that the theory of the *Trauerspiel* introduction was to be "put to the test" in the subsequent discussion of Baroque allegory.[88] The fact that Scholem himself never commented on this "test" is unfortunate, because for him the evaluative standard lay close at hand. It was Scholem who had shared his youthful enthusiasm for Kabbalist thought with Benjamin, beginning in 1917.[89] His scholarship was then just beginning to unearth the socially radical ideas of this tradition of Jewish mysticism which, because it challenged both orthodoxy and rational reformism,[90] had fallen into disrepute in the course of the nineteenth century, and was dismissed by Jewish even more than by Christian scholars.

The Kabbalah and the Messianic Idea to which it gave expression would become Scholem's lifelong study. As a scholar, he would remain centrally concerned with rescuing this tradition within the specifically Jewish intellectual heritage. But as a philosopher, Benjamin saw its significance elsewhere. Kabbalist thought (which had experienced a rebirth precisely in the Baroque era) provided an alternative to the philosophical antinomies of not only Baroque Christian theology, but also subjective idealism, its secular, Enlightenment form. Specifically, Kabbalism avoided the split between spirit and matter which had resulted in the Baroque dramatists' "treacherous" abandonment of nature, and it rejected the notion that redemption was an antimaterial, otherworldly concern. Scholem has written:

A totally different concept of redemption determines the attitude to Messianism in Judaism and Christianity [. . .]. Judaism, in all its forms and manifestations, has always maintained a concept of redemption as an event which takes place publicly, on the stage of history and within the community [. . .]. In contrast, Christianity conceives of redemption as an event in the spiritual and unseen realm, an event which is reflected in the soul, in the private world of each individual, and which effects an inner transformation which need not correspond to anything outside.[91]

It is no secret that the Jewish Messianic conception, which already has the attributes of being historical, materialist, and collective, translates readily into political radicalism in general and Marxism in particular. The redemptive task of the proletariat was articulated in Messianic terms by close contemporaries of Benjamin, such as Georg Lukács and Ernst Bloch, and Benjamin also understood it in this way.[92] Bloch had argued forcefully that Christianity itself had a tradition of chiliastic Messianism anticipatory of Marx's communist goals, embodied most particularly in the teachings of Thomas Münzer (called by Martin Luther the "archdevil," but called by Bloch the "theologian of the revolution" in his 1921 book on Münzer, with which Benjamin was familiar).[93] Unique about the Kabbalah was less its Messianism than its epistemology. It was a mystical mode of cognition that revealed previously concealed truths within nature, which were meaningful only in the context of a Messianic Age (in secular, Marxist terms, a socially just, classless society). Kabbalists read both reality and the texts,[94] not to discover an overarching historical plan (*vid.* Lukács' Hegelian-Marxist teleology), but to interpret their multiple, fragmentary parts as signs of the Messianic potential of the present. The truth thus revealed was expressed in the Kabbalist writings inventively, indirectly, in riddles, providing an antiauthoritarian form of pedagogy. Kabbalist cognition replaced the dogmatism of institutionalized religion with "a novel and living experience and intuition" of the doctrines it contained.[95]

In their interpretation of the material world the Kabbalists did not deny its fallen state, and the consequent "abysmal multiplicity of things" when compared to the unity of Divine Reality.[96] Here they agreed with the Baroque allegoricists. But their texts describe "with an infinite complexity"[97] the ten "Sefiroth," the spheres and stages of God's attributes as these appear within nature *despite* that broken unity.[98] Where, faced with a transitory and ambiguous reality, the Christian allegoricists give up on material nature, the Kabbalists only begin.

5

My thinking relates to theology as the blotter to ink. It is totally saturated with it. But if it were up to the blotter, nothing that is written would remain.[99]

The Kabbalah, a theology of mystical metaphysics (that has had, it may be noted, Christian as well as Jewish adherents[100]) differs from the entire tradition of idealist philosophy, whether in theological or secular form, in terms of the structure of cognitive experience. Moreover, it does so in ways compatible with the philosophic goal described in the *Trauerspiel* book's introduction, "to transform historical, material content" into "truth content."[101] But Benjamin's analysis of the tragic dramas is not itself "Kabbalist." Rather, in this early study, the Kabbalah is the hidden, theological alternative that shapes Benjamin's critique of the Baroque Christian allegoricists, while the critique, at least for the initiate, functions as the alternative's defense. It is first in the *Passagen-Werk* that the paradigmatic status for Benjamin of the Kabbalah is brought to expression, because it is first in this project that he employs certain of its fundamental premises as the mode of his philosophical exegesis. This is true not in spite of, but because of the project's Marxism.

To connect the philosophy underlying the *Passagen-Werk* with theology in general and the Kabbalah in particular is to invite controversy. Sectarian battles marking the reception of Benjamin have polarized the Marxist and theological sides of his thinking, claiming them to be incompatible antitheses.[102] In these battles, Scholem has been one of the most partisan fighters, defending the "theological" in Benjamin against all attacks. However, in his determination to secure Benjamin's position within the particularistic, Judaic intellectual tradition, Scholem underestimates the deepest sense in which theology permeates Benjamin's thought, that is, precisely in his theology-free, manifestly "Marxist" writings. Meanwhile, Marxists, although rightly claiming Benjamin as their own, have generally failed to recognize the enormity of the challenge that this appropriation poses to their own theoretical presuppositions.

The very charged term "theological" is perhaps less misleading if it is understood as having a precise philosophical function within Benjamin's theory. Important elements of the Kabbalist paradigm provided Benjamin with a metaphysical base for revolutionary pedagogy vital to Marxian politics, but it is expressed in the fully secular, historically specific discourse of women's fashions and street traffic, in which every trace of positive theology has been extinguished. (Thus Scholem was unwittingly closer to Benjamin's understanding of the "theological" when in 1920 he playfully suggested for the catalogue of their jointly founded, fictional "University of Muri," a course, the title of which was a takeoff on a work of Kabbalist scholarship: "Cosmic Cloak and Heavenly Canopy" (*Weltmantel und Himmelszelt*). Scholem's "course" was called: "Ladies' Coats and Beach Cabanas [*Damenmantel und Badezelt*] in Religio-Historical Illumination."[103]) Because its material is so thoroughly profane, one can indeed describe the *Passagen-Werk* without mentioning theology or the Kabbalah. Yet the whole project is only arbitrary and aesthetic, carrying no *philosophical* conviction, if the invisible theological armature is ignored.

Basic features of Scholem's research in the Kabbalah[104] find an undeniable echo in what might appear to be the most idiosyncratic aspects in Benjamin's theory of dialectical images. Scholem tells us that the word Kabbalah means "that which is received through tradition"; yet its relationship to tradition is inherently paradoxical. As is true of most theology, it is first and foremost a hermeneutic method of reading the sacred texts. But as mysticism, it reads them for hidden meanings that could not have been known at the time of their writing, rejecting the historicist approach of interpreting texts in terms of authorial intent. Unconcerned with recapturing original meanings or with extrinsic concerns of historical accuracy, these mystics took delight in invention, often interpreting passages in a manner as remote as possible from that which Rabbinical philosophy had come to accept as correct. Their concern for tradition is in the interest of its transformation rather than preservation. They interpret the texts in order to illuminate their own era, in order to discover within it clues of the coming Messianic Age. Scholem speaks of the "fate of sacred writings" to become "divorced from the intentions of their authors" as "what may be called their afterlife, which, discovered by later generations, frequently becomes of greater importance than their original meaning [. . .]."[105] But for radical interpretation, this hermeneutic difficulty becomes a virtue. Note that there is no "disappearance of the object": Without present-day material referents, the ancient texts are indecipherable. Hence the paradox: one cannot interpret the truth of present reality without past texts, but this reality transforms radically the way these texts are read. The result is that "old combinations will be interpreted in an entirely new way,"[106] as traditional symbols demonstrate "their explosive power in shattering tradition."[107] In short, the Kabbalah reveres the past in order to break from it.

Clearly, as Scholem points out, a thin line separated Kabbalism from heresy, as revelation might (and did) disclose truths in violation of religious law.[108] This is particularly true of Sabbatianism, the Messianic movement of believers in Sabbatai Zevi, which spread rapidly in 1665, and which persisted in the face of Zevi's antinomial act of apostasy, his scandalous conversion to Islam in 1666. Sabbatians argued that the laws of the Torah were not valid in the Messianic Era which had begun; indeed, they affirmed the "holiness of sin."[109] By challenging the absolutist claims of religious dogma, their very fanaticism encouraged secularization, and tended to undermine all established authority. Thus, Scholem maintains that these believers were in fact the true forerunners of the Enlightenment and of political radicalism among Jewish thinkers, not the medieval rationalists as has commonly been asserted[110]:

To the anarchic religious feeling of these new Jews [the Sabbatians], all the three great institutional religions have no longer an absolute value.[. . .] When the outbreak of the French Revolution again gave a political aspect to their ideas, no great change was needed for them to become the apostles of an unbounded political apocalypse. The urge towards revolutionizing all that existed [. . .] assumed an intensely practical aspect in the task of ushering in the new age.[111]

According to the Messianic idea, the new age will end the historical era of human suffering that began with the Fall. The Age of Redemption is marked by a restoration of nature to its paradisiacal state. In keeping with Kabbalist exegetical understanding, however, this restoration is not literally a return,[112] because the worldly conditions to which the myth of Paradise would apply as truth have only now appeared. With the advent of the new age, the true meaning of the ancient story reveals itself for the first time, and in unexpected ways.

The centrality of the Creation story for Kabbalist thought has political implications. Because Adam and Eve were the parents of all humanity, Messianic redemption is understood as an event in universal history, ending the "exile" not just of the Jewish nation, but of the whole world, entailing "a fundamental transformation of the entire Creation."[113] The Messianic vision of a Paradise with an "'abundance of worldly goods'"[114] establishes the purpose of universal human history: to bring about "a utopia that as yet has never been, that as yet has never been capable of realization."[115] But because the Kabbalists believe there is "no progress in history leading to redemption,"[116] no developmental dynamic that guarantees the goal, the burden of ushering in the Messianic Age falls squarely on human beings, who for their part are not unwilling tools in realizing God's plan, but historical agents whose knowledge and understanding of what is at stake is indispensable.[117] Scholem describes the Messianic task:

At opposite poles, both man and God encompass within their being the entire cosmos. However, whereas God contains all by virtue of being its Creator and Initiator in whom everything is rooted and all potency is hidden, man's role is to complete this process by being the agent through whom all the powers of creation are fully activated and made manifest [. . .]. Man is the perfecting agent in the structure of the cosmos [. . .]. Because he and he alone has been granted the gift of free will, it lies within his power to either [sic.] advance or disrupt through his actions the unity of what takes place in the upper and lower worlds.[118]

In contrast to the idealist tradition, the Kabbalah understands alienation as ignorance of, not separation from God.[119] Moreover, it is with nature rather than God that humans are to be reconciled. Even in its fallen state, "under the penetrating gaze of the mystic,"[120] material nature is the sole source of divine knowledge: "[. . .] all [K]abbalists agree that no religious knowledge of God, even of the most exalted kind, can be gained except through contemplation of the relationship of God to creation."[121] Nature is not evil[122]; it is shattered and imperfect. According to Isaac Luria's Kabbalist doctrine of *Tikkun*, the breaking of the "vessels" of God's attributes scattered divine sparks in fragments throughout the material world. The task of healing these broken vessels, an enterprise in which "man and God are partners,"[123] reestablishes the "harmonious condition of the world" not as a restoration, but "as something new."[124]

For the Kabbalists, words have a mystical significance. Language plays a central role in the historical enterprise, for the Fall broke not only the unity of Creation, but the unity of the Adamic language of Names. In the latter there is no gap between word and referent, whereas the language of judgment which replaced it interprets nature abstractly as a sign of its fallen state. The whole thrust of humanity's moral obligation is a cognitive one, that is, to overcome ignorance of God by interpreting nature in terms of the divine sparks within it. The broken unity of both nature and language dictates the specifics of the interpretive method. Kabbalist exegesis is antisystemic. Each interpretive fragment has, monadologically, its own center; the macrocosm is read within the microcosm. No part of God's creation, no word of the sacred texts, is too small or insignificant not to manifest, as a monad, one of the ten attributes of God, and thus to be "'understood and explained in reference to redemption.'"[125] The divine knowledge revealed in nature is pluralistic; it exists in different, disconnected registers, presenting itself in metaphors, riddles, and mysteries. Nature's meaning is, in short, as disparate and ambiguous as the Baroque allegoricists insisted.

What prevents this knowledge from being arbitrary? What allows the Kabbalists to claim that their readings are not merely allegorical? Scholem discusses this question explicitly. He first defines allegory:

Allegory consists of an infinite network of meanings and correlations in which everything can become a representation of everything else, but all within the limits of language and expression. To that extent it is possible to speak of allegorical immanence. That which is expressed by and in the allegorical sign is in the first instance something which has its own meaningful context, but by becoming allegorical this something loses its own meaning and becomes the vehicle of something else. Indeed the allegory arises, as it were, from the gap which at this point opens between the form and its meaning. The two are no longer indissolubly welded together; the meaning is no longer restricted to that particular form, nor the form any longer to that particular meaningful content. What appears in the allegory, in short, is the infinity of meaning which attaches to every representation.[126]

Scholem then contrasts allegory's immanent meaning to the "transcendent" meaning of the theological symbol,[127] drawing, (precisely as Benjamin did in the *Trauerspiel* study[128]) on the first volume of Friedrich Cruezer's *Mythologie* (1819):

For the [K]abbalist, too, every existing thing is endlessly correlated with the whole of creation; for him, too, everything mirrors everything else. But beyond that he discovers something else which is not covered by the allegorical network: a reflection of the true transcendence. The symbol "signifies" nothing and communicates nothing, but makes something transparent which is beyond all expression. Where deeper insight into the structure of the allegory uncovers fresh layers of meaning, the symbol is intuitively understood all at once—or not at all. The symbol in which the life of the Creator and that of creation become one, is—to use Creuzer's words—"a beam of light which, from the dark and abysmal depths of existence and cognition, falls into our eye and penetrates our whole being." It is a "momentary totality" which is perceived intuitively in a mystical now—[*Nu*] the dimension of time proper to the symbol.

Of such symbols the world of Kabbalism is full, nay the whole world is to the Kabbalist such a *corpus symbolicum*.[129]

The Kabbalist may start out like the allegoricist, juxtaposing sacred texts and natural images; but when past text and present image come together in a way that suddenly both are illuminated in the Messianic light of redemption, so that the historical present becomes visible as pregnant with the potential for a worldly utopia, then allegory's arbitrariness is transcended. In the clarity of the *theological* symbol, "reality becomes transparent. The infinite shines through the finite and makes it more and not less real [. . .]."[130] This is "the profound difference" between the "allegorical inter-pretation of religion and its symbolical understanding by the mystics."[131]

6

What is valuable in me and in the other "Jews" is not Jewish.[132]

As a Jewish thinker, Benjamin was a heretic.[133] Sabbatai Zevi's apostasy, his blasphemous conversion to Islam in 1666, was enacted under threat of death. If Benjamin's avowal of Marxism lacked the element of forced conversion, it was nonetheless totally in keeping with what he had learned from Scholem was the Kab-balist tradition of antitraditionalism. The Sabbatians justified their leader's act as "a mission to lift up the holy sparks which were dispersed even among the gentiles and concentrated now in Islam."[134] Scholem refused to make similar concessions to his friend, telling Benjamin that his attempt to write as a Marxist was nothing more than "self-deception in an unusually intensive form."[135]

It must be emphasized that while Benjamin for his part con-tinued to find Scholem's work on the history of the Kabbalah "use-ful" and ventured even as a Marxist to say that he read it "with profit,"[136] he confessed neither general interest in,[137] nor great familiarity with the Kabbalist texts, referring in fact to the "abyss of ignorance" that was his "in this region."[138] If his earliest writings displayed "Kabbalist" elements, these may well have come to Benjamin indirectly, via the language philosophies of Johann Georg Haman and the German Romantics.[139] Moreover, by the time he began conceiving the *Passagen-Werk*, it was not the Kabbalist *Zohar*, but a Surrealist text that kept Benjamin awake nights with pounding heart. Moses de Leon, author of the *Zohar*, saw the face of God in the ten "mystical crowns" of the Sefiroth[140]; Louis Aragon, author of *Le paysan de Paris*, saw the face of God in a gas tank[141]. And if the *Zohar* contained meditations on the Tree of Life, the meditative objects of Breton's Surrealist novel *Nadja*[142] were objects of the "new" nature: a woman's glove, a cigarette lying in an ashtray, the luminous sign advertising Mazda lightbulbs on the boulevard. Yet that which distinguished the theological symbol, the "unity of sensory and supersensory object,"[143] is precisely what Benjamin found in these Surrealist texts. Aragon wrote in *Le paysan de Paris*:

It seemed to me that the essence of these pleasures was totally metaphysical, that it implied a kind of passionate taste for revelation. An object transfigured itself before my eyes, taking on neither the allure of allegory nor the character of the [aesthetic] symbol; it was less the manifestation of an idea than the idea itself. It extended deep into earthly matter.[144]

As with the *Trauerspiel* allegoricists, Benjamin considered the Surrealists' revelatory vision of historically transient objects a philosophical position rather than an aesthetic technique.[145] It was "profane illumination—of a material, anthropological inspiration."[146] The cognitive experience which the Surrealist images provided, while related to that of the mystics, was "dialectical" rather than "mysterious," and in fact more difficult to attain. Benjamin called it "the true, creative overcoming of religious illumination," for which religious experience (as well as hashish or falling in love) was merely the "preschool."[147]

But even as Benjamin affirmed this materialist revelation over the spiritual one, he still continued to insist that the metaphysical writings of his early years were related to "the method of observation of dialectical materialism" which he later adopted, even if by "a tense and problematic mediation."[148] Moreover, he formulated entries to *Konvolut* N of the *Passagen-Werk* that described the method of the "historical materialist" as "theology," appropriating in this context explicitly "political-theological categories"[149] (apokatastasis, redemption)—not just in the last years of his life when political disillusionment was intense,[150] but throughout the period of his work on the project. Writing in 1935 with regard to the *Passagen-Werk* exposé just completed, Benjamin attributed the slow tempo of its formulation to the fact that the "mass of thoughts and images" that were his from a much earlier time and that had their origins "in immediately metaphysical, indeed, theological thinking," had to undergo a "total revolution"—not in order to *eliminate* this thinking, but: "so that it might nourish my present conception with its entire energy."[151]

Through its "total revolution" theological tradition is to be saved. This is only an apparent contradiction. The paradox resolves itself if the ur-old utopian themes to which theology first gave expression are understood to have found, potentially, their true referents in the modern epoch of "new nature" which has only just begun.

"Ur-history of the nineteenth century"—this would have no interest if it were understood to mean that ur-historical forms are to be rediscovered within the inventory of the nineteenth century. The conception [. . .] has meaning only where the nineteenth century is presented as the originary form of Ur-history, the form, that is, in which all of Ur-history groups itself in new images, indigenous to the past century.[152]

Mythic, ur-historical themes are for the first time "legible"[153] as profane discourse, because they now have real, historical referents. As emblematic captions, they cohere to nineteenth-century images with a new and surprising adequacy.[154] The Fall that alienates nature from human beings describes accurately the production of commodities in its historical particularly—as Marx's early texts make clear.[155] Similarly, the Biblical loss of the language of Names identifies the essence of abstract labor that characterizes this production.[156] The devaluation of the old nature that found expression in Christian allegory is experienced *sui generis* by Baudelaire in the marketplace, where the "meaning" of commodities is not the act of their creation, but their extrinsic and arbitrary price.[157] Satanic qualities of death and eternal recurrence coalesce around this commodity world as fashion. But the new nature is not evil. Scattered throughout its objects, the "divine sparks" described by the doctrine of *Tikkun* take the form of socialist potential, a transcendent element, the existence of which is no less real than the capitalist social relations that prevent its actualization. As Benjamin says explicitly in the passage on "the Gambler," the only meaning of sin is to accept the given state of things, surrendering to it as fate.[158] In contrast, "the Name knows no greater opponent than fate."[159] Humanity's historical responsibility is an interpretive task, "naming" both the socialist potential of the new nature (now synonymous with nature's "redemption") and the failure of history to realize it. This task is the vital core of the *Passagen-Werk*. Benjamin writes:

The phrase "the Book of Nature" indicates that we can read reality like a text. That will be the approach here to the reality of the nineteenth century. We break open the book of what has come to pass.[160]

7

To read reality *like* a text is to recognize their difference.

One must keep making it clear how commentary on a reality [. . .] needs a totally different method than commentary on a text. In the former case theology is the fundamental science; in the latter it is philology.[161]

How can the *Passagen-Werk* make the metaphysical claim to be a commentary on "reality"? This brings us back to the heart of the philosophical problem. Why is the Arcades project not merely an arbitrary, aesthetic representation of the nineteenth century, a political allegory that appropriates theological themes for Marxist ends—in which case it would fall rightly to the domain of poetry (not to speak of propaganda), and Jauss' criticisms would be correct?

In the *Passagen-Werk* Benjamin defines allegory as the activity of the ponderer, whose reflective attitude is one of recollection:

The case of the ponderer is that of the man who already had the resolution to great problems, but has forgotten them. And now he ponders, not so much about the thing as about his past meditations over it. The thinking of the ponderer stands therefore in the sign of remembering. Ponderer and allegoricist are out of *one* piece of wood.[162]

The memory of the ponderer holds sway over the disordered mass of dead knowledge. Human knowledge is piecework to it in a particularly pregnant sense: namely as the heaping up of arbitrarily cut up pieces, out of which one puts together a puzzle. [. . .] The allegoricist reaches now here, now there, into the chaotic depths that his knowledge places at his disposal, grabs an item out, holds it next to another, and sees whether they fit: that meaning to this image, or this image to that meaning. The result never lets itself be predicted; for there is no natural mediation between the two.[163]

Benjamin sees the ponderer's behavior as closely connected to that of the collector,[164] who assembles things that have been set out of circulation and are meaningless as use values. Collecting the no longer useful object is an activity governed by the category of "completeness," which, says Benjamin, is

[. . .] a grand attempt to overcome the totally irrational fact of its merely being-here-at-hand by ordering it into a historical system, the collection, that he has himself created. And for the true collector every single item in this system becomes an encyclopedia of all knowledge of the epoch, the district, the industry, the owner, from whence it comes.[165]

Surely Benjamin's work brings him into affinity with both types; in his dealings with nineteenth-century phenomena he is both ponderer and collector. But he describes in very different terms his task as the historical materialist who "blasts apart" the continuum of history, constructing "historical objects" in a politically explosive "constellation of past and present," as a "lightning flash" of truth.

Allegorical image and dialectical image are distinct. The meaning of the former remains an expression of subjective intention, and is ultimately arbitrary. The meaning of the latter is objective, not only in the Marxist sense, as an expression of sociohistorical truth, but also, simultaneously, in the mystico-theological sense, as "a reflection of the true transcendence,"[166] to use Scholem's phrase. Benjamin's "dialectical images" resemble what Scholem describes as "theological symbols," in which even the most "insignificant" phenomena are "understood and explained in reference to redemption."[167] In the *Passagen-Werk*, these phenomena are the decaying objects of the nineteenth century, the mortified new nature that comes back to life with a brand new meaning as the mystical "*corpus symbolicum*." The code that unlocks their ideological meaning is the commodity form. But the code in which they are redeemed (and this begins to be recognized by social dreamers when the objects first appear in the nineteenth century) is the ur-old, theological myth of worldly utopia as the origin and goal of history.

In the Theses on History, Benjamin observes: "The Great Revolution introduced a new calendar."[168] He is referring to the act of the French Revolutionary Convention declaring 1792 the year 1 of a new world era, a gesture of the universal human significance of this particular historical event. Now, with the establishment of a new political discourse of human rights and democratic rule (and no matter how long the bourgeoisie pretends otherwise), class domination as the structure of society loses political legitimacy; with the advent of the industrial revolution, which has real potential to achieve universal material well-being, class domination loses economic legitimacy as well.[169] Once the Messianic promise is not a myth but historically "actual," in the sense that it is realizable, from this point on, time can be said to exist in two registers: as secular history, the sequence of (catastrophic) events that mark human time without fulfilling it; and as revolutionary "now-time," every moment of which is irradiated with the real anticipation of redemption—just as, "[f]or the Jews [. . .] every second was the narrow portal through which the Messiah was able to enter."[170]

These time registers do not follow one another sequentially in the new era; they overlap (display G), the one given, the other, continuously, a rational possibility. They remain disconnected until the act of political revolution cuts across history's secular con-

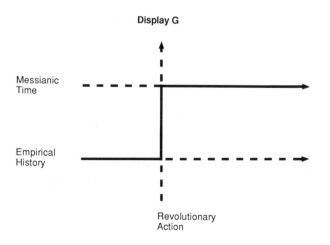

Display G

Messianic
Time

Empirical
History

Revolutionary
Action

tinuum and blasts humanity out of it, a "leap under the open skies
of history [. . .] which is how Marx conceived the revolution."[171]
In describing how the idea of progress is rejected by "the religious
view of history," Benjamin cites Lotze: "'[. . .] we would presume
too much to try to discover progress in history longitudinally, but
rather [. . .] in an upward direction at every single one of its
points.'"[172] His own conception of dialectical materialism has more
affinities to this view than to any notion—religious or secular—of
history as a teleological progression.

Political action is the link between the two registers of historical
time. This link is possible because the history of the individual re-
capitulates that of the cosmos. The metaphysical truth of history's
origin and goal—the loss of immediate presence and the socially
mediated task of its restoration—is verified by personal experience.
It is the unfulfilled potential for happiness of our own recollected
past that gives us insight into the Messianic drama of the cosmos.

Happiness is only conceivable to us in terms of the air which we have
breathed, among those people who have lived with us. In other words, the
idea of happiness—and here is what the remarkable fact [of our lack of
envy of the future] teaches us—resonates with the idea of redemption.
This happiness is founded precisely upon the despair and forsakenness
which were ours. In other words, our life is a muscle that has enough
strength to contract the whole of historical time. Or in still other words,
the authentic conception of historical time rests wholly and totally on the
image of redemption.[173]

Is unfulfilled utopian potential a psychological category (a wish of
the collective unconscious) or a metaphysical one (the very essence
of the objective world)? Perhaps Benjamin (who never thought of
metaphysics as a form of domination) means both. Contemporary
psychoanalytic theory might argue that the desire for immediate
presence can never be fulfilled. Perhaps Benjamin would respond
that it makes no difference. The point is, rather, that this utopian
desire can and must be trusted as the motivation of political action
(even as this action unavoidably mediates the desire)—can, because every experience of happiness or despair that was ours
teaches us that the present course of events does not exhaust reality's potential; and must, because revolution is understood as a
Messianic break from history's course and not its culmination. The
Messianic Age as "actual," that is, as potentially present, is the

temporal dimension that charges images in the collective unconscious with explosive power in the political sense. Plotting the
events of empirical history in relation to this time register provides
the third axis in the coordinate structure of dialectical images—the
crucial axis for both the political *and* the philosophical power of the
project.

8

If we are reading into Benjamin's texts at this point, it is according
to his instructions. *Konvolut* N states clearly: "The authentic concept of universal history is a Messianic one."[174] In "now-time,"

truth is laden with time to the point of explosion. The death of intention is
nothing else but this explosion, which thus coincides with the birth of
historical time, the time of truth.[175]

Recollected under the category of redemption, the empirically
finished suffering of history is unfinished:

This is theology; but in recollection we have an experience that forbids us
to conceive of history as fundamentally atheological, just as we are not
allowed to try to write it in immediately theological concepts.[176]

Why are "immediately theological concepts" forbidden? Benjamin
cannot mean here that it is because they violate the (Communist)
Party line. Rather, such concepts would distort theological truth by
dragging the new back into the discourse of the old; whereas the
true Messianic task is to resurrect the old within the discourse of
the new.

Were Benjamin to use theological concepts openly, he would be
giving Judaic expression to the goals of universal history; by
eschewing them, he gives universal-historical expression to the
goals of Judaism. The difference is crucial. Judaism proves its
chosen status by disappearing into secular, nonnationalist politics.
Disappearance is, paradoxically, the price paid for the survival of
any particularistic religion in the Messianic Age. Such a dialectical
"rescue" is antithetical to the eternal return of the same.

The allegoricist juxtaposes moral captions to images of a mortified nature. Benjamin's radical, "negative theology" (as Adorno
called it) replaces the lost natural aura of the object with a metaphy-

245

sical one that makes nature *as* mortified glow with political meaning. Unlike natural aura, the illumination that dialectical images provide is a mediated experience, ignited within the force field of antithetical time registers, empirical history and Messianic history. The airplane, miraculous object of the new nature, has no theological meaning in itself. That would be phantasmagoria (—one thinks of the image of Hitler's plane flying divinely though the clouds in Riefenstahl's film "Triumph of the Will"). The airplane's theological meaning in Benjamin's sense emerges only in its "construction" as a historical object. When the originary, ur-image of the airplane is brought together with its historically present form, the double focus illuminates both industrial nature's utopian potential and, simultaneously, the betrayal of that potential:

"Bomber planes make us remember what Leonardo Da Vinci expected of the flight of man; he was to have raised himself into the air 'In order to look for snow on the mountain summits, and then return to scatter it over city streets shimmering with the heat of summer.'"[177]

Today's bomb-dropping airplanes are the dialectical antitheses of Da Vinci's utopian anticipation. When the philosophical gaze scrutinizes the juxtaposition of these images, utopian and real, it is compelled not only to recognize technical nature's original state of innocence, but to study empirical history for the reasons why technology nonetheless came to terrorize humanity. Such knowledge leads to total, nihilistic mistrust in *this* history's progress, but it can transform the rage of a humanity betrayed into energy for political mobilization in order to break free of it.[178] Thus theological illumination that redeems past history, and political education that condemns it, are one and the same endeavor.

9

No point in Benjamin's philosophy has been more vehemently contested than his attempt to fuse theological and Marxist exegesis in the name of historical materialism. So vociferous a chorus of criticism needs to be confronted directly. We have already discussed Scholem's total skepticism regarding what we have called Benjamin's apostatic conversion to Marxism. Brecht, as a Marxist, was no less appalled:

benjamin is here [. . .]. he says: when you feel a gaze directed to you, even behind your back, you return it (!). the expectation that what you look at looks back at you provides the aura. [. . .] it is all mysticism, in a posture opposed to mysticism. it is in such a form that the materialistic concept of history is adopted! it is rather ghastly.[179]

It was Adorno to whom Benjamin communicated most accurately what he hoped the Arcades project would accomplish.[180] And it was Adorno who, at least at first, was most appreciative of precisely the "theological" pole of Benjamin's dialectical materialism, adopting it as his own.[181] In their correspondence, Adorno referred to the "negative" or "inverse theology" which they shared; and in response to Benjamin's essay on Kafka (1934), which made a distinction between cosmic epochs (*Weltalter*) and epochs of empirical history (*Zeitalter*), he noted that since "we recognize neither decadence nor progress in the overt sense," the concept of *Zeitalter* "[. . .] is for us truly nonexistent [. . .] but instead only the cosmic epoch, as an extrapolation out of the petrified present. And I know that no one would sooner grant me this theoretical point than you."[182] But the *Passagen-Werk* exposé completed just one year later dampened Adorno's enthusiasm considerably. He disapproved of Benjamin's strategy of trying to avoid theological terms by translating their contents into psychological categories that referred to the collective unconscious.[183] The philosophical problem which concerned Adorno increasingly was that between "myth" (the phantasmagoria of empirical history), and "reconciliation" (history's Messianic goal) "the subject evaporates."[184] Of course Benjamin clearly did affirm human subjects as autonomous agents in the sense that their political action was indispensable as the link between *Zeitalter* and *Weltalter*; it was their revolutionary praxis that would usher in the Messianic epoch. But for Adorno that was not enough. As he wrote in retrospect, Benjamin "reduces this autonomy to a moment of transition in a dialectical process, as with the tragic hero, and the reconciliation of man with the creation has as its condition the dissolution of all self-posited human existence."[185]

Theology, after all, was as much a category of empirical history as a category in opposition to that history, and the Enlightenment thinkers, including Marx, had not fought against it without good cause. Ultimately, Adorno turned to art, human creation, rather than nature, God's creation, in order to ground the transcendent element in his philosophy. He paid a price. His own theory can be subsumed within empirical history's cultural continuum. Revolving predictably around the binaries of Romanticism (art) and Enlightenment (critical reason), Adorno's philosophy can be read as an integral part of the bourgeois intellectual tradition—that *Zeitalter* which in 1934 Adorno had been so ready to dismiss. Benjamin was totally unwilling to give up the register of cosmic time as an axis for plotting both philosophy and political practice.

Of all the attempts to grapple with the "theological" in Benjamin's conception of historical materialism,[186] Rolf Tiedemann's 1975 essay on the Theses on History is the most scrupulous, philologically and intellectually.[187] With access as Benjamin's editor to the still unpublished manuscript of the Arcades project (and drawing specifically from entries in *Konvolut* N), Tiedemann argues convincingly[188] in regard to the Theses on History that when theological or mystical concepts appear there, they have "a materialist intent"[189]; there is "no thought here of a Messiah in the religious sense,"[190] as is clear from Benjamin's note for the Theses on History: "'In the concept of the classless society, Marx secularized the concept of the Messianic Age. And that was as it should be.'"[191] But Tiedemann knows that this is only half the issue:

[. . . A]n interpretation of the theses would stop halfway if it did not ask *why* Benjamin proceeds in this manner: at certain points he translates back into the language of theology that which Marx "had secularized"— which Benjamin thought was "as it should be."[192]

Tiedemann can find no *philosophical* reason for Benjamin's reverse translation. He searches instead for extrinsic causes, and finds them in the political situation, most urgently, "the [1939] alliance between Stalin and Hitler."[193] But if this explains for Tiedemann, Benjamin's retreat into theological language, it does not, in his view, justify it. Benjamin's effort to connect revolutionary destruction and the idea of redemption was ultimately "an attempt to unite the irreconcilable."[194] In it, Tiedemann sees a resurgence of Benjamin's early anarchism:

Benjamin's idea of political *praxis* in the 1940 theses has more of the enthusiasm of the anarchists than the sobriety of Marxism. It becomes a cloudy mixture of aspects of utopian socialism and of Blanquism, producing a political Messianism which can neither take Messianism really seriously nor be seriously transposed into politics.[195]

In an influential essay written in 1972 (before the *Passagen-Werk* was available), Jürgen Habermas finds Benjamin's philosophical position in the Theses similarly untenable, if for somewhat different reasons. Habermas argues that Benjamin's Messianic conception of history as a radical break from the past is incompatible with Marx's theory of history, because in the latter, precisely the development of empirical history creates the dynamic tension out of which socialism is born. One cannot, he protests, slip "an anti-evolutionary conception of history" over Marxism "like a monk's cowl": "This attempt must fail, because the anarchistic conception of 'now-times' that intermittently break through fate from above, as it were, cannot simply be inserted into the materialistic theory of social development."[196] Habermas understands the "redemptive" pole of Benjamin's method as an attempt to salvage the "semantic potential from which human beings draw in order to invest the experiential world with meaning."[197] He says that Benjamin believed if the "semantic energies of myth" were to be lost to humanity, "the poetic capacity to interpret the world in the light of human needs would thereby be denied."[198] Regardless of its merits, he continues, this is a "conservative-revolutionary understanding of critique"[199] because it has "no immanent relationship to political praxis."[200] It is antithetical to the Marxian method of *Ideologiekritik*, the critical attitude of which, according to Habermas, Benjamin fell behind.[201] In his recent book, Richard Wolin agrees that Benjamin's conservative, indeed, nostalgic[202] attitude toward tradition cannot be unambiguously reconciled with Marxist politics. He is, however, more sanguine than Habermas in judging Benjamin's "relevance for historical materialism"; it lies "precisely in the reverential attitude he assumed toward tradition,"[203] because this attitude provides "a decisive corrective to Marxism's customary devaluation" of culture as a superstructural phenomenon,[204] even if the attempt to combine this reverence with historical materialism resulted in philosophical ambivalence.[205]

Thus, despite differences among those who have taken Benjamin seriously as a philosopher, the overriding opinion is that his attempt to fuse "theology" and historical materialism failed, and perhaps was bound to. But if we are correct in understanding how, for Benjamin, theology functions as an axis of philosophical experience, and how this differs from the function of "religion" as part of the ideological superstructure, it would appear that this conclusion is not inevitable.

10

The hermeneutic method of the Kabbalah as Benjamin understood it was antihistoricist, unconcerned with showing things "'as they actually were.'"[206] It satisfied Benjamin's mandate that in the rescue of tradition, "historical objects are to be ripped out of context"[207] with "a firm, apparently brutal grasp."[208] In the spirit of the Kabbalah, Benjamin's redemption of the "semantic potential" of the past is in no way an act of nostalgia.[209] He believed that the elements of archaic myth have no true meaning in themselves, but only as "actual," as keys for deciphering what is absolutely new about modernity, that is, its real potential for a classless society. Archaic images are no longer mythic, but "genuinely historical,"[210] when they refer to real historical possibilities, and become capable thereby of charging even the most commonplace, secular phenomena with political significance. This is political vision. Simultaneously, on another interpretive axis, Marxism provides Benjamin with a method for analyzing the course of modernity's empirical history: Commodity production reifies the mythic elements, creating within the superstructure a cultural phantasmagoria which, for all its material reality, ensures that the utopian promise of myth remains *un*realized. This is political demystification.

Without theology (the axis of transcendence) Marxism falls into positivism; without Marxism (the axis of empirical history) theology falls into magic. Dialectical images indeed emerge at the "crossroads between magic and positivism," but at this nullpoint, both "roads" are negated—and at the same time dialectically overcome.

The problem, as Benjamin himself recognized, was in the construction: If the substance of dialectical images was to be found in everyday objects and profane texts, how were these to be contextualized in such a way that their theological (i.e., philosophico-political) meaning would be recognized? Explicitly theological formulations appear in the early notes of the *Passsagen-Werk*, including the passage on the gambler that refers to the "hellish" repetition of time, the "sin" of submitting to fate, and "the Name" as fate's greatest opponent. This passage impressed Adorno as "genial" in the project's "glorious first draft."[211] But by the time of the 1935 exposé, such discourse disappears. As *Konvolut* N makes clear,[212] theology never ceased to animate the work; but it was to become invisible. We have argued that Benjamin adopted this strategy lest his mode of expression draw the meaning of the "new nature" back into religious particularism, rather than this nature's pulling theology out of the ideological superstructure and into the realm of secular politics.

For all their affinity with Creuzer's description of theological symbols, dialectical images are described by Benjamin in modern metaphors: The "lightning flash" of cognition they provide is like illumination from a camera flashbulb; the images themselves— "dialectics at a standstill"[213]—are like camera shots, that "develop" in time as in a darkroom:

"The past has left images of itself in literary texts that are comparable to those which light imprints on a photosensitive plate. Only the future possesses developers active enough to bring these plates out perfectly."[214]

These images are to be juxtaposed like film[215]:

Regarding the modern-day rhythm which determines this work: Very characteristic in movies is the counterplay between the totally sporadic image sequence that gratifies the very deep need of this generation to see the "flow" of "development" disavowed, and the accompanying music. So, too, the tendency in this work is to banish "development" from the image of history down to the last detail, and to represent Becoming in sensation and in tradition though dialectical dismemberment, as a constellation of Being.[216]

The "shock" of recognition with which the juxtapositions of past and present are perceived is like electricity. (Note that the shock-like, fragmentary form of unconscious perception in the modern era is not compared regretfully to an organic-traditional totality, but mimicked, replicated at the level of conscious perception.) Benjamin compares his own activity in "constructing" dialectical images to that of an engineer,[217] who "blasts" things in the process of building them. He records that in a 1935 conversation with Ernst Bloch about the Arcades project: "I set forth how this project—as in the method of smashing an atom—releases the enormous energy of history that lies bound in the "once upon a time" of classical historical narrative."[218]

Cognitive explosiveness in a political sense occurs, not when the present is bombarded with "anarchistically intermittent," utopian "now-times" (Habermas), but when the present *as* now-time is bombarded with empirical, profane fragments of the recent past.[219] Moreover, the *Passagen-Werk* does not ignore history's empirical "developments." These are important for critical knowledge, even if they are not themselves, immediately, truth. A pronounced thematic goal of the entries in *Konvolut* N is to trace the history of the idea of progress from its original Enlightenment meaning as a *critical standard* against which history's actual course was judged and found wanting.[220] Benjamin notes: "The defamation of the critical spirit begins immediately after the victory of the bourgeoisie in the July [1830] Revolution."[221] Thenceforth, bourgeois thinkers who still had reservations were "placed on the defensive."[222] One alternative was to affirm progress only in the limited sense of science, not society:

With Turgot [1844] the concept of progress still had a critical function. He made it possible to turn people's attention above all to the retrogressive movements in history. Significantly enough, Turgot saw progress as guaranteed first and foremost in the realm of mathematical research.[223]

Another alternative was to judge historical progress against the critical *theological* standard of redemption. Benjamin cites the metaphysician Hermann Lotze (1864), who refused to equate the evolution of science or human society with truth:

"Even when inspired by noble sentiments, it is nonetheless a thoughtless and rash enthusiasm that dismisses the claims of individual eras or individual men, ignoring all their misfortune, so long as mankind in general progresses...Nothing can be...progress that would not entail an increase of happiness and perfection in the same souls who before suffered an imperfect lot."[224]

Benjamin's "Ur-history of the 19th Century" is an attempt to construct inner-historical images that juxtapose the original, utopian potential of the modern (in which archaic, mythic elements have found *non*mythical, historical content) and its catastrophic and barbaric present reality. It relies on the shock of these juxtaposed images to compel revolutionary awakening. Hence: "I have nothing to say, only to show."[225] And yet when Benjamin attempted, as in the first Baudelaire essay, to let the montage of historical facts speak for themselves, he ran the risk that readers could absorb these shocks in the same distracted manner, the same trancelike dream consciousness in which they absorbed sensations when walking on the crowded city streets or moving through aisles of department store merchandise. The danger was that the lay reader of the *Passagen-Werk* would miss the point, that it would be accessible only to initiates.

The Theses on History were not meant for publication as a separate essay, lest they "leave the door wide open for enthusiastic misunderstandings."[226] But they have a didactic intent, providing in fact the initiation through which the *Passagen-Werk* reader must pass. The first thesis is an allegorical image. It tells us that hidden within the chess-playing puppet of historical materialism, the "dwarf" of theology (a "master chess player") is pulling the strings. Theology "today, as everyone knows, is small and ugly and anyway, does not allow itself to be seen."[227] But the theses that follow then promptly proceed to drag out the dwarf and expose its attributes, lest we fail to recall that anything was hiding there at all. To remember that theology animates historical materialism, but to keep this knowledge invisible because to call it by name would cause its truth to vanish—this is Benjamin's last warning. Let us respect it and, again, put the dwarf of theology out of sight.

Dream World of Mass Culture

1

The visible theoretical armature of the *Passagen-Werk* is a secular, sociopsychological theory of modernity as a dreamworld, and a conception of collective "awakening" from it as synonymous with revolutionary class consciousness. We have already frequently encountered these formulations. In his commentary in the *Passagen-Werk*, Benjamin went quite far in developing these ideas as he struggled to provide for himself a theoretical base that would support, nontheologically, the project's increasingly elaborate construction. His attempt was not entirely successful. The theory merges elements of Surrealism and Proust, Marx and Freud, with those of historical generations and childhood cognition in a blend that is bound together more by literary than logical means. Yet the quality of historical experience that Benjamin was trying to capture in this theoretical montage *is* conveyed, and it is vital to his project. Moreover (and this justifies, despite some repetition, treating it here systematically), the theory is unique in its approach to modern society, because it takes mass culture seriously not merely as the source of the phantasmagoria of false consciousness, but as the source of collective energy to overcome it.

Based on the writings of Max Weber,[1] it has become a shibboleth in social theory that the essence of modernity is the demythification and disenchantment of the social world. In contrast, and in keeping with the Surrealist vision, Benjamin's central argument in the *Passagen-Werk* was that under conditions of capitalism, industrialization had brought about a *re*enchantment of the social world

8.1 Giovanni Battista Piranesi, Antichità romane II, eighteenth century.

(figures 8.1[2] and 8.2), and through it, a "reactivation of mythic powers."[3] Weber's thesis was based on the triumph of abstract, formal reason in the eighteenth and nineteenth centuries as the organizing principle of structures of production, markets, state bureaucracies, and cultural forms such as music and law. Benjamin would not have challenged these observations. But if social and cultural institutions had become rationalized in form, this process allowed content to be delivered up to very different forces.[4] Underneath the surface of increasing systemic rationalization, on an unconscious "dream" level, the new urban-industrial world had become fully reenchanted. In the modern city, as in the ur-forests of another era, the "threatening and alluring face"[5] of myth was alive and everywhere. It peered out of wall posters advertising "toothpaste for giants,"[6] and whispered its presence in the most rationalized urban plans that, "with their uniform streets and endless rows of buildings, have realized the dreamed- of architecture of the ancients: the labyrinth."[7] It appeared, prototypically, in the arcades, where "the commodities are suspended and shoved together in such boundless confusion, that [they appear] like images out of the most incoherent dreams."[8]

8.2 Building signs, Germany, twentieth century.

In the early nineteenth century, German Romantics, in protest against Enlightenment rationality, had called for a rebirth of mythology, and what Schelling termed a new, "universal symbolism," based on the "things of nature," which "both signify and are."[9] By the twentieth century, Benjamin was saying, the "new nature" of industrial culture had generated all the mythic power for a "universal symbolism" that these Romantics might have desired. But Romanticism had falsely assumed that art would be the source of a regeneration of mythology, rather than the creativity of industrialism, which was largely anonymous, and increasingly tied to technical skills. Whereas, for example, Wagner in the late Romantic era had envisioned individual artistic genius as fabricating a totalizing mythic world through art,[10] the producers of the modern "collective" imagination were, as the *Passagen-Werk* exposé emphasizes, photographers, graphic artists, industrial designers, and engineers—and those artists and architects who learned from them.

"Mythic forces" are present in abundance in the new industrial technology—indeed, "the gods are partial" to the transitional space of awakening in which we now live."[11] Benjamin is heir enough to the Romantic tradition to find the pervasive presence of the gods an auspicious sign. It augurs social change. Such powers can be affirmed if they are held free of the reifying constraints of mythological systematization. To speak of "gods" is to represent in human language the awesome, not-yet-known powers of technology. But mythic symbols are necessarily as transitory as the changing historical moment in which they are generated. Hence: "This pervading of space by the gods is to be understood as a lightning flash":

Neoclassicism's fundamental lack is that it builds for the gods just passing through an architecture that disavows the essential terms of their establishing contact. (A bad, reactionary architecture.)[12]

Not the presence of the gods is to be deplored, not their return to walk the earth, but the attempt to build them a permanent home.

The Romantics wanted to root their "new mythology" in preindustrial, traditional culture. Benjamin rejected totally the social conservatism that by his own era *völkisch* theories had assumed.[13] The Surrealists also spoke of a new mythology[14]—and got the matter straight. Rather than looking to folk culture for inspiration or, as with neoclassicism, tacking the symbols of ancient myths onto present forms, they viewed the constantly changing new nature of the urban-industrial landscape as itself marvelous and mythic. Their muses, as transitory as spring fashions, were stars of the stage and screen, billboard advertisements, and illustrated magazines. Benjamin names the "muses of Surrealism": "Luna, Cleo de Merode, Kate Greenaway, Mors, Friederike Kempner, Baby Cadum, Hedda Gabler, Libido, Angelika Kauffmann, the Countess Geschwitz."[15] In Louis Aragon's *Le paysan de Paris*, to which Benjamin still referred in 1934 as "the best book about Paris,"[16] the narrator, the "peasant" of Paris, wanders, intoxicated, in the company of these muses through the new, natural landscape of commodity fetishes, as his agrarian counterpart of a different era might have wandered through an enchanted forest. The Eiffel Tower appears to him as a giraffe; Sacre Coeur is an icthyosaurus.[17] Gas tanks rise up at filling stations, shimmering with the aura of divinities:

They are the great red gods, the great yellow gods, the great green gods [. . .]. Hardly ever have human beings submitted themselves to so barbarous a view of destiny and force. Anonymous sculptors [. . .] have constructed these metallic phantoms [. . .]. These idols bear a family resemblance, which renders them awesome. Decorated with English words and other words newly created, with one long and supple arm, a luminous, featureless head, a single foot, and a belly stamped with numbers—at times these gasoline dispensers have the allure of Egyptian gods, or those of cannibal tribes who worship nothing but war. O Texaco motor oil, Esso, Shell! Noble inscriptions of human potential! Soon we will cross ourselves before your founts, and the youngest among us will perish for having viewed their nymphs in the naphtha.[18]

Debunking irreverence toward traditional cultural values was fundamental to Surrrealist humor. Daumier and Grandville were precursors of this critical method, which has become characteristic of modern sensitivity generally. Whether the most up-to-date banalities of daily life are infused with the aura of the ancients (figure 8.3) or whether the ancients are themselves brought up-to-date (figures 8.4 and 8.5), the result is to bring myth, concrete nature, and history together in such a way that myth's claim to express transcendent, eternal truth is undermined—as is the logic that leads from this claim to conservative or reactionary politics. Benjamin notes: "Humankind is to depart reconciled from its past—and *one* form of being reconciled is gaiety."[19] He then cites Marx:

"History is radical, and passes through many phases when it carries an old form to the grave. The last phase of a world historical form is as comedy [*Komödie*]. The gods of Greece who had already been tragically wounded in Aeschylus' Prometheus Bound, had to die again comically in the dialogues of Lucien. Why this course of history? So that humanity parts from its past gaily."[20]

Benjamin comments: "Surrealism is the death of the last century through farce."[21]

But there is more to Surrealism's new mythology than the shock of humor. If the modernist sentiment trivializes that which is conventionally honored, the reverse is true as well: The trivial becomes the object of reverence. For Aragon's peasant, the miraculous

8.3 Modernity itself as ancient: Nils Ole Lund, "Classicism," 1984.

8 Dream World of Mass Culture

8.4 and 8.5 Bringing the ancients up to date: Herbert Bayer, 1930.

emanates from the most mundane phenomena: a furrier shop, a high hat, an electroscope with gold leaves, a hairdresser's display.[22] Far from escaping into old forms, Surrealist perception apprehends directly the "metaphysical" essence[23] of the new forms, which is not above history but within it:

> I began to realize that the reign [of these new objects] was predicated on their novelty, and that upon their future shone a mortal star. They revealed themselves to me, then, as transitory tyrants, as the agents of fate in some way attached to my sensibility. It dawned on me finally that I possessed the intoxication of the modern.[24]

What distinguishes the gods of this modern mythology is their susceptibility to time. They belong to the profane, noneternal world of human history, in which their powers are fleeting. In short, these gods can die. Indeed, transitoriness is the very basis of their power, as Aragon recognized:

> It became clear to me that humankind is full of gods, like a sponge immersed in the open sky. These gods live, attain the apogee of their power, then die, leaving to other gods their perfumed altars. They are the very

principles of any total transformation. They are the necessity of move-ment. I was, then, strolling with intoxication among thousands of divine concretions. I began to conceive a mythology in motion. It rightly merited the name of modern mythology. I imagined it by this name.[25]

If Aragon sees the modern world as mythic, he does not order this vision into a mythological system that would explain (and hence legitimate) the given.[26] Rather, Aragon is recording a fact that the theory of instrumental rationality represses: Modern reality in this still-primitive stage of industrialism *is* mythic,[27] and to bring this to consciousness in no way eliminates the possibility of a critique, for which, indeed, it is the prerequisite. Aragon himself suggests such a critique. He acknowledges that the new gas tank gods came into being because humans "delegated" their "activity to machines," transferring to them the "faculty of thought": "They do think, these machines. In the evolution of this thinking they have surpas-sed their anticipated use."[28] They work with such speed that they "alienate" people from "their own slow selves," engendering in them a "panicky terror" of mechanical fate: "There is a modern form of tragedy: It is a kind of great steering mechanism that turns, but no hand is at the wheel."[29]

2

Benjamin's enthusiastic response to Aragon did not prevent him from recognizing, from the start, the dangers of Surrealism as a model for his own work. Surrealists intentionally put themselves in a dream state of mind in order to record the images of what modern reality had become. They revelled in this dream experience, which, for all their public display of it, belonged to an individual, private world, wherein action had anarchistic political implications. Ben-jamin's insistence that the dream was "a collective phenomenon"[30] contrasted significantly with their conception. This "dreaming collective"[31] was, admittedly, "unconscious" in a double sense, on the one hand, because of its distracted dreaming state, and on the other, because it was unconscious of itself, composed of atomized individuals, consumers who imagined their commodity dream-world to be uniquely personal (despite all objective evidence to the contrary), and who experienced their membership in the collectiv-ity only in an isolated, alienating sense, as an anonymous compo-nent of the crowd.[32]

Here was a fundamental contradiction of capitalist-industrial culture. A mode of production that privileged private life and based its conception of the subject on the isolated individual had created brand new forms of social existence—urban spaces, architectural forms, mass-produced commodities, and infinitely reproduced "individual" experiences—that engendered identities and conformities in people's lives, but not social solidarity, no new level of collective consciousness of their commonality and thus no way of waking up from the dream in which they were enveloped.[33] Aragon unwittingly expressed this contradiction when he represented the new mythic experiences as individual even when they were sparked by common objects; his writing reflected the illusory experience of mass existence rather than transcending it.[34] Benjamin's goal was not to represent the dream, but to dispel it: Dialectical images were to draw dream images into an awakened state, and awakening was synonymous with historical knowledge:

In the dialectical image, the past of a particular epoch [...] appears before the eyes of [. . . a particular, present epoch] in which humanity, rubbing its eyes, recognizes precisely this dream *as* a dream. It is in this moment that the historian takes upon himself the task of dream interpretation.[35]

Surrealists became "stuck in the realm of dreams."[36] Benjamin's intent, "in opposition to Aragon," was "not to let oneself be lulled sleepily within the 'dream' or 'mythology,'" but "to penetrate all this by the dialectic of awakening."[37] Such awakening began where the Surrealists and other avant-garde artists too often stopped short, because in rejecting cultural tradition they closed their eyes to history as well. Against the "mythology" of Aragon, the *Passagen-Werk* "is concerned with dissolving mythology into the space of history."[38]

It was crucial for Benjamin's conception that this "space of history" referred not only to the previous century, but to the ontogenetic, "natural" history of childhood—specifically, the childhood of his own generation, born at the century's close.

What are the noises of the waking morning that we draw into our dreams? The "ugliness" [of nineteenth-century kitsch], the "out-of-date" [phenomena of that world], are only dissembled morning voices which speak from our childhood.[39]

Benjamin's theory of the dreaming collective as the source of present revolutionary energy requires an understanding of the significance of childhood generally for his theory of cognition, a detour that will return us to Surrealism with a clearer awareness of what Benjamin saw as this intellectual movement's political potential.

3

[The *Passagen-Werk*] has to do with [. . .] achieving the most extreme concreteness for an epoch, as appears now and again in children's games, in a building, a life situation.[40]

Game in which children construct out of given words a very short sentence. This game appears to have been made to order for goods on display. Binoculars and flower seeds, wood screws and banknotes, makeup and stuffed otters, furs and revolvers.[41]

Children, wrote Benjamin, are less intrigued by the preformed world that adults have created than by its waste products. They are drawn to the apparently valueless, intentionless things: "In using these things they do not so much imitate the works of adults as bring together, in the artifacts produced in play, materials of widely differing kinds in a new intuitive relationship."[42] Benjamin's cognitive approach to the discarded, overlooked phenomena of the nineteenth century was not different. No modern thinker, with the exception of Jean Piaget, took children as seriously as did Benjamin in developing a theory of cognition. Nineteenth-century children's books were one of the most valued parts of his one passionately held possession: his book collection.[43] He confessed that there were not many things "in the realm of the book to which I have a similarly close relationship."[44] Scholem attested to the significance of children for Benjamin and pointed out that he took seriously the cognitive process of remembering his own childhood.

It is one of Benjamin's most important characteristics that throughout his life he was attracted with almost magical force by the child's world and ways. This world was one of the persistent and recurring themes of his reflections, and indeed, his writings on this subject are among his most perfect pieces.[45]

Benjamin found children's play with words "more akin to the language of sacred texts than to the colloquial language of grownups."[46] He used to say of the notoriously difficult philosophical introduction to his *Trauerspiel* study that it had as the "secret motto" for entry into the text, the nursery rhyme injunction: "Hurtle over root and stone, [be]ware the boulder, break no bone."[47] Imagery of the child's world appears so persistently throughout Benjamin's opus that the omission of a serious discussion of its theoretical significance in practically all commentaries on Benjamin is remarkable—a symptom, perhaps, of precisely the repression of childhood and its cognitive modes which he considered a problem of the utmost political significance.

Piaget and Benjamin agreed that children's cognition was a developmental stage so completely overcome that to the adult it appeared almost inexplicable. Piaget was content enough to see childhood thinking disappear. The values in his epistemology were tipped toward the adult end of the spectrum. His thinking reflected, on the axis of ontogenetic development, that assumption of history-as-progress which Benjamin considered the trademark of bourgeois false consciousness. Predictably, Benjamin's own interest was not in the sequential development of stages of abstract, formal reason, but in what was lost along the way. Scholem wrote that he was fascinated by "[. . .] the as yet undistorted world of the child and its creative imagination, which [as metaphysician] he describes with reverent wonder and at the same time seeks conceptually to penetrate."[48]

What Benjamin found in the child's consciousness, badgered out of existence by bourgeois education and so crucial to redeem (albeit in new form), was precisely the unsevered connection between perception and action that distinguished revolutionary consciousness in adults. This connection was not causal in the behaviorist sense of a stimulus-response reaction. Instead it was an active, creative form of mimesis, involving the ability to make correspondences by means of spontaneous fantasy.

[The child's bureau] drawers must become arsenal and zoo, crime museum and crypt. "To tidy up" would be to demolish an edifice full of prickly chestnuts that are spiky clubs, tin foil that is hoarded silver, bricks that are coffins, cacti that are totem poles, and copper pennies that are shields.[49]

The revolutionary "signal" that proceeds "out of the world in which the child lives and gives commands"[50] is the capacity for inventive reception based on mimetic improvisation. Perception and active transformation are the two poles of children's cognition: "Every child's gesture is a creative impulse which corresponds exactly to the receptive one."[51]

Piaget's experiments tested for the universal and predictable response, privileging precisely that abstract-formal rationality which Weber argued was the hallmark of modern reason.[52] Benjamin was interested in the creative spontaneity of response that bourgeois socialization destroyed. Piaget's theory treated cognition tied to action only as the most primitive cognitive form (—in the preverbal, sensory-motor period—), and ignored mimetic cognition once the child acquired language. In Piaget's tests, the child's fantastic play, the constitution of merely possible worlds, was likely to be registered as cognitive error. For Benjamin, in contrast, the primordial nature of motor reactions was a reason to pay attention to them. Evidence of the "mimetic faculty," they were the source of a language of gestures which Benjamin considered more basic to cognition than conceptual language.[53] Benjamin's idea of an "experiment" was to watch children's gestures in painting, dance, and particularly theater, which allowed an "untamed release of children's fantasy."[54] In children's dramatic performances:

Everything is turned upside down, and just as master served slave during the Roman Saturnalia, so during the performance, children stand on stage and teach and educate their attentive educators. New forces and new impulses appear [. . .].[55]

Children's cognition had revolutionary power because it was tactile, and hence tied to action, and because rather than accepting the given meaning of things, children got to know objects by laying hold of them and using them creatively, releasing from them new possibilities of meaning. Paul Valéry (with whose works Benjamin was very familiar) has written:

If they're fit and well, all children are absolute *monsters* of activity [. . .] tearing up, breaking up, building, they're always at it! And they'll cry if they can't think of anything better to do [. . .]. You might say they're only conscious of all the things around them insofar as they can *act* on them, or through them, in no matter what way: the action, in fact, is all [. . .].[56]

Bourgeois socialization suppressed this activity: Parroting back the "correct" answer, looking without touching, solving problems "in the head," sitting passively, learning to do without optical cues[57]— these acquired behaviors went against the child's grain. It might follow, moreover, that the triumph of such cognition in adults at the same time signaled their defeat as revolutionary subjects.[58]

But, so long as there were children, this defeat would never be complete. Thus Benjamin avoided the pessimistic conclusion to which Adorno was led when he described the "extinction of the ego" as the tragic result of history's "progress."[59] Benjamin's theory acknowledged that the relationship between consciousness and society on a historical level was interspersed with another dimension, the level of childhood development, in which the relationship between consciousness and reality had its own history. In children, the capacity for revolutionary transformation was present from the start. Hence, all children were "representatives of Paradise."[60] Stripped of its metaphysical pretensions, history was the having of children,[61] and as such, it was always a return to beginnings. Here revolutions appeared, not as the culmination of world history, but as a fresh start: "The instant one arrives," Benjamin not accidentally wrote of his visit to Moscow, "the childhood stage begins," when, because of the icy streets, even "walking has to be relearned."[62]

4

Benjamin's appreciation of childhood cognition did not imply the romanticizing of childhood innocence.[63] On the contrary, he believed that only people who were allowed to live out their childhood really grew up[64]—and growing up was clearly the desired goal (figure 8.6[65]). Benjamin was fully aware of the limitations of the consciousness of the child, who "lives in its world as a dictator."[66] Thus education was necessary, but it was a reciprocal process: "Is not education above all the indispensable ordering of the relation between generations and therefore mastery, if we are to use this term, of that relationship and not of children?"[67]

In regard specifically to the mimetic capacity, adults who observed children's behavior learned to rediscover a previously possessed mode of cognition, that had deteriorated both phylogenetically and ontogenetically. A very brief piece, "On the Mimetic

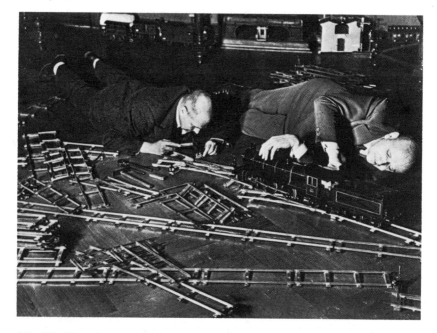

8.6 "Toy Train Society," photograph by Alfred Eisenstaedt, Berlin, 1931.

Faculty," written by Benjamin in 1933 and valued by him highly as a new, materialist formulation of his theory of language,[68] addresses this point precisely:

Nature produces similarities. One has only to think of mimicry [of, e.g., insects to leaves]. But the highest talent in producing similarities belongs to human beings. The gift of seeing similarities that they possess is merely a rudiment of the formerly powerful drive to make oneself similar, to act mimetically. Perhaps there is not one of the higher human functions that is not decisively determined, at least in part, by the mimetic capacity.

This capacity, however, has a history, and indeed in a phylogenetic as well as an ontogenetic sense. For the latter, play is in many regards the schooling. Children's play is permeated everywhere by mimetic forms of behavior; and its realm is in no way limited to what one person can mimic about another. The child not only plays shopkeeper or teacher but also windmill and railroad train.[69]

Mimetic cognitive skills have not been an anthropological constant:

One needs to consider that neither the mimetic powers, nor the mimetic objects and their themes have remained the same in the course of the centuries. Rather, we must suppose that the gift of producing similarities—for example, in dances, of which mimesis was the oldest function—and thus also the gift of recognizing them, have changed with changing history.[70]

The oldest cognitive apparatuses of "magical correspondences and analogies" were clearly based on this skill.[71] Indeed, as the practice whereby the expressive element in objects was brought to speech, human language was itself mimetic and magical in origin.[72] Benjamin speculates that astrology, the ancient science of "reading" similarities between the cosmos and the human being at the moment of birth, marked a change in the direction of mimetic powers toward "nonsensual similarities."[73] The latter were also the source of written script.[74] Benjamin suggests that what appears in the "signworld (*Merkwelt*) of modern man" to be the "decay of this capacity" of mimesis, may be, rather, a new stage in "its transformation."[75] He holds open the possibility of a future development of mimetic expression, the potentialities for which are far from exhausted. Nor are they limited to verbal language[76]—as the new technologies of camera and film clearly demonstrate. These technologies provide human beings with unprecedented perceptual acuity, out of which, Benjamin believed, a less magical, more scientific form of the mimetic faculty was developing in his own era. He noted in the Artwork essay that the camera arrests the flow of perception and captures the most subtle physical gestures. "Through it we first experience an optical unconscious, as in psychoanalysis we first experience the instinctual unconscious."[77] Film provides a new schooling for our mimetic powers: "Within the enlargement, space is stretched out; within slow motion, movement expands," revealing "entirely new structural formations of matter":

Thus it becomes clear that a different nature speaks to the camera than to the naked eye—different above all in this, that in place of space interwoven with the consciousness of human beings, one is presented with a space unconsciously interwoven.[78]

Now for the first time an analysis of this "unconsciously interwoven" space is possible. The film cameraman, like a surgeon, "operatively penetrates into" the material,[79] subjecting the actor's performance "to a series of optical tests."[80] Moreover, and of political importance, the world that opens up to the camera provides knowledge relevant to acting in it:

Through closeups of what it inventories, through accentuating the hidden details of props that for us are familiar objects, through exploration of banal milieus under the genial guide of the lens, film on the one hand increases our insight into the necessities that rule our lives, and on the other hand ensures for us an immense and unexpected field of action.[81]

It is in this way that technological *re*production gives back to humanity that capacity for experience which technological *production* threatens to take away. If industrialization has caused a crisis in perception due to the speeding up of time and the fragmentation of space, film shows a healing potential by slowing down time and, through montage, constructing "synthetic realities"[82] as new spatio-temporal orders wherein the "fragmented images" are brought together "according to a new law."[83] Both the assembly line and the urban crowd bombard the senses with disconnected images and shocklike stimulae. In a state of constant distraction, the consciousness of the collective acts like a shock absorber, registering sense impressions without really experiencing them: Shocks are "intercepted, parried by consciousness,"[84] in order to prevent a traumatic effect. Film provides the audience with a new capacity to study this modern existence reflectively, from "the position of a expert."[85] The printed word shows itself more vulnerable in contrast (figure 8.7): "Printing, having found in the book a refuge in which to lead an autonomous existence, is pitilessly dragged out onto the street by advertisements [. . . that] force the printed word entirely into the dictatorial perpendicular."[86]

Children instinctively mimic objects as a means of mastering their experiential world. Psychoanalytic theory tells us that the neurotic symptom, similarly, imitates a traumatic event in an (unsuccessful) attempt at psychic defense. Benjamin was suggesting that the new mimetic techniques could instruct the collective to employ this capacity effectively, not only as a defense against the trauma of industrialization, but as a means of reconstructing the capacity for experience that had been shattered by the process. The products of culture already showed signs of the development of this counterforce. Benjamin speculated:

8.7   London Street Advertising, early twentieth century.

Perhaps the daily sight of a moving crowd once presented the eye with a spectacle to which it first had to adapt. [. . . T]hen the assumption is not impossible that, having mastered this task, the eye welcomed opportunities to confirm its possession of its new ability. The method of impressionist painting, whereby the picture is assembled through a riot of flecks of color, would then be a reflection of experience with which the eye of a big-city dweller has become familiar.[87]

It is not surprising that Benjamin praised Charlie Chaplin's film performances on the same grounds. Chaplin rescued the capacity for experience by mimicking the fragmentation that threatened it.

What is new in Chaplin's gestures: He breaks apart human motions of expression into a series of the smallest innervations. Every single one of his movements is put together from a series of hacked-up pieces of motion. Whether one focuses on his walk, on the way [he] handles his cane, or tips his hat—it is always the same jerky sequence of the smallest motions which raises the law of the filmic sequence of images to that of human motor actions.[88]

To recreate the new reality of technology mimetically (—to bring to human speech its expressive potential—) is not to submit to its given forms, but to anticipate the human reappropriation of its power. Moreover, and this is the political point, such practice re-establishes the connection between imagination and physical innervation that in bourgeois culture has been snapped apart. Cognitive reception is no longer contemplative but tied to action. Just this refusal to separate body and mind within cognitive experience characterizes Aragon's imagistic representation in *Le paysan de Paris*. Just this insistence that action is the sister of the dream is what Benjamin found irresistibly compelling in Surrealism's political stance. Political space can "no longer be gauged by contemplation":

If it is the dual task of the revolutionary intelligentsia both to overthrow the predominance of the bourgeoisie and to gain contact with the proletarian masses, then it has fully misfired in regard to the second part of this task, because the latter is no longer to be accomplished contemplatively.[89]

Rather, the intellectual must place him- [or her-] self, "even at the cost of his [her] own creative development," in the "important points" of an "image-realm" in order to set this realm "into motion":

For it is no use; the admission is overdue: The metaphysical materialism [. . .of Marxist orthodoxy] observed by someone like Vogt or Bukharin does not transfer smoothly into anthropological materialism, as the experience of the Surrealists substantiates—and before them of Hebel, Georg Büchner, Nietzsche, or Rimbaud. There is something left over. The collective is also corporeal. And the technological nature which will organize in its behalf, because it is totally real, politically and materially, can only be produced in that image realm to which we have been acclimatized by profane illumination. Only within it, when body and image realm so interpenetrate that all revolutionary tension becomes bodily, collective innervation, and all the bodily innervations of the collective become revolutionary discharge, has reality surpassed itself to the extent demanded by the *Communist Manifesto*. For the moment, only the Surrealists have understood the commands that now emanate from that realm. All of them barter away their own facial expressions in exchange for the clockface of an alarm that in every minute rings for sixty seconds.[90]

8.8 "Tramp in Marseilles," photograph by Brassaï, 1930s.

We have said that the Arcades project was originally conceived as a "dialectical fairy scene" (*dialektische Feen*),[91] so that the *Passagen-Werk* becomes a Marxian retelling of the story of Sleeping Beauty, which was concerned with "waking up" (as the "best example of a dialectical overturning"[92]) from the collective dream of the commodity phantasmagoria (figure 8.8). We may note the key passage from *Konvolut* **K** which locates the source of the dreamworld that modern reality had become: "Capitalism was a natural phenomenon with which a new dream sleep fell over Europe and with it, a reactivation of mythic powers."[93] The arcades, as "houses without exteriors," were themselves "just like dreams."[94] Indeed: "All collective architecture of the nineteenth century provides housing for the dreaming collective"[95]: "arcades, winter gardens, panoramas, factories, wax-figure cabinets, casinos, railroad stations"[96]—as well as museums, apartment interiors, department stores, and public spas.[97] Benjamin referred to Sigfried Giedion's thesis that nineteenth-century architectural forms "'had the role of the subconscious'": "Is it not better to say that it had the role of body processes, and then place the 'arty' architecture like dreams about the scaffolding of these body processes?"[98]

Benjamin resurrects an image of the body politic, out of fashion in political discourse since the Baroque era,[99] in which the nineteenth-century dream elements register the collective's vital signs:

The XIX century: a time-space [*Zeitraum*] (a time dream [*Zeit-traum*]) in which individual consciousness maintains itself ever more reflectively, whereas in contrast the collective consciousness sinks into ever deeper sleep. But just as the sleeping person (here like someone insane) sets out on the macrocosmic journey through his body, and just as the sounds and sensations of his own insides—which to the healthy, awake person blend together in a surge of health (blood pressure, intestinal movements, heartbeat and muscle sensations)—due to his unprecedently sharpened senses generate hallucinations or dream images that translate and explain [these sensations], so it is too with the dreaming collective, which in the arcades sinks into its own innards. This is what we have to pursue, in order to interpret the nineteenth century in fashion and advertisement, building and politics, as the consequence of [the collective's] dream countenance.[100]

Benjamin notes: "The first stimulae for awakening deepen sleep."[101] He is referring to the kitsch of the end of the century that thickened the dream state. The proponents of *Jugendstil* rejected kitsch and tried to break out into "free air," but they understood this only as an ideational space, "the artificial brightness and isolation in which advertisements represented their objects": *Jugendstil* was thus only "the dream that one is awake."[102] It was Surrealism, with its "radical concept of freedom,"[103] that first sounded the rousing alarm; Benjamin's goal, within the "legacy of Surrealism,"[104] was to connect the shock of awakening with the discipline of remembering and thereby mobilize the historical objects: "We here construct an alarm clock that rouses the kitsch of the last century to 'assembly'—and this operates totally with cunning."[105]

"With cunning [*mit List*], not without it, we absolve ourselves from the realm of dreams."[106] The use of Hegel's term was intentional,[107] but Benjamin's meaning was unique. According to

Hegel, reason becomes conscious by working its way "with cunning" into history through the passions and ambitions of unwitting historical subjects. But in Benjamin's dialectical fairy tale, cunning is the capacity, through "awakening," to outwit history, which has placed a spell on the dreaming collective, and has kept its members *un*conscious.[108] Hegel's "cunning of reason" literally deifies history, affirming the myth of progress. For Benjamin, cunning is the trick whereby human subject get the better of mythic powers. "Fairy tales," Benjamin wrote in his (1934) essay on Kafka, "are the way of handing down the tradition of victory over the [forces of myth]:"[109] "Odysseus stands in fact on the threshold that separates myth and fairy tale. Reason and cunning have placed tricks within myths; their forces cease being invincible."[110]

The "trick" in Benjamin's fairy tale is to interpret out of the discarded dream images of mass culture a politically empowering knowledge of the collective's own unconscious past.[111] He believes he can do this because it is through such objects that the collective unconscious communicates across generations. New inventions, conceived out of the fantasy of one generation, are received within the childhood experience of another. Now (and this is where children's cognition becomes crucial), they enter a second dream state: "The childhood experience of a generation has much in common with dream experience."[112] We are thus presented with a double dream theory, based on the childhood of an epoch on the one hand and that of a generation on another. If capitalism has been the source of the historical dream state, the latter is of ontogenetic origins, and the two axes converge in a unique constellation for each generation. At this intersection between collective history and personal history, between society's dream and childhood dream, the contents of the collective unconscious are transmitted: "Every epoch has this side turned toward dreams—the childlike side. For the preceding century it emerges very clearly in the arcades."[113] Thus in the "arcades [. . .] we, as in a dream, once again live the life of our parents and grandparents [. . .].[114]

Childhood is not merely the passive receptacle for the historical unconscious. Even the most practical, technical inventions are transformed in accord with its own temporal index, and this entails their reversal from historically specific images into archaic ones. From the child's position the whole span of history, from the most ancient to the most recent past, occurs in mythic time. No history recounts his or her lived experience. All of the past lies in an archaic realm of ur-history. Within the phylogenetic axis, history manifests itself as progress, fashion, and newness. But it is just this that the cognitive experience of childhood reverses:

At first, granted, the technologically new gives the effect of being just that. But already in the next childhood memory it changes its characteristics. Every child accomplishes something great, something irreplaceable for humanity. Every childhood, through its interests in technological phenomena, its curiosity for all sorts of inventions and machinery, binds technological achievement [the newest things] onto the old world of symbols.[115]

The child's creative perception of the objects in fact recollects the historical moment when the new technology was first conceived— that "too-early" epoch when, onto a new nature still in the stage of myth, all kinds of archaic symbols were cathected.[116] The difference is that now the technical aspects of that nature have matured historically. Over the century, they have become "merely new," displaying only their "modern" or "dashing" side. But: "The child can in fact do something of which the adult is totally incapable: 'discover the new anew.'"[117] This discovery reinvests the objects with symbolic meaning and thus rescues for the collective memory their utopian signification.

Slumbering within the objects, the utopian wish is awakened by a new generation that "rescues" it by bringing the old "world of symbols" back to life. Here Benjamin's fairy tale may appear to come close to the theory posited by Jung of a collective unconscious containing innate, archetypal symbols. The difference is Benjamin's Marxist sensibility. When the child's fantasy is cathected onto the products of modern production, it reactivates the original promise of industrialism, now slumbering in the lap of capitalism, to deliver a humane society of material abundance. Thus, in terms of socialist, revolutionary politics, the rediscovery of these ursymbols in the most modern technological products has an absolutely contemporary relevance—and a politically explosive potential.

The biological task of awakening from childhood becomes a model for a collective, social awakening. But more: In the collective experience of a generation the two converge. The coming-to-consciousness of a generation is a politically empowering moment, historically unique, in which the new generation, in rebellion against the parental world, may awaken not only itself, but the slumbering, utopian potential of the epoch.

The fact that we have been children in this time is part of its objective image. It had to be thus in order to release from itself this generation. That means: we look in the dream-connection for a teleological moment. This moment is one of waiting. The dream waits secretly for the awakening; the sleeper gives himself over to death only until recalled; he waits for the second in which he wrests himself from capture with cunning. So it is too with the dreaming collective for whom its children become the fortunate occasion for its own awakening.[118]

A materialist history that disenchants the new nature in order to free it from the spell of capitalism, and yet rescues all the power of enchantment for the purpose of social transformation: this was to have been the goal of Benjamin's fairy tale. At the moment of the collective's historical awakening, it was to provide a politically explosive answer to the sociohistorical form of the child's question: "Where did I come from?" Where did modern existence, or, more accurately, the images of the modern dreamworld come from? Speaking of Surrealism, the aesthetic expression of that dreamworld, Benjamin wrote: "The father of Surrealism was Dada; its mother was an arcade."[119]

6

What Benjamin said and wrote sounded as if, instead of rejecting the promises of fairy tales and children's books with tasteful "maturity," thought took them so literally that actual fulfillment became itself conceivable to knowledge.[120]

In his 1936 essay, "The Storyteller," Benjamin described the fairy tale as a mode of cultural inheritance that, far from participating in the ideology of class domination,[121] keeps alive the promise of liberation by showing that nature—animals and animated forces— prefers not to be "subservient to myth," but rather, "to be aligned with human beings" against myth.[122] In this sense, merely by rescuing for historical memory Fourier's visions of society, the historian becomes a teller of fairy tales. Fourier's utopian plans, in which nature and humanity are in fact allied, challenge the myth that industrialization had to develop as it has, that is, as a mode of dominating both human beings and the natural world of which they are a part. A late entry to the *Passagen-Werk* makes this clear, and connects Fourier's theories specifically with children's play:

The distinguishing characteristic of the labor process' relationship to nature is marked by this relation's social constitution. If humans were not genuinely exploited, then one could spare oneself the *disingenuous* talk of the exploitation of nature. Such talk strengthens the illusion that raw material receives "value" only through an order of production which rests on the exploitation of human labor. If this order ceases, then human labor for its part will cast aside its characteristic exploitation of nature. Human labor will then proceed in accord with the model of children's play, which in Fourier is the basis of the *travail passionné* [passionate labor] of the *harmoniens* [dwellers in his utopian communities]. To have situated play as the canon of a form of labor that is no longer exploitative is one of the greatest merits of Fourier. Labor thus animated by play aims not at the production of value, but at an improved nature. And Fourier's utopia presents a model for it, one that can in fact be found realized in children's play. It is the image of an earth on which all places have become *Wirtschaften*. The double meaning of the word [economy/public inn] blossoms here: All places are cultivated by human beings, made useful and beautiful by them; all, however, stand like a roadside inn, open to everyone. An earth ordered according to such an image would cease to be part "*D'un monde où l'action n'est pas la soeur de rêve* [Baudelaire]." In it, activity would be the sister of the dream.[123]

Of course, it is not to children that the fairy tale of the Arcades is to be told, but to those whose childhood is itself only a dream memory. Benjamin writes:

That which the child (and the grown man in his faint memory) finds in the old folds of the dress into which he pressed himself when he held fast to the skirted lap of his mother—that must be contained by these pages.[124]

He adds to this the keyword: "Fashion." For it is precisely the ephemeral fashion of a mother's skirt that determines the physical experience of this childhood event. Even the most fundamental, ur-desire for the mother is thus mediated by historically transitory material, and it is the latter (as Proust knew[125]) that leaves its trace in memory. These memories are evidence that the "unfinished and commonplace, comforting and silly" world in which we have in fact lived is not without the momentary experience of utopia. Benjamin cites Kafka's description of Josephine, the singing mouse:

Something of our poor, brief childhood is in [her song], something of lost happiness, never to be rediscovered, but also something of our present daily life, of its small, inexplicable and yet existing, indestructible gaieties.[126]

At no time did Benjamin suggest that the child's mythic understanding was itself truth. But childhood caught the historical objects in a web of meanings so that the grown generation had, subsequently, a psychic investment in them, lending them a "higher degree of actuality" now than in the past.[127] Moreover— and this was no small part of Benjamin's "trick"—in the presence of the historical objects that populate a city, this generation not only "recognizes" its "own youth, the most recent one"; but also "an earlier childhood speaks to it," as if, through the "double floor" of the street pavement one could be dropped back in time as through a trap door, and "affected even by the knowledge of dead dates as something experienced and lived": It is thus "the same" whether the experience of recognition prompted by the objects is "of an earlier [childhood] or of one's own."[128] In either case it is as a memory trace that the discarded object possesses the potential for revolutionary motivation. Benjamin describes

[. . .] the two faces of the [Arcades] project: One, that which goes from the past into the present, and represents the arcades as precursors; and [the other], that which goes from the present into the past, in order to let the revolutionary completion of these "precursors" explode in the present, and this direction also understands the sorrowful, fascinated contemplation of the most recent past as its revolutionary explosion.[129]

7

[In the arcades] we relive, as in a dream, the life of our parents and grandparents, just as, in the mother's womb, the embryo relives animal life.[130]

"Who will live in the paternal home?"[131]

The cognitive axis of social history was necessary because it allowed one to "recognize the sea in which we are journeying and the shore from which we pushed off."[132] Moreover, the allegorical, "sorrowful" contemplation of the past underscored the transiency of mythic images. But even within the symbolic, cognitive axis of childhood, Benjamin took great pains to demonstrate that its images were mediated at every point by history. In the *Passagen-Werk* he cited Ernst Bloch's insistence that the unconscious is an "'acquired condition'" in specific human beings.[133] Exemplary were those images of his own childhood which he recorded in the early 1930s. They are less of people than of those historically specific, urban spaces of turn-of-the-century Berlin that provided the settings for his experiences.[134] They concern as well the material products of industrialism: a wrought-iron door, the telephone, a slot machine dispensing chocolates, Berlin's own arcades. The world of the modern city appears in these writings as a mythic and magical one in which the child Benjamin "discovers the new anew," and the adult Benjamin recognizes it as a rediscovery of the old.[135] The images of the unconscious are thus formed as a result of concrete, historical experiences, not (as with Jung's archetypes) biologically inherited.[136]

Benjamin observes that the dialectical interpenetration of generational and collective history is a specifically modern phenomenon: "This inexorable confrontation of the most recent past with the present is something historically new."[137] In fact, the intensification of mythic power in both dream states is itself a function of history. When capitalism's new dream sleep fell over Europe, *it* became the cause of a reactivation of mythic powers. Precisely the *city* landscape "confers on childhood memories a quality that makes them at once as evanescent and as alluringly tormenting as half-forgotten dreams."[138] In the premodern era, fashions did not change with such rapidity, and the much slower advances in technology were "covered over by the tradition of church and family"; but now: "The old prehistoric shudder already surrounds the world of our parents because we are no longer still bound to it by tradition."[139] Benjamin describes what is specific to his own historical era:

The worlds of memory replace themselves more quickly, the mythic in them surfaces more quickly and crassly, [and] a totally different world of memory must be set up even faster against them. From the perspective of today's ur-history, this is how the accelerated tempo of technology looks.[140]

In the premodern era, collective symbolic meaning was transferred consciously through the narration of tradition, which guided the new generation out of its childhood dream state. Given modernity's rupture of tradition, this is no longer possible.

Whereas [. . .] the traditional and religious upbringing of earlier generations interpreted these dreams for them, the present process of childrearing boils down simply to the distraction of children. Proust could appear as a phenomenon only in a generation that had lost all bodily, natural expediencies for remembering, and, poorer than before, was left to its own devices, and thus could only get a hold of the children's world in an isolated, scattered, and pathological fashion.[141]

Paralleling the "old-fashioned effect" of the arcades "on people of today," was the "antiquarian effect of the father on his son."[142] In a world of objects that changed its face drastically in the course of a generation, parents could no longer counsel their children, who were thus "left to their own devices." These devices remained "isolated," indeed "pathological," until they could be organized collectively. Benjamin's fairy tale was conceived in response to this need.

The rupture of tradition was irrevocable. Far from lamenting the situation,[143] Benjamin saw precisely here modernity's uniquely revolutionary potential. The traditional manner whereby the new generation was brought out of its childhood dreamworld had the effect of perpetuating the social status quo. In contrast, the rupture of tradition now frees symbolic powers from conservative restraints for the task of social transformation, that is, for a rupture of those social conditions of domination that, consistently, have been the source of tradition. Thus Benjamin insisted: "We must wake up from the world of our parents."[144]

8

The history of dreams has yet to be written [. . .].[145]

Benjamin maintained the double dream theory outlined above at least until 1935, the year he completed his exposé of the Arcades project. At this point the philological situation becomes murky. There are at least six copies of the 1935 exposé, with differences in wording significant enough to have caused the editor to include three of them in the published *Passagen-Werk*.[146] All of these versions refer to the following: dreamworld, utopian wish images, collective dream consciousness, generations,[147] and, most emphatically, the conception of dialectical thinking as historical awakening which is sparked by the residues of mass culture.[148] Noticeably absent is the image of the slumbering body politic, as well as any reference to a "dialectical fairy scene."

In a letter to Karplus (August 16, 1935), Benjamin explained that he had given up this earlier subtitle because it allowed only an "inexcusably literary" shaping of the material.[149] Did Benjamin give up his theory of the childhood dream state as well? In the same letter he spoke of the absolute distinction between the Arcades project and forms, such as *Berliner Kindheit um 1900*, that recounted childhood memories: "The ur-history of the 19th century which is reflected in the gaze of the child playing on its threshold has a much different face than that which it engraves on the map of history."[150] He added that "making this knowledge clear to me" had been "an important function of [writing the exposé]."[151] And yet, if not only the too-literary form but also the theoretical content of the original conception had been abandoned, it would be difficult to justify his simultaneous claim, against Adorno's criticism, that there had been "no word lost" from the original 1927–29 draft of the project.[152] In fact, Benjamin had not discarded the early notes and commentary dealing with the dream theory, and he never did.[153] Adorno's knowledge of these notes was limited to what Benjamin had read to him in Königstein in 1929.[154] We do not know whether their discussions there included the childhood dream state. We do know that its absence in the exposé was not what Adorno lamented when he accused Benjamin of betraying the early plan. It was the imagery of "negative theology"—the nineteenth-century commodity world as Hell—that Adorno missed, not that of childhood and fairy tales.

Ironically, had Benjamin included an elaboration of the theory of the childhood inheritance of the collective dream, he might have warded off another of Adorno's criticisms, that with the "sacrifice of theology," Benjamin had "disenchanted" the idea of dialectical images by psychologizing them to the point where the entire conception had become "de-dialectized."[155] The double dream theory was complex and its expression was perhaps indeed "inexcusably literary," but without it, the revolutionary power of "dream images" had to be situated solely within the sociohistorical axis, as if that power existed ready-made in the images of the nineteenth-century collective (un)conscious, rather than being created by the specific way the present generation inherited the "failed material" of the past. Adorno argued against the conception of a collective consciousness on Marxist grounds: "It should speak clearly and with sufficient warning that in the dreaming collective there is no room for class differences."[156]

There is no doubt that Benjamin took Adorno's criticisms of the 1935 exposé seriously.[157] There is little doubt that he attempted to stick to his position despite them.[158] The material relating to theoretical questions which he added to the *Passagen-Werk* after 1935 intensified a direction of research he had in fact already begun, to ground the basic premise of his dream theory—that the nineteenth century was the origin of a collective dream from which an "awakened" present generation could derive revolutionary signification—in the theories of Marx and Freud.[159] Strikingly (and dialectically), he found in Marx a justification for the conception of a collective dream, and in Freud an argument for the existence of class differences within it.

Of course Marx *had* spoken positively of a collective dream, and more than once. After 1935 Benjamin added to *Konvolut* N the well-known quotation from Marx's early writings:

"Our motto must... be: Reform of consciousness not by means of dogmas, but by analyzing the mystical consciousness unclear to itself, whether it appears religiously or politically. It will then become clear that the world has long possesssed in the form of a dream something of which it only has to become conscious in order to possess it in reality."[160]

And he chose as the inscription for this *Konvolut* (the major one on method) Marx's statement: "'The reform of consciousness consists *only* therein, that one wakes the world... out of its dream of itself.'"[161]

Class differentiations were never lacking in Benjamin's theory of the collective unconscious, which even in his earliest formulations he considered an extension and refinement of Marx's theory of the superstructure. The collective dream manifested the ideology of the dominant class:

The question is, namely, if the substructure to a certain extent determines the superstructure in terms of the material of thought and experience, but this determining is not simply one of copying, how is it [...] to be characterized? As its expression. The superstructure is the expression of the substructure. The economic conditions under which society exists come to expression in the superstructure, just as the over-filled stomach of someone who is sleeping, even if it may causally determine the contents of the dream, finds in those contents not its copied reflection, but its expression.[162]

It is of course the bourgeoisie, not the proletariat, whose dream expresses the uneasiness of an overly full stomach.

Benjamin claimed that Marx never intended a direct, causal relationship between substructure and superstructure: "Already the observation that the ideologies of the superstructure reflect [social] relations in a false and distorted form goes beyond this."[163] Freud's dream theory provided a ground for such distortion. Benjamin's direct references to Freudian theory remained limited and quite general.[164] But on this point, even if direct indebtedness cannot be proven,[165] there was a clear consensus. Freud had written that "ideas in dreams [. . . are] fulfillments of wishes,"[166] which, due to ambivalent feelings, appear in a censored, hence distorted form. The actual (latent) wish may be almost invisible at the manifest level, and is arrived at only after the dream's interpretation. Thus: "A dream is a (disguised) fulfillment of a (suppressed or repressed) wish."[167] If one takes the bourgeois class to be the generator of the collective dream, then the socialist tendencies of that industrialism which it itself created would seem to catch it, unavoidably, in a situation of ambivalent desire. The bourgeoisie desires to affirm that industrial production from which it is deriving profits; at the same time it wishes to deny the fact that industrialism creates the conditions that threaten the continuation of its own class rule.

Precisely this bourgeois class ambivalence is documented by a whole range of quotations that Benjamin included in the *Passagen-Werk* material at all stages of the project. Nineteenth-century utopian writings are the "depository of collective dreams,"[168] but they also come to the aid of the ruling class by fetishisticly equating technological development with social progress (Saint-Simon). Architectural constructions have "the role of the subconscious,"[169] but their facades camouflage the very newness of the technology they employ. In his research Benjamin finds a description of "future Paris" in which cafés are still ranked according to social classes.[170] Images of Paris projected into the twentieth century include visitors from other planets arriving in Paris to play the stock market.[171] Benjamin notes: "The operetta is the ironic utopia of a lasting domination by Capital."[172] On the manifest level, the future appears as limitless progress and continuous change. But on the latent level, the level of the dreamer's true wish, it expresses the eternalization of bourgeois class domination.

An early (pre–June 1935) *Konvolut* entry questions whether

[. . .] there could spring out of the repressed economic contents of the consciousness of a collective, similarly to what Freud claims for [the] sexual [contents] of an individual consciousness [. . .] a form of literature, a fantasy-imagining [. . . as] sublimation [. . .].[173]

A late formulation describes the ruling class' ambivalence that makes it block the realization of the very utopian dreams it has generated:

[. . . T]he bourgeoisie no longer dares to look in the eye the order of production that it has itself set into motion. The idea of [Nietzsche's] Zarathustra of eternal recurrence and the motto embroidered on pillow covers—"Just a quarter hour more"—are complementary.[174]

Benjamin notes similarly that the "phantasmagoria" of Baudelaire's *rêve parisian* "reminds one of the world expositions in which the bourgeoisie calls out to the order of property and production: 'Stay awhile. You are so lovely! [*Verweile doch, du bist so schön*].'"[175] The culture of the nineteenth century unleashed an abundance of fantasies of the future, but it was at the same time "a vehement attempt to hold back the productive forces."[176] If, on the dream's manifest level, changing fashion is a prefiguring of social transformation, on the latent level it is "a camouflage of very specific desires of the ruling class," a "figleaf" covering up the fact that, to cite Brecht: "'The rulers have a great aversion against violent changes.'"[177]

Commodity fetishism (as well as urban "renewal") can be viewed as a textbook case of Freud's concept of displacement: Social relations of class exploitation are displaced onto relations among things, thus concealing the real situation with its dangerous potential for social revolution. It is politically significant that by the late nineteenth century, the bourgeois dream of democracy itself underwent this form of censorship: Freedom was equated with the ability to consume. Benjamin writes that *egalité* developed its own "phantasmagoria,"[178] and "*la revolution*" came to mean "clearance sale" in the nineteenth century.[179]

By the end of the century, the dream, clearly of bourgeois origins (and bourgeois in the latent wish that it expressed) had in fact become "collective," spreading to the working class as well. The mass marketing of dreams within a class system that prevented their realization in anything more than the distorted form of dream symbols was quite obviously a growth industry. In his earliest notes, Benjamin interpreted "kitsch," the cluttered, aesthetic style of this mass marketing, as bourgeois class guilt: "the overproduction of commodities; the bad conscience of the producers."[180] The social goal of course *was* material abundance, which is why the dream functioned legitimately on the manifest level of collective wish image. But the commodity form of the dream generated the expectation that the international, socialist goal of mass affluence could be delivered by national, capitalist means, and that expectation was a fatal blow to revolutionary working-class politics.

9

The childhood of Benjamin's generation belonged to this end-of-the-century era of the first mass marketing of dreams. Benjamin recalled that his introduction to civic life had been as a consumer. He remembered his "sense of impotence before the city," and his "dreamy resistance" when, led by his mother, he walked through the streets of the city center:

In those early years I got to know the "city" only as the stage of "errands." [. . . I]t was not until the confectioner's that we felt better, having escaped the idolatrous worship that humbled our mother before idols with the names of Mannheimer, Herzog and Israel, Gerson, Adam, Esders and Madler, Emma Bette, Bud and Lachmann. A row of unfathomable masses, no, caves of commodities—that was the city.[181]

If, as has just been argued, Benjamin's theory of the collective dream did not disregard class distinctions, can the same be said of his theory of political awakening? In his earliest notes, Benjamin indicated that the bourgeoisie who had generated the dream remained trapped within it:

Did not Marx teach us that the bourgeoisie can never come to a fully enlightened consciousness of itself? And if this is true, is one not justified in connecting the idea of the dreaming collective (i.e., the bourgeois collective) onto his thesis?[182]

And in the entry immediately following:

Would it not be possible, in addition, to show from the collected facts with which this [Arcades] work is concerned, how they appear in the process of the proletariat's becoming self-conscious?[183]

Benjamin never implied that his own experience of the city was anything but class bound. In *Berliner Chronik*: "The poor? For rich children of his [Benjamin's] generation they lived at the back of beyond."[184] He admitted:

I never slept on the street in Berlin [. . .]. Only those for whom poverty or vice turns the city into a landscape in which they stray from dark till sunrise know it in a way denied to me.[185]

And in the *Passagen-Werk*: "What do we know of the streetcorners, curbstones, heat, dirt, and edges of the stones under naked soles [. . .]?"[186]

The class division was undeniable. Nevertheless, Benjamin felt that there was a confluence in the *objective* positions of intellectuals and artists as cultural producers and the proletariat as industrial producers, as a result of the specific constellation of economic and cultural history. The turn of the century experienced a cultural "crisis," and close on its heels there followed the economic one, a "shaking of commodity society"[187] that set off tremors in the collective dream. Around this historical constellation the experience of his generation coalesced, and well into the 1930s Benjamin found in it an extremely precarious cause for hope. Thus he could write to Scholem in 1935: "I believe that [the *Passagen-Werk*'s] conception, even if it is very personal in its origins, has as its object the decisive historical interests of our generation."[188]

For the proletariat, the discarded material of nineteenth-century culture symbolized a life that was still unattainable; for the bourgeois intellectual, it represented the loss of what once was. Yet for both classes, the revolution in style brought about by commodity culture was the dream form of social revolution—the only form possible within a bourgeois social context. The new generation experienced "the fashions of the most recent past as the most thorough anti-aphrodisiac that can be imagined."[189] But precisely this was what made them "politically vital," so that "the confrontation with the fashions of the past generation is an affair of much greater meaning than has been supposed."[190] The discarded props of the parental dreamworld were material evidence that the phantasmagoria of progress had been a staged spectacle and not reality. At the same time, as the stuff of childhood memories, these outmoded objects retained semantic power as symbols. Benjamin commented that for Kafka, "as only for 'our' generation [. . .] the horrifying furniture of the beginning of high capitalism was felt as the showplace of its brightest childhood experience."[191] The desire to recapture the lost world of childhood determined a generation's interest in the past. But it was the needs of its members as adults that determined their desire to wake up.

9
Materialist Pedagogy

1

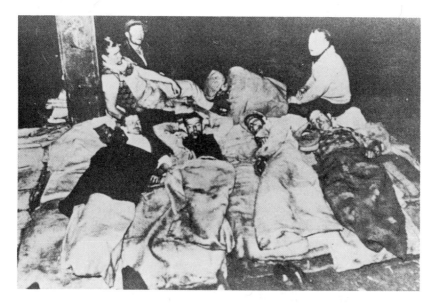

9.1 Sitdown strike, Paris, June 1936: Workers occupying a factory, some playing cards, others sleeping.

The contemporary who, in reading a work of history, recognizes with what a long hand the misery that befalls him [her] has been in preparation—and showing the reader this must lie close to the historian's heart—thereby acquires a high opinion of his [her] own powers. A history that teaches people in this manner does not make them melancholy, but provides them with weapons.[1]

The dialectical penetration and actualization of the past as it connects with the present is the test of the truth of present action.[2]

The Theses on History[3] make a pedagogic point, and it is expressly political. If, as Marx argued, the ruling ideas have always been those of the ruling class, what value can the historical materialist find in those "treasures" which make up the cultural inheritance?

For without exception the cultural treasures he surveys have a lineage which he cannot contemplate without horror. They owe their existence not only to the efforts of the great geniuses who have created them, but also to the anonymous toil of their contemporaries. There is never a document of culture that is not simultaneously a document of barbarism. And just as it is itself not free of barbarism, so barbarism taints the tradition through which it has been transmitted from owner to owner.[4]

The process of cultural transmission appears as a "triumphal procession," in which the present rulers step over those who today are lying prostrate."[5] Benjamin concludes: "A historical materialist therefore disassociates himself from it as far as possible. He regards it as his task to brush history against the grain."[6] This "task" of the historical materialist is vital for revolutionary pedagogy. In "Eduard Fuchs: Collector and Historian," an article which, as Tiedemann claims, is "without question one of the most significant works of Benjamin's later years"[7] (and which, like the Theses, draws heavily from *Konvolut* N) Benjamin writes that in the period before World War I, the Social Democrats made a serious theoretical error, one which was largely responsible for the co-opting of the working-class movement and the failure of the German revolution of 1918. The Social Democrats had a slogan: "Knowledge is power."

But [the Social Democratic Party] did not see through to its double meaning. It thought the same knowledge that ensured the rule of the bourgeoisie over the proletariat would enable the proletariat to free itself from this rule. In reality, knowledge that had no access to praxis and that could teach the proletariat nothing about its situation as a class was no danger to its oppressors. This was especially true of knowledge relating to the humanities. It lagged far behind economics, remaining untouched by the revolution in economic theory.[8]

It is important to realize that Benjamin was not simply attempting to build on the work of Mehring, Fuchs, and others in developing a new "Marxist" approach to the sociology of literature or art. He believed cultural history stood at the center of class education. He wrote concerning the Second International (sounding very much like Gramsci): "Very few at the time recognized how much in reality hinged upon the task of materialist education."[9] Since progress was not automatic in history, "materialist education," knowledge that provided "access to praxis" was crucial. Everything depended on it.[10]

In his notes to the Baudelaire book, Benjamin anticipated the criticism that this poet (who had acquired the status of a "classic"[11] among his own generation) might have *nothing* of revolutionary value to say in the present—and rejected it.[12]

It is a vulgar-Marxist illusion to [think one is] able to determine the social function of either mental or materialist products by viewing the circumstances and carriers of their historical transmission.[. . .] What speaks against confronting in a summary fashion the object of the inquiry, the poet Baudelaire, with today's society, and answering the question of what [. . .] he would have to say to its progressive cadres, in reply to a stocktaking of his works; without (. . .), mind you, proceeding to the question of whether he has anything to say to them at all? Actually, something important speaks against this uncritical interrogation [. . .] the fact that we are instructed in the reading of Baudelaire precisely by bourgeois society, and indeed, already long since not by its most progressive elements.[13]

It is because of the conservative way culture is transmitted in history that it has a reactionary effect: "Culture appears reified. Its history then becomes nothing but the residue of memorabilia that have been unearthed without ever entering into human consciousness through any authentic, that is, political experience."[14] The purpose of a materialist education is to provide this political experience, giving the revolutionary class the strength to "shake off" those cultural treasures that are "piled up on humanity's back"— "so as to get its hands on them."[15]

2

[The historical researcher must] give up the tranquil, contemplative attitude toward the object in order to become conscious of the critical constellation in which precisely this fragment of the past is positioned with regard to precisely this present.[16]

Dialectical images as "critical constellations" of past and present are at the center of materialist pedagogy. Short-circuiting the bourgeois historical-literary apparatus, they pass down a tradition of *dis*continuity. If all historical continuity is "that of the oppressors,"[17] this tradition is composed of those "rough and jagged places" at which the continuity of tradition breaks down, and the objects reveal "cracks" providing "a hold for anyone wishing to get beyond these points."[18] It is "the tradition of new beginnings,'"[19] and it corresponds to the understanding that "the classless society is not the final goal of progress in history, but its so frequently unsuccessful, yet ultimately accomplished interruption."[20]

As early as *One Way Street*, Benjamin made clear the connection between cognitive images and revolutionary praxis:

Only images in the mind vitalize the will. The mere word, by contrast, at most inflames it, to leave it smoldering, blasted. There is no intact will without exact pictorial imagination. No imagination without innervation.[21]

The will that counted for Benjamin was the collective, political will of the proletariat, and its motivation was mobilized by looking backward. The historian who constructed dialectical images drew, unavoidably, on cultural material produced by the bourgeoisie, expressing the experience of this class. Yet Baudelaire actually had more of revolutionary significance to "teach" readers about the present than writers like Pierre Dupont or Victor Hugo who had glorified the worker in their writings. Benjamin criticized as romanticism "the old and fatal confusion—perhaps it begins with Rousseau—" whereby the descriptive term "edifying" came to be attached to the "special simplicity" of the life led by those "dispossessed and dominated."[22] He chided the present-day "intellectual" who "adopts a kind of mimicry of proletarian experience without thereby being in the least allied to the working class."[23] More crucial was the kind of images he constructed: "In truth, it is far less a matter of making the creative person of bourgeois background into a master of 'proletarian art' than of deploying him [. . .] at important points in this image realm."[24]

It is inconceivable that in the *Passagen-Werk* Benjamin did not intend to fulfill what these major essays (written in 1928, 1934, 1937, and 1940) define repeatedly as the task of the politically committed intellectual. And in fact, *Konvolut* N makes explicit reference to the present, political meaning of dialectical images, the construction of which is described as "telescoping the past through the present"[25]: "It is not that the past throws its light on the present, or the present its light on the past, but [the dialectical] image is that wherein the past comes together with the present in a constellation."[26] Moreover, the "style for which one should aim" was accessible rather than esoteric, consisting of " 'everyday words [. . .] common language [. . .] frank style.' "[27]

If we take Benjamin at his word, then those elements of the nineteenth century that he chose to record must be seen as having a very specific political import for his own era. Such connections are rarely explicit in the *Passagen-Werk*, where direct references to the contemporary world are few. Still, we can, and indeed must assume their existence. *Konvolut* N leaves no doubt about it:

The events surrounding the historian and in which he takes part will underlie his presentation like a text written in invisible ink. The history that he lays before the reader gives form, so to speak, to the quotations in this text; and only quotations shaped in this way lie before anyone and everyone in a legible fashion.[28]

In order to do the politics of the *Passagen-Werk* justice, we need to make visible the *in*visible text of present events that underlies it, that for Benjamin's generation would have been "legible" for "anyone and everyone."

[. . . J]ust as Giedion teaches us we can read the basic features of today's architecture out of buildings of the 1850s, so would we read today's life, today's forms out of the life {and} the apparently secondary, forgotten forms of that era.[29]

We will expect "today's life" to provide the answer to why Benjamin represented *these* phenomena and not others in his "Ur-history of the 19th Century." And we will not be disappointed.

3

The appearance of closed facticity that adheres to the philosophical investigation and holds the researcher in its spell disappears to the degree that the object is constructed in historical perspective. The vanishing lines of this perspective converge in our own historical experience. It is thereby that the object constitutes itself as a monad. In the monad everything becomes alive which as facts in a text lay in mythical fixedness.[30]

Benjamin described the "pedagogic" side of his work: "'to educate the image-creating medium within us to see dimensionally, stereoscopically, into the depths of the historical shade.'"[31] A stereoscope, that instrument which creates three-dimensional images, works not from one image, but two. On their own, the nineteenth-century facts collected by Benjamin are flat, bordering indeed on "positivism," as Adorno complained. It is because they are only half the text. The reader of Benjamin's generation was to provide the other half of the picture from the fleeting images of his or her lived experience.[32] In the case of the arcades, Benjamin explicitly evoked these images. In the earliest *Passagen-Werk* notes (1927) he connects the decaying arcades with a description of the fashionable, new ones on the Avenue des Champs Elysées, that were just then having their grand opening:

In the Avenue Champs-Elysées among new hotels with Anglo-Saxon names, arcades were opened recently as the newest Parisian *passage*. A monstrous orchestra in uniform played at its opening among flowerbeds and flowing fountains. People groaned as they pressed together to cross over the sandstone thresholds and pass along mirrored walls; they viewed artificial rain falling on the copper innards of the latest automobiles as proof of the quality of the material, observed gears oscillating in oil, and read on black placards in street letters the prices of leather goods, gramophone records, and embroidered kimonos. In the diffused light that came from above, they glided over tile floors. While here a new passageway was prepared for fashionable Paris, one of the oldest arcades in the city disappeared, the Passage de l'Opera, swallowed up when construction of the Boulevard Haussman broke through it. As was true of this remarkable covered walkway until recently, several arcades still today, in their stark and gloomy corners, preserve history-become-space. Outmoded firms maintain themselves in these interior rooms, and the commodity display has an indistinct, multiple meaning [. . .].[33]

These original arcades are "the mold from which the image of 'the modern' is cast."[34] When juxtaposed to the dazzling commodity displays of the present, they express the essence of modern history as a riddle: Where the arcades and their contents remain mythically unchanged, history becomes visible in them; where they have been superseded historically by new commodity phantasmagorias, their mythic form lives on. Such juxtapositions of past and present undercut the contemporary phantasmagoria, bringing to consciousness the rapid half-life of the utopian element in commodities and the relentless repetition of their form of betrayal: the same promise, the same disappointment. "That which is 'always-again-the-same' is not the event, but the element of newness in it [. . .]."[35] The temporal dialectic of the new as the always-the-same, the hallmark of fashion, is the secret of the modern experience of history. Under capitalism, the most recent myths are continuously superseded by new ones, and this means that newness itself repeats mythically.

4

The past haunts the present; but the latter denies it with good reason. For on the surface, nothing remains the same. World War I was a turning point in the fashions of everything from office buildings to women's clothing, from printing type to children's book illustrations (figures 9.2 to 9.16). By the 1920s, in every one of the technical arts, and in the fine arts affected by technology, the change in style was total. In Germany, Walter Gropius' Bauhaus heralded this transformation.[36] In Paris, Le Corbusier's work epitomized the functional side of the new style, while Surrealism signaled its reflection in the imagination. Benjamin wrote: "To embrace Breton and Le Corbusier. That would mean to span the spirit of contemporary France like a bow out of which knowledge [of the past] hits to the heart of the present."[37] The *Passagen-Werk* was to provide the historical data for such knowledge. Benjamin describes the old style:

It understood living as the encasing of human beings, and embedded them with all their possessions so deeply within it that one is reminded of the interior of a compass case, where the instrument lies there with all its

9.2 Illustration by G. Alboth, German fairy tales, 1846 (top).

9.3 Illustration by Theodor Herrmann, German children's book, 1910 (bottom).

alternative parts nestled, typically, in violet-colored velvet or satin-lined hollows. It is scarcely possible to discover anything for which the nineteenth century did not invent casings: for pocket watches, slippers, egg cups, thermometers, playing cards—and in lieu of casings, then covers, carpet runners, linings and slipcovers.[38]

Ornamentation was a kind of casing. It will be recalled[39] that in the early, mythic stage of technology, newly processed iron was used as linear, surface decoration to hide structural forms. Its strength was made to look like lace, as in the Eiffel Tower, or in the omnipresent wrought-iron railings on balconies and banisters (figure 9.4). The twentieth-century stylistic revolution changed all this. Masks, casings, and surface ornamentation disappeared. Function became visible. The new sensibility penetrated the most habitual experiences of everyday life, and thereby into the collective unconscious.

9.4 Interior, GUM, Moscow department store.

9.5 Nineteenth-century window bolt, Coudrue, Paris, 1851 (top).

9.6 Twentieth-century doorknob, Le Corbusier, Frankfurt am Main, 1920s (bottom).

9 Materialist Pedagogy

9.7 Exhibition Hall, Paris, Gustav Eiffel, 1878 (top).

9.8 Bauhaus, Dessau, Walter Gropius, 1926 (bottom).

9.9 Chair with velvet upholstery, August Kitschelt, Vienna, 1851 (top).

9.10 Work table, C. F. Grubb, Banbury, England, 1851 (bottom).

9 Materialist Pedagogy

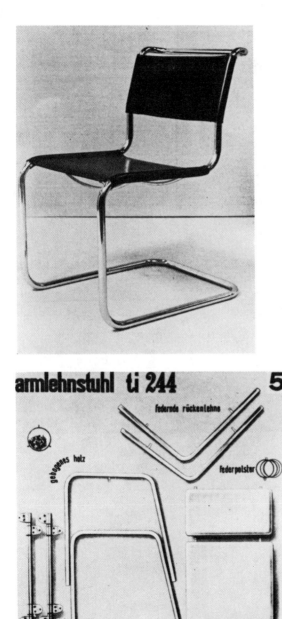

9.11 Variant of the cantilever tubular steel chair, Marcel Breuer, Bauhaus, 1928 (top).

9.12 Dismountable chair, Josef Albers, Bauhaus, 1929 (bottom).

9.13 Nineteenth-century interior, Paris (Sarah Bernhardt at home).

9.14 Twentieth-century interior, Villa Savoye, Poissy, France, Le Corbusier, 1929–31.

9.15 Martin Lewis, "Shadow Dance," 1930 (top).

9.16 Constantin Guys, "Coquette," 1850s (bottom).

Exteriors of buildings were themselves casings. Here the modern reversal of aesthetic form made a grand-scale visual difference (figures 9.7 and 9.8). "The twentieth century, with its porosity, transparency, light and free air made an end to living in the old sense."[40]

It is in juxtaposition to the villas built by Le Corbusier that images of nineteenth-century interiors take on the force of dialectical extremes. The latter made a distinct separation between public space and living space. Interiors were closed off, draped and dark, musty, and, above all, private (figure 9.11). Le Corbusier's villas broke definitively out into the open air, and "privacy" became old-fashioned (figure 9.12). Under the glass roofs of the last century, flowers and whole gardens were transposed indoors. In contrast: "Today the slogan is not transposing, but transparency. (Corbusier!)"[41]

Women's clothing, which had also been a casing (of corsets, crinolines, bustles, and trains), became as airy as interiors (figure 9.15). Erotic fashion changed with it. Benjamin notes: "The corset as the passage of the torso. What today is common among cheap prostitutes—not to take off their clothes—seems at that time to have been true of the most elegant ones."[42]

5

Necessity of a theory of history from which fascism can become visible.[43]

The experience of our generation: That capitalism will die no natural death.[44]

In the early stages of the *Passagen-Werk* (1927–33) this stylistic revolution was arguably Benjamin's central concern.[45] He affirmed the new, modernist aesthetics for the transparency of its "social content" as well as social function.[46] During the potential charged years of the late twenties, when capitalism was in crisis and social unrest had not yet congealed into reactionary or fascist forms, Benjamin seems to have seen the change in cultural forms as anticipatory, illuminating the tremendous social(ist) potential of the new nature, and he believed it therefore to be politically instructive.[47] As a precursor Fourier had particular relevance. He adopted the arcades building style in his "phalansteries," as the first vision of public housing—with the galleries as a connecting walkway ("rue-galerie"[48]) of public space. And it was Fourier whose wildest imaginings (ridiculed in his own time) were prophetic of the telegraph,[49] radio,[50] even television[51]—not to mention satellites[52] and space travel![53]

As long as the "present" still had revolutionary potential, Benjamin could conceive of it positively—indeed, teleologically—as "the waking world toward which the past was dreaming."[54] But events of the thirties drew the past into quite different constellations. Particularly after 1937,[55] the images recorded in the *Konvoluts* have a less utopian luster. Rather than being "anticipatory of a more humane future,"[56] they flash out in the present as urgent warnings, images far less of new political possibilities than of recurring political dangers.

Indicative of this change are Benjamin's comments on the figure of the flâneur, the nineteenth-century stroller on the city streets who was the origin of Benjamin's own class of literary producers, and the "ur-form" of the modern intellectual. The flâneur's object of inquiry is modernity itself. Unlike the academic who reflects in his room, he walks the streets and "studies" the crowd. At the same time, his economic base shifts drastically, no longer protected by the academic's mandarin status. As a specific historical figure, Baudelaire embodies the qualities of the flâneur. Indeed, his acute awareness of his highly ambivalent situation—at once socially rebellious bohemian and producer of commodities for the literary market—is precisely what accounts for Baudelaire's ability to "teach" Benjamin's generation of intellectual producers about their own objective circumstances, in which their interests in fact converge with those of the proletariat.

In the late 1920s, Benjamin seems to have affirmed this public orientation of the flâneur, as well as the public spaces of the city and the crowd that moves through them. An early (1927–29) *Passagen-Werk* note begins with the formulation:

Streets are the dwelling place of the collective. The collective is an eternally restless, eternally moving essence that, among the facades of buildings endures (*erlebt*), experiences (*erfährt*), learns, and senses as much as individuals in the protection of their four walls. For this collective the shiny enameled store signs are as good and even better a wall decoration as a

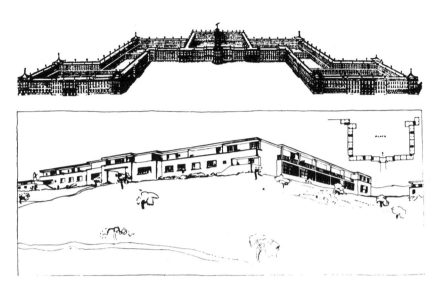

9.17 Charles Fourier, phalanstery, conceived 1808 (drawing, 1844) (top).

9.18 Le Corbusier, "Domino" housing project, plan, 1915 (bottom).

salon oil painting is for the bourgeoisie. Walls with the *"defense d'afficher"* are its writing desk, newspapers are its libraries, letterboxes its bronzes, benches its bedroom furniture—and café terraces the balcony from which it looks down on its domestic concerns after work is done.[57]

The same passage appears in Benjamin's 1929 review of Franz Hessel's book *Spazieren in Berlin*, except that the subject (who still has Benjamin's approval) is not the *Kollektiv*, but "the masses [*die Masse*]—and the flâneur lives with them [. . .]."[58] By the time of the first Baudelaire essay (1938), however, this motif has undergone a significant change. The flâneur alone is depicted on the streets (without sleeping on its benches) and the walls are now *his* desk, against which he "presses his notebooks." The passage has a new conclusion:

That life in all its multiplicity and inexhaustible wealth of variations can thrive only among the grey cobblestones and, above all, against the grey background of despotism—this, politically, stood in the background of those writings, of which the physiologies [written by flâneurs] were a part.[59]

The tone of this version is clearly critical, and it functions as a warning to the intellectual "flâneurs" of his own era. Benjamin describes the more modern forms of this social type: The reporter, a flâneur-become-detective, covers the beat[60]; the photojournalist hangs about like a hunter ready to shoot.[61] The later entries emphasize that the flâneur is not truly a person of leisure (*Musse*). Rather, loitering (*Müssigang*) is his trade. He is the prototype of a new form of salaried employee who produces news/literature/advertisements for the purpose of information/entertainment/persuasion—these forms are not clearly distinguished. Posing as a reporter of the true conditions of urban life, he in fact diverts his audience from its tedium.[62] His mass-marketed products fill the "empty" hours that time off from work has become in the modern city. At the same time, the flâneur as bohemian himself becomes a café attraction. Viewed by the public while he "works" at loitering,[63] he "takes the concept of being-for-sale itself for a walk. Just as the department store is his last haunt, so his last incarnation is as sandwichman."[64]

The sandwichman (figure 9.19) is paid to advertise the attrac-

9.19 Sandwichman, Paris, 1936.

tions of mass culture. The cultural producer, similarly, profits by peddling the ideological fashion. Benjamin mentions as the "true salaried flâneur" and "sandwichman" Henri Beraud,[65] protofascist journalist for *Gringoire*, whose nationalist and anti-Semitic attack on Roger Salengro, Léon Blum's minister of the interior, led the latter to suicide. Benjamin comments that intimations of such politics could already be found in Baudelaire, whose diary contained the "joke": "'A lovely conspiracy could be organized with the goal of exterminating the Jewish race.'"[66] Like a sandwichman, the financially successful Beraud peddled the fascist line, which camouflaged class antagonisms by displacing hostility onto the Jewish "race," allowing the attack on the Left to be concealed under the jargon of patriotism. In a late note, Benjamin makes the association: "Flâneur—sandwichman—journalist-in-uniform. The latter advertises the state, no longer the commodity."[67]

Clearly, Benjamin's view of both the flâneur and the crowd had changed:

In fact this "collective" is nothing but illusory appearance [*Schein*]. This "crowd" on which the flâneur feasts his eyes is the mold into which, 70 years later, the "*Volksgemeinschaft*" was poured. The flâneur, who prided himself on his cleverness [. . .] was ahead of his contemporaries in this, that he was the first to fall victim to that which has since blinded many millions.[68]

But, even in the late 1930s, his view of the proletariat had not changed:

The audience of the theater, an army, the inhabitants of a city [form] the masses, which as such do not belong to a particular class. The free market increases these masses rapidly [. . .] in that every commodity collects around itself the mass of its customers. The totalitarian states drive everything out of individuals that stands in the way of their complete assimilation into a massified clientele. The only unreconciled opponent [. . .] in this connection is the revolutionary proletariat. The latter destroys the illusion of the crowd (*Schein der Masse*) with the reality of the class (*Realität der Klasse*).[69]

6

The pre–1848 era (the epoch of the first arcades and Fourier[70]) had provided Benjamin with a rich source of images of utopian anticipation. But it was the period of the Second Empire that became increasingly "legible"[71] in the 1930s. Napoleon III was the first bourgeois dictator[72]; Hitler was his present-day incarnation. Hitler advertised his rule as historically unique: "'This happens only once; it never comes again.' Hitler did not assume the title of President of the Reich; he had in view impressing upon the people the one-time-only nature of his appearance'"[73]—so Benjamin notes in 1934. Not accidentally, Marx's history of Napoleon's coup d'état, *The 18th Brumaire*, begins to be cited heavily in the *Passagen-Werk* entries. Marx's text showed that Hitler's formula for success was *not* unique. Louis Napoleon followed the coup with a plebiscite to justify his illegal dissolution of the Republic.[74] Hitler employed precisely this tactic in August 1934. What concerns Benjamin is not only the parallel in political strategy, but the prototypical constellation of elements that provided the social cement of the Second Empire, including the use of new technologies of cultural production for the goal of social control rather than liberation. A 1936 entry to *Konvolut* d ("Literary History, Hugo") cites a contemporary French journalist:

"A perspicacious observer said one day that fascist Italy is managed like a large newspaper, and moreover, by a great pressman: one idea per day, competition, sensationalism, adroit and insistent orientation of the reader toward certain disproportionately vulgar aspects of social life, a systematic distortion of the reader's comprehension, in order to achieve certain practical ends. In sum, fascist regimes are regimes of publicity."[75]

That same year Benjamin composed the Artwork essay which asserts the tremendous progressive potential of the mass communications media, an argument designed to function as a *criticism* of its present use. Similarly the *Passagen-Werk* connects Mickey Mouse (a "star" in Paris cinema in the thirties[76]) with the fantasies of Grandville[77] and Fourier[78] as precursors—and yet the notes to the Artwork essay acknowledge: "the applicability of Disney's methods for fascism"[79] (figure 9.20).

Konvolut T on "Types of Lighting" records how original projects for city lighting were based on the eighteenth-century Enlightenment's "'idea of universal illumination'"[80]; but its reactionary potential was anticipated as early as the 1830s: "'1836 Jacques Fabien publishes *Paris en songe*. He develops here how electricity,

9.20 Mickey Mouse decal on German weapon.

through the overabundance of light, produces multiple blindings, and through the tempo of news sending brings on insanity.'"[81] A century later, urban illumination characteristically obfuscated reality, dazzling the masses rather than aiding them in seeing clearly. Commercial lighting turned shop facades into fairy scenes (figure 9.21). Light advertisements created "new types of writing"[82] (figure 9.22). The use of light bulbs in displays suggested an image of the fungibility of mass man: "Comparison of human beings with a control panel on which are thousands of electric light bulbs; first these die out, then others light themselves anew"[83] (figure 9.23). Here again, fascism was not an alternative to commodity culture, but appropriated its most sophisticated techniques—while robbing them of material content: "'[A]bstraction for [. . .] modern means of expression (lighting, modes of construction, etc.) can be dangerous"[84] (figure 9.24).

Fascism appealed to the collective in its *un*conscious, dreaming state. It made "historical illusion all the more dazzling by assigning

9.21 Lighting display, Grands Magazins du Louvre, Paris, 1920s (top).

9.22 Aux Galleries Lafayette: Night display of neon and electric lighting, Paris, 1930s (bottom).

9 Materialist Pedagogy

9.23 German Solstice Festival in the Berlin Stadium, 1938 (top).

9.24 "Dome of Lights," Nazi Party rally at Nuremberg, 1935 (bottom).

to it nature as a homeland."[85] Far from "'compensating for the one-sided spirit of the times'"[86] (as Jung had argued), this reaction was totally permeated by it.

Benjamin asked the question: "Should it be empathy (*Einfühlung*) in exchange value which first makes people capable of the total *Erlebnis* [of fascism]?"[87] To the eye that shuts itself when faced with this experience [of the "inhospitable, blinding age of big-scale industrialism"] there appears an experience of complementary nature as its almost spontaneous afterimage".[88] Fascism was that afterimage. While condemning the contents of modern culture, it found in the dreaming collective created by consumer capitalism a ready-at-hand receptacle for its own political phantasmagoria. The psychic porosity of the *un*awakened masses absorbed the staged extravaganzas of mass meetings as readily as it did mass culture.[89] And if the sandwichman was the last, degraded incarnation of the flâneur, he himself underwent a further metamorphosis (figure 9.25).

9.25 Munich, 1933: "I am a Jew, but I have no complaints about the Nazis."

7

An early *Passagen-Werk* entry cites Le Corbusier's criticisms of the urban projects of Haussmann during the Second Empire: "'The works of Haussmann were all arbitrary: They were not the rigorous conclusions of urbanism. They were the measures of a financial and military order.'"[90] Later entries emphasize how Haussmann's public works programs drew political support for the state, controlled labor through state employment, and economically benefited the capitalist class.[91] Parallels to the ambitious plans for public works projects in Hitler's Germany (or Blum's France, or Roosevelt's United States[92]) could not have gone unrecognized by readers in the thirties (figure 9.26).

Benjamin made note of an engraving of a regiment of soldiers under Napoleon I who became a "regiment of workers" during the Restoration.[93] In Hitler's Germany, it was already possible to anticipate that the stages would be reversed (figure 9.27).

9.26 Army of unemployed as construction workers for the Frankfurt Autobahn.

9.27 "Hitler 'solves' the unemployment problem: German workers! If you don't want this to be your fate, come over to the side of the Russian workers and peasants!"—Communist poster

9.28 (Top) Model of the renovation of Berlin, structured along two monumental avenues, running north and south, and east and west.

9.29 (Bottom) Model of the "People's Hall," planned as a German Pantheon glorifying Hitler, designed by Albrecht Speer as the centerpiece of Hitler's renovation of Berlin.

If the predecessor of Haussmann was less the social dreamer Fourier than the technocratic planner Saint-Simon,[94] his most self-conscious successors were urban architects like Robert Moses, New York's commissioner of buildings who made use of New Deal funds to demolish large sections of the city with the philosophy: "When you operate in an overbuilt metropolis, you have to hack your way with a meat axe"[95]—or like Albrecht Speer, who was put in charge of a colossal rebuilding project for Berlin which, employing a neo-classical style,[96] was to manifest the Third Reich's Imperial grandeur (figures 9.28 and 9.29). Benjamin wrote: "Empire style is the style of revolutionary terrorism, for which the state is an end in itself."[97]

It is important that Benjamin's data make it possible to distinguish between a nostalgic, conservative opposition to demolitions in general (which he did not endorse), and a specific criticism of the political and economic interests that guide those destructions. Benjamin did not criticize the Paris Communards for the damage to Paris caused by their incendiary revolt (figure 9.30), but rather, for their falsely equating the city's destruction with that of the social order.[98] For him the political choice was not between historically preserving Paris and modernizing it, but between destruction of the

9.30 Burning of Paris by the Communards, 1871.

historical record—which alone makes revolutionary consciousness possible—and destruction in remembrance of this record. In short, it was a choice between obliterating the past, or actualizing it.

If the *Passagen-Werk* entries can be seen to demonstrate a change in Benjamin's position over time, it is less one of increasing disillusionment as to the socialist potential of modern "nature," than of increasing awareness as to the ways that potential could be systematically distorted by those in power.[99] What had "progressed" in urban renewal were the technical capacities for destruction: "[A]long with the growth of the big cities there developed the means of razing them to the ground. What visions of the future are evoked by this!"[100] This development benefited the state, not those in revolt against it. In an early entry, Benjamin cited Le Corbusier, who found it "remarkable" that Haussmann's enormously extensive demolitions were accomplished by the most primitive of tools: "Very important: 'The tools of Haussmann,' illustration in Le Corbusier, *Urbanisme*, p. 150. The various spars, pickaxes, carts, etc."[101] (figure 9.31).

"In 1830, the populace used rope to barricade the streets,"[102] and threw chairs out of windows to stop the government's soldiers.[103] In Benjamin's time, technological advances made resistance to the state far more precarious:

"Today war in the streets has its technics: it was perfected after the recapture of Munich by armed combat, in a curious little work published confidentially, with great secrecy by the government of Berlin. You no longer advance on the streets, you let them remain empty. You tramp into the interiors, piercing through the walls. As soon as you are master of a street, you organize it; the telephone unrolls across the gaps of the walls of defense; meanwhile, in order to avoid a return of the adversary, you mine the conquered territory immediately. . . . One development that is most clear is that you will no longer be at all burdened with sparing buildings or lives. Alongside the civil wars of the future, the [construction of barricades on the] rue Transnonnain will appear an . . . innocent and archaic incident."[104]

That warning, written in 1926, was recorded by Benjamin in the *Passagen-Werk* before 1935, with a cross-reference to Haussmann. Several years later Benjamin observed: "Haussmann's activity is today accomplished by very different means, as the Spanish Civil War demonstrates"[105] (figure 9.32).

Les moyens d'Haussmann.

9.31 Haussmann's tools, from Le Corbusier, *Urbanisme*, 1931.

9.32   Spanish Civil War: Bomb exploding on Madrid street, 1936.

8

Every historical perception can be visualized as a scale, the one side of which is weighted down with the past, the other with the perception of the present. Whereas the facts collected in the former cannot be too insignificant or numerous enough, those on the other side should be only a few heavy, massive weights.[106]

"The dignity of a person demands that one submit one's concepts to these [. . .] single and primordial facts: that the police face the workers with cannons, that there is the threat of a war, and fascism already reigns [. . .]."[107]

In February 1934, as the effects of the economic Depression intensified, street demonstrations broke out in Paris. The strongest protest came from the Right; the French parliament felt itself threatened with a fascist Putsch. Benjamin observed the events from his hotel, which was located on the Boulevard Saint-Germain in the thick of the disturbances.[108] At the time, in connection with his planned article on Haussmann,[109] he was reading "an excellent history of Paris" that drew him "fully into the tradition of these struggles and disturbances."[110] In fact, he was learning that since the construction of Haussmann's boulevards (of which Saint-Germain was one), barricade fighting had become obsolete as revolutionary praxis.[111] To believe that such street confrontations could overturn a state armed with modern weaponry was to succumb to a revolutionary romanticism and nostalgia that already in the nineteenth century had proven fatal.[112] Perhaps it was his research that led Benjamin, unlike the French Left generally, to believe in February 1934 that "the present movements would not materialize into anything."[113]

The events of February unified the Left, which feared fascism as the greatest danger. But Benjamin saw danger as well in the nature of the Left's political response. The Communist Party joined Socialists and others to "save the Republic," organizing a Popular Front against fascism. The Front's program combined workers' demands with patriotic loyalty to the state. Its first great success was to organize a demonstration of hundreds of thousands on July 14, 1935, commemorating the Great (bourgeois) Revolution as a repetitive, patriotic cult.[114] Led by the Socialist Léon Blum, the Popular Front won the national elections the following year. But at this point something happened that the Left leadership had not foreseen. In May, shortly after the elections, in one after another of the factories in the suburbs of Paris, workers spontaneously staged sitdown strikes, indicating that they would not be content if the Popular Front continued governmental business as usual. The strikers' mood was festive and jubilant, but the threat of revolution appeared no less real.[115] Communist and Socialist trade-union and party leadership refused to join the strikers; instead they hammered out an accord with frightened business leaders, who were willing to make concessions to workers so long as property relations remained unchanged. But the strikes continued even after these "Matignon agreements" were signed, spreading to the big department stores, cafés, restaurants, and hotels. By June, one and a half million workers in Paris were on strike. Leon Trotsky proclaimed from exile: "'The French Revolution has begun. . . . These are not just strikes, this is *the* strike. . . .'"[116] Still, the French Communist

Party leaders held fast to the Comintern policy of the Popular Front. Blum's government seized the Trotskyite newspaper that had published Trotsky's call for French revolutionary soviets, and (in a repetition of 1848 and 1871) prepared the *gardes mobiles* for advancing into Paris should it be necessary. In the end the strikers capitulated and bloodshed was avoided. Blum was given a free hand to realize his programs, which put socialist goals aside in the name of national unity, and for the sake of economic recovery.

Benjamin's published correspondence is silent on the June strikes.[117] He might have despaired of their lack of clear direction and their trade-unionist demands. But he would have supported sit-down strikes that interrupted the course of things, and he would have deduced from the strikes' duration, despite the lack of leaders, that working-class consciousness still possessed a revolutionary potential.[118] In his speech, "The Author as Producer," composed during the critical year 1934, he emphasized the responsibility of intellectuals and literary writers with regard to the task of political education. At the same time, he began noting in the *Konvoluts* how much political *mis*education had been provided by nineteenth-century writers—Lamartine, for example, whose nationalist sentiment and preference for social order over social justice was prototypical. Indeed: "Lamartine's political-poetical program" was "the model of today's fascist one."[119] Benjamin's disapproval of the Popular Front was expressed in a July 1937 letter: "They all cling solely to the fetish of the 'left' majority, and they are not concerned that this majority executes a kind of politics which, if it was being done by the Right, would lead to insurrection."[120]

The Popular Front claimed national unity could override class differences. It argued that recovery of the capitalist economy would benefit workers by providing jobs, commodities, and the wages to buy them. It passed laws for worker benefits rather than worker ownership, and secured for the first time paid vacations for French workers. In contrast, Benjamin notes that in the utopian communities conceived by Fourier in the 1820s, the "harmonists neither know of vacations nor wish for them."[121] Blum was an admirer of Franklin Roosevelt and modeled his policies after the New Deal. In fact, Hitler's regime also had the goal of increasing consumption by increasing employment[122] (and German workers under fascism were the first to receive the benefit of paid vacations[123]). What Benjamin's research was uncovering was just how familiar this political formula of national unity, patriotism, and consumerism was in history, and how it inevitably resulted in the betrayal of the working class.

9

"The phrase that corresponded to this fantasized transcendence of class relations [in the 1848 revolution] was *fraternité*."[124]

The ur-form of Popular Front politics can be found at the birth of industrial capitalism in the social theories of Saint-Simon.[125] The decisive political characteristic of this early nineteenth-century thinker was the conception of workers and capitalists as a single "'industrial class,'" and an insistence that the "'interests of the directors of industrial businesses was actually in accord with those of the masses of people,'" so that the problem of social antagonisms could be resolved by "'a peaceful erection of the new social system.'"[126] In a reaction that paralleled that of Blum's Popular Front during the Paris strikes of June 1936, The Saint-Simonian newspaper *Le Globe* opposed the worker uprising in Lyons in 1831, fearing that "a raise in wages might place the industry there in jeopardy.'"[127] The Saint-Simonian solution to workers' problems involved the intervention of the state in terms of social legislation and a certain level of planned economy. Capitalism was relied upon to deliver technological innovation, as well as consumer goods that improved the quality of life of the working class. In short, Saint-Simonianism prefigured state capitalism in its leftist (Popular Front and New Deal) as well as rightist (national-socialist) forms:

"The major task of an industrial system was to be the setting up of a . . . work plan which was to be executed by the society . . . But . . . [Saint-Simon's] ideal was closer in meaning to state capitalism than to socialism. With Saint-Simon there is no talk of eliminating private property, of expropriation. The state subsumes the activities of the industrialists under a general plan only to a certain degree. . . ."[128]

When Benjamin commented critically on the Saint-Simonian faith in technological progress, whereby class conflict was denied and wished away,[129] he was indirectly attacking the prevailing politics of his own time.

World expositions, those popular phantasmagorias of patriotism and consumerism that glorified capitalism's technological progress, provided a perfect vehicle of expression for Saint-Simonian ideology. As we have seen, Benjamin documents this connection clearly in the *Passagen-Werk* entries,[130] and devotes considerable space to the nineteenth-century expositions themselves. In this case, the parallels with his own time are as striking as the fact that in the *Passagen-Werk* they are never made explicit. Nowhere does Benjamin so much as mention what were the most obvious of "present" images that entered into a constellation with the ur-forms of the nineteenth century. This silence, far from refuting contemporary connections, in fact supports the claim that the present underlay the project very literally, even if "written in invisible ink." For no one in Europe (or the United States) could have lived through the decade of the thirties without being aware that international expositions, having become less frequent after World War I, suddenly came back with a vengeance during these Depression years. They were seen as a means of enhancing business, creating jobs for the unemployed, and providing state-subsidized, mass entertainment that was at the same time public "education." Major expositions occurred almost yearly:

Stockholm 1930

Paris 1931

Chicago 1933

Brussels 1935

Paris 1937

Glascow 1938

New York 1939

San Francisco 1939

The "Colonial Exposition," held in Paris in 1931, exhibited not only the commodities but the people of the French colonies as exotica on display. Breton, Eluard, Aragon, and other members of the Surrealist movement urged a boycott of this exposition because it was racist and imperialist, justifying the "millions of new slaves" created by colonialism and the destruction of non-Western cultures in the name of progress, and because the nationalist sentiment it encouraged undermined international solidarity.[131] The 1937 exposition in Paris, announced years in advance, was to be a unity of artists and technology, artisans and industry—a "grand, peaceful" demonstration of nations which, despite their competition, contributed to the peaceful progress of humanity.[132] It glorified the latest "advances" in technology, which included this time not only radio, cinema, television, phonographs, electricity, gas, and air travel, but also biogenetics, x-ray technology and the new, wonder insulation, asbestos.[133] This exposition, planned long before the 1936 national elections, suited perfectly the ideology of the Popular Front. Léon Blum presided over its opening ceremonies, which were delayed by a strike of those constructing the exhibition as the "last gasp" of the workers' autonomous movement.[134] The fair's "Avenue de la Paix" was flanked by the pavilions of Germany and the USSR (figure 9.33[135]). In two years these countries would sign a Non-Aggression Pact; in four, they would be at war. Now they faced each other at Trocadéro, Albrecht Speer's neoclassical design complementing that of the Soviet Pavilion, despite efforts on both sides to distinguish between them.

In light of Benjamin's search for ur-forms, the 1937 exposition's Pavilion of Solidarity, dedicated to French workers, was significant. Its political message expressed the Popular Front line of national solidarity *with* labor, rather than the international solidarity *of* labor, and evoked nineteenth-century tradition not to challenge the present but to justify it:

Humans cannot consider themselves as isolated. Each is an associate. The association of all like beings [. . .]. Since the middle of the nineteenth century, action for bringing about social solidarity in France has taken a new form. . . Saint-Simon and Fourier are introducers of conceptions of social cooperation.[136]

The following, post–1937 *Passagen-Werk* entry records the ur-form of this ideology, citing a verse composed in 1851 for London's first international exposition:

The rich, the learned, the artists, the proletariat—
Each works for the well-being of all
And uniting like noble brothers
All desire the happiness of each.[137]

9.33 German (left) and Soviet (right) pavilions, International Exposition, Paris, 1937.

Benjamin's research uncovered as well the origins of the contemporary ideology of the small investor:

" ' . . .] the poor person, even if he possesses only one Thaler, can participate in the holding of public stock (*Volksaktien*) which is divided into very small portions, and can thus speak of *our* palaces, *our* factories, *our* treasures.' Napoleon III and his accomplices in the coup d'etat were very much taken by these ideas . . . believing] they could interest the masses in the solidity of public credit and preclude political revolution.' "[138]

Germany hosted no international expositions in the thirties. Instead, Hitler presided over the new form of mass spectacle that would supersede them in our own era (when world expositions have become unprofitable). The Olympic Games were held in Berlin in 1936 at the new eighty-five thousand-seat "Olympic Stadium" (figure 9.34). Here the fittest in human bodies, rather than the latest in industrial machines, were put on display, performing for mass audiences. Television was used experimentally at these

9.34 Olympic Stadium, Berlin, built by Werner March, 1934–36.

Olympics, and Leni Riefenstahl captured the games on film, demonstrating the new technical ability to create a mass audience out of individuals isolated in space.

The modern Olympics, begun in 1896, were part of the ideology of neoclassicism, a supposed return to the natural, athletic prowess of the ancient ("Aryan") Greeks. In a note to the 1936 Artwork essay, Benjamin compared them instead to the industrial science of Taylorism that employed the stopwatch to analyze minutely the bodily actions of workers for the purpose of setting norms for worker productivity in mechanized production. Precisely this was the distinctive characteristic of the new Olympics—hence the purportedly ancient event revealed itself to be absolutely modern. The athletes in Berlin ran against the clock. Their performances were measured in "seconds and centimeters": "It is these measurements that establish the sports records. The old form of struggle disappears [. . .]."[139] Such measurement is a form of test, not competition: "Nothing is more typical of the test in its modern form as measuring the human being against an apparatus."[140] And whereas these tests cannot themselves be displayed, the Olympics provide for them a representational form. For these reasons: "Olympics are reactionary."[141]

9.35 Triumphal arch sketched by Hitler, 1924–26, given to Speer for use in the plan of Berlin (top).

9.36 German troops entering Paris, June 1940 (bottom).

Part III

10

"The remarkable thing [. . .] is that Paris still exists."[142]

At the 1867 Paris Exposition celebrating the peaceful competition between nations, Bismarck was hosted by Napoleon III, whom in three years he would meet, and defeat on the battlefield. Hitler chose to forgo the exposition of 1937. Three years later he entered the city as its conquerer. It was his first trip to Paris. With him was Albrecht Speer, in charge of Hitler's project to rebuild Berlin in the image of Paris, but grander. They arrived by airplane at 6:00 a.m. For barely three hours they drove the deserted streets, stopping at Paris' cultural "treasures": the Opéra built under Haussmann, which he wanted most to see; the Champs Elysées with its shopping arcades, the Arc de Triumph, Trocadéro, the tomb of Napoleon, the Pantheon, Notre Dame, Sacré Coeur, and the Eiffel Tower (figure 9.37). He told Speer that it was his "life's dream" to see Paris, and said to him afterward:

Wasn't Paris beautiful? But Berlin must be made far more beautiful. In the past I often considered whether we would not have to destroy Paris, but when we are finished in Berlin, Paris will only be a shadow. So why should we destroy it?[143]

Thus Paris survived, due to the eagerness of this new, and most barbaric of conquerers to take his place in the line of cultural inheritance, that "triumphal procession" in which rulers "step over those who are lying prostrate."[144]

Hitler's trip to Paris was on June 25, 1940. Benjamin had fled the city only weeks before, not able to carry with him "more than my gas mask and toilet articles."[145] Throughout August, he was in Marseilles, still without an exit visa. In September he joined a small group that left France illegally by crossing into Spain. Days before, the German *Luftwaffe* had begun its aerial attacks on London. The fire bombing demonstrated the extreme vulnerability of the modern city. Soon this, not Hitler's urban planning, would be Berlin's fate as well (figure 9.38).

Cities would survive the war. They would be rebuilt reflecting the most modern urbanist design; their nineteenth-century facades would be restored as historical treasures. But the significance of the

9.37 Hitler before the Eiffel Tower, June 25, 1940, photograph sent to Eva Braun.

9.38 Ruins of the Reichstag, Berlin, 1945.

modern metropolis as the ideological centerpiece of national imperialism, of capital and consumption, disappeared with these air attacks. The planet's metropolitan population has never been greater. Its cities have never appeared more similar. But in the sense that Benjamin recorded in his history of the city of Paris, there can be no "Capital City" of the late twentieth century. The *Passagen-Werk* records the end of the era of urban dream worlds in a way the author never intended.

Afterword

Revolutionary Inheritance

For Kim and Mona Benjamin

1

From what are the phenomena rescued? Not only, not so much from the discredit and disregard into which they fall, as from the catastrophe of how a particular form of tradition so often represents them, their "appreciation as heritage."[1]

Professor Chimen Abramsky was on sabbatical leave in Stanford, California, in 1980, when he met Lisa Fitko, a seventy-year-old, Berlin-born woman, who told him she had led Walter Benjamin over the Pyrénées to Spain forty years before. She remembered well that he had carried a heavy briefcase, containing a manuscript more important, so Benjamin said, than his life. Mindful of the potential significance of her account, Professor Abramsky notified Gershom Scholem in Israel, who telephoned Lisa Fitko and recorded from her the following story:

I remember waking up in that narrow room under the roof where I had gone to sleep a few hours earlier. Someone was knocking at the door. [. . .] I rubbed my half-closed eyes. It was one of our friends, Walter Benjamin—one of the many who had poured into Marseille when the Germans overran France.

[. . .] *Gnädige Frau*, he said, "please accept my apologies for this inconvenience." The world was coming apart, I thought, but not Benjamin's *politesses*. "*Ihr Herr Gemahl*," he continued, "told me how to find you. He said you would take me across the border into Spain."

Afterword

[. . .]

The only truly safe crossing that was left [. . .] meant that we had to cross
the Pyrénées farther west, at a greater altitude, it meant more climbing.
"That would be all right," Benjamin said, "as long as it is safe. I do have
a heart condition," he continued, "and I will have to walk slowly. Also,
there are two more persons who joined me on my trip from Marseille and
who also need to cross the border, a Mrs. Gurland and her teenage son.
Would you take them along?" Sure, sure. "But Mr. Benjamin, do you
realize that I am not a competent guide in this region? [. . .] You want to
take the risk? "Yes," he said without hesitation. "The real risk would be
not to go."

[. . .]

I noticed that Benjamin was carrying a large black briefcase [. . .] It
looked heavy and I offered to help him carry it. "This is my new manuscript," he explained. "But why did you take it for this walk?" "You must
understand that this briefcase is the most important thing to me," he said.
"I cannot risk losing it. It is the manuscript that must be saved. It is more
important than I am."

[. . .]

Mrs. Gurland's son, José—he was about 15 years old—and I took turns
carrying the black bag; it was awfully heavy. [. . .] Today, when Walter
Benjamin is considered one of the century's leading scholars and critics—
today I am sometimes asked: What did he say about the manuscript? Did
he discuss the contents? Did it develop a novel philosophical concept?
Good God, I had my hands full steering my little group uphill; philosophy
would have to wait till the downward side of the mountain was reached.
What mattered now was to save a few people from the Nazis; and here I
was with this—this—*komischer Kauz, ce drôle de type*—this curious eccentric. Old Benjamin: under no circumstances would he part with his
ballast, that black bag; we would have to drag the monster across the
mountains.

Now back to the steep vineyard. [. . .] Here for the first and only time
Benjamin faltered. More precisely, he tried, failed, and then gave formal
notice that this climb was beyond his capability. José and I took him
between us, with his arms on our shoulders we dragged him and the bag
up the hill. He breathed heavily, yet he made no complaint, not even a
sigh. He only kept squinting in the direction of the black bag.

[. . .]

We passed a puddle. The water was greenish and slimy. Benjamin knelt down to drink. [...] "Listen to me," I said. [...] "We have almost arrived [...] to drink this mud is unthinkable. You will get typhus..." "True, I might. But don't you see, the worst that can happen is that I die of typhus...AFTER crossing the border. The Gestapo won't be able to get me, and the manuscript will be safe. I do apologize." He drank.

[...]

"That is Port-Bou down there! The town with the Spanish border control where you will present yourselves [...]. I must go now, *auf Wiedersehen.*"

[...]

In about a week the word came: Walter Benjamin is dead. He took his life in Port-Bou the night after his arrival.[2]

His companions—Mrs. Henny Gurland and her son José—reached America successfully. She wrote to a cousin on October 11, 1940, about that last night:

For an hour, four women and the three of us sat before the officials [at Port Bou] crying, begging and despairing as we showed them our perfectly good papers. We were all *sans nationalité* and we were told that a few days earlier a decree had been issued that prohibited people without nationality from traveling through Spain. [...]. The only document I had was the American one; for José and Benjamin this meant that they would be sent to a camp. So all of us went to our rooms in utter despair. At 7 in the morning Frau Lipmann called me down because Benjamin had asked for me. He told me that he had taken large quantities of morphine at 10 the preceding evening and that I should try to present the matter as illness; he gave me a letter addressed to me and Adorno TH. W.... {sic.} Then he lost consciousness. I sent for a doctor [...]. I endured horrible fear for José and myself until the death certificate was made out the next morning. [...] I had to leave all papers and money with the *juge*[,] and asked him to send everything to the American consulate in Barcelona [...]. I bought a grave for five years, etc. [...] I really can't describe the situation to you any more exactly. In any case, it was such that I had to destroy the letter to Adorno and me after I had read it. It contained five lines saying that he, Benjamin, could not go on, did not see any way out, and that he [Adorno] should get a report from me, likewise his son.[3]

Mrs. Gurland later wrote to Adorno that Benjamin's letter had said: "Please transmit my thoughts to my friend Adorno and explain the situation in which I find myself placed."[4] Did these "thoughts" refer to the manuscript in the briefcase?

In October 1940, Horkheimer requested detailed information from the Spanish border police. He was told Benjamin's death was "not suicide but from natural causes,"[5] and that his personal effects taken into custody consisted of

[. . .] a leather briefcase of the type used by businessmen, a man's watch, a pipe, six photographs, an X-ray photograph (*radiografia*), glasses, various letters, periodicals and a few other papers, the contents of which are not noted, as well as some money [. . .].[6]

No mention of a "heavy" manuscript. The "few other papers" have not been preserved.[7] Nor was his grave marked or tended.[8]

Henny Gurland, who married Erich Fromm in 1944, died in Mexico in 1952. Her son "José," Joseph Gurland, is a professor of engineering in the United States. Benjamin's editor, Rolf Tiedemann, contacted him and reports:

Although his memory has preserved precisely many details, much has also been forgotten, or remembered only darkly and unsurely. In the decisive question he is not able to be helpful: He no longer knows whether or not Benjamin carried with him a briefcase, can just as little remember seeing any manuscript by Benjamin, and also never heard his mother mention anything about it later.[9]

Scholem believes the possibility cannot be ruled out "that for reasons connected with what happened after Benjamin's death, to which she referred only vaguely in her letter, Mrs. Gurland might have destroyed this manuscript [. . .]."[10] Tiedemann "cannot agree with this conclusion."[11] He grants that in the "more than a quarter of a year" that Benjamin spent in southern France before crossing the border he had "time enough to complete a short or even somewhat lengthy manuscript," and that "it could have concerned scarcely anything else than a text on the Arcades project."[12] But "given his 'microscopic handwriting,'" even a longer text could have fit on the "few other pages" delivered to the Spanish officials. Had it been a new text, it is difficult to understand why Benjamin would not have mentioned it in his correspondence during these last months. Tiedemann's own conjecture is that the "manuscript" was in fact the Theses on History, finished just before he left Paris, where Benjamin had left his papers in "'*total uncertainty*'" as to whether they would survive.[13]

Ironically, Hitler's decision not to destroy Paris means that we now have Benjamin's massive assembly of notes for the *Passagen-Werk* as part of our cultural inheritance. But what if Scholem has guessed correctly that the manuscript in the briefcase represented some form, however preliminary, of a completed *Passagen-Werk*? Then this opus, which might now be valued by our own generation as not only the most important cultural commentary on modernity, but one of the greatest literary achievements of the twentieth century (as, in its absence, has often been conjectured), was destroyed by a woman who feared desperately for her son's safety, and for her own.

One month before Benjamin's suicide, his own son Stefan, five years older than José Gurland, escaped with his mother to England. He survived the aerial bombings, settled in London as a book collector, married, and had his own children. This afterword is dedicated to them, Benjamin's granddaughters, and to the memory of an evening in their London home when we read to each other from their grandfather's collection of nineteenth-century children's books.

2

[. . . D]anger affects both the content of tradition and its receivers. The same threat hangs over both: that of becoming a tool of the ruling classes. In every era the attempt must be made anew to wrest tradition away from a conformism that is about to overpower it. [. . . *E*]*ven the dead* will not be safe from the enemy if he wins. And this enemy has not ceased to be victorious.[14]

In 1982, an international conference at the University of Frankfurt (where Benjamin had been denied a position in 1926) marked the appearance of the *Passagen-Werk* as volume V of Benjamin's *Gessammelte Schriften*. The morning after the formal presentations, in an open discussion with students, Benjamin's interpreters argued for "their" Benjamin from opposing intellectual camps. I remember nothing of these debates, perhaps because they have been so often repeated. The wisdom came not from us that morning, but from a German student who suddenly spoke of those missing from the room—those German Jews who might have been a part of his generation of students. He felt their lack, and expressed sadness at their absence. All at once the room filled with ghosts. We shivered.

Can we, taking hold of our cultural heritage, be made mindful of the violence in the wake of which these "treasures" have been gathered up and preserved, whereas others have disappeared, and countless others not even been created? Can academicians (—I count myself—), for whom scholarly meticulousness is all that is required of intellectual responsibility, be trusted as the guardians and transmitters of the cultural heritage? And more, can we view seriously, with reverence, the discarded material objects of mass culture as monuments to the utopian hope of past generations, and to its betrayal? Who will teach us *these* truths, and in what form shall they be passed on to those who come after us?

3

[The story] is one of the oldest forms of communication. It does not aim at transmitting the pure in-itself of the event (as information does) but anchors the event in the life of the person reporting, in order to pass it on as experience to those listening.[15]

In *One Way Street* Benjamin wrote:

[. . . A]lready today, as the contemporary mode of knowledge production demonstrates, the book is an obsolete mediation between two different card filing systems. For everything essential is found in the note boxes of the researcher who writes it, and the reader who studies it assimilates it into his or her own note file.[16]

In the *Passagen-Werk*, Benjamin has left us his note boxes. That is, he has left us "everything essential." The *Passagen-Werk* is a historical lexicon of the capitalist origins of modernity, a collection of concrete, factual images of urban experience. Benjamin handled these facts as if they were politically charged, capable of transmitting revolutionary energy across generations. His method was to create from them constructions of print that had the power to awaken political consciousness among present-day readers. Because of the deliberate unconnectedness of these constructions, Benjamin's insights are not—and never would have been—lodged in a rigid narrational or discursive structure. Instead, they are easily moved about in changing arrangements and trial combinations, in response to the altered demands of the changing "present." His legacy to the readers who come after him is a nonauthoritarian system of inheritance, which compares less to the bourgeois mode of passing down cultural treasures as the spoils of conquering forces, than to the utopian tradition of fairy tales, which instruct without dominating, and so many of which "are the traditional stories about victory over those forces."[17]

The Theses on History is not a fairy tale in any traditional sense. And yet its imagery tells the same story that had always motivated the *Passagen-Werk*. In the Theses, Benjamin speaks of "shock" rather than awakening, but they are different words for the same experience. "Images of the past" replace the term "dream images," but they are still dialectically ambivalent, mystifying and yet containing "sparks of hope."[18] The revolution, the "political world-child," has yet to be born,[19] but the utopia it would usher in is understood in the childlike terms of Fourier, whose most fantastic daydreams of cooperation with nature "prove to be surprisingly sound."[20] "The subject of historical knowledge is the struggling, oppressed class itself,"[21] but the entire "generation" possesses "Messianic power."[22] History appears as catastrophe, a hellish, cyclical repetition of barbarism and oppression. But Blanqui's "resignation without hope"[23] is absent from Benjamin's own voice; instead he speaks of the need to "improve our position in the struggle against fascism."[24] It leads to an apocalyptic conception of breaking out of this historical cycle, in which the proletarian revolution appears under the sign of Messianic Redemption.[25]

In the Theses on History, Benjamin explicitly rejected the historicist's "once upon a time"; the historical materialist "leaves it to others to expend themselves" with this whore in "the bordello of historicism. He remains master of his power, adult enough to blast open the continuum of history."[26] And yet, there was a way of storytelling that was not this prostituted one, because its imagery broke this continuum rather than replicating it.

The first of the Theses on History, with its image of the dwarf and the puppet, begins: "*Bekanntlich soll es* [. . .] *gegeben haben* [. . .]." It has been translated: "The story is told [. . .]."[27] Benjamin's last position was that of the storyteller. He returned to this form when the continuous tradition of world war left only the hope that, within the *dis*continuous tradition of utopian politics, his story would find a new generation of listeners, one to whom the dreaming collective of his own era appears as the sleeping giant of the past "for which its children become the fortunate occasion of its own awakening." Consider in the light of the original plan for the *Passagen-Werk*, the second thesis:

There is a secret agreement between past generations and the present one. Our coming was expected on earth. Like every generation that preceded us, we have been endowed with a *weak* Messianic power, a power to which the past has claim. That claim cannot be settled cheaply. The historical materialist is aware of this.[28]

4

The wisest thing—so the fairy tale taught mankind in olden times, and teaches children to this day—is to meet the forces of the mythical world with cunning and with high spirits.[29]

Unavoidably, historical events are written about in terms of what comes after them. The proposed goal of historical scholarship, to see "'with purity into the past'" without regard for "'everything that has intervened' [. . .] is not so much difficult as impossible to attain.[30] This fact, lamented by bourgeois scholars, is to be affirmed by the historical materialist. His purpose, wrote Benjamin, is to accomplish a "Copernican Revolution" in the writing of history:

The Copernican Revolution in historical perception is this: Before one held the past for the fixed point and saw the present as an effort to advance knowledge gropingly to this point. Now this relationship is to be reversed, and the past becomes the dialectical turnabout that inspires an awakened consciousness. Politics maintains preeminence over history.[31]

But if bourgeois history writing is to be overturned, then it is not a question of replacing it with a Marxist narrative. Rather, the goal is to bring to consciousness those repressed elements of the past (its realized barbarisms and its unrealized dreams) which "place the present in a critical position."[32] In the dialectical image, the present as the moment of revolutionary possibility acts as a lodestar for the assembly of historical fragments. Benjamin writes in the *Passagen-Werk*:

Comparison of the others' attempts to setting off on a sea voyage in which the ships are drawn off course by the magnetic north pole. To discover *this* north pole. What for the others are deviations are for me the data that set my course.[33]

The present as "now-time" keeps the historical materialist on course. Without its power of alignment, the possibilities for reconstructing the past are infinite and arbitrary.

This criticism is relevant to "deconstruction,"[34] the form of cultural hermeneutics most in vogue in our own present. Granted, deconstruction as a hermeneutic method denies the past as a "fixed point," draws the present emphatically into interpretation, and claims to be both anti-ideological and philosophically radical. But it cannot bring to a standstill what is experienced as a continuous restlessness of meaning, because there is no image of the present as the moment of revolutionary possiblity to arrest thought.[35] In the absence of any "magnetic north pole" whatsoever, deconstructionists "decenter" the texts as a series of individualist and anarchist acts. Change appears eternal, even while society remains static. Its revolutionary gesture is thereby reduced to the sheer novelty of interpretations: Fashion masquerades as politics.

In contrast, Benjamin's dialectical images are neither aesthetic nor arbitrary. He understood historical "perspective" as a focus on the past that made the present, as revolutionary "now-time," its vanishing point. He kept his eyes on this beacon, and his interpreters would do well to follow suit. Without its constant beam, they risk becoming starry-eyed by the flashes of brilliance in Benjamin's writings (or in their own), and blinded to the point.

5

In reality, there is not one moment that does not bring with it *its own* revolutionary possibility—it only wants to be defined as a specific one, namely as the chance for a totally new resolution in view of a totally new task.[36]

"One should never trust what an author himself says about his work," wrote Benjamin.[37] Nor can we, because if Benjamin is correct, the truth content of a literary work is released only after the fact, and is a function of what happens in that reality which becomes the medium for its survival. It follows that in interpreting the *Passagen-Werk* our attitude should not be reverence for Benjamin that would immortalize his words as the product of a great author no longer here, but reverence for the very mortal and precarious reality that forms our own "present," through which Benjamin's work is now telescoped.

Today the Paris arcades are being restored like antiques to their former grandeur; the bicentennial celebration of the French Revolution has at least threatened to take the form of another great world exposition; Le Corbusier-inspired urban renewal projects, now in decay, have become the desolate setting for a film like *Clockwork Orange*, while the "postmodernist" constructions that reject his heritage bring both wish image and fetish into quite different constellations; "Walt Disney Enterprises" is constructing technological utopias—one on the outskirts of Paris—in the tradition of Fourier and Saint-Simon. When trying to reconstruct what the arcades, expositions, urbanism, and technological dreams were for Benjamin, we cannot close our eyes to what they have become for us. It follows that in the service of truth, Benjamin's own text must be "ripped out of context,"[38] sometimes, indeed, with a "seemingly brutal grasp."[39]

The responsibility for a "theological" reading of the *Passagen-Werk* (one which concerns itself not only with the text, but also with the changing present that has become the index of the text's legibility) cannot be brushed aside. This means simply that politics cannot be brushed aside. By way of concluding this study, the following images provide material for such a reading, urging that readers begin this interpretive project on their own.

Afterimages

1988 Postcard

Walter Benjamin in Ibiza, 1932. Photograph © Theodor W. Adorno Archiv, Frankfurt am Main

Arcades: Continuity/Discontinuity

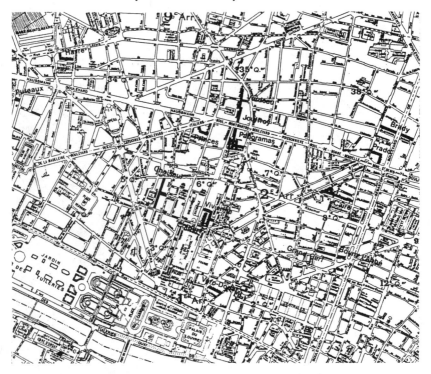

It is not difficult through our own flânerie to reconstruct Benjamin's work day. Arriving by metro, he would have surfaced through the art-nouveau portal at rue 4. Septembre, and traversed the Passage Choiseul, exiting near the lush Square de Louvois, the quiet peace of which ends abruptly at the rue de Richelieu. Crossing its speeding lanes of traffic, he reached the safety of the Bibliothèque Nationale. He worked "the whole day there," accustoming himself to the "annoying regulations" in the main reading room (V, 1100). When tired of reading, a short stroll from the library brought to view all of central Paris, first and foremost, the surviving arcades in which he discovered the modern world in miniature: Choiseul, Vivienne, Colbert, Puteaux, Havre, Panoramas, Jouffrey, Verdeau, Princes, Brady, Prado, Caire, Bourg l'Abée, Grand-Cerf, Vero-Dodat.

The restored Paris arcades still function as dreamworlds, but now instead of celebrating urban modernity, they provide fantasies of escaping from it: English tea rooms, antique shops, old bookstores, and travel agencies find their natural homes in today's passages.

Passage Vivienne, built in 1832, a historical monument since 1974, restored in 1982.

Dialectics of a Social Type: The Flâneur

Traffic circle proposed in 1906 by Eugène Hénard

"Around 1840 it was elegant to take turtles for a walk in the arcades, (This gives a conception of the tempo of flânerie)" (V, p. 532). By Benjamin's time, taking turtles for urban strolls had become enormously dangerous for turtles, and only somewhat less so for flâneurs. The speedup principles of mass production had spilled over into the streets, waging "'war on flânerie'" (V, p. 547). The "'flow of humanity . . . has lost its gentleness and tranquility,'" *Le temps* reported in 1936: "'Now it is a torrent, where you are tossed, jostled, thrown back, carried to right and left'" (V, p. 547). With motor transportation still at an elementary stage of evolution, one already risked being lost in the sea.

Today it is clear to any pedestrian in Paris that within public space, automobiles are the dominant and predatory species. They penetrate the city's aura so routinely that it disintegrates faster than it can coalesce. Flâneurs, like tigers or preindustrial tribes, are cordoned off on reservations, preserved within the artificially created environments of pedestrian streets, parks, and underground passageways.

The utopian moment of flânerie was fleeting. But if the flâneur has disappeared as a specific figure, the perceptive attitude that he embodied saturates modern existence, specifically, the society of mass consumption.

Hénard's "simple and elegant solution" in practice. Image juxtaposition by Nora Evenson

In the flâneur, concretely, we recognize our own consumerist mode of being-in-the-world. (The same can be argued for all of Benjamin's historical figures. In commodity society all of us are prostitutes, selling ourselves to strangers; all of us are collectors of things.)

Benjamin wrote: "the department store is [the flâneur's] last haunt" (V, p. 562). But flânerie as a form of perception is preserved in the characteristic fungibility of people and things in mass society, and in the merely imaginary gratification provided by advertising, illustrated journals, fashion and sex magazines, all of which go by the flâneur's principle of "look, but don't touch" (V, p. 968). Benjamin examined the early connection between the perceptive style of flânerie and that of journalism. If mass newspapers demanded an urban readership (and still do), more current forms of mass media loosen the flâneur's essential connection to the city. It was Adorno who pointed to the station-switching behavior of the radio listener as a kind of aural flânerie. In our time, television provides it in optical, nonambulatory form. In the United States, particularly, the format of television news programs approaches the distracted, impressionistic, physiognomic viewing of the flâneur, as the sights purveyed take one around the world. And in connection with world travel, the mass tourist industry now sells flânerie in two- and four-week packets.

The flâneur thus becomes extinct only by exploding into a myriad of forms, the phenomenological characteristics of which, no matter how new they may appear, continue to bear his traces, as ur-form. This is the "truth" of the flâneur, more visible in his afterlife than in his flourishing.

Shopping Bag Lady, 1980

Photograph © Ann Marie Rousseau

Benjamin noted in a 1934 book, this "portrayal of suffering, presumably under the Seine bridges. . . 'A bohemian woman sleeps, her head bent forward, her empty purse between her legs. Her blouse is covered with pins which glitter from the sun, and all her household and personal possessions: two brushes, an open knife, a closed bowl, are neatly arranged . . . creating almost an intimacy, the shade of an interior around her" (V, p. 537). In the United States today her kind are called "bag ladies." They have been consumed by that society which makes of Woman the prototypical consumer. Their appearance, in rags and carrying their worldly possessions in worn bags, is the grotesquely ironic gesture that they have just returned from a shopping spree.

The flâneur inhabits the streets as his living room. It is quite a different thing to need the streets as a bedroom, bathroom, or kitchen, when the most intimate aspects of one's life are in view of strangers and ultimately, the police. For the oppressed (a term that this century has learned is not limited to class), existence in public space is more likely to be synonymous with state surveillance, public censure, and political powerlessness.

The World of Things

Woodcut, Albrecht Dürer, 16th century

Just what is it that makes today's homes so different, so appealing?

Montage © Richard Hamilton, 1956

"The span between emblem and advertising image allows one to measure what changes have gone on since the seventeenth century in regard to the world of things" (V, p. 440).

Little Treasure Cupboard, seventeenth century

Painting by Johann Georg Hainz, 1666

Afterimages

Twentieth-century treasures

From the collection of the Museum of Modern Mythology, 693 Mission Street, San Francisco. Photograph © Matthew Selig

Afterimages

The Collector

The Object as Fetish:

"'Private property has made us so stupid and passive that an object is only *ours* if we *possess* it, i.e., if it exists for us as capital, or is *used* by us...'" (Marx, cited V, p. 277).

"'The need to accumulate is a sign of coming death for people as for societies'" (Morand, cited V, p. 275).

The Fetish Redeemed:

"But contrast with this collecting by children!" (V, p. 275).

"Collecting is an ur-phenomenon of studying: the student collects knowledge" (V, p. 278).

"In collecting the important thing is that the object is taken out of all the original functions of its use [...]" (V, p. 1016).

"One must understand: To the collector, in every one of his [her] objects, the world is present, and indeed, ordered—but according to a surprising relationship, incomprehensible in profane terms" (V, p. 274).

Like involuntary memory, collecting is a "productive disorder" (V, p. 280), "a form of practical remembering" (V, p. 271) wherein the things "step into *our* lives, not we into theirs" (V, p. 273). "Therefore, in a certain sense, even the smallest act of political reflection marks an epoch in the trade of antiques" (V, p. 271).

"In a practical sense, I can behave in a human way toward an object only when the object behaves in a human way toward human beings'" (Marx, cited V, p. 277).

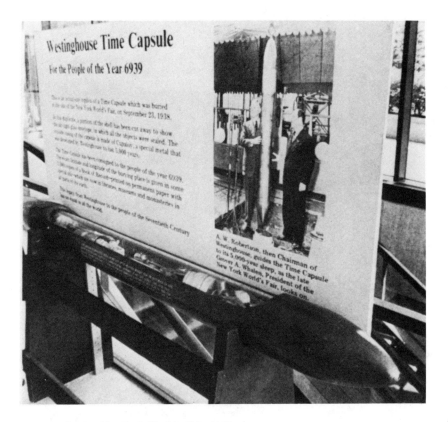

Exhibition Catalog, New York World's Fair, 1939

TIME CAPSULE, 1938, "For the People of the Year 6939," assembled and deposited by the Westinghouse Electric Corporation. A replica was exhibited at the 1939 New York World's Fair.

Among the items are a Mickey Mouse child's cup; a Woolworth rhinestone clip; "The Story of Rockefeller Center"; reproductions of paintings by Picasso, Mondrian, Dali, and Grant Wood; the sheet music of Flat Foot Floogie; *Gone With the Wind*; photographs of a radio broadcast; the *Daily Worker* for August 30, 1938 (along with eight other New York dailies); the Sears, Roebuck catalog for 1938–39; a newsreel including films of the veterans' reunion on the 75th anniversary of the Battle of Gettysburg, Howard Hughes' July 1938 record-breaking round-the-world flight in his Lockheed 14 called "New York World's Fair 1939," Jesse Owens winning the 100-meter dash at the 1936 Berlin Olympics, football and baseball games, military displays, the bombing of Canton by Japan (June 1938), a fashion show, and the World's Fair Preview Motorcade of April 30, 1938.

Ur-forms of Postmodernism

Arundel Castle. Photograph © Joan Sage

AT&T building, New York City, designed by Philip Johnson and John Burgee, 1983
Photograph © Danielle Moretti

Premodern:

In his home, the bourgeois citizen creates a "fictive setting" for his life (V, p. 69), a task of the imagination "all the more pressing," Benjamin tells us, "in that he does not dream of grafting onto his business affairs a clear conscience of his social function" (V, p. 67). And yet—even in so small a detail as the diagonal positioning of rugs and chairs which echoes the diagonal corners of medieval castles (V, p. 285), there are signs of a class under siege. Bedframes " 'bristle' " with battlements in eighteenth-century style; closets are girded with "medieval fortifications" (V, p. 281). " 'The stairway has remained something that resembles more a military construction for preventing the enemies from invading a home than a means of communication and access offered to friends' " (V, p. 512). "The fortification character in cities as well as in furniture persisted under the bourgeoisie' " (V, p. 284). In 1833, a proposal to surround the city of Paris with a " 'circle of separate forts' " led to " 'universal opposition' " and " 'an immense popular demonstration' " (V, pp. 197–98). Le Corbusier noted: " 'The fortified city was up to the present the constraint that always paralyzed urbanism' " (V, p. 143).

Postmodern:

Atlanta, Georgia, 1983: "Downtown Atlanta rises above its surrounding city like a walled fortress from another age. [. . .] The sunken moat of I[nterstate highway]-85, with its flowing lanes of traffic, reaches around the eastern base of the hill from south to north, protecting lawyers, bankers, consultants and regional executives from the intrusion of low-income neighborhoods" (Carl Abbot, *The New Urban America*, p. 143).

Los Angeles Bonaventure Hotel, 1985: "Portman [the architect] has only built large vivariums for the upper middle classes, protected by astonishingly complex security systems.

"[. . .W]here the aim of Portman is to dissimulate and 'humanize' the fortress function of his buildings, another postmodernist vanguard is increasingly iconizing that function in its designs. Recently opened off Wall Street, 33 Maiden Lane by Philip Johnson is a 26-story imitation of the Tower of London, advertised as the 'state of the art in luxury accommodation . . . with emphasis on security.' Meanwhile Johnson and his partner, John Burgee, are working on the prospective 'Trump Castle' [. . .]. According to its advance publicity, Trump Castle will be a medievalized Bonaventure, with six coned and crenellated cylinders, plated in gold leaf, and surrounded by a real moat with drawbridges" (Mike Davis, *New Left Review* no. 151, pp. 112–13).

In the 1930s, Philip Johnson's minimalist architecture helped define the tenets of architectural modernism, in the spirit of Le Corbusier. By the late 1970s, his skyscrapers, classic examples of "postmodernism," had decorated tops referencing historical styles—here the characteristic curve of Chippendale furniture—and combined conflicting styles from various historical eras. At ground level, the AT&T building incorporates the glass architecture of the arcades style (right). Photograph © Danielle Moretti

Premodern:

On early nineteenth-century fashion: " 'We have seen something that was never before presented: marriages of styles that one had formerly thought unmarriageable [. . .]' " (V, p. 283).

On the nineteenth-century interior: "The change of styles: Gothic, Persian, Renaissance, etc. That means: Superimposed over the interior of the bourgeois dining room is laid a banquet room of Caesara Borgia; out of the bedroom of the housewife there arises a Gothic chapel; the workroom of the master of the house shimmers iridescently, transformed into the chamber of a Persian sheik. Photomontage, which fixes such images for us, corresponds to the most primitive form of perception of these generations" (V, p. 282).

On architecture: " 'The architectonic aspects of later world's fairs: 'marrying together the most contrary tastes' [Gothic, Oriental, Egyptian, and classical Greek] in the most varied geometric forms' " (V, p. 264).

Afterimages

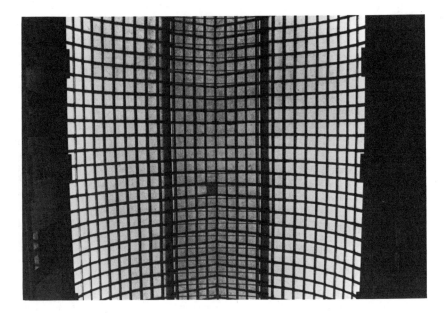

Photograph © Johann Friedrich Geist

Photograph © Danielle Moretti
Above: Galleries St. Hubert, Brussels, first monumental arcades construction, mid-nineteenth century. *Below*: AT&T building, detail of monumental arcade at ground level.

The *Passagen-Werk* suggests that it makes no sense to divide the era of capitalism into formalist "modernism" and historically eclectic "postmodernism," as these tendencies have been there from the start of industrial culture. The paradoxical dynamics of novelty and repetition simply repeat themselves anew.

Modernism and postmodernism are not chronological eras, but political positions in the century-long struggle between art and technology. If modernism expresses utopian longing by anticipating the reconciliation of social function and aesthetic form, postmodernism acknowledges their nonidentity and keeps fantasy alive. Each position thus represents a partial truth; each will recur "anew," so long as the contradictions of commodity society are not overcome.

Media Stars: Politics and the Entertainment Industry

Les Miserables   Reaganomics

ÉLECTIONS DU 7 JANVIER

Le COMITÉ ÉLECTORAL DE LA RUE BRÉA, le COMITÉ ÉLECTORAL DES TRAVAILLEURS, le COMITÉ RÉPUBLICAIN RADICAL, le COMITÉ DE LA LIGUE D'UNION RÉPUBLICAINE DES DROITS DE PARIS, de l'UNION et de l'ALLIANCE RÉPUBLICAINE, de l'ASSOCIATION DES TRAVAILLEURS et les COMITÉS RADICAUX DES ARRONDISSEMENTS DE PARIS

Ont choisi pour candidat aux élections du 7 janvier le citoyen

VICTOR HUGO

Ce nom est pour eux l'affirmation la plus nette des principes républicains. Dans les circonstances actuelles, ce nom signifie particulièrement

AMNISTIE

ABOLITION DE LA PEINE DE MORT

DISSOLUTION DE L'ASSEMBLÉE

RENTRÉE DU GOUVERNEMENT A PARIS

LEVÉE IMMÉDIATE DE L'ÉTAT DE SIÈGE

Career Opportunities: President

BEDTIME FOR BONZO

8:00   limited to the college communities $3.00+$.50
Uris
directed by Frederick de Cordova
with Ronald Reagan, Walter Slezak
In this camp classic, Reagan plays a more lively professor of psychology who sets out to prove that a monkey can be taught morality and ethics (too bad he didn't try the same experiment on Ollie North). "That Bonzo doesn't sink in its own silliness is due mainly to the unyielding dignity, professionalism, and low-key charm of Ronald Reagan the actor. Reagan's ability to project a generous amiability in the most ridiculously trying situations would serve him well three decades later when he was to make the most reactionary and greed-oriented program in the history of the Republic seem as quintessentially American as mom's apple pie. In the end, Bonzo's trainer has made monkeys of us all" (Andrew Sarris, Village Voice).   Co-sponsored with Senior Week.
1951   b/w   1 hr. 23 min.   USA

Photomontage © Michael Busch and Leslie Gazaway

The Literary Market

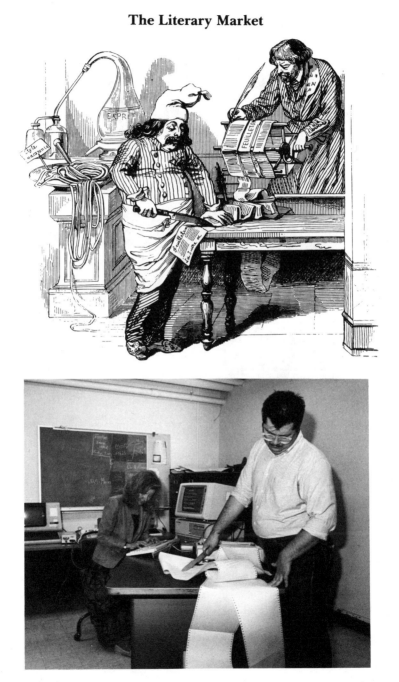

Above: Grandville, *Un autre monde*, 1844   *Below*: Photograph © Joan Sage, 1988

Landmark in Robotic Design

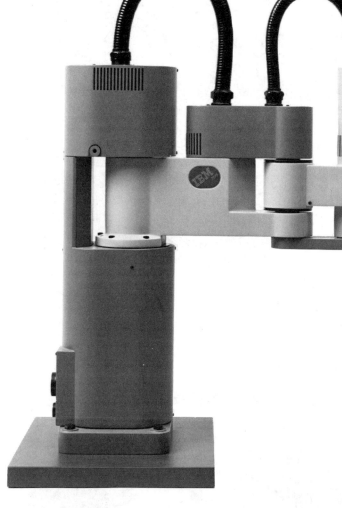

IBM's 7575 Robot, designed by Randall Martin, winner of the 1987 IDEA for machinery.
Courtesy of IBM

Ur-form of Robotics

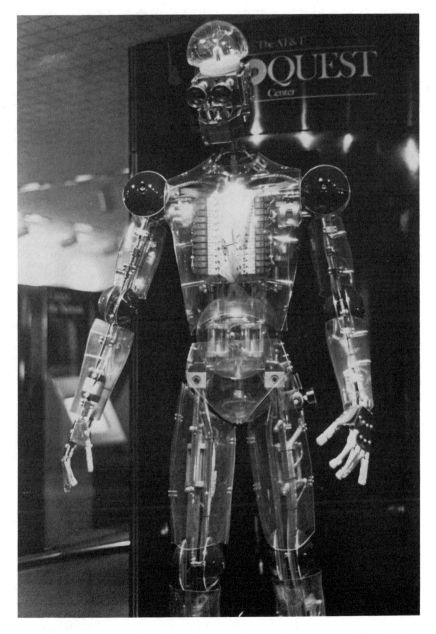

"Gor-don," latest of a long line of robots in human form, explains computer software in the "InfoQuest Center," AT&T building, New York. Photograph © Danielle Moretti

Childhood Reception

Above: Street hawkers with wind-up toys outside a Paris Arcade, 1936. *Miroir du monde*

Below: "Gor-don" talking with children in the AT&T InfoQuest Center, 1988. Photograph © Danielle Moretti

Automatons

Photograph © Grant Kester

Mechanical dolls were an invention of bourgeois culture. In the nineteenth century, these automatons were common. As late as 1896 "the doll motif had a socially critical meaning. Thus: 'You have no idea how these automatons and dolls become repugnant, how one breathes relief in meeting a fully natural being in this society'" (V, p. 848). Ironically, if playing with dolls was originally the way children learned the nurturing behavior of adult social relations, it has become a training ground for learning reified ones. The goal of little girls now is to become a "doll." This reversal epitomizes that which Marx considered characteristic of the capitalist-industrial mode of production: Machines that bring the promise of the naturalization of humanity and the humanization of nature result instead in the mechanization of both.

Thin Line Between Fact and Fiction

THE NEW YORK TIMES, SUNDAY, NOVEMBER 20, 1983

A host of small labs grapples with the changing technologies of the new field.

By N. R. KLEINFIELD

A woman whose job was final inspection grabbed something resembling a bracket for wall bookshelves that for some reason had a shiny doorknob stuck onto the end. It was actually an artificial hip. "Here's a shoulder," remarked a co-worker, plucking what looked like a skinny faucet out of a rack. "I believe this is a wrist."

This was in Rutherford, N.J., at the Howmedica Inc. artificial parts factory, one of many stops in a wide-ranging odyssey into the real-life world of the bionic man. They make hips here. And knees. Some shoulders. A few wrists, elbows, ankles, toes, thumbs. Every so often, a jaw.

In the main, the parts were being fabricated out of a rugged chrome cobalt alloy. "Some surgeons think that these things are made in some sort of carpentry shop," remarked David Fitzgerald, Howmedica's executive vice president. "We use space-age materials. We could manufacture fan blades for jet airplanes here if we wanted to." He was not kidding. The material for hips and knees is used by the aerospace industry to make fan blades.

Most parts come in several stock sizes, like sweaters: small, medium, large and extra-large. Hard-to-fit people are the domain of the custom department. Somebody there was working on an awfully big knee. Someone else was assigned to a job for Goodyear. The tire people had recently happened upon a giant sea turtle minus a flipper that had been dinner for a shark. Could Howmedica perhaps produce an artificial giant sea turtle wing? Well, it would try.

"We've done some stuff for famous people," said one of the custom men. "Arthur Godfrey had one of our hip cups in him. We made a skull plate for a gangster. I made Casey Stengel's hip. I also made up an ashtray for Casey with the same kind of hip on it. Got a kick out of that [. . .]."

The industry is highly amorphous. Sales and profit figures are closely guarded, though executives admit that the money is good in duplicating the body. When one tallies the estimated sales of all the body parts, the number exceeds 1 billion. Billions more are the carrots of the future.

"Everybody is a potential customer," one executive remarked. "If you live to be 70 or 80, then the odds are pretty good that something inside you is going to go. Your hip could go tomorrow."

"The third proposal was long-range and far more drastic. It advocated ectogenesis, prostheticism and universal transception. Of man only the brain would remain, beautifully encased in duraplast; a globe equipped with sockets, plugs and clasps. And powered by atomic battery—so the ingestion of nutriments, now physically superfluous, would take place only through illusion, programmed accordingly. The brain case could be connected to any number of appendages, apparatuses, machines, vehicles, etc. This prostheticization process would be spread out over two decades, with partial replacements mandatory for the first ten years, leaving all unnecessary organs at home; for example, when going to the theater one would detach one's fornication and defecation modules and hang them in the closet [. . .]. Mass production would keep the market supplied with custom-made internal components and accessories, including brain-tracks for home railways, that would enable the heads themselves to roll from room to room, an innocent diversion."

—From *Futurological Congress*, a science fiction novel by Stanislaw Lem, 1971

The Archaic as Anticipatory: Ur-forms of Feminism

In the context of the technological revolution, the utopian image of the Amazon woman returns with a brand new meaning, suggesting technology's capacity to liberate both nature and humanity.

Wish Image as Ruin: Eternal Fleetingness

"No form of eternalizing is so startling as that of the ephemeral and the fashionable forms which the wax figure cabinets preserve for us. And whoever has once seen them must, like André Breton [*Nadja*, 1928], lose his heart to the female form in the Musée Gravin who adjusts her stocking garter in the corner of the loge" (V, p. 117).

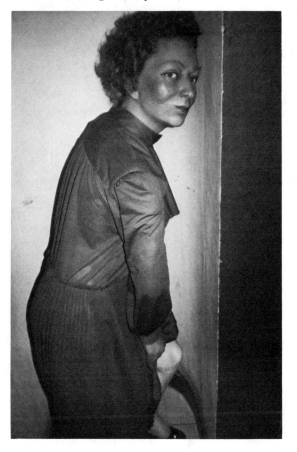

Wax figure in the corner of the loge, Musée Gravin, 1984. Photograph © Susan Buck-Morss

The wax woman to whom both Breton and Benjamin lost their hearts still adjusts her garter, as she has for half a century. Her ephemeral act is frozen in time. She is unchanged, defying organic decay. But her dress is musty; her figure and hair are no longer fashionable; she has clearly aged.

Unrealized Potential

Solar-powered printing press, built by Abel Pifre, 1880. At an exhibition that year in the Jardin des Tuilleries, it printed out 500 copies of the *Solar Journal*.

Realized Fiction

Nuclear Power, from the science fiction magazine, *Amazing Stories*, October, 1939.
Illustration © Frank R. Paul

"Only hunting and nomad people could sustain life there. Northern cities of once great importance were deserted. The population streamed southward." Illustration © Frank R. Paul, from Bruno Burgel, "The Cosmic Cloud," *Wonder Stories Quarterly* 3 (fall 1931):6. (Reprinted by permission of the representative of the Estate of Frank R. Paul, Forrest J. Ackerman, Hollywood, CA.)

The Persistence of Memory

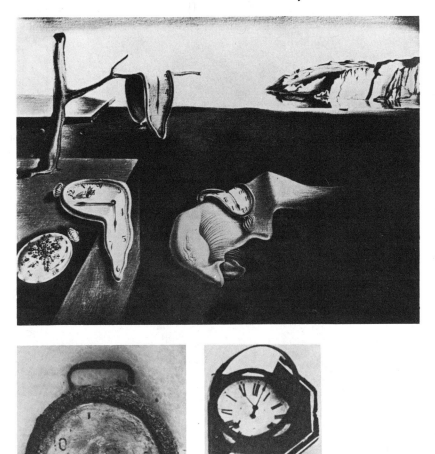

Above: "The Persistence of Memory," 1931. Painting by Salvador Dali. Oil on canvas, $9\frac{1}{2} \times 13''$. Collection, The Museum of Modern Art, New York. Given anonymously.

Below: August 9, 1945. *Left*: The hands on the watch show the time the atomic bomb hit Hiroshima: 8:15 a.m. (Peace Memorial Museum, Hiroshima) *Right*: A clock records the instant of the bomb blast at Nagasaki: 11:02 a.m. (Atomic Bomb Materials Center, Nagasaki)

Empty Time

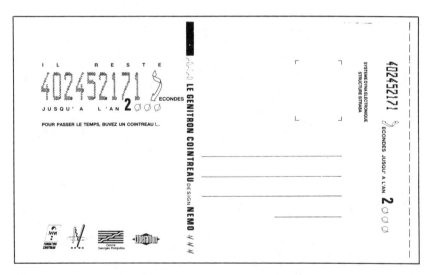

Postcard dispensed from a time machine outside the Centre Pompidou, Paris, that records the seconds remaining until the year 2000—"To pass the time, drink a cointreau!" (Spring 1987).

"Fashion: Mr. Death, Mr. Death!" (V, p. 110)

Presentation de quelques nouveautés

Magazin de Nouveauté

Fashion is the "eternal recurrence of the new" in the mass produced form of the "always the same" (I, p. 677).

These photographs of the newest fashions in weaponry were published in 1911, in an exposure of the financial interests behind the arms build-up, and a warning against the possibility of World War I. They were reprinted in 1933 in a special issue of *Crapouillot* on armaments, as an exposure of the persistence of these financial interests, and a warning against the possibility of World War II.

"There is a recorded tradition that is catastrophe" (V, p. 591).

"That it 'keeps going on like this' *is* the catastrophe" (V, p. 592).

Notes

Introduction to Part I

1. Walter Benjamin, *Gesammelte Schriften*, 6 vols., eds. Rolf Tiedemann and Hermann Schweppenhäuser, with the collaboration of Theodor W. Adorno and Gershom Scholem (Frankfurt am Main: Suhrkamp Verlag, 1972—), vol. V: *Das Passagen-Werk*, ed. Rolf Tiedemann (1982), p. 83 (Al, 1). Citations of Benjamin's *Gesammelte Schriften* will hereafter be by volume number (I–VI). Within citations, my own ellipses are distinguished from those of Benjamin by being enclosed in brackets: [. . .].

2. V, p. 83 (Al, 1).

3. Letter, Benjamin to Gershom Scholem, 15 March 1929, V, p. 1091.

4. The Arcades project was to embody "a theory of the consciousness of history. It is there that I will find Heidegger in my path, and I expect something scintillating from the connecting shock between our two very different ways of envisioning history" (letter, Benjamin to Scholem, 20 January 1930, V, p. 1094).

5. Letter, Benjamin to Scholem, 23 April 1928, V, p. 1086.

6. Early notes (1928–29), V, p. 1045 (a°, 3).

7. The phrase is Adorno's (see letter, Adorno to Benjamin, 6 November 1934, V, p. 1106).

8. Letter, Benjamin to Scholem, 30 January 1928, V, p. 1083.

9. Letter, Benjamin to Scholem, 23 April 1928, V. p. 1086.

10. He used the term *"Passagenarbeit,"* or simply *"Passagen."* The title *"Passagen-Werk"* has been given to the manuscript by the editors of Benjamin's *Gesammelte Schriften*.

11. Gershom Scholem, *Walter Benjamin: The Story of a Friendship*, eds. Karen Ready and Gary Smith (London: Faber & Faber, Ltd. 1982), p. 135.

12. Letter, Benjamin to Scholem, 24 May 1928, V, p. 1086.

13. Letter, Benjamin to Scholem, 30 November 1928, V, p. 1089.

14. Tiedemann's annotations are the guiding thread for any reading of the *Passagen-Werk*. Without them, even as competent a reader as Theodor Adorno was unable to decipher the material (see V, pp. 1072–73). As anyone who has worked on the *Passagen-Werk* will readily perceive, I am indebted to Tiedemann's editorial work immeasurably.

15. Among these I count my own earlier work, *The Origin of Negative Dialectics: Theodor W. Adorno, Walter Benjamin and the Frankfurt Institute* (New York: Macmillan Free Press, 1977). For the best intellectual biographies on Benjamin, see Richard Wolin, *Walter Benjamin: An Aesthetics of Redemption* (New York: Columbia University Press, 1982), Bernd Witte, *Walter Benjamin* (Reinbek bei Hamburg: Rowohlt, 1985) and Julian Roberts, *Walter Benjamin* (Atlantic Highlands, N.J.: Humanities Press, 1983).

16. *Ursprung des deutschen Trauerspiels*, I, p. 704.

1 Temporal Origins

1. *Ursprung des deutschen Trauerspiels*, I, p. 226.

2. Scholem reports that their marriage was held together by their son Stefan in whom Benjamin took "great interest," economic need (Dora supported the family as a translator during the worst inflation years), their common Jewish background, and their circle of friends in Berlin. The latter were mostly assimilated Jews (Scholem's own Zionism was the exception), radical more in a cultural than a political sense. Nonetheless, already by April 1921, "the disintegration of Walter's and Dora's marriage became evident." In the nine years "until their divorce, this situation remained unchanged and was interrupted only by Walter's long trips and by periods in which he took a separate room for himself" (Gershom Scholem, *Walter Benjamin: The Story of a Friendship*, eds. Karen Ready and Gary Smith [London: Faber & Faber, Ltd., 1982], pp. 93–94).

3. Scholem, *Walter Benjamin*, p. 85 (see also ibid., p. 54). In the fall of 1923 (for those who wish to find significance in the event), "Benjamin's father became gravely ill and had to have his right leg amputated" (ibid., p. 121). In 1924, Benjamin saw the archaic torso of Apollo in the Museum at Naples that had inspired Rilke's poem of the same name (ibid., p. 64). Not long afterward he wrote an aphorism entitled "torso": "Only he who knows how to view his own past as the monstrous product of compulsion and need would be capable of making it of utmost value for himself in the present. For that which one has lived is a best comparable to a lovely statue that has had all of its limbs broken off in transit, and now yields nothing but the costly block, out of which he has to hew the image of his future" (*Einbahnstrasse*, IV, p. 118).

4. Letter, Benjamin to Scholem, I, p. 875.

5. The inflation severely affected the finances of Benjamin's father, who put pressure on him, the eldest son, to take a position in a bank (see the excellently researched article by Gary Smith, "Benjamins Berlin," *Wissenschaft in Berlin*, eds. Tilmann Buddensieg et al. [Berlin: Gebr. Mann Verlag, 1987], p. 101).

6. At the time Scholem noted in his diary: "If some day Benjamin lectures on philosophy in a substantial way, not a soul will understand him, but his course could be tremendous if there were true *questioning* instead of label-sticking" (Scholem, *Walter Benjamin*, p. 34).

7. Scholem, *Walter Benjamin*, p. 79.

8. Letter, Benjamin to Scholem, 31 January 1918, Walter Benjamin, *Briefe*, 2 vols., eds. Gershom Scholem and Theodor W. Adorno (Frankfurt am Main: Schrkamp Verlag, 1978), vol.1, p. 169 (see also p. 171).

9. Benjamin had rather surprising academic tastes. While dismissing more acclaimed contemporary philosophers like the neo-Kantians Heinrich Rickert and Hermann Cohen, or the phenomenologists Husserl and Heidegger, he found Franz von Baader "more impressive than Schelling" (Scholem, *Walter Benjamin*, p. 22), and admired greatly the "gnostic Christian" Florens Christian Range (ibid., p. 115–17) and the Jewish mystic Franz Rosenzweig (ibid., p. 138). While in Munich in 1916, he had hoped to study with the *Lebensphilosoph* Ludwig Klages, whose writings on graphology "attracted him greatly," but the latter had left for Switzerland (ibid., pp. 19–20). Nonetheless, even in Benjamin's student years, at no time had a professor played the role of mentor. Intellectual stimulation came mainly from his friends (who for their part were repeatedly impressed by his "genius"). Scholem, as one of the closest, recalled: "We did not take the philosophy teachers very seriously [. . .]. We followed our stars without academic guides" (ibid., p. 21).

10. Benjamin, letter to Scholem, 10 May 1924, *Briefe*, vol. 1, pp. 344–45. The most famous Naples philosophy professor, Benedetto Croce, "was present at the meeting only at an effectively ostentatious distance" (ibid., p. 344).

11. As for Benjamin's future colleagues at the Frankfurt *Institut für Sozialforschung*, he did not yet have contact with Horkheimer, Löwenthal, or Marcuse, and only met the eleven-year-younger Adorno briefly through their mutual friend Siegfried Kracauer in 1923. Adorno remembered his first "impression of Benjamin as one of the most significant human beings who ever confronted me" (Theodor W. Adorno, "Erinnerungen," *Über Walter Benjamin*, ed. Rolf Tiedemann [Frankfurt am Main: Suhrkamp Verlag, 1970], p. 70).

12. Benjamin had no desire to teach. Students and lectures, he feared, would "assail my time murderously" (letter, Benjamin to Scholem, 19 February 1925, *Briefe*, vol. 1, p. 373). Adorno has written: "the antiquarian in him felt itself drawn to the academic life in much the same ironic manner as Kafka felt drawn to insurance companies" (Theodor W. Adorno, "A Portrait of Walter Benjamin," *Prisms*, trans. Samuel and Shierry Weber [London: Neville Spearman, 1967] p. 232).

13. His major works had been a study of Goethe's *Wahlverwandschaften*, and a dissertation on "The Concept of Criticism in German Romanticism" (I).

14. "Imperial Panorama: A Tour of German Inflation" went through several revisions before being published in *One Way Street* (*Einbahnstrasse*) in 1928. Benjamin's editor has distinguished the versions as follows (see IV, p. 907):

M^1 = manuscript presented to Scholem in fall 1923 (untitled): IV, pp. 928–35.

M^2 = "earlier, much more extensive manuscript" (IV, p. 907) entitled "Thoughts toward an Analysis of the Condition of Central Europe": IV, pp. 916–28.

J^7 = 1927 Dutch version, including sections (differently ordered) found in M^1 and *a* (we are not told which sections are found in which source), and a newly written preface (not found in any other version), a German translation of which is included: IV, p. 935.

a = text published in *Einbahnstrasse* in 1928: IV, pp. 85–148.

Because these revisions document Benjamin's move to Marx between 1923 and 1928, excerpts from "Imperial Panorama: A Tour of German Inflation" cited below will be identified as to the specific version in which they appear, and the differences compared to the final version of 1928 (*a*) will be noted. What becomes evident throught this procedure is how much—or, rather, how little—Benjamin needed to change the text in order to incorporate a Marxist orientation (and thus how close he was already in 1923 to that orientation—or, rather, how his loose interpretation of Marxism allowed it to fit his previous thinking).

15. "Instead of, at the very least, achieving a competent assessment of the impotence and implicatedness of one's own existence, whereby one might possibly detach it from the background of universal delusion, a blind determination to save the prestige of one's personal existence is triumphing everywhere" ("Imperial Panorama" [M²], IV, p. 928. Essentially unchanged in *Einbahnstrasse* [*a*], IV, p. 98).

16. "Imperial Panorama" (M¹), IV, p. 928. Essentially the same in *Einbahnstrasse* (*a*), IV, pp. 94–95, except for the significant substitution of "classes" [*Schichten*] for "millions" in the last sentence. Note, however, that the continuation of M¹ (1923) has, surprisingly, an explicit reference to revolution that has been *omitted* in *a* (1928). It grants that "oppressed people" from their "own authority," by forming "an authentic conception of liberation, might set a time limit to the continuation of such stability through the idea of revolution. But such intentions are far from the bourgeois manner of speaking. Even trying to restrain the [. . .] process of decline doesn't come to their minds, precisely because they consider the disintegration of a society or a nation as an exceptional circumstance that will restore itself automatically, even though history clearly shows the opposite" (M¹, IV, pp. 928–29).

17. M¹, IV, p. 935. Essentially unchanged in *Einbahnstrasse* (*a*), IV, p. 96.

18. Scholem, *Walter Benjamin*, p. 119.

19. From 1915 to "at least" 1927, "the religious sphere assumed a central importance for Benjamin that was utterly removed from fundamental doubt [. . .]. God was real for him [. . .]" (Scholem, *Walter Benjamin*, p. 56). Cf. chapter 7.

20. Scholem, *Walter Benjamin*, p. 116.

21. In Benjamin's earliest confrontation with Zionism (1912), he took the position: "'The best Jews today are linked to a valuable process in European culture [. . .]'"; "'[. . .] our cultural consciousness forbids us *ideally* from ever restricting the concept of culture to any single part of humanity'"; "'cultural Zionism [. . .] sees Jewish values *everywhere* and works for them. Here I will stay, and I believe I must stay.'" These excerpts, from Benjamin's correspondence with Ludwig Strauss (in the Strauss collection of the Jewish National and University Library, Jerusalem), are cited and translated by Anson Rabinbach in his important article (which corrects and modifies Scholem's account of Benjamin's early Judaism): "Between Enlightenment and Apocalypse: Benjamin, Bloch and Modern German Jewish Messianism, " *New German Critique* 34 (Winter 1985): 78–124 (see pp. 94–97). Rabinbach rightly concludes that for Benjamin, Zionism "was an alternative *only* if it remained in the sphere of ideas—as the utopian promise of cultural universality, not politics" (ibid., p. 98). A partial publication of the Benjamin-Strauss correspondence can be found in II, pp. 836–44.

22. Scholem reports a 1916 conversation with Benjamin, when "for the first time the question arose whether it was one's duty to go to Palestine. Benjamin criticized the 'agricultural Zionism' that I championed, saying that Zionism would have to wean itself of three things: 'the agricultural orientation, the racial ideology, and [Martin] Buber's "blood and experience" arguments'" (Scholem, *Walter Benjamin*, pp. 28–29). Scholem explains that Buber took a "positive stance" toward "the so-called 'experience' of the war" then in progress (ibid., p. 7), whereas Benjamin (feigning illness) managed to avoid military service, although he was, Scholem insists, against "this particular war," and not a pacifist by ideological conviction. "That simply was not his style" (ibid., pp. 24–25).

23. Benjamin, cited in Scholem, *Walter Benjamin*, p. 122.

24. Scholem, *Walter Benjamin*, p. 122.

25. Asja Lacis, *Revolutionär im Beruf: Berichte über proletarisches Theater, über Meyerhold, Brecht, Benjamin und Piscator*, ed. Hildegaard Brenner (Munich: Regner & Bernhard, 1971), p. 431.

26. Letter, Benjamin to Scholem, 7 July 1924, *Briefe*, vol. 1, p. 351.

27. See Benjamin's writings from that period, particularly I, pp. 7–104; also Richard Wolin, *Walter Benjamin: An Aesthetics of Redemption* (New York: Columbia University Press, 1982), pp. 4–13.

28. Scholem recalls that generally Benjamin had an "utter aversion to discussing the political events of the day" (*Walter Benjamin*, p. 23). Benjamin then still completely rejected "the idea of a dictatorship of the proletariat: "I would say that our sympathies were to a great extent with the Social Revolutionary Party in Russia [. . .]" (ibid., p. 78). And on the attempted Socialist Revolution in Hungary in 1919: "He regarded the Hungarian soviet republic as a childish aberration, and the only thing that touched him was the fate of Georg Lukács, Bloch's closest friend; at that time people (mistakenly) feared that he had been arrested and might be shot" (ibid., p. 80).

29. Scholem, *Walter Benjamin*, p. 7.

30. In 1927 Benjamin observed: "I belong to the generation that is today between thrity and forty. The intelligentsia of this generation is surely the last to have enjoyed a thoroughly apolitical upbringing. The war drove those elements which were farthest Left into the camp of a more or less radical pacifism [. . .]; [its] radicalization [. . . owed] more to the Revolution of 1918 which failed due to the petty-bourgeois parvenu spirit of German Social Democracy, than to the war itself." In the twenties it became increasingly evident that "consciously or unconsciously," the allegedly "free" intelligentsia "worked for a class" (VI, p. 781).

31. Letter, Benjamin to Ludwig Strauss, 7 January 1913, II, p. 842. Two years after Benjamin's encounter with Lacis, he still spoke in similar terms: "[. . .] I [. . .] consider the communists 'goals' to be nonsense and non-existent; but this doesn't take away from the value of communist action one iota, because the latter is the corrective of the communist goals, and because meaningful *political* goals do not exist" (letter, Benjamin to Scholem, 29 May 1926, *Briefe*, vol. 1, p. 426).

32. Scholem reports that reading *Geist der Utopie* made Benjamin impatient because he could not approve of everything about it. Benjamin admired some of Bloch's writings; others "made him fly into a rage" (Scholem, *Walter Benjamin*, p. 109.) On Benjamin's reception of Bloch, see Rabinbach, "Between Enlightenment and Apocalypse," pp. 109–21.

33. Scholem, *Walter Benjamin*, p. 56.

34. Scholem, *Walter Benjamin*, p. 13. This is from an early conversation (1915) with Scholem, in which Benjamin discussed "the question of what a historical work would look like if it were actually based on history" (ibid.).

35. Not history, but material nature was meaningful, and in this sense, mysticism and even animism were more adequate interpretive schemata than Hegel's philosophical abstraction (cf. Scholem, *Walter Benjamin*, pp. 30–31).

36. Scholem, *Walter Benjamin*, p. 37.

37. Scholem, *Walter Benjamin*, p. 37.

38. Benjamin, cited in Scholem, *Walter Benjamin*, p. 59 (cf. p. 13).

39. Ernst Bloch, "Erinnerung," *Über Walter Benjamin*, mit Beiträgen von Theodor W. Adorno et al., (Frankfurt am Main: Suhrkamp Verlag, 1968), p. 17.

40. See "Über Sparache Überhaupt und Über die Sprache des Menschen," II, pp. 140–57; see also VI (published 1986) for previously unavailable material on this notoriously difficult side of Benjamin's early philolsophy of language. Two monographs that deal intelligently with Benjamin's *Sprachphilosophie* are Winfried Menninghaus, *Walter Benjamins Theorie der Sprachmagie* (Frankfurt am Main: Suhrkamp Verlag, 1980) and Liselotte Wiesenthal, *Zur Wissenschaftstheorie Walter Benjamins*' (Frankfurt am Main: Athenaüm, 1973). See also the (dubiously) nihilist reading of Benjamin's language theory (which ends with a brilliant reading of a *Passagen-Werk* entry on the *place du Maroc*) by Michael W. Jennings in Chapter 3 of his recent, extremely well-written book, *Dialectical Images: Walter Benjamin's Theory of Literary Criticism* (Ithaca: Cornell University Press, 1987), pp. 82–120. On Benjamin's theory of language, I have learned much from papers by Daniel Purdy, "Walter Benjamin's Blotter: Soaking up the Dialectical Image" (Cornell University, Department of German Studies, 1986), and Christiane von Bülow, "History, Metaphor and Truth in Benjamin" (University of California, Irvine, Department of English and Comparative Literature).

41. M^1, IV, p. 931.

42. *a*, IV, p. 97 (italics mine).

43. Scholem dismisses the changes thus (without stating precisely what they are) in *Walter Benjamin*, pp. 118–19.

44. "The change can stand as the motto of his political radicalization" (publ. note, Walter Benjamin, *One Way Street and Other Writings*, trans. Edmund Jephcott and Kingsley Shorter [London: NLB, 1979], p. 34). Yes. But consider the following. As late as 1927, the Dutch translation of "Imperial Panorama" (J^7) contained an introduction that, undoubtedly by Benjamin, "has a counterpart in no other version" (ed. note, IV, p. 935), and which combines images of theology and politics (as well as nature and history), fusing them quite effortlessly into one: "With the end of the four-year war, inflation began in Germany. It has been raging now for eight years, striking first one country then another, stopping only for a few months or weeks. But for the ruling class in all of Europe these months and weeks are already enough to keep proclaiming the restoration of "stable prewar relations." But the fact that the war itself (which they want to forget) *was* the stabilization of these relations— followed consequently to the point of madness—and that its end coincides with the end of just these relations, this they don't understand. What irritates them, like bad weather that won't go away, is in fact and truth the downfall of their world. the low barometric pressure of the economic situation that has lasted in Germany for years, for the first time, due to this indicator, makes consideration of a new flood possible.

"To incite this flood is the business not of history but politics; the affair not of the chroniclers, but of the prophets" (J^7, IV, p. 935).

45. "[. . . F]our years ago I could have made Judaism a maxim. Now I can no longer do that"; "For Judaism is for me in no way an end in itself, but instead a most distinguished bearer and representative of the intellect" (letter, Benjamin to Strauss, November 1912, II, p. 838). Of course, the same was true of Benjamin's reception of Marx. He found not Marxist "dogma," but the "attitude" (*Haltung*) of Communism "obligatory" (letter, Benjamin to Max Rychner, 7 March 1931, *Briefe*, vol. 2, p. 524).

46. Text written 1 May 1927, intended as an introduction for a published version of Benjamin's "Moskauer Tagebuch" (VI, p. 782). This publication did not take place.

47. "Programm eines proletarischen Kindertheaters" II, p. 768. "The proletariat cannot pass its class interests onto the young generation through the unfair means of an ideology which is geared to suppress the child's suggestibility. [. . .] Proletarian education proves its superiority by guaranteeing to children the fulfillment of their childhood" (ibid.). These quotations are from a description of the philosophy behind the proletarian children's theater, written collaboratively by Lacis and Benjamin in 1928. Lacis has described her conception: "I was convinced that one could awaken and develop children by means of play" (Lacis, *Revolutionär im Beruf*, p. 22), and in Capri, Benjamin showed "an extraordinary interest in it" (ibid., pp. 25–26).

48. Lacis, *Revolutionär im Beruf*, pp. 43–44. Lacis continued: "At that time I wasn't satisfied with his answers. I asked whether he also saw analogies in the world views of the Baroque dramatists and Expressionists, and what class interests they expressed. He answered vaguely and then submitted that he was at the moment reading Lukács and was beginning to become interested in a materialist aesthetics. At the time, in Capri, I didn't understand correctly the connection between allegory and modern poetry. In retrospect, I now see how perceptively Walter Benjamin saw through the modern problem of form. Already in the 1920s allegory emerges in the 'Agit-prop' pieces and in the plays of Brecht ('Mahagonny,' 'Das Badener Lehrstück vom Einverständnis') as a fully valued means of expression. In plays in the West, for example in the dramas of Genet, also those by Peter Weiss, ritual is an important factor" (ibid., p. 44).

49. Benjamin, letter to Scholem 13 June 1924, *Briefe*, vol. 1, p. 347. It was in this letter that Benjamin first mentioned meeting Lacis (not yet by name).

50. See letter, Benjamin to Scholem, 22 December 1924, *Briefe*, vol. 1, p. 365.

51. Letter, Benjamin to Scholem, 22 December 1924, *Briefe*, vol. 1, p. 368.

52. Letter, Benjamin to Scholem, 22 December 1924, *Briefe*, vol. 1, p. 367.

53. I, pp. 209.

54. I, p. 208.

55. IV, p. 85.

56. IV, p. 85.

57. IV, p. 85.

58. IV, p. 85.

59. "The treatise is an Arabic form. Its exterior is continuous and unmarked like the facades of Arabian buildings, the articulation of which begins only in the inner courtyard. So too, the articulated structure of the treatise is not perceptible from the exterior, but opens itself up only from within. If it is constructed as chapters, these are noted, not by verbal titles but by numerals." (*Einbahnstrasse*, IV, p. 111).

60. IV, p. 125.

61. M², IV, p. 917 (not in *a*).

62. IV, p. 109.

63. IV, p. 146.

64. Witte calls it "one of the most significant works of the German language avant-garde literature of the twenties" (Bernd Witte, *Walter Benjamin* [Reinbek bei Hamburg: Rowohlt, 1985], p. 65). Devoid, however, of futurist sensitivities despite the prevalence of technological images, this work does not claim for modernist aesthetics any intrinsic merit. Even as it adopts the "ready language" of the placard, it acknowledges that the revolution in print has taken a toll (IV, p. 103). And, while *One Way Street* is at times identifiably Marxist—Scholem refers to "Marxist terminology" in it as still "merely a kind of distant thunder" (Scholem, *Walter Benjamin*, p. 34)—it warns against romanticizing the class struggle by projecting it onto the screen of history as a modern myth, a drama of proletarian heroes vanquishing bourgeois foes: "The concept of class warfare can lead to error. It does not have to do with a trial of strength in which is decided: who wins? [. . .] To think thus is to romanticize and ignore the facts. For whether the bourgeoisie wins or is defeated in the struggle, it is condemned to decline due to internal contradictions that will become fatal as they develop. The question is only whether its downfall will come from itself or from the proletariat. [. . .] Political intervention, danger and timing are technical—not knightly" (IV, p. 122). The irreversibility of the bourgeoisie's decline is for Benjamin simply a statement of fact; but so is the emergence of new cultural forms, and as an engineer in the service of the proletariat, he is experimenting with their expressive potential. Thus, although modernist aesthetics and Marxist politics both function in the text, they are not presented as identical. Rather, the revolutionized media and the cultural producer are "allies," as he says in his criticism of Karl Kraus, the Viennese writer whose literary journal *Die Fackel* singlehandedly took on journalism's degenerating effects on language: "In ur-old armor, grinning with wrath, a Chinese idol brandishing drawn swords in both hands, he [Kraus] dances a war dance before the burial vault of the German language [. . .]. What is more helpless than his conversion? What more impotent than his humanity? What is more hopeless than his struggle against the press? What does he know of the forces that are in fact and truth his allies?" (IV, p. 121).

65. Cf. I, pp. 329–33.

66. "In an aversion to animals the dominant sensitivity is a fear of being recognized by them through contact" (IV, p. 90).

67. In his *Trauerspiel* study, Benjamin referred to "the most current dramatic experiments" (i.e., Expressionism) that attempted to "rehabilitate" the "best parts" of Baroque drama; he judged these attempts as "indeed, in vain" (I, p. 390).

68. Benjamin describes the city, traditionally the fortress of the bourgeoisie, as crumbling, besieged from without by highways and from within by new architectural "monstrosities" (IV, p. 100). For the centrality of crumbling ruins in Baroque allegory, see I, pp. 353–55.

69. "Freedom of conversation is being lost. [. . . I]t is now replaced by asking the price of the other person's shoes or umbrella [. . .]. It is as if one were trapped in a theater and had to follow the play on the stage whether one wanted to or not, and make it again and again the subject of one's thoughts and speech" (IV, p. 98).

70. "Warmth is ebbing out of things [. . .]. Their coldness must be compensated by [people's] own warmth in order not to freeze to death [. . .]" (IV, p. 99).

71. Here again, *One Way Street* provides a practical demonstration of what the *Trauerspiel* study presents theoretically, namely, the distinction between allegory and symbol as different modes of experiencing transitoriness: "Whereas in the symbol passing away is transformed

and the transfigured face of nature is fleetingly revealed in the light of redemption, in allegory there lies before one's gaze the *facies hippocratica* [deathmask] of history as a petrified, primitive landscape." (I, pp. 342–43) See chapter 6, section 2.

72. IV, p. 92, trans. by Edmund Jecphcott and Kingsley Shorter, *One Way Street and Other Writings* (London: NLB, 1979), p. 52. This passage was written for Lacis, to whom he read it during his trip to Moscow ("Moskauer Tagebuch," VI, p. 297).

73. IV, p. 113, trans. Jephcott and Shorter, *One Way Street*, pp. 71–72.

74. IV, p. 107. The same statement occurs in the *Trauerspiel* study: "Every completed work is the deathmask of its intention" (I, p. 875).

75. IV, p. 138, trans. Jephcott and Shorter, *One Way Street*, p. 95.

76. IV, p. 83.

77. I, p. 203.

78. Letter, Benjamin to Scholem, 30 January 1928, *Briefe*, vol. 1, p. 455.

79. Interestingly, this is true as well of Benjamin's research procedure. He wrote to Scholem in 1924 of the "eccentric acribie" he had employed in the *Trauerspiel* study: "I have alone at my disposal over 600 quotations, in the best order and most easily perused arrangement" (*Briefe*, p. 339), and that "the written text is composed almost totally out of quotations" (ibid., p. 366). He prepared the *Passagen-Werk* with this same "eccentric acribie," but, to cite him, with "fiendish intensification," as the quotations numbered in the thousands.

80. Scholem, *Walter Benjamin*, p. 124.

81. Benjamin's notes for the *Trauerspiel* study, I, p. 918.

82. See below, chapter 7.

83. Lacis, *Revolutionär im Beruf*, p. 45.

84. See the chapter, "The Failed Project, 1928–29," in Scholem, *Walter Benjamin*, pp. 143–56.

85. "Speaking again of my trip [to Capri], in Berlin everyone agrees that the change I have undergone is apparent" (letter, Benjamin to Scholem, 22 December 1924, *Briefe*, vol. 1, p. 368).

86. Asja went (via Paris) to Berlin as well, but accompanied by Bernhard Reich (Lacis, *Revolutionär im Beruf*, p. 48).

87. Letter, Benjamin to Scholem, 19 February 1925, *Briefe*, vol. 1, p. 372.

88. Lacis said it showed "how naive Walter was. Although the work looks properly academic, laden with learned quotations, even in French and Latin, and relates to a vast material, it is still fully clear that no scholar wrote this book, but a poet who is in love with language and applies hyperboles in order to construct a brilliant aphorism" (Lacis, *Revolutionär im Beruf*, p. 45).

89. Hans Cornelius, cited in the detailed, definitive account by Burkhardt Lindner, "Habilitationsakte Walter Benjamin: Über ein 'akademisches Trauerspiel' und über ein Vorkapitel der 'Frankfurter Schule' (Horkheimer, Adorno)," *Zeitschrift für Literaturwissenschaft und Linguistik* 53/54 (1984), p. 155.

90. Letter, Benjamin to Scholem, 5 April 1926, *Briefe*, p. 416.

91. *Briefe*, p. 418. When Benjamin read this "preface" to the *Trauerspiel* book to Lacis during his visit to Moscow two years later, "Asja thought, in spite of everything, I should simply write [on the manuscript to be published]: 'Rejected by the University of Frankfurt am Main'" ("Moskauer Tagebuch," VI, p. 326).

92. Bloch, "Erinnerungen," *Über Walter Benjamin*, p. 22.

93. V, p. 578 (N3, 2).

94. Bloch, "Erinnerungen," *Über Walter Benjamin*, p. 16. Bloch recalled that as foreigners in Paris they were perhaps too dependent on each other's company (ibid.). By the 1930s, Benjamin felt somewhat distanced from Bloch, and expressed concern that Bloch was plagiarizing his ideas, particularly those that belonged to the constellation of the *Passagen-Werk* (see V, p. 1082).

95. "Diary of my Loire Trip" (1927), VI, p. 410.

96. Letter, Benjamin to Adorno, 31 May 1935, V. p. 1117.

97. Letter, Benjamin to Scholem, 25 April 1930, *Briefe*, vol. 2, p. 513.

2 Spatial Origins

1. "Moskauer Tagebuch," VI, p. 306, trans. Richard Sieburth, Walter Benjamin, *Moscow Diary*, ed. Gary Smith (Cambridge, Mass.: Harvard University Press, 1987), p. 25.

2. Asja Lacis, *Revolutionär im Beruf: Berichte über proletarisches Theater, über Meyerhold, Brecht, Benjamin und Piscator*, ed. Hildegaard Brenner (Munich: Regner & Bernharad, 1971), pp. 44–5.

3. "Neapel," IV, p. 314.

4. IV, p. 314.

5. IV. p. 309.

6. IV, p. 313.

7. IV, p. 308.

8. IV, p. 313.

9. IV, p. 310.

10. "Everything that the foreigner desires, admires and pays for is 'Pompeii.' 'Pompeii' makes the gypsum imitations of the temple ruins, the necklaces out of lumps of lava, and the louse-filled personage of the tour guide irresistible" (IV, p. 308).

11. IV, p. 311.

12. IV, p. 311.

13. IV, p. 315.

14. IV, p. 312. Benjamin and Lacis make no mention of the fascism that had reigned in Italy for several years (but see Walter Benjamin, *Briefe*, 2 vols., eds. Gershom Scholem and Theodor W. Adorno [Frankfurt am Main: Suhrkamp Verlag, 1978], vol. 1, pp. 364–65).

15. Letter, Benjamin to Martin Buber, 23 February 1927, *Briefe*, vol. 1, pp. 442–43.

16. Letter, Benjamin to Hugo von Hofmannsthal, 5 June 1927, *Briefe*, vol. 1, pp. 443–44.

17. "Moskau," IV, p. 343.

18. IV, p. 325.

19. IV, pp. 325–26.

20. IV, pp. 324–25.

21. "Here there is nothing of the dreary, repressed attitude of the few proletarians who barely dare to show themselves in the pubic space of our museums. In Russia the proletariat has really begun to take possession of bourgeois culture; with us such undertakings appear as if it were planning a burglary" (IV, p. 323).

22. IV, p. 343.

23. An otherwise sober and nonpredictive English trade-unions report mentions the possibility that in the future Lenin "'may even be pronounced a saint'"; Benjamin adds: "Even today, the cult of his picture has gone immeasurably far" (IV, p. 348).

24. "Moscow as it presents itself at the present moment allows all possibilities to be recognized in schematic abbreviation: above all, those of the failure and of the success of the revolution" (letter, Benjamin to Martin Buber, 23 February 1927, *Briefe*, vol. 1, p. 443). "[. . . W]hat will ultimately evolve from [the revolution] in Russia is totally unpredictable. Perhaps a truly socialist community, perhaps something totally different" (letter, Benjamin to Jula Radt, 26 December 1926, ibid., p. 439).

25. "Moskau," IV, p. 333.

26. IV, pp. 335–36, trans. Jephcott and Shorter, "Moscow," *One Way Street* (London: NLB, 1979), pp. 195–96.

27. "Moskauer Tagebuch," VI, pp. 367–68.

28. "Moskau," IV, p. 320.

29. IV, pp. 337–38.

30. IV, pp. 338–39.

31. He attended theater, films ("on average not all that good" [IV, p. 340]), museums, literary debates, and very often, giving in to his mania for collecting, he shopped.

32. He wrote to Scholem before the trip that he planned to join the Communist Party "by all means sooner or later" (letter, Benjamin to Scholem, [20–25] May 1925, *Briefe*, vol. 1, p. 382); but that such a move was for him experimental, a question "less of yes or no, but of how long" (letter, Benjamin to Scholem, 29 May 1926, ibid., p. 425).

33. The "Moskauer Taagebuch" (VI, pp. 292–409) combines drafts for parts of the published "Moscow" essay with the most personal reflections on Benjamin's own circumstances.

34. VI, p. 319, trans. Richard Sieburth, *Moscow Diary*, p. 73. "It is becoming clearer and clearer to me that my work needs some sort of solid frame for the immediate future. [. . .] Only purely external considerations hold me back from joining the German Communist Party. This would seem to be the right moment now, one which it would be perhaps danger-ous for me to let pass. For precisely because membership in the Party may very well only be an episode for me, it is not advisable to put it off any longer" (ibid., p. 72 [VI, p. 358]).

35. VI, p. 358, trans. Richard Sieburth, *Moscow Diary*, p. 72.

36. VI, p. 294.

37. Lacis, *Revolutionär im Beruf*, p. 54.

38. Benjamin knew of their relationship from the start, as Reich had accompanied Lacis to Capri in the summer of 1924, when (during Reich's absence for a few weeks in Munich) she had come to know Benjamin (see Lacis, *Revolutionär im Beruf*, p. 41). Both Reich and Lacis seem to have had other affairs while Benjamin was in Moscow, Lacis with a Red Army officer, and Reich with Lacis' sanitorium roommate. And, of course, Benjamin was still living with Dora, to whom he sent a birthday greeting from Moscow.

39. "Moskauer Tagebuch", VI, p. 317.

40. See Bernd Witte, *Walter Benjamin: Der Intellektuelle als kritiker. Untersuchungen zu seinem Frühwerk* (Stuttgart: J. B. Metzlerische Verlagsbuchhandlung, 1976).

41. "Moskauer Tagebuch," VI, p. 409, trans. Richard Sieburth, *Moscow Diary*, p. 121.

42. Letter, Benjamin to Jula Cohn Radt, 26 December 1926, *Briefe*, vol. 1, pp. 439–40. Jula Cohn was a sculptor whom Benjamin had known (and loved) since his student years. It may be that she was with him in Capri when he returned there in September 1925 (see ibid., p. 423); the same year she married Fritz Radt. Benjamin saw her again in southern France in the summer of 1926 (ibid., p. 439).

43. "Goethe," II, pp. 705–39.

44. Benjamin had begun work on the article before his Moscow trip, and brought an outline of it with him to Moscow to discuss with the editors. They were wary. Their interest tempo-rarily increased in 1928, and Benjamin completed the Goethe entry that fall. The following spring it was definitively rejected. Reviewing Benjamin's article in March 1929, during his last days as Soviet Commissar for Education, Anatoly Lunacharsky wrote (29 March 1927) to the *Encyclopedia* editors that it was "inappropriate": "It displays considerable talent and contains occasional insights that are surprisingly acute, but it draws no conclusions of any sort. What's more, he explains neither Goethe's place within European cultural history nor his place for us in—so to speak—our cultural pantheon" (published in *Literaturnoe nasledstvo* [Moscow 1970], trans. Richard Sieburth, in Benjamin, *Moscow Diary*, p. 131). The article on Goethe that ultimately appeared in the *Great Soviet Encyclopedia* paralleled Benjamin's original manuscript by an estimated 12 percent (see ed. note, II, p. 1472).

45. Letter, Benjamin to Hugo von Hofmannsthal, 5 June 1927, *Briefe*, vol. 1, p. 444; see also letter, Benjamin to Scholem, 23 February 1927 (ibid., pp. 441–42).

46. A fragment of several pages entitled *"Passagen"* (V, pp. 1041–43) is "the only thoroughly formulated and coherent text from this earliest stage of the work, which dates to mid-1927, when Benjamin together with Franz Hessel still wanted to write a journal article" (ed. note, V, p. 1341). Notes of this early collaboration found in Benjamin's papers are printed in V, pp. 1341–48. They include themes later dropped from the project, and are significantly

different from the other early series of notes (series A° and a°), which correspond more closely to the developed conception of the project.

47. Earlier, Benjamin had not been so favorably impressed with the Surrealists. In July 1925 he wrote to Scholem that he was becoming acquainted with the "marvelous writings of Paul Valéry (*Variété*, *Eupalinos*) on the one hand, and the dubious books of the Surrealists on the other" (II, p. 1018). His altered perception following his Moscow trip is documented in his letter to Hofmansthal, 5 June 1927: "Whereas in Germany among people of my generation I feel totally isolated from my efforts and interests, in France there are specific phenomena—as authors Giraudoux and particularly Aragon—as a movement Surrealism, in which I see at work my own concerns" (*Briefe*, vol. 1, p. 446).

48. Letter, Benjamin to Adorno, 31 May 1935, *Briefe*, vol. 2, pp. 662–63. Benjamin found Hessel's company more comfortable than that of more genial acquaintances. Although it is impossible to say for certain which ideas of the Arcades project were Hessel's, from the latter's book, *Spazieren in Berlin*, published in 1929, it is clear that Benjamin's conception, particularly in its philosophical complexity, far outstripped the original idea which they conceived together.

49. V, pp. 993–1039 and 1044–59.

50. The essay criticized the rest of the French left-wing intelligentsia, "just as their Russian counterparts," for their "feeling of obligation not to the revolution, but to the tradition of culture ("Der Sürrealismus: Die letzte Aufnahme der europäischen Intelligenz," II, p. 304). 304).

51. "Der Sürrealismus," II, p. 306.

52. "Der Sürrealismus," II, p. 307. Benjamin did not rule out the importance of drug-induced states for such illumination; the latter came about through reflection *on* such states, not the states themselves (ibid.) Benjamin's own experiments with hashish began in 1927, were more frequent in 1930–31, and occurred as late as 1934. See "Protokolle Zu Drogenver-suchen," VI, pp. 558–618.

53. "Der Sürrealismus," II, p. 300.

54. Scholem reports that Surrealism was "the first bridge to a positive evaluation of psychoanalysis" (II, p. 1019). See below, chapter 8.

55. Notes for the essay, "Der Sürrealismus," II, p. 1024.

56. Early notes (1927–29), V, p. 1026 (0°, 4).

57. "Der Sürrealismus," II, p. 307.

58. It was in fact his third retelling. Not only had he retold it in his "preface" to the *Trauerspiel* study several years earlier; in 1908, as a member of Weyneken's *Jugendbewegung* and an editor of its student journal, *der Anfang*, the sixteen-year-old Benjamin had written in its second edition: "But youth is the Sleeping Beauty, asleep without suspecting the prince who approaches in order to awaken it. And in order that youth awaken, that it take part in the struggles surrounding it, it is to this that our journal desires to contribute its powers"—by interpreting past literature (Schiller, Goethe, Nietzsche) as instructive for the moral task of a coming "*Zeitalter* of youth": "For how can a young person, above all from a metropolis, confront the deepest problems, the social misery, without, at least for a time, being overcome by pessimism? [. . . Yet,] no matter how bad the world may be, you [i.e., youth] came to it to raise it up. That is not pride but only consciousness of one's duty" ("Das Dornröschen," II, pp. 9–10).

59. Letter, Benjamin to Scholem, 17 April 1931, *Briefe*, vol. 2, p. 531.

60. On this success (and, generally on Benjamin in Berlin) see the essay by Gary Smith, "Benjamins Berlin," *Wissenschaften in Berlin*, eds. Tilmann Buddensieg, et al. (Berlin: Gebr. Mann Verlag, 1987), pp. 98–102.

61. Ernst Bloch, "Erinnerungen," *Über Walter Benjamin*, mit Beiträgen von Theodor W. Adorno et al. (Frankfurt am Main: Suhrkamp Verlag, 1968), p. 22.

62. The significance of these reviews is discussed in Witte, *Walter Benjamin: Der Intellektuelle als Kritiker*.

63. The scripts of several of these broadcasts were first published in Walter Benjamin, "Radiofeuilletons für Kinder und Jugendliche," *Sinn und Form* 36, 4 (July/August 1984): 683–703. A more complete collection has appeared as *Aufklärung für Kinder: Rundfunkvorträge*, ed. Rolf Tiedemann (Frankfurt am Main: Suhrkamp Verlag, 1985). See also "Hörmodelle," examples of Benjamin's radio shows for the Frankfurt am Main station, *Sudwestdeutscher Rundfunk*, (IV, pp. 627–720). An empirical study of the broadcasts which mainfests excellent, original research in radio history, is provided in Sabine Schiller-Lerg, *Walter Benjamin und der Rundfunk: Programarbeit zwischen Theorie und Praxis*, vol. 1 of *Rundfunkstudien*, ed. Winfried B. Lerg (New York: K. G. Saur, 1984). For a discussion of the program contents, see Susan Buck-Morss, "Verehrte Unsichtbare! Walter Benjamins Radiovortäge," *Walter Benjamin und die Kinderliteratur*, ed. Klaus Dorderer (Weinheim and Munich: Juventa Verlag, 1988).

64. Radio broadcast, 24 April 1931, Frankfurt am Main, *Aufklärung für Kinder*, p. 116.

65. "Theodor Hosemann," *Aufklärung für Kinder*, p. 69.

66. See IV, pp. 671–73.

67. The Brechtian influence is particularly pronounced in the series of "Hörmodelle" for adult radio in Frankfurt am Main. One broadcast problematized an event from "everyday life," asking one's boss for a raise, presenting it as a "confrontation between example and counterexample" of how they might be resolved, and in the process revealing the context of class in which such "resolutions" occur ("Gehaltserhöhung? Wo denken Sie hin!" [1931] IV, pp. 629–40).

68. Letter, Benjamin to Brecht (February 1931), VI, p. 826 (italics, his), written to explain why Benjamin was withdrawing from the board, which had accepted articles that did not live up to what they had agreed would be the journal's intent. The project was never realized (ibid., pp. 826–27). The previous year, Benjamin planned to "establish a very small reading circle, led by Brecht and myself, [. . .] to destroy Heidegger," but it also seems to have failed to materialize (letter, Benjamin to Scholem, 25 April 1930, *Briefe*, vol. 2, p. 514).

69. "Moskauer Tagebuch," VI, pp. 358–59.

70. Letter, Benjamin to Scholem, 20 January 1930, *Briefe*, vol. 2, p. 505. Benjamin describes recreating his genre from within: "[. . .] the popular nature [*Volkstümlichkeit*] of writing is deposited not in consumption, but in production, that is, professionally. In a word, it is through the literalization of life's relations that the irresolvable antinomies are mastered under which all of aesthetic creativity stands today, and it is the arena of the deepest degradation of the printed word, that is, the newspaper, upon which, in a new society, the word's restoration will take place. It is, indeed, not the most contemptuous Cunning of the Idea. Necessity—which today with unbelievable atmospheric pressure compresses precisely the creativity of the best people so that it has a place in the dark belly of a *feuilleton*, as in that of a wooden horse, in order one day to set the Troy of this press aflame" ("Tagebuch vom 7.8.1931 bis zum Todestag," VI, p. 446).

71. On 3 October 1931, Benjamin wrote to Scholem that the extreme unemployment turned workers who had jobs by this fact alone into a "labor aristocracy," and he noted that the Communists "probably could hardly handle [the situation] otherwise than the Social Democrats were doing"; in fact the National Socialists were becoming recognized as the delegates of the unemployed: "The Communists have as yet not found the necessary contact to these [unemployed] masses and thereby to the possibilities for revolutionary action [. . .]" (*Briefe*, vol. 2, pp. 537–38).

72. Letter, Benjamin to Max Rychner, 7 March 1931, *Briefe*, vol. 2, p. 523.

73. Letter, Benjamin to Scholem, 20 January 1931, *Briefe*, vol. 2, p. 506.

74. See "Diary from 7 August 1931 to the Date of Death," which begins: "This diary does not promise to be very long" (VI, p. 441).

75. Letter, Benjamin to Scholem, 20 December 1931, *Briefe*, vol. 2, p. 544.

76. Letter, Benjamin to Scholem. 26 July 1932, *Briefe*, vol. 2, p. 556.

77. Letter, Benjamin to Scholem. 20 March 1933, *Briefe*, vol. 2, p. 566.

78. Letter, Benjamin to Scholem. 28 February 1931, *Briefe*, vol. 2, p. 562.

79. "Die Mississippi-Überschwemmung 1927," *Aufklärung für Kinder*, p. 188.

80. Letter, Benjamin to Scholem. 17 April 1931, *Briefe*, vol. 2, p. 532.

81. Hessel, cited in the brilliant study by Johann Friedrich Geist (inspired by Benjamin), *Arcades: The History of a Building Type*, trans. Jane O. Newman and John H. Smith (Cambridge, Mass.: The MIT Press, 1983), pp. 157–58 (trans. modified).

82. *Berliner Chronik* (begun 1931), ed. Gershom Scholem (Frankfurt am Main: Suhrkamp Verlag, 1970) and "Berliner Kindheit um Neunzehn Hundert" (begun 1932), IV, pp. 235–403.

83. Letter, Benjamin to Scholem. 15 January 1933, *Briefe*, vol. 2, pp. 560–61.

84. See the note in Benjamin's papers in the Bibliothèque Nationale: "In the year 1932, as I was abroad [in Spain], it began to be clear to me that I soon would have to take leave of the city in which I was born, perhaps permanently. I had experienced the procedure of immunization several times in my life as healing; I adhered to it again in this situation and called forth in myself intentionally those images that in exile are wont to awaken homesickness most strongly, those of childhood. The feeling of nostalgia was not allowed to dominate my spirit any more than the immunizing material [is allowed to dominate] over a healthy body. I attempted this by limiting my examination to the necessary, social irretrievability of the past, rather than the arbitrary biographical one" (Envelope no. 1, Benjamin Papers, Georges Bataille Archive, Bibliothèque Nationale, Paris).

85. Letter, Benjamin to Gretel Karplus Adorno, March 1934, V, p. 1103.

86. "Zum Bilde Prousts," II, p. 311.

87. V, p. 497 (K2a, 3).

88. V, p. 580 (N4, 4; also 0°, 76).

Introduction to Part II

1. Benjamin was often explicit regarding the connection: The Surrealism essay was "an opaque paravent before the Arcades project" (V, p. 1090), to which it could serve as the introduction (II, p. 1020); the Proust and Kafka essays could "pass to the account of the Arcades project" (II, p. 1020); the Artwork essay was "anchored" in the *Passagen-Werk*'s historical research (V, p. 1150), fixing "the present-day position" (V, p. 1152) of art, from which it was first possible to recognize what had been decisive about its historical "fate" (V, p. 1148). (Benjamin occasionally spoke of the Artwork essay as the "second exposé" of the Arcades project, "a kind of counterpiece to the 1935 exposé [V, p. 1151]). The "first quarter" of the Fuchs article contained "a number of important considerations on dialectical materialism that are provisionally synchronized with my [Arcades] book" (V, p. 1158). The two Baudelaire essays (1938 and 1939), for which "Central Park" provided a crucial theoretical armature, were intended to provide a "model" for the Arcades project as part of a book on Baudelaire (V, p. 1165). And finally, the Theses on History drew heavily on the methodological notes that appear in *Konvolut* N of the *Passagen-Werk*, "On Epistemology; Theory of Progress" (see I, p. 1225).

2. See V, pp. 1041–43.

3. Ed. note, V, p. 1341. For their collaborative notes, see pp. 1341–47.

4. This fragment of text (V, pp. 1060–63) was found inserted at the front of *Konvolut* G. Parts of it had found their way into one of Benjamin's radio programs, "Die Eisenbahnkatastrophe von Firth of Tay" in Walter Benjamin, *Aufklärung für Kinder: Rundfunkvorträge*, ed. Rolf Tiedemann (Frankfurt am Main: Suhrkamp Verlag, 1985), pp. 178–83.

5. V, p. 1033 (0°, 70).

6. Letter, Benjamin to Gretel Karplus, 16 August 1935 (V, p. 1138).

7. Letter, Benjamin to Adorno, 31 May, 1935, V, p. 1118.

8. Letter, Benjamin to Scholem, 17 October 1934, V, p. 1104.

9. Letter, Benjamin to Adorno, 18 March 1934, V, p. 1102.

10. The Arcades project from this point on figured in the official program of the exiled Frankfurt Institute under the English title, "The Social History of the City of Paris in the 19th Century" (ed. note, V, p. 1097).

11. Benjamin notes that his friendship with Brecht after 1929 was influential (letter, Benjamin to Adorno, 31 May 1935, V, p. 1117). He lived with Brecht in Denmark during the summer of 1934 when he was working intensively on the notes for the exposé.

12. Letter, Benjamin to Scholem, 20 May 1935, V, p. 1112.

13. This argument is considered in detail in the Introduction to Part III below.

14. In all, the books cited in the research material number 850 (see the bibliography compiled by the editor, V, pp. 1277–1323).

15. V, p. 1349.

16. Although he announced in March 1936 that the "preliminary material studies" were finished except for "a few small areas" (letter, Benjamin to Horkheimer, 28 March, 1936, V, p. 1158), he was to add to the *Konvoluts* continuously until forced to leave Paris.

17. The list (V, pp. 81–82) is Benjamin's own. The letters c, e, f, h, etc. without titles suggest that he had plans for further *Konvoluts* (see ed. note, p. 1261). *Konvolut* Z ("Doll, Automaton") was never photocopied; nor were the series D5 and B8 (omissions marked by an asterisk in the list of *Konvoluts*; for dating and photocopying of the entires, see p. 1262). Some of the entries were cross-referenced, at times to keywords that never had their own *Konvoluts*, but were incorporated as subtopics within others (e.g., "Hashish," "Velvet," "World of Things," "Dust," "Weather," "Predecessor," "Mythology," "Dream Structure").

18. Letter, Benjamin to Horkheimer, fall 1934.

19. Letter, Benjamin to Adorno, {?} May 1935, V, p. 1112.

20. Letter, Benjamin to Scholem, 20 May, 1935, V, p. 1112.

21. Letter, Benjamin to Brecht, 20 May 1935. Benjamin was capable of a degree of bluff in his correspondence, particularly when, as was the case with the Institute, his audience was the source of his very precarious funding. Nonetheless, his high optimism concerning the project's immanent completion was clearly genuine. That optimism may have been diminished by the critical reception which Adorno gave the exposé, particularly as he had been the most enthusiastic supporter of the project's early stage (see V, p. 1128 and 1140). Horkheimer, however, was more complimentary in his comments (V, p. 1143) and in Benjamin's major articles for the Institute's journal, he continued to develop the conceptions formulated as part of the Arcades complex.

22. Letter, Benjamin to Karplus, {?} March 1934, V, p. 1103.

23. Adorno wrote: "The division of chapters on the basis of men seems to me not totally felicitous: From it there proceeds a certain compulsion for a systematic exterior architecture with which I do not feel comfortable" (letter, Adorno to Benjamin, 2 August 1935, V, p. 1130).

24. Note that the 1939 version of the exposé modified its contents significantly (see below, Introduction to Part III).

25. Letter, Adorno to Benjamin, 2 August 1935, V, p. 1128.

26. "I have thereby, in a decisive example, realized my theory of knowledge that is crystallized in the concept I have [previously] handled very esoterically, the 'now of recognition.' I have discovered those elements of the art of the nineteenth century that are only 'now' recognizable, that never were before and never will be again" (letter, Benjamin to Gretel Karplus, 9 October 1935, V, p. 1148).

27. See ed. note, V, p. 24n.

28. See below, chapter 10.

29. V, p. 1009 (G°, 3).

30. See V, p. 1014 (I°, 2).

31. V, p. 416 (J56a, 7).

32. Benjamin himself used this term in the *Trauerspiel* study to describe his method of reconstructing philosophically the historical origins of German tragic drama: "Philosophical history (*die philosophische Geschichte*) as the knowledge of origins is that form which allows the configuration of the idea to emerge out of the remote extremes, the apparent excesses of development, as the totality characterized by the possibility of a meaningful juxtaposition of such contradictions" (I, p. 227).

33. Benjamin defines philosophical ideas as "discontinuous" in the *Trauerspiel* study: "These stand by themselves in complete isolation as words never could" (I, p. 217); and in the *Passagen-Werk*'s early notes he says that he is describing "a world of strict discontinuity" (V, p. 1011 [G°, 19]).

34. Here, particularly, Benjamin's research as a historian of mass consumer culture was pathbreaking. It can be appreciated even alongside the excellent studies that have recently appeared, and that corroborate his findings. I am referring in particular to the following books on nineteenth-century France, from which I have learned much that has been beneficial for this study: Susanna Barrows, *Distorting Mirrors: Visions of the Crowd in Late Nineteenth-Century France* (New Haven: Yale University Press, 1981); Nora Evenson, *Paris: A Century of Change, 1878–1978* (New Haven: Yale University Press, 1979); Johann Friedrich Giest, *Arcades: The History of a Building Type*, trans. Jane O. Newman and John H. Smith (Cambridge, Mass.: The MIT Press, 1983). Michael B. Miller, *The Bon Marché: Bourgeois Culture and the Department Store, 1869–1920*. (Princeton: Princeton University Press, 1981); Rosalind Williams, *Dream Worlds: Mass Consumption in Late Nineteenth-Century France* (Berkeley: University of California Press, 1982).

35. Letter, Benjamin to Karplus, 16 August 1935, V, p. 1138.

36. Letter, Adorno to Scholem, 9 May 1949, V, pp. 1072–73.

3 Natural History: Fossil

1. Theodor W. Adorno, "Charakteristik Walter Benjamin," *Über Walter Benjamin*, ed., Rolf Tiedemann (Frankfurt am Main: Suhrkamp Verlag, 1970), p. 17.

2. Benjamin would in fact not be pleased with my use of Sternberger to make this point, for although there was a direct influence, it was his own on Sternberger rather than vice versa, in a manner Benjamin considered nothing less than (unskillful) plagiarism. He wrote to Scholem 2 April 1939: "You should some time get yout hands on Sternberger's book, *Panorama of the Nineteenth Century*. It won't be lost on you that this is an outright attempt at plagiarism" (V, p. 1168). The second sentence is deleted with ellipses in the version published in Walter Benjamin, *Briefe*, 2 vols., eds. Gershom Scholem and Theodor W. Adorno (Frankfurt am Main: Suhrkamp Verlag, 1978), p. 802.

In a letter to Adorno twelve days later, Benjamin's vituperative attack continued (indicating that Sternberger had in fact "plagiarized" his ideas only too well). Only in the title, he wrote, was Sternberger able even to plagiarize correctly. "The idea of the *Passages* appears, having undergone two forms of filtering—first, that which could penetrate through Sternberger's skull [. . . and second,] that which was allowed to pass the [Third] Reich's Board of Literature. You can easily imagine what has survived [. . .]. The indescribably meager conceptual apparatus of Sternberger is stolen from [Ernst] Bloch, from him and me together [. . .]. Perhaps you can discuss with Max [Horkheimer] whether I should review—that means denounce—it" (V, pp. 1164–65).

Benjamin later sent a review to the Institute for Social Research in New York, where it was received in silence. He wrote to Gretel Adorno, 26 June 1939, that he had taken heavily to heart the "silence on all sides that my review of Sternberger's *Panorama* has encountered.

Even you didn't break it when you finally wrote to me yourself about the book" (*Briefe*, vol. 2, p. 828). Adorno seems to have had a more positive view of Sternberger (see V, p. 1107). Although Sternberger's journalistic commentaries still appeared in the Frankfurter *Zeitung* after Hitler came of power, he ultimately suffered persecution because of his Jewish wife. The Institute did not publish Benjamin's review (which was preserved, however, and appears in III, pp. 572–79).

3. Dolf Sternberger, *Panorama, oder Ansichten vom 19. Jahrhundert* [first published, Hamburg, 1938] (Frankfurt am Main: Suhrkamp Verlag, 1974), pp. 108–09.

4. Theodor W. Adorno, "Die Idee der Naturgeschichte," *Gesammelte Schriften*, vol. 1: *Philosophische Frühschriften*, ed., Rolf Tiedemann (Frankfurt am Main: Suhrkamp Verlag, 1973), p. 355.

5. Adorno argued that what appeared to be natural objects were not truly natural insofar as they were produced historically by human subjects; and history was not "historical," because of the blind destructiveness to nature (including physical, human bodies) which had thus far characterized its course. I discuss in detail Adorno's argument in this speech, and its specific debt to Benjamin, in Susan Buck-Morss, *The Origin of Negative Dialectics: Theodor W. Adorno, Walter Benjamin and the Frankfurt Institute* (New York: Macmillan Free Press, 1977), chapter 3.

6. Adorno, *Gesammelte Schriften*, vol. 1, pp. 360–61.

7. V, p. 1034 (0°, 80).

8. *John Heartfield: Photomontages of the Nazi Period* (New York: Universe Books, 1977), p. 11. "Like Eisenstein's films, Heartfield's photomontages use diametrically opposed images to provoke a conflict in the spectator which will give rise to a third synthetic image that is often stronger in its associations than the sum of its parts" (ibid., p. 13). Heartfield has been compared to the nineteenth-century lithographer Daumier (ibid.). Benjamin, in tracing the "origins" of the present, makes Daumier a significant figure in the *Passagen-Werk*. But it is the artist Antoine Wiertz, Benjamin says, who "can be described as the first who, even if he did not foresee it, demanded montage as the agitational utilization of photography" (1935 exposé, V, p. 49).

9. It appears that he knew the man rather later than his work. Benjamin's 1934 essay, "The Author as Producer," praises Heartfield's political use of photography (see II, pp. 692–93). But he does not mention meeting Heartfield until a letter written from Paris, 18 July 1935: "[. . . S]eldom is there among my new acquaintances one as delightful as John Heartfield [whom I met] not long ago, with whom I had a really excellent conversation about photography" (*Briefe*, vol. 2, p. 670). Heartfield was in Paris for the exhibition of his works that opened in May 1935 under the sponsorship of Louis Aragon and others in the left wing of the avant-garde, as a gesture of solidarity for this artist, exiled by Hitler in 1933. Heartfield's 1934 exposition in Prague had become a political issue when, under direct pressure from Hitler, some of the posters most critical of Nazism were removed (see *Heartfield*, p. 14).

10. "Heartfield's photomontages represent an entirely different type [than the formal-modernist collages of the Cubists]. They are not primarily aesthetic objects, but images for reading [*Lesebilder*]. Heartfield went back to the old art of the emblem and used it politically" (Peter Bürger, *Theory of the Avant-Garde*, trans. Michael Shaw, foreword Jochen Schulte-Sasse, *Theory and History of Literature*, vol. 4 (Minneapolis: University of Minnesota Press, 1984), p. 75. Cf: "Like emblems of old, these photomontages merge in a powerful fusion of picture and motto, and like emblems they became engraved in the mind and eye of a generation" (*Heartfield*, p. 11).

11. See note no. 9 above.

12. Letter, Benjamin to Kitty Steinschneider, cited in Gershom Scholem, *Walter Benjamin: The Story of a Friendship*, eds. Karen Ready and Gary Smith (London: Faber & Faber, Ltd., 1982), p. 64.

13. The debilitating effects on the German working class of the popular acceptance of Darwinism, which, merged with Marxism, resulted in an evolutionary theory of socialism, has been explored by Alfred H. Kelly in his book *The Descent of Darwin: The Popularization of Darwin in Germany, 1860–1914* (Chapel Hill: University of North Carolina Press, 1981).

14. IV, pp. 95–96. Essentially the same in versions M^2 (p. 929) and M^2 (pp. 918–19), (see chapter 1, note no. 14).

15. IV, p. 147.

16. The long-held belief that Marx had wanted to dedicate vol. 2 of *Capital* to Darwin, but that the latter did not allow it because he did not want his name associated with atheism, has recently been proven false (see Lewis S. Feuer, "The Case of the 'Darwin-Marx' Letter: A Study in Socio–Literary Detection," *Encounter* 51, 4 [October 1976]: 62–78).

17. V, p. 1250 (1935 exposé note no. 24).

18. V, p. 1045 (a°, 3). Note that Proust, too, spoke of the pre–1914 world as "prehistoric."

19. V, p. 670 (R2, 3).

20. V, p. 993 (A°, 5).

21. V, p. 670 (R2, 3).

22. V, p. 1048 (c°, 1).

23. V, p. 93 (A3a, 7; see also R2, 3).

24. V, p. 1048 (b°, 2).

25. "Earth atmosphere as submarine" (V, p. 1013 [H°, 4; cf. 0°, 46]).

26. V, p. 1047 (b°, 2; see also a°, 3; c°, 4; H°, 4).

27. "Das Paris des Second Empire bei Baudelaire," I, p. 549 (cf. V, p. 1035 [P°, 3] and p. 292 [I 4, 4]).

28. V, p. 1056 (f°, 3).

29. Cf. V, p. 496 (K2a, 1).

30. V, p. 1215 (again H2, 6).

31. Adorno, *Gesammelte Schriften*, vol. 1, p. 359.

32. Cf. Buck-Morss, *The Origins of Negative Dialectics*, chapter 9. Adorno, too, used the term "dialectical image," and particularly in his study of Kierkegaard (1933) it played a major role (in a passage Benjamin cites in V, p. 576 [N2, 7]). But after 1935 he became increasingly critical of Benjamin's "dialectical images" as "static" and "unmediated" (see ibid., chapter 9).

33. Such a perspective was characteristic of "idealism's image of history" (letter, Benjamin to Adorno, 31 May 1935, V, p. 1117).

34. II, pp. 697–98.

35. V, p. 572 (N1, 10).

36. In the early stages of the *Passagen-Werk*, Benjamin's treatement of panoramas was not merely critical. In particular, Prévost's mimetic replication of cities provided a "true image of the city," as a "windowless monad" (V, p. 1008 [F°, 24; also Q1a, 1]). Moreover, although Benjamin connected them with the "dream world" of the nineteenth century, he also considered them anticipatory ur-forms of photography and film (K°, 9; K°, 17; K°, 18). The form of their reception was particularly ambiguous: Due to the "peephole" through which the viewer gazed (see chapter 4, figure 4.1), it remained private and individual; due to the panorama of images that moved past the viewers sequentially, it was public and collective.

37. See above, note no. 2.

38. Sternberger, *Panorama*, p. 83.

39. "What we must require of photographers is the ability to give to their shots the captions that will rescue them from the corrosion of fashion and confer upon them revolutionary use-value" (II, p. 693).

40. "There is no shallower, more helpless antithesis than that which reactionary thinkers like Klages try to set up between the symbolic space of nature and that of technology"; technology is "fundamentally" a "form of nature [*Naturgehalt*]" (V, p. 493 [K1a, 3]).

41. Adorno, *Gesammelte Schriften*, vol. 1, pp. 356ff. It was in Capri in June 1924 that Benjamin read Lukács' newly published *History and Class Consciousness*, which he considered "important particularly for me" (letter, Benjamin to Scholem, 13 June 1924, *Briefe*, vol. 1, p. 350). He noted in September that what struck him about this book was "that beginning from political reflections Lukács comes to statements in his theory of knowledge that are at least partially, and perhaps not so thoroughly as I first suspected, very familiar, confirming my position" (letter, Benjamin to Scholem, 7 July 1924, *Briefe*, vol. 1, p. 355). Thus, while impressed with Lukács' work, Benjamin came early to realize that their intellectual positions were not so close as it might first have seemed.

42. In *History and Class Consciousness*, Lukács went so far as to proclaim that all nature is a social category, that is, no objective matter exists outside of consciousness or history. He later criticized this position as an attempt to "out-Hegel Hegel," and noted that his more recent familiarlity with Marx's 1844 manuscripts had convinced him that Marx himself had meant no such thing (see p. 234 and 1967 preface to Georg Lukács, *History and Class Consciousness* [1923], trans. Rodney Livingstone [Cambridge, Mass.: The MIT Press, 1971]).

43. His conception is perhaps closer to that of the early Marx, who spoke in the 1844 manuscripts (heavily cited in the *Passagen-Werk*) of industry's transformative effects on nature. Cf.: "'Industry is nature, and hence natural science, in its true historical relationship to humanity'" (Marx, 1844 mss., cited in Landshut and Mayer [1932], cited V, p. 800 [X1, 1]).

44. V, p. 282 (I1, 6).

45. Below, chapter 5.

46. V, p. 595 (N11, 1).

47. Letter, Benjamin to Gretel Karplus [Adorno], 10 September 1935, V, p. 1142.

48. Michel Melot, V, p. 1324. Melot reports that the material Benjamin had to work with was a series, *Topographie de Paris*, that had "around 150,000 images of every variety" (drawings, maps, press clippings, postcards, photographs, posters) classified by arrondissement, and by an alphabetical ordering of streets, and another series on the history of France, which included several hundred volumes on the nineteenth century. He also worked with the series *Enseignement des arts*, concerning the workshops and lives of the artists, the Salon, etc. He did not content himself with studying those series to which there was ready access, but pursued material the classification of which was very complex (ibid.).

49. Alfred Sohn-Rethel, to the ed., V, p. 1324.

50. Ed. note, V, p. 1324. Certain entries in the *Passagen-Werk* refer to specific images that Tiedemann has tracked down in the archives, and has included in V, along with several contemporary photographs of the Paris arcades taken by a friend of Benjamin, the photographer Germaine Krull (see the end of vol. 1 of V).

51. V, p. 575 (N2, 6).

52. V, p. 574 (N1a, 6).

53. "Um verlorenen Abschluss der Notiz über die Symbolik der Ekenntnis" VI, p. 38.

54. VI, p. 38.

55. Georg Simmel, *Goethe* [first published 1913], 3rd ed. (Leipzig: Klinkhardt & Biermann, 1918), pp. 56–57.

56. Simmel, *Goethe*, p. 57 (cf. above, chapter 2).

57. Simmel, *Goethe*, p. 56.

58. Simmel, *Goethe*, p. 57 (italics, Simmel's).

59. V, p. 577 (N2a, 4). (The phrase in braces, absent from the *Passagen-Werk* entry, is in the "addendum" to the *Trauerspiel* book, I, p. 953.) The entry continues: "'Origin'—that is the concept of the *Urphänomen* {historically differentiated, alive both theologically and historically, and} brought out of the pagan context of nature and into the Judaic context of history" (V, p. 577 [N2a, 4]). (The phrase in braces is in the addendum, I, p. 954). The meaning for Benjamin of "theological" as it relates to the "Judaic context of history," and the relation of the new nature to the old nature in this context is discussed below in chapter 7.

60. V, p. 592. Such nonsubjective metaphysical symbols might also be called "theological" (see chapter 7 below, section 7).

61. V, p. 577 (N2a, 4).

62. V, p. 1033 (0°, 73).

63. V, p. 574 (N1a, 8).

64. Adorno, cited V, p. 1072.

65. Letter, Adorno to Horkheimer, 9 May 1949, V, p. 1072.

66. Ed. note, V, p. 1073.

67. V, pp. 226–27 (F6, 2). It was invented by Sir David Brewster in 1815.

68. "The *'casse-tête* [Chinese Puzzle]' that arises during the Empire reveals the awakening sense of the century for construction [. . .] the first presentiment of the principle of cubism in pictoral art" (V, pp. 226–27 [F6, 2]).

69. A. G. Meyer (1907), cited V, p. 223 (F4a, 2).

70. V, p. 575 (N2, 6).

71. VI, p. 39.

4 Mythic History: Fetish

1. It is handled thematically in *Konvolut* N, "On Epistemology: Theory of Progress," V, pp. 570–611. This crucial *Konvolut* has been excellently translated into English by Leigh Hafrey and Richard Sieburth, as "Theoretics of Knowledge, Theory of Progress," in *The Philosophical Forum*, special issue on Walter Benjamin, ed. Gary Smith, XV, nos. 1–2 (fall–winter 1983–84): 1–40.

2. V, p. 1013 (H°, 16).

3. V, p. 1026 (0°, 5). These early notes also contain the critique appearing in Benjamin's Theses on History (1940), which describes von Ranke's attempt to show history " 'as it actually was' " as "the strongest narcotic of the nineteenth century" (V, p. 1033 [0°, 71]).

4. V, p. 574 (N2, 2).

5. V, p. 596 (N11a, 1).

6. Theses on History, I, p. 699.

7. V, p. 596 (N11a, 1).

8. V, pp. 598–99 (N13, 1).

9. V, p. 596 (N11a, 1). Cf.: "From where does the conception of progress come? From Condorcet? At any rate it doesn't yet seem to be very firmly rooted at the end of the eighteenth century. In his *Eristik*, Hérault de Séchelles, under advice for ridding oneself of one's enemy, suggests the following: 'Lead him astray into questions of moral freedom and infinite progress' " (V, p. 828 [Y2a, 1]).

10. Appleton, cited in Norma Evenson, *Paris: A Century of Change, 1878–1978* (New Haven: Yale University Press, 1979), p. 1.

11. " 'With the magical title *Paris*, a drama, revue or book is always sure of success' " (Gautier [1856], cited V, p. 652 [P4, 3]).

12. Evenson, *Paris*, p. 1.

13. V, p. 1049 (C°, 1).

14. See *Konvolut* T, "Beleuchtungsarten," V, pp. 698–707.

15. "It is only the particular social relation between people that here takes on the phantasmagoric form of a relation between things" (Marx, *Capital*, cited V, p. 245 [G5, 1]).

16. V, p. 86 (A2, 2; also L°, 28).

17. V, p. 700 (T1a, 8).

18. V, p. 614 (O1a, 2; also c°, 2).

19. V, p. 90 (A3, 3).

20. V, p. 45 (1935 exposé).

21. Cf. V, p. 239 (G2a, 7; G2a, 8). The length of the Crystal Palace measured 560 meters (G8, 5).

22. Lothar Bacher (n.d.), cited by Julius Lessing, cited V, p. 248 (G6–6a).

23. Julius Lessing (1900), cited V, pp. 248–49 (G6–6a).

24. Already beginning in 1798 there had been national industrial expositions in Paris "'to amuse the working class'" (Sigmund Engländer [1864], cited V, p. 243 [G4, 7]); after 1834 these were held every five years (cf. V, pp. 242–43 [G4, 2—G4, 4]).

25. (1855), cited V, p. 257 (G11, 1).

26. Paul Morand (1900), cited V, p. 243 (G4, 5).

27. Théophile Gautier (1867), cited V, pp. 253–54 (G9, 2).

28. Cf. V, p. 243 (G4, 4) and p. 268 (G16a, 3).

29. V, p. 238 (G2, 3).

30. V, p. 267 (G16, 7).

31. V, p. 267 (G16, 6; again m4, 7). Other aspects of the pleasure industry were spawned by the fairs—the first amusement parks, and perhaps the first form of international mass tourism as well, as foreign pavilions provided cultures-on-display for visual consumption: "In 1867 the 'Oriental quarter' was the center of attraction" (V, p. 253 [G8a, 3]); the Egyptian exhibition was in a building modelled after an Egyptian temple (V, p. 255 [G9a, 6]).

32. "'These expositions are the first actually modern festivals'" (Hermann Lotze [1864], cited V, p. 267 [G16, 5]).

33. The Eiffel Tower cost six million francs to build, and in less than a year, it had earned 6,459,581 francs from the sale of entry tickets (V, p. 253 [G9, 1]). Fittingly, given the stress on spectacle over commerce, the task of organizing the first world exposition in New York City, 1853, fell to Phineas Barnum, whose business was circuses (V, p. 249 [G6a, 2]).

34. V, p. 255 (G9a, 5).

35. V, p. 253 (G8a, 4).

36. V, p. 250 (G7, 5).

37. Cf. Walpole's description of the exhibition of machines in London's Crystal Palace: "'In this hall of machines there were automated spinning machines [...,] machines that made envelopes, steam looms, models of locomotives, centrifugal pumps and a locomobile; all of these were laboring like crazy, whereas the thousands of people who were beside them in top hats and workers' caps sat quietly and passively, and without suspecting that the age of human beings on this planet was at an end'" (Hugh Walpole [1933], cited V, p. 255 [G10, 2]).

38. V, p. 252 (G8, 4).

39. Cf. the "myth" of the proletariat as the "child born in the workshops of Paris [...] and brought to London [during the exposition] for nursing" (S. Ch. Benoist [1914], cited V, p. 261 [G13, 3]).

40. The King of Prussia protested against the London exposition of 1851, refusing to send a royal delegation. Prince Albert who, in fact, had endorsed the project (which was financed and organized by private entrepreneurs) related to his mother the spring before the fair opened that opponents of the exposition believed "'foreign visitors will begin a radical revolution here, will kill Victoria and myself, and proclaim the red republic. A breakout of the plague [they believe] will certainly result from the concourse of such a huge multitude, and devour those whom the accumulated costs of everything have not driven away" (cited V, p. 254 [G9, 3]). During the fair there was continuous police surveillance of the crowd (V, p. 255 [G10, 1]). At the 1855 Paris exposition: "Workers' delegations this time were totally barred. It was feared that it [the exposition] would provide the workers with a chance for mobilizing" (V, p. 246 [G5a, 1]).

41. Cf. V, p. 256 [G10a, 2]).

42. Cf. V, p. 252 [G8a, 1]).

43. David Riazanov (1928), cited V, pp. 245–46 (G5, 2).

44. Plekhanov (1891), cited V, p. 244 (G4a, 1).

45. The text in figure 4.3 is from "Exposition Universelle Internationale de 1900 à Paris," advance publicity for the 1900 exposition, cited in *Le Livre des Expositions Universelles, 1851–1889* (Paris: Union Centrale des Arts Décoratifs, 1983), p. 105.

46. "'1851 was the time of free trade...Now for decades we find ourselves in a time of ever-increasing tariffs [...] and whereas in 1850 the highest maxim was no government interference in these affairs, now the government of every country has come to be viewed as itself an entrepreneur'" (Julius Lessing [1900], cited V, p. 247 [G5a, 5]).

47. V, p. 247 (G5a, 6).

48. Cf. V, p. 1219 (note no. 19).

49. Cf. ed. note, V, p. 1218: "The second stage of work on the *Passagen* began in early 1934 with plans for an article in French on Haussmann...for *Le Monde*." Some notes for this never completed article have been preserved (see V, pp. 1218–19, 1935 exposé, note no. 19). Benjamin wrote to Gretel Adorno in 1934 of plans for the Haussmann article, mentioning that Brecht considered it an important theme, and that it was "in the immediate proximity of my *Passagenarbeit*" (V, p. 1098).

50. V, p. 188 (E3, 6).

51. Cf. V, p. 187 (E3, 2).

52. Benjamin cites Engels: "'I understand under 'Haussmann' the now general practice of turning the workers' districts into rubble, particularly those lying at the center of our great cities. . . . The result is everywhere the same . . . their disappearance with the great self-congratulations of the bourgeoisie . . . , but they spring up again at once somewhere else [. . .] .'" (V, p. 206 [E12, 1]).

53. "'The great ladies are out for a stroll; behind them play the little ladies'" (Nguyen Trong Hiep [1897], cited V, p. 45 [1935 exposé]).

54. Cf. V, p. 182 (E1a, 4).

55. V, p. 182 (E2a, 5).

56. Benjamin notes: "For the architectonic image of Paris the [Franco-Prussian] war of the 70s was perhaps a blessing, as Napoleon III intended further to redesign whole areas of the city" (V, p. 1016 [K°, 5, again; E1, 6]).

57. Benjamin notes: "Illusionism settles into the image of the city: perspectives" (V, p. 1211 [1935 exposé, note no. 5]).

58. J. J. Honegger (1874), cited V, p. 181 (E1a, 1).

59. Dubech-D'Espezel (1926), cited V, p. 189 (E3a, 6).

60. V, p. 57 (1935 exposé); cf. V, p. 190 (E4, 4, also E8, 1).

61. Newspaper obituary of Hugo, cited V, p. 905 (d2, 3).

62. V, p. 905 (d2, 2). Benjamin notes elsewhere: "A telltale vision of progress in Hugo: Paris incendié (L'année terrible): 'What? scarifice everything? Even the granary of bread? What? The library, this ark where the dawn arises, this unfathomable ABC of ideals, where Progress, eternal reader, leans on its elbows and dreams . . .'" (V, p. 604 [N15a, 2]).

63. V, p. 736 (U14, 3).

64. Michel Chevalier (1853), cited V, p. 739 (U15a, 1). "Chevalier was the disciple of [the Saint-Simonian] Enfantin [. . . and] Editor of the *Globe*" (V, p. 244 [G4a, 4]).

65. Cf. V, pp. 717–18 (U5, 2).

66. V, p. 716 (U4, 2).

67. V, p. 733 (U13, 2).

68. V, p. 716 (U4a, 1).

69. "Lebende Bilder aus dem modernen Paris" (1863), cited V, pp. 236–37 (G2, 1).

70. Dubech-D'Espezel (1926), cited V, p. 193 (E5a, 2).

71. Rattier (1859), cited V, p. 198 (E7a, 4). "'The universe does nothing but pick up the cigar butts of Paris'" (Gautier [1856], cited V, p. 652 [P4, 4]).

72. V, p. 1217 (1935 exposé note no. 14).

73. Notes to the Theses on History, I, p. 1232.

74. Theses on History, I, pp. 697–98 (italics Benjamin's).

75. Henri de Pène (1859), cited V, p. 165 (D1a, 1).

76. "'[. . . T]he rue Grange-Bateliére is particularly dusty, and [. . .] one gets terribly dirty on the rue Réamur'" (Louis Aragon [1926], cited V, p. 158 [D1a, 2]).

77. "With dust, the rain gets its revenge on the Passages" (V. p. 158 [D1a, 1]).

78. "Velvet as a trap for dust. The secret of dust playing in the sunlight. Dust and the parlor" (V, p. 158 [D1a, 3]).

79. V, p. 1006 (F°, 8).

80. Cf. V, p. 158 (D1a, 3).

81. V, p. 158 (D1a, 1). Benjamin's evidence is the following dusty scene of history-stopped-in-its tracks. It occurred twelve years after the 1830 revolution (which began with a desertion of the National Garde, and went no further than ousting the House of Bourbon and replacing it with the House of Orleans and the "bourgeois king" Louis-Philippe), on the occasion of the planned marriage of the young Prince of Orleans: "'[. . .] a great celebration was held in the famous ballroom where the first symptoms of revolution had broken out. In cleaning up the room for the young bridal pair, it was found just as the Revolution [of 1830] had left it. Still on the ground were traces of the military banquet—broken glass, champagne corks, trampled cockades of the Garde du Corps and the ceremonial ribbons of the Officers of the regiments of Flanders" (Karl Gutzkow [1842], cited ibid.).

82. Leon Daudet (1930), cited V, p. 155 (C9a, 1).

83. V, p. 487 (J91a, 1). "'The old Paris exists no more. The form of a city changes more quickly—alas! than the mortal heart.' These two lines of Baudelaire could be placed as an epigraph on the collected works of Meyron" (Gustave Geffroy [1926], cited V, p. 151 [C7a, 1]).

84. V, p. 1010 (G°, 17).

85. V, p. 1213 (1935 exposé note no. 7).

86. V, p. 177 (D10, 3).

87. V, pp. 1010–11 (G°, 17).

88. V, p. 1011 (G°, 17).

89. Benjamin writes that fashion was unknown to antiquity (V, p. 115 [B2, 4]), as it is to revolutionary, communist societies, which, as Cabet anticipated (V, p. 120 [B4, 2]), experience an "end of fashion" (V, p. 1211 [1935 exposé note no. 5]): "Does fashion die perhaps—in Russia for example—because it can no longer keep up with the tempo—in certain areas at least?" (V, p. 120 [B4, 4]; cf. pp. 1028–29 [0°, 20]). But Benjamin also observes that the capitalist form of fashion is not the only one imaginable. The nineteenth-century social utopian Charles Fourier envisioned fashion's variety and abundance, but in goods of such excellent quality that they would last indefinitely: "'even the poorest has . . . a closetful of clothes for each season'" (cited v, p. 129 [B8a, 1]).

90. Benjamin wrote to Hofmannsthal, 17 March 1928: "I am presently working on that which, scanty and meager, has been attempted up to now as a philosophical presentation and exploration of fashion: What is it that this natural and totally irrational time division of the course of history is all about" (V, pp. 1084–85).

91. V, p. 997 (C°, 2).

92. See Angus Fletcher, *Allegory: The Theory of a Symbolic Mode* (New York: Cornell University Press, 1982), pp. 131; 132–33n.

93. Edouard Foucaud (1844), cited V, p. 125 (B6a, 3; see also B8, 3).

94. Egon Friedell (1931), cited V, p. 125 (B6a, 2).

95. Charles Blanc (1872), cited V, pp. 123–24 (B5a, 3).

96. An early entry recognizes the anticipatory potential of fashion generally: "The most burning interest of fashion for the philosopher lies in its extraordinary anticipations. [. . . Fashion is in] contact with what is to come, due to the strength of the incomparable scent which the feminine collective has for that which lies ready in the future. In its newest creations, every season brings some sort of secret flag signals of coming things. The person who understands how to read them would know in advance not only about the new currents of art, but also about new laws, wars and revolutions" (V, p. 112 [B1a, 1]). Benjamin refers to the tendency of fashion to reveal the body at times when revolution is imminent (see V, p. 119 [B3a, 5]); in contrast, the fashion of the crinoline in the early years of the Second Empire, its conical shape, was mimetic of the shape of imperial bureaucratic hierarchies. He cites Friedrich Theodor Vischer (1879): The crinoline "'is the unmistakable symbol of the imperialist reaction [. . . that] threw its might like a bell over the good and the bad, the just and unjust of the revolution'" (V, p. 116 [B2a, 7; again, B7, 5]).

97. Later entries omit euphoric references to the predictive power of "the feminine collective," and are more critical. Benjamin cites Simmel's observation "'that fashions are always class fashions, that the fashions of the higher class are distinct from those of the lower, and are abandoned the moment the latter begins to appropriate them'" (Georg Simmel [1911], cited V, p. 127 [B7a, 2]). Entries from the 1930s point out the crucial role of capital in distorting the utopian aspects of fashion. Benjamin cites Fuchs: "'It must be reiterated that the interests of class divisions are only one cause for fashion's frequent change, and that the second, frequent change in fashions as a consequence of the mode of production of private capital . . . is just as significant, as it must constantly increase their possibility for replacement in the interests of profits'" (Edward Fuchs [1926?], cited V, p. 128 [B7a, 4]). On the connections between fashion, class divisions and the needs of capitalist production, see also V, pp. 124–29 (D, 6; B6a, 1; B7, 7; B7a, 3; B8a, 1; B8, 2).

98. V, p. 51 (1935 exposé).

99. Cf. Benjamin's note: "Fashion/Time // Lethe (Modern)" (V, p. 1001 [D°, 5]).

100. V, p. 131 (B9a, 1).

101. Benjamin cites Rudolph von Jhering (1883): "'[. . .] the third motive of our fashion today: its . . . tyranny. Fashion contains the external criterion that one . . . belongs to "good society." Whoever does not want to do without this must go along with it [. . .]'" (V, p. 125 [B6a, 1]).

102. Paul Valéry (1935), cited V, p. 123 [B5a, 2]).

103. V, p. 115 (B2, 4).

104. "'The fashion of buying one's wardrobe in London only pertained to men; the fashion for women, even for foreigners, was always to outfit oneself in Paris'" (Charles Seignobos [1932], cited V, p. 126 [B7, 3]).

105. V, p. 694 (S9a, 2).

106. Helen Grund (1933), cited V, p. 123 (B5, 3).

107. Georg Simmel (1911), cited V, p. 127 (B7, 8). Why else is it weak but for the social implications of her natural potency?

108. V, p. 1213 (exposé note no. 7; again p. 1211, and B2, 5).

109. V, p. 115 (B2, 5).

110. Benjamin refers to the "cult of love: Attempt to lead the technical force of production into the field against the natural force of production" (V, p. 1210 [1935 exposé note no. 5]).

111. V, p. 1015 (I°, 7). The reference is to Baudelaire.

112. "Friedell explains with reference to the woman: 'that the history of her clothing manifests surprisingly few variations, and is not much more than a change of [. . .] nuances: length of the train, height of the hairdo, length of the sleeve, fullness of the skirt, degree of decolletage, position of the waist. Even radical revolutions like today's bobbed haircut are only the "eternal recurrence of the same" [. . .].' Thus according to the author, female fashion contrasts to the more varied and decisive masculine one" (Egon Friedell [1931], cited V, p. 120 [B4, 1]). See also V, pp. 1207 and 1032 (0°, 60).

113. In connection with world expositions and commodity display, Benjamin studied Grandville's midnineteenth-century lithographs closely. The imagery of Heaven and Hell in connection with Paris occurs in Grandville's *Un autre Monde* when the hero Krackq dreams he is visiting the pagan heaven, the "Elysian Fields," and finds there famous personages of his own era enjoying the material pleasures of Paris' Champs Elyseés; Krackq then moves to the lower regions, where Charon's ferry boat business across the river Styx is ruined by the construction (as then in Paris) of an iron footbridge (V, p. 215 [F2, 3]).

114. "Focillon [1934] on the phantasmagoria of fashion" (cited V, p. 131 [B9a, 2]).

115. V, p. 115 (B2a, 5).

116. V, pp. 117–18 (B3, 5; also B1, 5).

117. Apollinaire (1927), cited V, pp. 118–19 (B3a, 1).

118. V, p. 132 (B10a, 2).

119. V, p. 1207 (1935 exposé note no. 2).

120. Auguste Blanqui (1885), cited V, p. 129 (B8a, 3). Cf.: "Re: the section on flowers. The fashion magazines of the time contained instructions on how to conserve bouquets" (V, p. 1035 [P°, 1]).

121. V, p. 130 (B9, 2).

122. V, p. 130 (B9, 2)

123. V, p. 118 (B3, 8).

124. V, p. 111 (B1, 4).

125. V, p. 118 (B3, 8).

126. V, p. 126 (B6a, 4).

127. Benjamin notes that this fragmentation, which "secretly values the image of the corpse," can be found in Baroque literature as well as in Baudelaire (V, p. 130 [B9, 3]). See below, chapter 6.

128. V, p. 139 (B8, 4).

129. V, p. 111 (B1, 4).

130. V, p. 51 (1935 exposé). The passage continues: Fashion "affirms the rights of the corpse over the living. Fetishism, which lies at the base of the sex appeal of the inorganic, is its vital nerve, and the cult of the commodity recruits this into its service" (ibid.; again B1a, 4, and B9, 1).

131. "'[. . . I]t becomes difficult to distinguish merely by the clothing an honest woman from a courtesan'" (Charles Blanc [1872], cited V, p. 124 [B5a, 3]). Indeed: "'The fashionable type [in the Second Empire] is the *grande dame* who plays at being a cocotte'" (Egon Friedell [1931], cited V, p. 125 [B6a, 2]).

132. V, p. 111 (B1, 4; again F°, 1). The figure of the prostitute within the setting of the aracades, in connection with fashion and commodities, death and desire, echoes Aragon's description in *Le Paysan de Paris*.

133. V, p. 137 (C2, 1).

134. J. F. Benzenberg (1805), cited V, p. 143 (C3a, 2).

135. Victor Hugo (1881), cited V, p. 146 (C5a, 1).

136. Sigmund Engländer (1864), cited V, p. 142 (C3a, 1).

137. "'The cold in these subterranean galleries is so great that many of the prisoners [from the June insurrection] could keep the warmth of life only by continuous running or moving their arms, and no one dared to lay down on the cold stones. The prisoners gave all the passages names of Paris streets and exchanged addresses with each other when they met'" (Sigmund Engländer (1864), cited V, p. 142 [C3a, 1]).

138. Dubech-D'Espezel (1926), cited V, p. 142 (C3, 8).

139. V, pp. 135–36 (C1a, 2).

140. V, p. 1020 (L°, 22; again C2a, 2).

141. V, p. 1019 (L°, 7; cf. C1a, 2). Benjamin compares the typography of the Paris Passages to Pausanias' typography of Greece, written in 200 A.D., "as the cult places and many of the other monuments began to decay" (V, p. 133 [C1, 5]).

142. V, p. 178 (D10a, 4).

143. V, p. 1008 (F°, 31; again C1, 4).

144. V, p. 1033 (0°, 74; cf. O3, 6).

145. Gambling, like prostitution, was not new, but capitalism changed its form: Just as big-city prostitution became emblematic of the commodity form, so: "Speculation on the stock exchange caused the forms of gambling that had come down from feudal society to recede. [. . .]. Lafargue defined gambling as a replication of the mysteries of the market situation in miniature" (V, pp. 56–57 [1935 exposé]).

146. V, p. 1046 (g°, 1; again O1, 1).

147. Criticizing the concept of progress, Benjamin refers to "Strindberg's thought: Hell is nothing that might stand before us—but this life here" ("Zentralpark," I, p. 683).

148. V, p. 1056 (g°, 1).

149. See V, p. 114 (B2, 1).

150. V, p. 1057 (g°, 1).

151. V, p. 1057 (g°, 1).

152. See Benjamin's philosophical interpretation of the first chapter of Genesis in "Über Sprache überhaupt und über die Sprache des Menschen" (II, pp. 140–57), where Adam, who named God's creatures in Paradise, is called the "first philosopher." There is a tension here between the receptive and spontaneous poles of human "naming" (a tension expressed in the double sense of the German word "*heissen*": to mean, and to be named). Benjamin wants to insist that the meaning of nature is revealed to (rather than created by) humans. The latter bring the "linguistic essence" of things to speech, by translating their nameless, mute language into the sound-language, the name-language of humans. But it is God's language that created them and "made things knowable in their names" (ibid., pp. 142–49). Without the prop of the Genesis story (which, it could be argued, gives mythic expression to a philosophical desire rather than philosophical truth), maintaining a philosophical distinction between the creation and the interpretation of meaning is problematic. This is a question to which we will return in chapter 7.

153. V, p. 962 (m1a, 5).

154. Jean Vaudal (1937), cited V, p. 168 (D5, 6).

155. It is a world of strict discontinuity: "The always-again-new is not the old that remains, nor the past that recurs, but the one-and-the-same crossed by countless interruptions. (The gambler lives in the interruptions) [. . .] and what results from it: Time of Hell [. . .]" (V, p. 1011 [G°, 19]).

156. V, p. 165 (D3a, 4).

157. V, p. 167 (D4a, 3).

158. Louis Veuillot (1914), cited V, p. 160 (D2, 2). Benjamin cites from Haussmann's memoirs (1890) a late conversation between him and Napoleon III: "Napoleon: 'How right you are to maintain that the French people who are considered so changeable are at bottom the most routine prone in the world!'—[Haussmann:] 'Agreed, Sir, if you permit me the qualification: As far as things are concerned!. . . I have supposedly myself committed the double injustice of having greatly disturbed the population of Paris, in disrupting

(*bouleversant*), in "boulevardizing" (*boulevardisant*) almost all sections of the city, and of having Parisians weary of seeing the same scene in the same setting nonetheless'" (cited V, p. 187 [E3, 3]).

Cf. Blanquis' criticism of Haussmann: "'Nothing so sad as this immense rearrangement of stones by the hands of despotism, without social spontaneity. There is no more gloomy symptom of decadence. As Rome fell more deeply into its death-throes, its monuments sprang up more numerous and more gigantic. It was building its tomb, making itself beautiful for death'" (Auguste Blanqui, cited V, pp. 205–06 [E11a, 1]).

159. V, p. 178 (D10a, 2). A "metaphysics of waiting" was planned for the *Passagen-Werk*, under the key word "Boredom."

160. Cf. Konvolut D, entitled "Boredom, Eternal Recurrence." (Baudelaire refers to the dandy as "an unemployed Hercules" [D5, 2]).

161. Jules Michelet (1846) refers to the first specialization of unskilled labor as "'"the hell of boredom" at the textile looms: "Forever, forever forever" is the invariable word that the automatically turned wheel [. . .] sounds in our ear. One never gets used to it"'" (Michelet, cited in Friedman [1936], cited V, p. 166 [D4, 5]).

162. V, p. 164 (D3, 7). Cf.: "Boredom is always the outer surface of unconscious happenings" (V, p. 1006 [F°, 8; again, D2a, 2]).

163. V, p. 161 (D2, 7; cf. F°, 11).

164. "Waiting and making people wait. Waiting is the form of existence of [society's] parasitic elements" (V, p. 1217 [1935 exposé notes no. 12 and 13]).

165. It is the source of Baudelaire's "spleen." His Paris is rainy, somber (cf. V, p. 157 [D1, 4]).

166. "Nothing bores the average man more than the cosmos. Hence the most intimate connection for him between boredom and the weather" (V, p. 157 [D1, 3]; cf. D2, 8]). Benjamin notes "the double meaning of '*temps*' in French [time and weather]" (V, p. 162 [D2a, 3]).

167. V, p. 162 (D2a, 4).

168. "The gambler. Time squirts out of his every pore" (V, p. 164 [D3, 4]).

169. V, p. 164 (D3, 4).

170. V, p. 161 (D2, 7).

171. "L'Eternite par les astres" (Paris, 1872).

172. See letter, Benjamin to Horkheimer, 6 January 1938, cited I, p. 1071.

173. "Blanqui submits to bourgeois society. But he comes to his knees with such force that its throne begins to totter" (V, p. 168 [D5a, 2]).

174. The passage concludes "The piece, which linguistically has great strength, bears the most remarkable relation to both Baudelaire and Nietzsche" (V, p. 169 [D5a, 6], see also letter, Benjamin to Horkheimer, 6 January 1938, I, pp. 1071–72 and below, chapter 6, section 5).

175. Auguste Blanqui (1872), cited V, p. 170 (D6, 1).

176. Auguste Blanqui (1872), cited V, p. 170 (D6, 1).

177. Auguste Blanqui (1872), cited V, p. 170 (D6a, 1).

178. Auguste Blanqui (1872), cited V, p. 171 (D7, D7a).

179. V. p. 429 (J62a, 2).

180. V, p. 429 (J62a, 2). Benjamin calls "the theory of eternal recurrence" a "dream of the amazing discoveries yet to come in the area of reproduction technology" ("Zentralpark," I, p. 680).

181. See V, pp. 174–78 (series D9 and D10). Given Nietzsche's then well-known theory of eternal recurrence (cited in the early notes, D1°, 1), it is difficult to see how Benjamin's excitement in discovering Blanqui's texts could have been sparked by the ideas themselves (even if Blanqui's description of endless repetition expresses more transparently the mass production characteristic of commodity society). The texts of Blanqui, the great proletarian revolutionary (and the great adversary of Marx's theories) lent themselves to being woven into the fabric of the *Passagen-Werk* not merely as a critique of the bourgeois ideology of progress (also found in Nietzsche), but as (Marxist) pedagogy vital for the revolutionary awakening of the proletarian class. Benjamin noted: "There is a version in which Caesar rather than Zarathustra is the bearer of Nietzsche's theory. That is significant. It underlines the fact that Nietzsche had an inkling of the complicity of his theory with imperialism" (V, p. 175 [D9, 5]). Nietzsche, scornful of the masses, never intended to champion the proletarian cause. The fact that Blanqui, on the contrary, was their tireless supporter, makes his own resignation all the more powerful from a pedagogic point of view.

182. V, p. 177 (D10a, 1): "Life in the magic circle of eternal recurrence perceives an existence that doesn't step out of the auratic."

183. V, p. 1256 (see also 1939 exposé, p. 61).

184. V, p. 1010 (G°, 8).

185. V, p. 1023 (M°, 14).

186. V, p. 591 (N9, 5).

187. V, p. 178 (D10a, 5).

5 Mythic Nature: Wish Image

1. V, p. 1212 (1935 exposé note no. 5).

2. V, p. 560 (M16a, 3).

3. "My analysis deals with this thirst for the past as its main object" (V, p. 513 [L1a, 2]).

4. Friedrich Theodor Vischer (1861), cited V, p. 115 (B2a, 3).

5. V, p. 1017 (K°, 20).

6. V, p. 110 (B1, 2 and B1, 3).

7. "Über einige Motive bei Baudelaire," I, p. 634.

8. "One can describe the phalansterie as a human machine. That is not a criticism, nor does it mean something mechanistic; instead it describes the great complexity of his construction. It is a machine out of human beings" (V, p. 772 [W4, 4]).

9. 1935 exposé, V, p. 47.

10. V, p. 838 (Y7, 5).

11. V, p. 228 (F7, 3).

12. " 'In the mid–[18] 30s, the first iron furniture appears, as bedposts, chairs [. . .], and it is very characteristic of the times that advertised as their particular advantage was the fact they were capable of being mistaken for every kind of wood' " (Max von Boehn [1907], cited V, p. 212 [F1, 3; see also F5a, 2]. CF.: " 'Cabinet making in iron rivals that in wood [. . .] ' " (Foucaud [1844], cited V, p. 225 [F5a, 2]).

13. V, p. 287 (I2a, 3, and I2a, 4).

14. V, p. 1011 (G°, 22).

15. V, p. 152 (C8, 2).

16. V, p. 260 (G12a, 2).

17. V, p. 216 (F2, 8).

18. V, p. 216 (F2, 8).

19. V, p. 105 (A10a, 1; also F4, 5).

20. V, p. 98 (A7, 5).

21. V, p. 1044 (a°, 1; again, F3, 2).

22. V, p. 1052 (d°, 2; again F1, 2 and F3, 2).

23. V, p. 1031 (0°, 42).

24. V, p. 46 (1935 exposé; also F2, 7). Cf. an 1875 project for a railroad station: " 'Rails supported by elegant arches elevated 20 feet above the ground and 615 meters long' "—" 'a sort of Italian mansion' "; " 'How little it divined the future of the railroad' " (Maxime DuCamp [1875], cited V, p. 214 [F2, 1]).

25. Sigfried Giedion (1928), cited V, p. 215 (F2, 5).

26. V, p. 497 (K2a, 4).

27. V, pp. 46–47 (1935 exposé). There are several versions of the exposé. This version is M^2 (the latest version, published in V as the most definitive).

28. See Bloch's discussion of Benjamin's *Einbahnstrasse*, "Revueform der Philosophie" [1928] in *Erbschaft dieser Zeit* [1935], vol. 4 of Ernst Bloch, *Gesamtausgabe* (Frankfurt am Main: Suhr-

kamp Verlag, 1962), pp. 368–71. Bloch claimed that in Benjamin's writing "ever-new 'I's" appear and then "efface themselves"; in place of a recognizeable " 'I' " or " 'we' " there is "only the body dawdling along, not first and foremost ear and eye, not warmth, goodness, wonder, but instead climatically sensitized touch and taste [. . .] philosophemes of the world are placed in window displays under glass" (ibid., pp. 369–70). Precisely in this book by Bloch, however, Benjamin saw his own ideas expressed so closely that he stopped sharing them with Bloch, out of fear of plagiarism (see letter, Benjamin to Scholem, 9 August 1935, V, p. 1137).

29. V, pp. 1224–25 (1935 exposé, M¹ version, n.d. [see ed. note, p. 1252]).

30. Marx, cited V, p. 217 (F2a, 5).

31. V, p. 217 (F2a, 5).

32. The Artwork essay (composed in the fall of 1935) uses the Lukácsian term "second nature" that rarely appeared in Benjamin's writing: "Our emancipated technology, how-ever, confronts today's society as a second nature, and indeed, as economic crises and wars demonstrate, no less elemental than that nature which was given to ur-society. Confronted with this second nature, the humanity that of course has invented it but long since ceased to master it, is forced to undergo just such a learning process as it was with the first nature" (I, p. 444).

33. V, p. 139 (C2a, 2).

34. V, p. 1225 (1935 exposé, M¹ version).

35. This is the wording of the later version of the exposé cited above.

36. V, p. 777 (W7, 4).

37. Victor Hugo, cited by George Betault (1933), cited, V, p. 907 (d3, 7).

38. V, pp. 765–66 (W1a).

39. V, p. 47 (1935 exposé).

40. Langle and Vanderbusch (1832), cited V, p. 50 (1935 exposé).

41. Cf. V, p. 852 (a1, 1).

42. Commenting on the midnineteenth-century mania among tradesmen to metamorphize their products so that they took another form, as if in the age of industrialism anything could be made out of anything (even bakers took to building cakes like architectural or sculptural edifices), Benjamin wrote that this had its source in a "helplessness" which "sprang in part from the overabundance of technological methods and new materials with which people had been presented overnight. Where they attempted to make these more fully their own it re-sulted in misconceived, deficient endeavors." But it is here that he adds: "From another side, however, these attempts are the most authentic witness of just how caught in a dream tech-nological production was in its beginnings. (Technology, not just architecture, is witness in a certain stage to a collective dream)" (V, p. 213 [F1a, 2]).

43. For example, in a section added in the the 1939 exposé Benjamin considered it important to point out that Marx defended Fourier, and that: "One of the most remarkable traits of the Fourierist utopia is that the idea of the exploitation of nature by human beings, which subse-quently became so prevalent, is foreign to it. [. . .] The later conception of the *de facto*

exploitation of nature by human beings is the reflection of the exploitation of people by the owners of the means of production. If the integration of technology into social life has failed, the fault lies in this exploitation" (V, p. 64; see also below, chapter 8, section 6).

44. V, pp. 1224–25 (M[1] version of the 1935 exposé).

45. V, p. 245 (G5, 1) cites the well-known passage from chapter 1 of *Capital*, which Benjamin has taken from Otto Ruhle, *Karl Marx: Leben und Werk* (1928).

46. Marx and Engels, "The Holy Family" [1843], published 1932, cited V, p. 778 (W7, 8).

47. Adorno received a version (T[1]) in some ways different from both of the ones cited here (ed. note, V, p. 1252); but the passage we are considering is the same in T[1] and the first version (from the 1935 exposé, pp. 46–47) cited above.

48. Letter, Adorno to Benjamin, 2 August 1935, V, p. 1128.

49. Letter, Adorno to Benjamin, 2 August 1935, V, p. 1128.

50. Letter, Adorno to Benjamin, 2 August 1935, V, p. 1128.

51. Letter, Adorno to Benjamin, 2 August 1935, V, p. 1113.

52. Letter, Benjamin to Gretel Karplus, 16 August 1935, V, p. 1138.

53. See above, chapter 4.

54. These passages (see above, note no. 45) were recorded in *Konvolut* "G" in the early section "assuredly written before June 1935" (ed. note V, p. 1262), that is, before Benjamin received the letter with Adorno's remonstrances.

55. Letter, Adorno to Benjamin, 2 August 1935, V, p. 1132.

56. See above, chapter 3.

57. Karl Marx, "Der 18[te] Brumaire des Louis Napoleon," *Die Revolution* (1852), Karl Marx and Friedrich Engels, *Werke*, vol. 8 (Berlin: Dietz Verlag, 1960), p. 115.

58. Marx, "18[te] Brumaire," p. 116. Later Marx would endorse enthusiastically the Paris Commune, because the working class voiced its own interests. Benjamin documents, however, that even the Communards, who had everything to lose from such "self-deception" regarding the class content of the struggle, fell victim to the revolutionary phantasmagoria; the Commune "felt itself thoroughly the inheritor of 1793" (V, p. 950 [k1a, 3]). "The illusions that still underlay the Commune come to expression in a striking way in Proudhon's formulation, appealing to the bourgeoisie: 'Save the people; save yourselves, as did your fathers, by the Revolution'" (V, p. 952 [k2a, 1]).

59. Marx, "18[te] Brumaire," p. 116.

60. Marx, "18[te] Brumaire," p. 116.

61. Marx, "18[te] Brumaire," p. 115.

62. V, pp. 500–01 (K3a, 2), cf. the earlier entry (0°, 32) which has in place of "clear to us," "ur-historical." The K3a, 2 version adds: "Of course: within the dialectical essence of technology this throws light on only one moment. (Which one it is difficult to say: antithesis if not synthesis.) In any case there exists in technology the other moment: that of bringing about

goals that are alien to nature, also with means that are alien, even hostile to nature, that emancipate themselves from nature and subdue it."

63. See V, pp. 451–54 (J72a, 4–J74, 3). Instead, in regard to the role of farce in preparing humanity to separate from its past, he cites a related passage from Marx's *Critique of Hegel's Philosophy of Right*, V, p. 583 (N5a, 2).

64. Marx, "18te Brumaire," p. 116.

65. See above, chapter 2.

66. The close connection between the Artwork essay and the *Passagen-Werk* is documented in a letter written by Benjamin just after completing the Artwork essay to an unnamed Dutch woman (with whom he fell in love in 1933): "[. . .T]he center of gravity of my work [. . .] still concerns my big book [the *Passagen-Werk*]. But I now only seldom work on it in the library. Instead, I have interrupted the historical research [. . .] and have begun to concern myself with the other side of the scale. For all historical knowledge can be conceptualized in the image of a pair of scales [. . .] the one tray of which is weighted with the past, the other with knowledge of the present. Whereas in the first tray the facts assembled cannot be mi- nute and numerous enough, in the second, only a few heavy, significant weights are allowed. It is these that I have secured in the last two months through considerations of that which determines the life of art in the present. In the process I have arrived at extraordinary formulations, emanating from totally new insights and concepts. And I can now declare that the materialist theory of art, about which one had heard much but seen nothing with one's own eyes, now exists.

Because it is the best thing I've found since I found you, I sometimes think about showing it to you" (letter, November 1935, VI, p. 814).

67. Artwork essay, II, p. 435.

68. Benjamin is cautious to say that a retrospective analysis of this process cannot tell us in advance what art will be like after the proletariat seizes power, "not to mention art in a classless society," but instead it makes certain prognostic claims possible regarding present tendencies in art (Artwork essay, II, p. 435).

69. Cf. Benjamin's assertion: "[. . .] history is not only a science, but no less a form of recollection. What science has 'established,' recollection can modify. Recollection can make the incomplete (happiness) into something finished, and that which is finished (suffering) into something incomplete. That is theology; but in recollection we have an experience which forbids us to conceive of history as fundamentally atheological, just as little as we are allowed to attempt to write it in terms of immediately theological concepts" (V, p. 189 [N8, 1]). For why Benjamin is "not allowed" to use theological concepts, see below, chapter 7.

70. Given the eliptical language of the exposé, and the fact that the abundant historical data in the *Passagen-Werk* material on the relationship of art and technology are assembled with minimal commentary, a rigorous, systematic reconstruction of Benjamin's argument is im- possible on the basis of the *Passagen-Werk* alone. In the following analysis, I have drawn on related essays which Benjamin published in the years just before and just after the exposé: "The Author as Producer, " II, pp. 683–701, and "The Work of Art in the Age of Its Technical Reproduction," I, pp. 435–508.

71. Except for a few references to Kracauer's work on Offenbach, material and commentary relevant to music are noticeably lacking in the *Passagen-Werk*, perhaps because among the Frankfurt Institute members, this was clearly Adorno's intellectual preserve. Yet the earliest notes (1927 A° series) do make these observations: "Music in the Passages. It appears to have first settled into these spaces with the decline of the arcades, that is, just at the same

time as the age of mechanically reproduced music. (Gramophone. The "Theatrephone" is to a certain extent its predecessor.) And yet there was music written in the spirit of the Passages, a panoramic music that one now only gets to hear at respectably oldfashioned concerts, like those by the *Kurkapelle* in Monte Carlo: the panoramic compositions of David ('Le désert,' 'Herculanum')" (V, pp. 1005–06 [F°, 3]; see also 0°, 61 ["In jazz noise is emancipated"]; and H1, 2; H1, 5, Q1a, 6, Q4a, 1).

72. Benjamin clearly considered Marx's theory of the superstructure inadequate (see e.g., V, p. 581 [N4a, 2]), and one of the purposes in the *Passagen-Werk* was to make up for this lack.

73. V, p. 59 (1935 exposé).

74. Marx's theory that the superstructure is distinct from the forces of production presumes the division between art and technology as a social constant rather than a specifically bourgeois phenomenon. It neglects to consider the possibility (as an application of his own argument that forms of socialism begin to appear within the existing relations of capitalism), that the effects of industrial capitalism may have been precisely to undermine this division.

75. The term *"ingénieur"* was first used in France in the 1790s, applied to officers trained in the art of military siege and fortications (V, p. 218 [F3, 6]).

76. " 'The characteristic of *l 'Ecole polytechnique*... was the coexistence of purely theoretical training with a series of *applied courses*, relevant to civil works, building construction, military fortifications, mining, even shipbuilding... Napoleon decreed the requirement that the students live in barracks' " (de Lapparent [1894], V, p. 982 [r1, 3]).

77. V, p. 219 (F3, 6).

78. Cf. Balzac's critical judgment: " 'I do not believe that an engineer from *l 'Ecole [polytechnique]* would ever be able to build one of the miracles of architecture that Leonardo da Vinci knew how to erect [; the latter was a] mechanic, architect and painter all at once, one of the inventors of hydraulics and tireless constructor of canals. Formed at a young age by the absolute simplicity of theorems, the persons coming out of *l 'Ecole* lose the sense of elegance and ornament; a pillar appears useless to them; by not departing from utility, they regress to the point where art begins' " (Balzac, cited V, p. 986 [r3, 2]).

79. Giedion (1928), cited V, p. 217 (F3, 1).

80. " 'The *Halle au blé* built in 1811 [which, anticipating the arcades, had a central glass skylight] received its complicated construction out of iron and copper... from the architect Bellangé and the engineer Brunet. As far as we know, it is the first time that architect and engineer were no longer united in one person' " (Giedion [1928], cited V, p. 215 [F2, 6]).

81. V, p. 217 (F3, 1).

82. Johann Friedrich Geist, *Arcades: The History of a Building Type*, trans. Jane O. Newman and John H. Smith (Cambridge, Mass.: The MIT Press, 1983), p. 64.

83. V, p. 222 (F4, 5).

84. " 'The most important step toward industrialization: the construction of specific forms (sections) out of wrought iron or steel on mechanical roadways. The spheres interpenetrate: one began, not with structural components, but with railroad tracks... 1832. Here lies the beginnings of sectional iron, that is, the fundamental basis of steel frames [out of which modern skyscrapers were built]' " (Sigfried Giedeon [1928], cited V, p. 216 [F2, 8]).

85. "'The way from the Empire-form of the first locomotives to the consummated new objec-tivity (*Sachlichkeitsform*) of today identifies a revolution'" (Joseph August Lux [1909], cited V, p. 224 [F4a, 7]).

86. Giedion (1928), cited, V, p. 218 [F3, 5]).

87. V, p. 1016 (K°, 6).

88. V, p. 218 (F3, 5). Benjamin refers specifically to nos. 61–63 of Giedion's illustrations. Reproduced here (figure 5.4) is no. 62.

89. Joseph August Lux (1909), cited V, p. 224 (F4a, 7).

90. Journalist (1837), cited V, p. 219 (F3a, 2).

91. V, p. 229 (F7a, 1).

92. Emile Levasseur (1904), cited V, p. 214 (F1a, 4).

93. V, p. 56 (1935 exposé).

94. Fritz Stahl (1929), cited V, p. 231 (F8a).

95. A. G. Meyer (1907), cited V, p. 219 (F3a, 1).

96. Meyer (1907), cited V, p. 219 (F3a, 1).

97. Meyer (1907), cited V, p. 220 (F3a, 4; cf. F3a, 1).

98. From a "much-published" polemic by Paris architects in 1805, cited V, p. 228 (F6a, 3; also F4, 3).

99. Benjamin notes that neoclassical buildings could house any purpose precisely because their architectural "style" had nothing to do with utility. He cites Victor Hugo's observation that the pseudo-Greek temple built to house the Bourse could just as well contain "'a king's palace, a House of Commons, a city hall, a college, a merry-go-round, an academy, a ware-house, a court, a museum, a barracks, a tomb, a temple, a theater'" (Hugo, cited V, p. 227 [F6a, 1]). In contrast, the public responded to a newspaper query as to how the Crystal Palace might be *used* after the London Exposition by suggesting everything from a hospital to public baths to a library (V, p. 225 [F5a, 1]). Benjamin comments: "The Bourse could *mean* anything; the Crystal Palace could be *used* for everything" (ibid.). On the arbitrariness of meaning as a characteristic of commodity society, see chapter 6 below.

100. Meyer (1907), cited V, p. 221 (F4, 1; also F2a, 1).

101. He was confronted with the practical problem of enclosing "'marvelous elm trees which neither the Londoners nor Paxton wanted to tear down'" (Meyer [1907], cited V, p. 221 [F4, 2]).

102. V, p. 216 (F2a, 1; also F6a, 2).

103. Meyer (1907), cited V, p. 222 (F4, 5).

104. Meyer (1907), cited V, p. 222 (F4a, 1).

105. Dubech-D'Espezel (1926), cited V, p. 223 (F4a, 5). The "gothic" iron style referred to here is Eiffel's 1878 Paris Exhibition Hall (pictured below, chapter 9, figure 9.7).

106. Perret (1935), cited V, p. 230 (F8, 4).

107. Cited V, p. 222 (F4, 6).

108. V, p. 1062 ("Der Saturnring, oder etwas von Eisenbau").

109. V, p. 223 (F4a, 4).

110. V, p. 216 (F2, 8).

111. Chéronnet (1937), cited V, p. 230 (F8, 2).

112. V, p. 826 (Y1a, 4).

113. V, p. 826 (Y1a, 4; also Q2, 7). "The first Panorama of Paris was directed by an American from the United States . . . by the name of Fulton . . . [He was] the engineer [who invented the steamboat . . .]" (Louis Lurine [1854], cited V, p. 664 [Q4, 2]).

114. V, p. 658 (Q1a, 8).

115. V, p. 655 (Q1, 1).

116. V, p. 659 (Q2, 2).

117. V, p. 659 (Q2, 5).

118. V, p. 658 (Q1a, 8; also Q2, 6).

119. V, p. 48 (1935 exposé). In the same year (1839) that Daguerre's panorama burned down, he made his discovery of daguerreotype (ibid.; cf. Q2, 5.).

120. V, p. 49 (1935 exposé).

121. "When daguerreotype, that giant child, will have attained the age of maturity, when all its force, all its power will have been developed, then the genius of art will suddenly grab it by the collar and cry: 'Mine! You are mine now! We are going to work together'" (Antoine Wiertz [1870], cited V, p. 824 [Y1, 1]).

122. Benjamin's Artwork essay tells us that photographic reproduction transformed images from aesthetic objects into a practical language of communication: "[T]he process of pictorial reproduction was accelerated so enormously that it would keep pace with speech" (I, p. 475). Photographic images expanded the range of cognitive experience: "For example, in photography the process of reproduction can bring out aspects of the original not attainable to the naked eye, but only to the lens, which is adjustable and chooses its focus at will. And with the aid of certain processes such as enlargement or slow motion, photographic reproduction can capture images which escape natural vision totally" (ibid., p. 476).

123. Marx. *Early Writings*, cited V, p. 802 (X1a, 3).

124. Marx, *Early Writings*, cited V, p. 802 (X1a, 3).

125. Marx, *Early Writings*, cited V, p. 801 (X1a, 2).

126. V, p. 49 (1935 exposé).

127. Gisèle Freund (1930 ms.), cited V, p. 826 (Y1a, 4).

128. V, p. 827 (Y2, 2).

129. V, p. 827 (Y2, 3).

130. Arago, cited in Freund (1930 ms.), cited V, pp. 830–31 (Y4, 1).

131. Benjamin describes: the "photographic reproduction of art as one phase in the struggle between photography and painting" (V, p. 826 [Y1a, 3]).

132. Benjamin challenged the description of his friend Gisèle Freund, whose 1930 manuscript on the history of photography he otherwise cited without criticism, precisely on the point of photography's democratizing impact: " 'Photography . . . was adopted first within the dominant class . . . : industrialists, factory owners, and bankers, men of state, literary figures and the intellectuals.' " Benjamin expressed doubt: "Is this true? Should not, rather, the succession be reversed?" (V, p. 829 [Y3, 2]).

133. Interpreters of Benjamin have insisted that he lamented the "disintegration of the aura" of artworks. This was, rather, Adorno's postion, part of his apprehension regarding mass culture generally. The *Passagen-Werk* material demonstrates quite unequivocably that Benjamin was no more (nor less) swayed by nostalgia in his description of these objective developments than, say, Marx, when he wrote in the 1848 Manifesto of the Communist Party that the bourgeoisie "has pitilessly torn asunder the motley feudal ties that bound man to his 'natural superiors' [. . .]."

Aesthetic aura was subjective illusion. The metaphysical aura of objects, however, was another matter. The latter, rather than veiling truth, only shone forth when the truth of objects was exposed. For a discussion of the difference, see below, chapter 7.

134. Walter Crane (1895/96), cited V, p. 828 (Y2a, 5).

135. V, p. 832 (Y4a, 4).

136. V, p. 832 (Y4a, 3).

137. V, p. 838 (Y7, 5). Benjamin's example is from Galimard (1805): " 'We will be one with the opinion of the public in admiring . . . the fastidious artist who . . . represents himself this year with a painting that in its finesse could contend with the proofs of daguerreotypes.' "

138. V, p. 832 (Y4a, 2). Action photography, first possible in 1882, inaugurated photojournalism (Y7, 8).

139. V, p. 49 (1935 exposé).

140. V, p. 45 (1935 exposé); see as example V, p. 98 (A7, 1).

141. Cabinet des Estampes, Bibliothèque Nationale (n.d.), cited V, p. 908 (d3a, 7).

142. Cabinet des Estampes, cited V, p. 908 (d3a, 6).

143. " " "In Marseilles around 1850, there was a total of four or five miniature painters, of whom only two enjoyed the particular reputation of finishing fifty portraits in the course of a year. These artists earned just enough to make a living . . . A few years later there were in Marseilles forty to fifty photographers . . . Each produced yearly an average of 1,000 to 1,200 negatives which they sold for 15 francs a piece, receiving 18,000 francs, so that the group of them constituted a business turnover of close to a million. And one could confirm the same development in all the large cities of France" ' " (Vidal [1871], cited in Freund, cited V, p. 830 [Y3a, 2]).

144. V, p. 49 (1935 exposé). In "The Author as Producer," Benjamin criticizes the fact that photography "can no longer depict a tenement block or a garbage heap without transfiguring it. [. . .] For it has succeeded namely in making even misery, by recording it in a fashionably perfected manner, an object of enjoyment" (II, p. 693).

145. Commercially successful photographers used props, backdrops, and retouching, trying to mimic painters (cf. V, p. 831 [Y4, 4]). Disderi suggested that by means of such props one could imitate historical "genre" paintings (V, pp. 831–32 [Y4a, 1]).

146. "Invention of the high-speed press 1814. It was first applied by the [London] *Times*" (V, p. 835 [Y5a, 8]).

147. II, pp. 683–701. This was a speech delivered at the *Institut zum Studium des Fascismus* in Paris, a front organization for the Communist Party.

148. As early as 1822 Sainte-Beuve recognized this potential: " 'With our electoral and industrial habits of life, everyone, at least once in his life, will have had his page, his speech, his prospectus, his toast—he will be an author [. . . . B]esides, in our day, who can say that he does not write a bit in order to live . . . ?' " (cited V, pp. 725–26 [U9, 2]).

149. "The Author as Producer," II, pp. 686–88 and 696.

150. Artwork essay, II, pp. 688–89.

151. II, p. 688.

152. II, p. 688.

153. II, p. 688.

154. II, p. 688.

155. II, p. 688. The central core of Benjamin's argument (the whole of p. 688) is in fact a self-quotation of the earlier piece, "die Zeitung" (II, pp. 623–24), which he wrote as part of a supplement, or addendum to *Einbahnstrasse*, with the one difference that "die Zeitung" does not equate the ideal socialist press with the actual one in the USSR. Adorno wrote to Benjamin that he considered the piece, "die Zeitung," "exceptional" (II, p. 1437). Benjamin never sent Adorno "The Author as Producer."

156. Already Balzac lamented: " ' "We have products, we no longer have works" ' " (Balzac, cited in Curtius [1923], cited V, p. 926 [d12a, 5]).

157. Friedrich Kreyssig (1865), cited V, p. 824 (Y1, 2).

158. Friedrich Kreyssig (1865), cited V, p. 825 (Y1, 2).

159. "Jacquot de Mirecourt publishes a book: *Alexandre Dumas and Co., Factory of Novels* (Paris: 1845)" (V, p. 908 [d3a, 8]).

160. J. Lucas-Dubreton (1928), cited V, p. 908 (d4, 2).

161. Paulin Limyrac (1845), cited V, p. 903 (d1, 4). Not all writers followed this path to success (and some of the most famous still relied on state patronage.) Benjamin notes the increasing economic precariousness of independent writers during the century. Whereas the first generation, the "guilded bohemians," were from solid bourgeois backgrounds (Gautier, de Nerval, Houssaye) and indulged in social nonconformism without risking grave

economic insecurity, " 'the true Bohemians, ' " who were still in their twenties in 1848, represented " 'a veritable intellectual proletariat: Murger was the son of a *concierge tailleur*; the father of Champfleury was secretary of a town hall at Laon . . . that of Delvau a tanner from the faubourg Saint-Marcel; the family of Courbet was a demi-peasant . . . Champfleury and Chintreuil handled packages for a bookdealer; Bonvin was a typography worker' " (Martino [1913], cited V, p. 921 [d10, 1], cf. p. 725 [U8a, 5]). Benjamin's prime example of the autonomous writer was, of course, Baudelaire, considered in detail in chapter 6 below.

162. V, p. 717 (U4a, 7).

163. The fact that newspapers first reached working-class audiences through individual sales worked against another mode of reception, the reading rooms (*cabinets de lectures*)which were frequently found in the arcades. They were places where for a small fee books and newspapers could be read in a collective setting. These reading rooms, having to compete with cheap publications, declined after 1850 (as did the arcades).

164. V, p. 725 (U9, 1).

165. V, p. 731 (U12, 3).

166. V, p. 734 (U13, 4).

167. Cf. the yearly statistics of new journals launched, V, p. 737 (U14, 6).

168. V, p. 726 (U9a, 1).

169. Benjamin notes the "connection between revenues [Hugo 300,000 francs for *Les Misérables*; Lamartine 600,000 for *Les Girondins*] and political aspirations" (V, p. 913 [d6a, 1]). Sociopolitical impact was not limited to the electoral arena: "The novels of George Sand led to an increase in divorces, almost all of which were applied for from the side of the woman. The authoress carried on a large correspondence in which she functioned as advisor to the women" (V, p. 914 [d6a, 7]).

170. Exemplifying this fundamentally idealist stance: Victor Hugo saw in the shape of Notre Dame an "H," as the gigantic projection of his own name (see V, p. 935 [d17a, 1]).

171. J. Lucas-Dubreton (1927), cited V, p. 903 (d1, 3).

172. "Meant ironically: 'It was a fortunate idea of M. de Balzac to predict a peasant revolt and demand the reestablishment of feudalism! What do you want? It is his own brand of socialism. Mme. Sand has another. Likewise M. Sue: to each novelist his own' " (Paulin Limayrac [1845], cited V, p. 903 [d1, 5], cf, V, p. 926 [d12a, 6]).

173. Albert Malet and P. Grillet (1919), cited V, p. 904 (d1a, 3).

174. " " "[. . .T]he red flag which you bring to us has never done anything but tour the Champ de Mars, dragged in the blood of the people in '91 and '93, and the tricolor has made a tour of the globe with the name, the glory and the liberty of the nation" ' " " (Lamartine, speech [at the Hôtel de Ville], 25 February 1848, cited in Albert Malet and P. Grillet [1919], cited V, p. 903 [d1, 2]).

175. Friedrich Szarvody (1852), cited V, p. 904 (d1a, 2).

176. On 6 April 1848, Lamartine assured a Russian diplomat that the French population had " " "such healthy common sense, such a respect for the family and for property" ' " " that " ' "order in Paris" ' " would be maintained; moreover, the bourgeois National Guard who

were called back to the city (and who ten days later were to put down a workers' demonstration by violence) would, he maintained, " ' "keep in check the fanatics of the clubs, who are supported by several thousand bums and criminal elements [. . .]" ' " (Lamartine, cited in Pokrowski [1928], cited V, p. 925 [d12, 2]).

177. "Decisive facts in *Les Miserables* are based on real occurrences" (V, p. 925 [d12, 1]).

178. V, p. 907 (d3, 6).

179. Eugène Spuller, cited in E. Meyer (1927), cited V, p. 918 (d8a, 5).

180. V, p. 935 (d17, 3).

181. V, p. 918 (d8a, 5). When Hugo subsequently participated in the resistence to Louis Napoleon's *coup d'état*, he was rewarded with exile from France.

182. As one critic satirized Hugo speaking: " 'I make a revolutionary wind rustle. I place a red bonnet on the old dictionary. No more words, senator! No more words, commoner! I make a tempest at the bottom of the ink-pot' " (Paul Bourget [1885], cited V, p. 905 [d2a, 3]). A June '48 revolutionary passed this judgment: "Citizen Hugo has made his debut in the tribune of the National Assembly. He was as we predicted: quack of gestures and phrases, orator of bombastic and hollow words [. . .]" (political sheet, cited, V, p. 904 [d1a, 2]).

183. V, p. 917 (d8, 4).

184. J. Lucas-Dubreton (1928), cited V, p. 908 (d4, 1).

185. Alphonse de Lamartine (n. d.), cited V, p. 937 (d18, 5).

186. "Der Autor als Produzent," II, p. 687.

187. Cf. V, p. 926 (d12a, 2).

188. The *Passagen-Werk* thus provides the historical research in support of Benjamin's political-cultural pronouncement at the end of the Artwork essay that fascism "aestheticizes politics; communism responds by politicizing art" (Artwork essay, I, p. 508).

189. Balzac, cited in Batault (1934), cited V, p. 907 (d3, 5).

190. Gautier, cited in Alfred Michiels (1863), cited V, p. 906 (d3, 1).

191. V, p. 216 (F2, 8). The "difficulties and criticisms" levied against technology were of a degree "no longer easily comprehended": It was thought that " 'steam carriages' " should run on "streets of granite" rather than railroad ties ("Der Saturnring . . .," V, p. 1061).

192. Cited, V, p. 906 (d2a, 5).

193. V, p. 826 (Y1a, 5).

194. Dubech-D'Espezel (1926), cited V, p. 826 (Y1a, 5). The development of railroads " 'surprised everyone' " (ibid.). Politicians were no more perceptive in recognizing the significance of the new railroads. " 'Thiers, thinking railroads would never function, had gates constructed at Paris at the moment when he ought to have been building train stations' " (idem, cited V, p. 220 [F3a, 6]). " 'Haussmann didn't know how to adopt what one could call a policy for [the construction of] train stations' " (idem, cited V, p. 223 [F4a, 3]).

Notes to pages 142–146

195. V, p. 834 (Y5a, 2).

196. This was the crucial point. Benjamin's reason for assembling these historical facts was to demonstrate to the writers and artists of his own era that their objective interests, as "technicians," would "sooner or later" lead them to make assessments that would "ground their solidarity with the proletariat in the most passionate way" ("Der Autor als Produzent," II, p. 699).

197. In its early years the *Ecole polytechnique* was receptive to the theories of Saint-Simon (V, p. 728 [U10a, 3]). Marx noted in regard to the insurrection of workers in 1848: " 'In order that the people's last illusion disappear, in order that the past be broken with totally, the customarily poetic ingredient of the enthusiastic bourgeois youth, the pupils of the *Ecole polytechnique*, the three-brimmed hats, had to stand on the side of the oppressors' " (Marx, cited V, p. 987 [r3a, 2]).

198. V, p. 828 (Y2a, 6).

199. V, p. 232 (G1, 1).

200. V, p. 59 (1935 exposé).

201. "Der Autor als Produzent," II, p. 693.

202. Hence the "phantasmagoria" of the flâneur (V, p. 540 [M6, 6], whose perceptions, blended with daydreams, paralleled those of the hashish smoker (M2, 3; M2, 4).

203. V, p. 1062 ("Der Saturnring . . . ").

204. V, p. 692 (S8a, 1). Benjamin mentions Realism as the first attempt to fuse the two in a self-conscious response to the threat from technology (see S5, 5). By the time of *Jugendstil* this threat had "fallen into repression"; *Jugendstil's* "aggression" against technology, because hidden, occurred "all the more aggressively" (S8a, 1).

205. V, p. 693 (S8a, 7).

206. Marxists have traditionally envisioned socialism as an overcoming of the division between mental and manual labor in that each member of society will do some of both. Benjamin's conception is that the technological revolution will make both kinds of labor the same. While mental work is mediated by an increasingly technologized production apparatus, "manual" labor becomes intellectualized. He notes that at the building site of the Eiffel Tower, " 'thought dominated over muscle power,' " as human energy found a substitute in " 'sturdy scaffolding and cranes' " (V, p. 1063 ["Der Saturnring . . . "]).

207. V, p. 560 (M16a, 3).

208. These are cited heavily in the pre–1937 entries to *Konvolut* X, "Marx" (V, pp. 800–804).

209. V, pp. 500–01 (K3a, 2), cf. the earlier entry (0°, 32), which has in place of "clear to us," "ur-historical". The K3a, 2 version adds: "Of course: within the dialectical essence of technology this throws light on only one moment. (Which one it is difficult to say: antithesis if not synthesis.) In any case there exists in technology the other moment: that of bringing about goals that are alien to nature, also with means that are alien, even hostile to nature, that emancipate themselves from nature and subdue it."

210. V, p. 578 (N3, 1).

211. *Trauerspiel* study, I, p. 211.

212. In caricature, " 'the bourgeois society of that century was opened up for art' " (Eduard Fuchs [1921], cited V, p. 899 [b1, 4]).

213. Edouard Drumont (1900), cited V, p. 899 (b1, 1).

214. Daumier was himself not without nostalgia for the classical ideal: "On the artistic idea of the Empire. Regarding Daumier: 'He was to the highest degree enchanted by muscular agitation. Tirelessly, his pencil glorified the tension and activity of the muscle . . . Yet the public realm of which he dreamed had another measure than that of this worthless . . . shopkeeper society. He yearned for a social milieu which, like Greek antiquity, gave people a basis on which they raised themselves as on pedestals in powerful beauty . . . There was bound to occur . . . a grotesque distortion if one was observing the bourgeoisie from the perspective of such presuppositions' " (Schulte [1913/14], cited V, p. 224 [F5, 2]).

215. Baudelaire, cited V, p. 901 (b2, 3; see also b2, 1).

216. "Der Autor als Produzent," II, pp. 698–99.

217. V, p. 218 (F3, 2).

218. V, pp. 216–17 (F2a, 5).

219. V, p. 1022 (M°, 3).

220. V, p. 51 (1935 exposé).

221. V, p. 51 (1935 exposé).

222. V, p. 246 (G5a, 2; again, 1935 exposé).

223. V, p. 51 (1935 exposé).

224. V, p. 267 (G16, 4).

225. V, p. 51 (1935 exposé).

226. In *Un autre monde*, Grandville has his character see that " 'the ring of this planet [Saturn] is nothing else but a circular balcony onto which Saturnites come in the evening to take a breath of air' " (Grandville, [1844], cited V, p. 212 [F1, 7]; cf. p. 1060 ["Der Saturnring . . . "]).

227. Benjamin asks whether, indeed, one could see in this commodified nature the "soul" of the worker who had been sacrified to produce it (V, p. 260 [G12a, 3]).

228. V, p. 120 (B4, 5).

229. He cites Georg Simmel's criticism (1900) of the " 'totally childish concept,' " the " 'mythological manner of thinking' " that " 'we conquer or dominate nature,' " and praises Fourier for his "entirely different reception of technology" (V, pp. 812–13 [X7a, 1]).

230. "Neues von Blumen" review of Karl Blossfeldt's *Urformen der Kunst. Photographische Pflanzenbilder* (1928), III, p. 152.

231. "Neues von Blumen," III, p. 153.

232. "Neues von Blumen," III, P. 152.

233. "Neues von Blumen," III, p. 152. Benjamin cites Moholy-Nagy on photography: " 'Here everything is still so new that the very seeking itself leads to creative results' " (ibid., p. 151).

234. "Neues von Blumen," III, p. 152.

6 Historical Nature: Ruin

1. Cf. Adorno's definition (which draws on Benjamin's *Trauerspiel* study) of *Naturgeschichte* as "a kind of enchantment of history" (Adorno, "Die Idee der Naturgeschichte," *GS* I, p. 361).

2. V, p. 698 (T1, 4; also T1a, 8; cf. D°, 6; a°, 2).

3. V, p. 1046 (a°, 4). The novel opens with a description of the Passage du Pont Neuf: "[. . .] a narrow, dark corridor [. . .] paved with yellowish flagstones, worn and loose, which always exude a damp, pungent smell, and it is covered with a flat glazed roofing black with grime.
"On fine summer days, a whitish light does fall through the dingy glass roofing and hang dismally about this arcade [. . .]. The murky shops behind are just so many black holes in which weird shapes move and have their being. [. . .] The Passage du Pont Neuf is no place to go for a nice stroll" (Emile Zola, *Thérèse Raquin*, trans. Leonard Tancock [New York: Penguin Books, 1978], pp. 31–32).

4. V, p. 1215 (1935 exposé note no. 9; cf. C2a, 9). "All that [about which we are speaking here] never lived, just as truly as no skeleton has ever lived, but only a human being" (V, p. 1000 [D°, 3]).

5.Theodor W. Adorno, "Die Idee der Naturgeschichte" (1932), *Gesammelte Schriften*, vol. 1: *Philosophische Früschriften*, ed. Rolf Tiedemann (Frankfurt am Main: Suhrkamp Verlag, 1973), p. 356. Adorno cites, not the now-famous discussion of "second nature" in Lukács' *History and Class Consciousness*, which uses the term as synonymous with Marx's concept of commodity fetishism, but Lukács' earlier use of the (Hegelian) term in *Theory of the Novel*: " 'The second nature of human creation has no lyrical substantiality. Its forms are too fixed for the symbol-creating moment to nestle in them, [. . .] This nature is not mute, obvious and meaningless like first nature; it is a frozen sense-complex that has become alien, no longer awakening the soul. It is a hill of skulls [*Schädelstätte*] of decaying inwardness, and could therefore—if this were possible—only be awakened through the metaphysical act of a reawakening of the psychical that it created or contained in its former or supposed existence, never, however, capable of being experienced by another inwardness' " (cited in ibid., pp. 356-57).

6. Adorno, "Die Idee. . . ," *GS* I, p. 357.

7. Adorno, "Die Idee. . . ," *GS* I, p. 357. Cf. Benjamin's comment in a letter to Scholem that he and Lukács came to similar conclusions, despite different ways of getting there (*Briefe* I. p. 355).

8. Adorno, "Die Idee. . . ," *GS* I, p. 357.

9. Adorno, "Die Idee. . . ," *GS*, p. 358.

10. Benjamin considered the emblem books of the Baroque "the authentic documents of the modern allegorical way of looking at things" (*Trauerspiel* study, I, p. 339).

11. *Trauerspiel* study (I, p. 343), cited by Adorno, *GS* I, pp. 358–59.

12. *Trauerspiel* study, I, p. 354.

13. *Trauerspiel* study, I, p. 353.

14. *Trauerspiel* study (I, p. 343), cited by Adorno, *GS* I, p. 359.

15. This emblem has been described by the Baroque scholar Gottfried Kirchner: "The *lemma* [title] of the emblem—'*Vivitur ingenio*'—emphasizes continual life through the mind. The *pictura* [image] shows the skeleton of death in front of a landscape-in-ruins of the fate/vanity-filled world, who holds in his hand or touches with his foot the crown and scepter, transitory attributes of earthly power. Next to it one sees on a flat rock a book overgrown with ivy, and on which lies the snake in a circle, both emblematic signs of eternal lastingness. The *subscriptio* [caption] makes evident the connection between the separate levels of the graphic composition [. . .]. For the decline of empires and the destruction of their major cities, the position on Rome is exemplary in the seventeenth century; of its earlier grandeur there remains only an empty concept" (Gottfried Kirchner, *Fortuna in Dichtung und Emblematik des Barok: Tradition und Bedeutungswandel eines Motivs* [Stuttgart: J. B. Metzlerische Verlagsbuchhandlung, 1970], p. 78).

16. Baroque publisher's preface to the dramas of Jakob Ayrer, cited *Trauerspiel* study, I, p. 320.

17. V, p. 1216 (1935 exposé note no. 11).

18. See, e.g., V, p. 153 (C8a, 2; C8a, 3).

19. See, e.g., V, p. 152 (C7a, 4).

20. *Trauerspiel* study, I, p. 354.

21. "The [Baroque] poet must not conceal the fact that he is arranging, since it was not so much the mere whole which was the center of all intentional effects, but rather, its obviously constructed quality" (*Trauerspiel* study, I, p. 355).

22. V, p. 1215 (1935 exposé note no. 10; again H2, 6).

23. V, p. 344 (J22, 5).

24. "Zentralpark" (1939–40), I, p. 677. This fragmentary text was formulated specifically with reference to Benjamin's planned book on Baudelaire. The controversial relationship of this "book" to the *Passagen-Werk* is discussed in the Introduction to Part III, below.

25. *Trauerspiel* study, I, p. 354.

26. "'The man-made ruins [. . .] appear as the last heritage of an antiquity that is visible in the modern world really only as a picturesque field of ruins'" (Karl Borinski, cited *Trauerspiel* study, I, p. 354).

27. "For it was absolutely decisive for the development of this [Baroque] mode of thought that not transitoriness alone, but also guilt must appear to have an obvious home in the province of idols as in the realm of the flesh" (*Trauerspiel* study, I, p. 398).

28. *Trauerspiel* study, I, p. 399.

29. *Trauerspiel* study, I, p. 399.

30. Benjamin considers this debasement a hallmark of "modern allegory," as opposed to secular allegorical forms that appeared in Renaissance humanism, and in the animal fables of antiquity itself. In Benjamin's idiosyncratic schematization, this "modern" form has its roots in the late (Christian) era of the Holy Roman Empire, which was "part of an intensive preparation for allegory" (*Trauerspiel* study, I, p. 397), whereas the secular humanism of the Renaissance appears as an atavistic recurrence of the most ancient form of allegory.

31. Baroque allegory is based on this Christian attitude toward classical antiquity; the Apollonian conception of this era came only later, with the Enlightenment. Benjamin cites Warburg's observation: " 'The classically ennobled world of the ancient divinities has, of course, been impressed upon us so deeply since the time of Winckelmann as the sign of antiquity in general that we entirely forget that it is a new creation of the scholars of humanist culture: This "Olympic" aspect of antiquity had first to be wrested from the demonic side that tradition had brought to it [. . .]' " (Aby Warburg, cited *Trauerspiel* study, I, p. 400).

32. *Trauerspiel* study, I, p. 400 (cited V, p. 409 [J53a, 1]).

33. *Trauerspiel* study, I, p. 395.

34. *Trauerspiel* study, I, pp. 399–400.

35. *Trauerspiel* study, I, pp. 398–99. "[. . . A]llegorical exegesis tended above all in two directions: it was designed to establish the true, demonic nature of the ancient gods as viewed by Christianity, and it served the pious mortification of the body. Thus it is not by chance that the Middle Ages and the Baroque took pleasure in the meaning-filled juxtapositions of images of idols and the bones of the dead" (ibid., p. 396).

36. *Trauerspiel* study, I, p. 398.

37. *Trauerspiel* study, I, p. 397. Notice that the rescue of antiquity had nothing to do with ahistorical, eternal truth (as nineteenth-century neoclassicism would have it), but with its radical reconstruction within a totally changed historical present.

38. *Trauerspiel* study, I, pp. 338–39, discussed above, chapter 1, section 3.

39. *Trauerspiel* study, I, p. 342.

40. *Trauerspiel* study, I, p. 342.

41. "[W]ith the radiance of sunset, the transfigured countenance of nature reveals itself fleetingly in the light of redemption" (*Trauerspiel* study, I, p. 343).

42. *Trauerspiel* study, I, p. 342.

43. *Trauerspiel* study, I, p. 355.

44. *Trauerspiel* study, I, p. 339.

45. In the *Trauerspiel* study allegory is connected with "stations of decline" (I, p. 343).

46. *Trauerspiel* study, I, p. 397.

47. *Trauerspiel* study, I, p. 244. "Historical life"—indeed, social "catastrophe"—was its "true object. In this it is different from tragedy," the object of which "is not history, but myth" (I, pp. 242–43).

48. *Trauerspiel* study, I, p. 405.

49. See especially chapter 7 below.

50. *Trauerspiel* study, I, p. 319.

51. *Trauerspiel* study, I, p. 346.

52. "What else than the theological conviction that the hieroglyphs of the Egyptians contain a traditional wisdom that illuminates every obscurity of nature [. . .] is expressed in the following sentence of Pierio Valerianos: 'Since speaking in hieroglyphs is nothing other than unveiling the nature of things human and divine'" (*Trauerspiel* study, I, p. 347).

53. As emblematics developed: "Egyptian, Greek, and Christian pictorial languages interpentrated" (*Trauerspiel* study, I, p. 348).

54. *Trauerspiel* study, I, p. 349.

55. Karl Giehlow, cited *Trauerspiel* study, I, p. 350.

56. *Trauerspiel* study, I, p. 390.

57. *Trauerspiel* study, I, p. 398.

58. *Trauerspiel* study, I, p. 398.

59. *Trauerspiel* study, I, p. 400.

60. *Trauerspiel* study, I, p. 401.

61. *Trauerspiel* study, I, p. 398.

62. *Trauerspiel* study, I, p. 402.

63. "For in this [Baroque] poetry, it is a common characteristic to pile up fragments ceaselessly without any strict idea of a goal, with stereotypes taken for intensification, in the unremitting expectation of a miracle" (*Trauerspiel* study, I, p. 354).

64. *Trauerspiel* study, I, p. 363. Benjamin's analysis of the problem of modern allegory is well summarized by Wiesenthal: "In the allegoricists's power over meanings there lies at the same time his impotence [. . .]. The material objects observed by him are 'incapable' of 'radiating a single meaning' [WB]. In its most extreme stamp, allegory becomes the expression of senseless combinations of emblems that have been 'hollowed out.' Every emblem can be dismissed; for in their meaninglessness the emblems are arbitrarily exchangeable." (Liselotte Wiesenthal, *Zur Wissenschaftstheorie Walter Benjamins* [Frankfurt am Main: Athenaum, 1973]), p. 120.

65. *Trauerspiel* study, I, pp. 380–84.

66. *Trauerspiel* study, I, p. 404.

67. *Trauerspiel* study, I, p. 404.

68. "Thus in allegory an ambivalence occurs between the power to lend meaning to things on the one hand, and the inability to fix this meaning essentially on the other" (Wiesenthal, p. 58).

69. *Trauerspiel* study, I, p. 405.

70. *Trauerspiel* study, I, p. 405.

71. *Trauerspiel* study, I, p. 406.

72. Daniel Caspers von Lohenstein, cited *Trauerspiel* study, I, p. 406.

73. *Trauerspiel* study, I, p. 406.

74. See particularly "Über Sprache überhaupt und Über die Sprache des Menschen" (1916), passages of which are incorporated into the *Trauerspiel* book (I, pp. 398 and 407); also "Zur Kritik der Gewalt" (1921), and "Theologisch-Politisches Fragment" (1920–21) [perhaps 1937–38], all in II. However, the first of these essays is problematic. Benjamin draws directly from it in the closing pages of the *Trauerspiel* study (I, p. 407) without making it clear where his description of the allegoricists ends and his own theory begins, so that it sometimes appears that he is affirming the Baroque solution. More probably he means to affirm a *theological* solution, but not the Christian one (see also below, chapter 7).

75. *Trauerspiel* study, I, p. 260. (This was the medieval view.)

76. *Trauerspiel* study, I, p. 334.

77. *Trauerspiel* study, I, p. 406.

78. "The vain activity of the intriguer was regarded as the undignified counter image of passionate contemplation [. . .]" (*Trauerspiel* study, I, p. 320.)

79. *Trauerspiel* study, I, p. 246.

80. *Trauerspiel* study, I, p. 406.

81. *Trauerspiel* study, I, p. 406.

82. *Trauerspiel* study, I, p. 406.

83. Cited *Trauerspiel* study, I, p. 406.

84. *Trauerspiel* study, I, p. 406.

85. *Trauerspiel* study, I, pp. 406–07. Benjamin had made the same criticism of the German Romantics in his (1917) dissertation, "Der Begriff der Kunstkritik in der deutschen Romantik," II, pp. 7–122.

86. Rolf Tiedemann, *Studien zur Philosophie Walter Benjamin*, intro. by Theodor W. Adorno (Frankfurt am Main: Suhrkamp Verlag, 1973), p. 38.

87. Letter, Benjamin to Max Rychner, 7 March 1931, Walter Benjamin, *Briefe*, 2 vols., eds. Gershom Scholem and Theodor W. Adorno (Frankfurt am Main: Suhrkamp Verlag; 1978), vol. 2, p. 523. See below, chapter 7, for a fuller discussion of the connection.

88. Letter, Benjamin to Adorno, 31 May 1935, *Briefe*, vol. 2, p. 644 (and V, pp. 1117–18); see also letter, Benjamin to Scholem, 20 May 1935, V, pp. 1112–13.

89. Letter, Adorno to Benjamin, 10 November 1938, *Briefe*, vol. 2, p. 783 (see above, chapter 1, section 5).

90. V, pp. 1022–23 (M°, 5).

91. See Susan Buck-Morss, *The Origin of Negative Dialectics: Theodor W. Adorno, Walter Benjamin and the Frankfurt Institute* (New York: Macmillan Free Press, 1977), pp. 20–23 and passim.

92. See discussion, chapter 7.

93. See above, chapter 1.

94. Benjamin mentions Kierkegaard in the closing pages of the *Trauerspiel* study in connection with the "subjectivism" of Christian allegory (I, p. 407).

95. See Buck-Morss, *Origin of Negative Dialectics*, chapter 7, pp. 111–21.

96. Benjamin cites Adorno's passage on the bourgeois interior from the Kierkegaard study in his *Konvolut* entitled, "The Interior; Trace" (*Konvolut* I), V, pp. 290–91 (I3a).

97. Compare Buck-Morss, *Origin of Negative Dialectics*, pp. 116–21, with *Konvolut* I, "Interieur, der Spur," (V, pp. 281–300). The image of the bourgeois interior is interpreted by both Adorno and Benjamin as an emblem of bourgeois consciousness, which retreats into a subjective, inward realm (see letter, Adorno to Benjamin, 2 August 1935 [V, p. 1128]).

98. See in particular the entry N2, 7 (V, pp. 575–76), to which Benjamin returned repeatedly in trial arrangements of the *Passagen-Werk* material for the Baudelaire book (discussed below, Introduction to Part III).

99. V, p. 405 (J51a, 5).

100. Cited V, p. 313 (J7, 3).

101. V, p. 460 (J77, 2).

102. "But it is the Dante of a fallen epoch, a Dante modern and atheist, a Dante come after Voltaire" (Barbey d'Aurevilly [1857], cited V, p. 306 [J3a, 1; see also J3, 1; J11, 3; J11, 4; J23a, 2; J26, 1; J33a, 10; J37, 3]).

103. Baudelaire, cited V, p. 273 (H2, 1).

104. Thus Benjamin writes: "If one could be permitted a conjecture, it would be this, that little would have been able to give [Baudelaire] so high an understanding of his own originality as reading the Roman satirists" ("Zentralpark" [1939–40], I, p. 658).

105. "Zentralpark," I, p. 677.

106. Honoré de Balzac (1846), cited V, p. 84 (A1, 4). This fragment is noted in the material for the Baudelaire book in the Bataille Archive, Bibliothèque Nationale (under the keyword "Commodity"), as are virtually all of the fragments cited in the discussion of Baudelaire that follows. (For a clarification as to the status of the Baudelaire "book" vis-à-vis the *Passagen-Werk*, see below, Introduction to Part III.)

107. Although Benjamin records the changes in Baudelaire's professed political positions (including his brief enthusiasm for the revolution in June 1848) it is not these that Benjamin believes provide the interpreter with the key to the political meaning of his poems. The latter is not subjectively intended; it has an objective source.

108. V, p. 309 (J5, 1).

109. Charles Baudelaire, "Le Cygne," *The Flowers of Evil* [*Les Fleurs du mal*] ed. Marthiel and Jackson Mathews, revised ed. (New York: New Directions Book, 1962), pp. 329–30 (trans. mine). On this poem see V, p. 450 (J72, 5), and *passim*.
A note on the Baudelaire translations: the standard English translations in the edition cited above are by poets who take considerable license with the wording, juxtaposed to which Benjamin's comments are often mystifying. This is true as well of the justly praised, recent translation of *Les Fleurs du mal* by Richard Howard. I have therefore made my own translations, more literal, if less elegant, referring when possible to Benjamin's own translations of significant portions of *Les Fleurs du mal* in IV, pp. 23–82.

110. "Zentralpark," I, p. 658.

111. There is reason to believe that Benjamin was inspired by a comment of Adorno in his (critical) response to the 1935 exposé. Adorno wrote: "The commodity is on the one hand the alienated object in which use value dies out; on the other, however, that which survives [. . . .T]he fetish—to carry further the connection you justifiably establish in the Baroque [*Trauerspiel*] book—is for the nineteenth century a faithless final image comparable only to the human skull" (letter, Adorno to Benjamin, 2 August 1935, V, p. 1130). On the margin next to this passage, Benjamin wrote: "How does meaning stand in relation to exchange value?" (original letter sent to Benjamin, envelope no. 5, Benjamin papers, Bataille Archive, Bibliothèque Nationale, Paris). His answer is in fact what follows here.

112. V, p. 409 (J53a, 1).

113. "Zentralpark," I, p. 660.

114. Karl Marx (1843), cited V, p. 805 (X3, 6).

115. "Zentralpark," I, p. 681. For a comparison of the Baroque view toward God's "production" of human beings and assembly line production under capitalism, see V, p. 463 (J78, 4).

116. [Marx, cited in] Otto Rühle (1928), cited V, p. 245 (G5, 1).

117. V, p. 466 (J80, 2/J80a, 1).

118. "The allegorical intuition that in the seventeenth century shaped a style, no longer did so in the nineteenth" ("Zentralpark," I, p. 690). Hence: "Baudelaire's allegorical mode of conceptualizing was not understood by any of his contemporaries, and thus in the end not even commented upon" (V, 426 [J61, 3]).

119. Benjamin interprets Baudelaire as an "unwilling detective," in secret dissatisfaction with his own bourgeois class (I, p. 543). Before "the tribunal of history," his work bore witness, however unintentionally, to the criminal effects of that class's domination: His flânerie and his observations of the crowd and the market made him "an expert in the facts of the case" (V, p. 459 [J76a, 2]). The return of the same motifs in his poems "can be truly compared to the compulsion which draws the criminal repeatedly back to the scene of his crime" (I, p. 669). "The *Fleurs du mal* have three of [the detective story's] decisive elements as *disjecta membra*: the victim and the scene of the crime ('Une Martyre'), the murderer ('Le Vin de l'assassin'), the masses ('Le Crépescule du soir'). The fourth element is lacking, the power of understanding that could pierce through this affect-laden atmosphere" (I, p. 545). The "signature" of Baudelaire's "class betrayal" was not political but productive: His work was "incompatible with the fashionable customs of journalism" (V, p. 416 [J56a, 5]).

120. V, p. 71 (1939 exposé).

121. Adorno (1935), cited V, p. 582 (N5, 2).

122. V, p. 582 (N5, 2).

123. "Confession," *Les Fleurs du mal*, trans. mine.

124. Edmond Jaloux (1921), cited V. p. 366 (J33, 2).

125. "Zentralpark," I, p. 671.

126. V, p. 414 (J55a, 3).

127. V, p. 344 (J22, 5).

128. This comment is made by Benjamin with reference to J22, 4 (cited below), in the "Notes to the Baudelaire Book," under the keyword "Allegory" (Bataille Archive, Bibliothèque Nationale).

129. "Annotations to poems of Baudelaire" (1937–38), I, pp. 1144–45 (again, V, p. 419 [J57a, 3]).

130. V, p. 344 (J22, 4). The poem was one of the 23 in *Les Fleurs du mal* written by the summer of 1843 (J38, 1). Benjamin says: "The morning of *Vormärz* dawns in this poem" (J22, 4).

131. Baudelaire, "Le Crépescule du matin," *Les Fleurs du mal*, trans. mine.

132. "Annotations to poems of Baudelaire," I, 1145.

133. Baudelaire, "Le Crépescule du matin," *Les Fleurs du mal*, trans. mine.

134. See Hugo, cited V, p. 364 (J32, 1); cf. Baudelaire on Hugo (1865): "'One can simultaneously possess a special genius and be a fool. Victor Hugo proves that to us well—the Ocean itself is tired of him'" (cited, V, p. 338 [J19a, 7]).

135. "Are the flowers soulless? Does that play into the title 'The Flowers of Evil?'" With other words, are flowers symbols of the whore? Or are flowers to be banished with this title to their true place?" (V, p. 348 [J24, 5]).

136. V, pp. 465–66 (J80, 1). Cf.: "Machinery becomes in Baudelaire the sign of destructive powers. Not the least of such machinery is the human skeleton" ("Zentralpark," I, p. 684). The French word *armature*, which means both human skeleton and construction scaffolding, fuses these (cf. J71, 1).

137. V, p. 415 (J56, 3).

138. V, p. 365 (J32a, 5).

139. Charles Baudelaire, cited V, p. 365 (J32a, 5). The translation here of Charles Baudelaire, "The Salon of 1859," is by Jonathan Mayne in *Art in Paris: 1845–1862. Salons and Other Exhibitions* (Ithaca: Cornell University Press, 1981), p. 173.

140. "The span between emblem and advertising image lets one measure the changes that have taken place since the seventeenth century in the world of things" (V, p. 440 [J67a, 2]).

141. "Zentralpark," I, p. 671.

142. "Zentralpark," I, p. 671.

143. "Zentralpark," I, p. 671.

144. "Zentralpark," I, p. 671.

145. Cf. V, p. 455 (J75, 1; also J67, 5; J67a, 1). Benjamin intended to include in his "Baudelaire book" a description of the origins of the "labor market" (see V, pp. 715–16 [U4, 1], listed in the notes under the keyword "Commodity" in the Bataille Archive, Bibliothèque Nationale, Paris).

146. See section 3 above.

147. Marx, *Capital*, cited V, p. 807 (X4, 3). Cf. Marx's statement in the 1844 Manuscripts: "'Prostitution is only a *specific* expression of the *general* prostitution of the laborer [. . .]'" (cited X2, 1).

148. Cf. "Tearing things out of the context of their usual interconnections—which is the norm with commodities at the stage of their being exhibited—is a procedure very characteristic of Baudelaire. It is related to the destruction of the organic interrelations in the allegorical conception" ("Zentralpark," I, p. 670).

149. V, p. 422 (J59, 10).

150. V, p. 55 (1935 exposé).

151. "Zentralpark," I, pp. 687–88.

152. "Zentralpark," I, p. 687, cf. V, p. 425 (J60a, 2).

153. Baudelaire, cited V, p. 341 (J21, 2).

154. V, p. 416 (J56a, 3).

155. "La Muse vénale," *Les Fleurs du mal*, trans. mine.

156. "From early on he viewed the literary market totally without illusions" ("Das Paris des Second Empire bei Baudelaire" [1938], I, p. 535).

157. "It has been estimated that [Baudelaire] earned with his entire work no more than 15,000 francs" ("Das Paris des Second Empire bei Baudelaire," I, p. 535, cf. V, p. 386 [J42a, 3; see also J78a, 1]).

158. "Das Paris des Second Empire bei Baudelaire," I, p. 536, cf. V, p. 54 (1935 exposé).

159. "Notes sur les tableaux parisiens de Baudelaire" (1939), I, p. 746, cf. V, p. 383 (J41, 3).

160. "Le Soleil," *Les Fleurs du mal*, trans. mine.

161. V, p. 437 (J66a, 6). "A remark by Leiris: for Baudelaire the word '*familier*' is full of mystery and unrest; it stands for something for which it has never stood before" ("Zentralpark," I, p. 678)—in the poem "Obsession": "familiar gazes"; in the poem "Bohémiens en voyage": "the familiar empire."

162. Suffering was basic to the notion of Baudelaire's "aesthetic passion" (cf. V, p. 420 [J58a, 1]).

163. "In allegory the original interest is not linguistic but optic. [Baudelaire:] 'The images, my grand, my primitive passion.' Question: When did the commodity become prominent in the image of the city? It could be crucial to have statistical information about the intrusion of the shop window with facades" ("Zentralpark," I, p. 686, cf. V, p. 302 [J1, 6]). Although the arcades do not appear in Baudelaire's images, Benjamin compares the experience of reading a poem like "Le Crepescule du matin" with walking through an arcade (J88a, 2).

164. V, p. 424 (J60, 1).

165. V, p. 54 (1935 exposé).

166. V, p. 723 (J59a, 4). Benjamin notes his frequent changes of address (J29, 11).

167. Baudelaire, cited V, p. 555 (M14, 3; again M15a, 3). In his 1939 article on Baudelaire, Benjamin gives a striking example with reference to the poem "A une passante," in which an unknown woman, graceful, majestic, in a widow's veil, passes the poet on the "deafening street": The glance that they share before each passes by the other is, writes Benjamin, "love, not so much at first sight as at last [. . .]. What makes the body [of the poet] contract in a spasm—*crispé comme un extravagant*—is not the rapture of the person in whom eros has seized possession of every corner of his being; it is more the kind of sexual shock that can overcome a lonely man" ("Über einige Motive bei Baudelaire" [1939], I, p. 623).

168. "Jules Renard wrote of Baudelaire: "'His heart [. . .] more alone than an ace of hearts in the middle of a playing card'" (cited V, p. 440 [J67a, 5]).

169. V, p. 466 (J80a, 1).

170. V, p. 423 (J59a, 4).

171. V, p. 466 (J80a, 1).

172. See section 3 above.

173. Baudelaire, cited V, p. 395 (J47, 2; see also J44, 3).

174. V, p. 413 (J55, 12). The closing verse beings: "'Clear emblems, perfect tableau'" (cited, J70, 4).

175. "L'Irrémédiable," cited V, p. 446 (J70, 4).

176. V, p. 466 (J80a, 10).

177. V, p. 419 (J57a, 4).

178. "Zentralpark," I, p. 665.

179. V, pp. 441–42 (J68, 4).

180. "Zentralpark," I, p. 662; also V, p. 415 (J56, 5).

181. "Les Sept Vieillards," cited V, p. 461 (J77a, 3): "The hero who stands his ground on the scene of modernity is in fact more than anything else an actor" (ibid.).

182. *Trauerspiel* study, cited V, p. 409 (J53a, 4). "'Laughter is satanic, and thus profoundly human,'" Baudelaire, *L'Essence du rire*, cited V, p. 409 [J53a, 3]).

183. V, p. 409 (J53a, 4).

184. "Zentralpark," I, p. 680, cf. V, p. 414 (J55a, 8).

185. "L'Héautontimorouménos," cited V, p. 411 (J54a, 3).

186. "Zentralpark," I, p. 689.

187. "[In Baudelaire's poem] 'La Destruction' on the devil: 'I . . . sense him burning in my lungs,/Filling them with endless, guilty desire.' The lungs as the seat of a wish is the most daring transcription of the impossibility of its being fulfilled that one could think of" (V, pp. 440–41 [J68, 1]).

188. "In the erotology of the condemned—as one might call that of Baudelaire—infertility and impotence are the decisive givens. These *alone* are that which gives the cruel and discredited instinctual moments in sexuality its purely negative character" (V, p. 438 [J66a, 9]).

189. "Baroque detailing of the female body. 'Le beau navire'" (V, p. 415 [J56, 7]). On "the detailing of female beauty of which Baroque poetry is so fond": "This fragmentation of female beauty into its most fame-worthy parts is like an autopsy, and the popular comparisons of the body parts with alabaster, snow, jewels or other, mostly inorganic forms does it one better. (Such fragmentation is found also in Baudelaire: 'Le beau navire')" (B9, 3. The poem praises the "diverse beauties" of a woman who walks like a "splendid ship," her bosom jutting like a prow, her skirts billowing like sails, and details her legs like sorcerers, arms like pythons, neck, shoulders, head, etc.)

190. Cf. the courtesan: "her heart bruised like a peach" ("L'Amour du mensonge"); or the little old women: "debris of humanity" ("Les Petites Vieilles").

191. "La Destruction," *Les Fleurs du mal*, trans. mine.

192. V, p. 441 (J68, 2). Benjamin continues: "The poem breaks off abruptly; it creates the impression—doubly surprising for a sonnet—of itself being something fragmentary" (ibid.).

193. V, p. 440 (J67a, 7; cf. "Zentralpark," I, p. 670).

194. "Une Martyre," *Les Fleurs du mal*, trans. mine.

195. V, p. 440 (J67a, 7).

196. V, p. 415 (J56, 2).

197. V, p. 413 (J55, 13).

198. "L'Examin de minuit," cited by Benjamin as an example of "lived experiences that are emptied, robbed of their substance" (V, p. 410 [J54, 7]).

199. V, p. 464 (J79, 5).

200. V, p. 440 (J67a, 5).

201. "Zentralpark," I, p. 681.

202. V, p. 405 (J51a, 6).

203. "Zentralpark," I, p. 681.

204. "Zentralpark," I, p. 689.

205. "Zentralpark," I, p. 681. Benjamin explains: "The capacities of the soul as they appear in Baudelaire are 'souvenirs' [*Andenken*] of human beings, in the way the medieval allegories are souvenirs of the gods. Claudel once wrote: 'Baudelaire made his object the only inner experience that was still possible for people of the nineteenth century: remorse.' But that is painting too rosy a picture. Among inner experiences, remorse was no less rotted out [*ausgestorben*] than the others canonized beforehand. Remorse in Baudelaire is only a souvenir, just as repentance or virtue, hope or even anxiety [. . .]" (V, pp. 407–08 [J53, 1; cf. J33, 8]). Cf.: "What is sold in the arcades are souvenirs" (V, p. 1037 [0°, 76]).

206. "Zentralpark," I, 669.

207. The "souvenir" is the schema of the transformation. The correspondences are the "endlessly multiple resonances of each souvenir with all the others" ("Zentralpark," I, p. 689).

208. "Spleen (II)," *Les Fleurs du mal*, trans. mine, cf. V, p. 447 (J71, 2).

209. Here is a clear parallel to Adorno's Kierkegaard study, which argues that what Kierkegaard intended as a metaphorical description was actually the intrusion of reality into his own subjective inwardness (see Buck-Morss, *The Origin of Negative Dialectics*, chapter 7). Benjamin cites Adorno's study (or Kierkegaard directly) in several entries, V, pp. 422–31.

210. V, p. 360 (J30, 8).

211. "Avec ses vêtements . . . " (written to Jeanne Duval), cited V, p. 411 (J54a, 5).

212. "Je te donne ces vers . . . " (written to Jeanne Duval) cited V, p. 416 (J56, 9).

213. "Zentralpark," I, p. 675.

214. "Zentralpark," I, p. 675.

215. "Tu mettrais l'univers entier dans ta ruelle" (addressed to Jeanne Duval), cited V, p. 447 (J71, 1, cf. J80, 1).

216. V, p. 450 (J72a, 2).

217. "Je t'adore a l'égal de la voûte nocturne," *Les Fleurs du mal*, trans. mine.

218. "Zentralpark," I, p. 668.

219. V, p. 437 (J66, 8; also J61a, 1).

220. "Zentralpark," I, p. 687.

221. Cf. V, p. 427 (J61a, 1).

222. V, p. 436 (J66, 4).

223. Baudelaire, cited V, p. 369 (J34a, 3).

224. V, p. 474 (J84, 4).

225. V, p. 71 (1939 exposé).

226. "Les Sept vieillards," *Les Fleurs du mal*, trans. mine.

227. V, p. 413 (J55, 10).

228. V, p. 417 (J56a, 10).

229. V, p. 71 (1939 exposé).

230. V, p. 401 (J50, 1).

231. Cf. V, p. 370 (J35, 2).

232. V, p. 474 (J84a, 5).

233. Baudelaire, "Perte d'auréole," cited in "Über einige Motive bei Baudelaire," I, pp. 651–52.

234. V, p. 422 (J59, 7).

235. V, p. 475 (J84a, 5).

236. "Zentralpark," I, p. 686.

237. V, p. 429 (J62, 5).

238. V, p. 433 (J64, 4). "The lack of illusory appearances (*Scheinlosigkeit*) and the decline of aura are identical phenomena. Baudelaire places the artistic means of allegory at their service" ("Zentralpark," I, p. 670).

239. V, pp. 342–43 (J21a, 1; see also J58a, 3).

240. V, p. 433 (J64, 4).

241. "Crépescule du soir," *Les Fleurs du mal*, trans. mine.

242. "Zentralpark," I, p. 670. On the renunciation of the magic of distance: "It found its supreme expression in the first verse of 'Le Voyage'" (V, p. 417 [J56a, 12]). That verse is: "For the small boy in love with maps and stamps,/The universe equals his vast appetite!/Ah, how grand the world when viewed by lamplight!/In the eyes of memory, how small it has become!" ("Le Voyage," *Les Fleurs du mal*, trans. mine).

243. "Zentralpark," I, p. 670. Also: "Where in Ovid is the place where it is said that the human countenance was created to send out the reflection of the stars?" (V, p. 336 [J18a, 8]). Baudelaire commented on this passage in Ovid that, on the contrary, the human countenance "'speaks (?![WB]) no more than an expression of foolish ferocity'" (cited, J69a, 3).

244. "L'Amour du mensonge," *Les Fleurs du mal*, trans. mine. "Re: the extinction of illusory appearance: "L'Amour du mensonge" ("Zentralpark," I, p. 670). Also: "The gaze in which the magic of distance is extinguished:
'Plunge your eyes into the fixed eyes of Satyresses or Nymphs'"
("L'Avertisseur," cited V, p. 396 [J47a, 1]).

245. "Tu mettrais l'univers . . . ," cited V, p. 447 (J70a, 9).

246. "Über einige Motive bei Baudelaire," I, p. 649.

247. V, p. 429 (J62a, 1).

248. V, p. 414 (J55a, 2).

249. "Zentralpark," I, p. 658.

250. "Zentralpark," I, p. 658.

251. V, p. 424 (J60, 6; also J59a, 2; J59a, 3).

252. V, p. 306 (J3a, 4; cf. J24a, 5; J59a, 2).

253. V, p. 423 (J59a, 1; cf. J52, 6).

254. "Zentralpark," I, pp. 664–65; cf. V, p. 420 (J58, 4).

255. "With the production of mass articles, there arose the concept of the specialty" (V, p. 93 [A4, 2]).

256. V, p. 470 (J82, 6; J82a, 1).

257. Baudelaire, cited V, p. 369 (J34a, 1).

258. V, p. 71 (1939 exposé).

259. V, p. 56 (1935 exposé). Baudelaire had earlier rejected *l'art pour l'art* in favor of "useful" art. But Benjamin contends: "It would be a great mistake to see the substance of a development in the art-theoretical positions of Baudelaire after 1852 [. . .]. This art [*pour l'art*] is [still] useful in that it is destructive. Its disturbing fury is directed not the least against the fetishistic concept of art" (J49, 1). Consistent in Baudelaire's position throughout his life was "renouncing the application of art as a category of the totality of existence [*Dasein*]" (J 53, 2). Benjamin explains: "Allegory sees both existence and art under the sign of brittleness and ruins. *L'art pour l'art* erects the realm of art outside that of profane existence. Common to both is the renunciation of the idea of the harmonious totality in which art and profane existence interpenetrate, as they do in the theories of both German idealism and French eclecticism" (J56a, 6).

260. V, p. 55 (1935 exposé).

261. V, p. 55 (1935 exposé).

262. "Zentralpark," I, p. 673.

263. "Zentralpark," I, p. 687. Cf.: " 'The idea of progress. This gloomy beacon, invention of present-day philosophizing, licensed without guarantee of nature or of God—this modern lantern throws a stream of darkness on all the objects of knowledge: liberty melts away, discipline vanishes' " (Baudelaire [1855], cited V, p. 397 [J48, 6; see also J38a, 7 and J38a, 8], trans by Jonathan Mayne, Baudelaire, *Art in Paris*, pp. 125–26).

264. Proust (1921), cited V, p. 390 (J44, 5).

265. V, p. 444 (J69a, 1). Cf. Benjamin on "L'Horloge": "The decisive thing about this poem is that time is empty" ("Annotations to poems of Baudelaire," I, p. 1141).

266. " 'The human being does not live for a moment/Without submitting to a warning signal . . . ' " ("L'Avertisseur," cited V, p. 411 [J54a, 1]).

267. V, p. 423 (J59a, 4).

268. Jaloux (1921), cited V, p. 366 (J33, 4).

269. V, p. 71 (1939 exposé).

270. "Zentralpark," I, p. 668.

271. V, p. 418 (J57, 5).

272. "Zentralpark," I, p. 673. Similarly, Benjamin sees a strong similarity between Kierkegaard's "aesthetic passion" (concerning which he cites Adorno's study) and Baudelaire's own. (See especially V, pp. 430–31 [J62a, 3–J62a, 4 and J63, 1–J63, 6]).

273. "Zentralpark," I, p. 670; cf. V, p. 174 (D9, 1).

274. V, p. 414 (J55a, 4).

275. V, p. 429 (J62a, 2). Benjamin compares Blanqui's vision of our "doubles" repeated in every detail on other planets to Baudelaire's "Seven Old Men" (J76, 3).

276. V, p. 425 (J60, 7). "For Baudelaire it is much more an attempt to wrest the 'new' from the always-the-same with heroic effort" (ibid.). (For Nietzsche's vision of eternal recurrence cf. Blanqui, see J74a, 4, cf. "Zentralpark," I, p. 673).

277. See above, chapter 4, section 5.

278. "Über einige Motive bei Baudelaire," I, p. 652.

279. "Le Reniement de Saint Pierre," *Les Fleur du mal*, trans. mine (cited in shortened form, V, p. 456 [J75, 2]).

280. V, p. 414 (J55a, 5). Gottfried Keller attaches this phrase to the image of the shield of Medusa, which he sees as an image of "lost justice, lost happiness"; This image is evoked at the close of Baudelaire's "La Destruction" (V, p. 402 [J50a, 5]). Again, Benjamin avoids psychologistic explanations, interpreting the theme of sexual impotence in Baudelaire as emblematic of social impotence. Similarly: "In the pose of a recipient of charity Baudelaire tested uninterruptedly the example set by bourgeois society. His arbitrarily induced (if not arbitrarily sustained) dependency on his mother had not only a cause emphasized by psychoanalysis, but a social one" (V, p. 427 [J61, 7]).

281. See section 3 above.

282. *Trauerspiel* study, cited V, p. 410 (J54, 5).

283. "Zentralpark," I, p. 684.

284. "Zentralpark," I, p. 682.

285. "Zentralpark," I, p. 683.

286. V, p. 352 (J26, 2).

287. V, p. 352 (J26, 2).

288. V, p. 352 (J26, 2).

289. V, p. 401 (J50, 2).

290. "Zentralpark," I, p. 671.

291. Benjamin cites a verse by Verhaeren (1904): "And of what consequence are the evils and demented hours/And vats of vice in which the city ferments/If someday . . ./A new Christ arises, sculpted in light/Who lifts humanity toward him/And baptizes it by the fire of the stars?" Benjamin comments: "Baudelaire knows no such perspectives. His concept of the fragility of the metropolis is the source of the permanence of the poems which he has inscribed on Paris" ("Das Paris des Second Empire bei Baudelaire," I, p. 586; cf. V, p. 458 [J76, 6]).

292. V, p. 415 (J56, 1).

293. V, p. 417 (J57, 3; also J56, 1).

294. "Zentralpark," I, p. 660 (cf. p. 1139).

Introduction to Part III

1. See ed. note, V, p. 1262. The entries of "J" cannot be dated by the same means as the other *Konvoluts*, since none of the "Baudelaire" material was photocopied (whereas only the post-December, 1937, material of the other *Konvoluts* remained uncopied.) The editor gives no explanation for this singular status of *Konvolut* "J." One can presume, however, that the real burgeoning of this file did not occur until the mid-thirties when Benjamin conceived of a separate Baudelaire "book."

2. Letter, Benjamin to Horkheimer, 16 April 1938, V, p. 1164. Benjamin wrote that he had "foreseen" this relationship to the *Passagen-Werk* as a "tendency" in the Baudelaire study during his discussions with "Teddie" (Adorno) during their visit together in San Remo, December 1937–January 1938.

3. Letter, Adorno to Benjamin, 10 November 1938, I, p. 1096. Adorno tried to excuse Benjamin by suggesting that he, misreading the position of the Institute, had applied Marxist categories in an unmediated way "in order to pay tribute to Marxism" (ibid.).

4. The discovery was announced in spring 1982—just before the appearance of the *Passagen-Werk* as Volume V of Benjamin's *Gesammelte Schriften*—by Agamben, editor of the Italian edition of Benjamin's works. See Giorgio Agamben, "Un importante ritrovamento di manoscritti di Walter Benjamin," *Aut . . . Aut . . .* (189/90 [1982]), pp. 4–6.

5. Benjamin proceeded as follows: He first read through the entire *Passagen-Werk* material, marking in a sign and color code (see note no. 7) any entries that *might* prove relevant to "Baudelaire." He then listed these entries under the code ideas or categories, adding short notations as to their meaning within these particular contexts. That their meanings were not fixed is demonstrated by the fact that several entries appear under more than one code concept.

6. Although this second essay's historical material is also drawn from the *Passagen-Werk*, interestingly, much of what was new in this second version, notably the theoretical references to Freud and Bergson, as well as Dilthey, Krauss, Valery, and Proust, is not found anywhere in the *Passagen-Werk*. (The texts of Freud, "Beyond the Pleasure Principle," and Bergson, "Matter and Memory," had been noted by Benjamin as crucial "points of support" for "the dialectical illumination of Kafka," on which Benjamin was working simultaneously in the

late 1930s as a possible means of support should he immigrate to Israel after all [see II, p. 1255]).

7. On this folder, Agabem first penned the misleading title "Fiches et notes pour le 'Passagen-Werk' (1983–40)." Tiedemann has since added, justifiably, "Et pour 'Charles Baudelaire. Ein Lyriker im Zeitalter des Hochkapitalismus.'" Agabem's original claim that these notes made the published version of the *Passagen-Werk* obsolete even before it appeared, is simply unfounded. What *is* clarified by the find are the mysterious "color signs" that Benjamin drew next to various *Passagen-Werk* entries (described by Tiedemann, V, pp. 1264–77). The archive material contains the key to these color signs as the code for the Baudelaire book, and indicates under what headings the color coded entries were to be assembled.

8. Michael Espagne and Michael Werner, "Vom Passagen-Projekt zum 'Baudelaire': Neue Handschriften zum Spätwerk Walter Benjamin," *Deutsche Vierteljahresschrift für Literaturwissenschaft und Geistesgeschichte* (4 [1984]): 593–657. As far as I have been able to verify from my own perusal of the find, their reporting is excellent and exact; my disagreements are, rather with their interpretation, as will become clear below.

9. Espagne and Werner, p. 648.

10. Their one suggestion as to "a possible cause of the failure: the dialectical image" (ibid., p. 622), will be discussed in section 2 below.

11. "For Benjamin, realization of the *Passagen-Werk* project as intended, as a philosophical summation of the 'Ur-history of the 19th Century,' was [after 1936/37] pushed ever further into the future because of his journalistic writing which was a financial necessity [*journalistische Brotarbeit*], and so the plan of a Baudelaire book really represented an attempt to nail down safely the most essential thoughts and material of the *Arcades* project in the form of a 'miniature model,' in view of the increasing darkness of the historical situation and the related threat to Benjamin's naked survival" (Espagne and Werner, p. 596). Between the lines of their account (and explicitly on p. 598), the authors raise up the familiar specter of the Institute for Social Research as the culprit, implying that the Institute forced Benjamin to write the Baudelaire essay when his true interests lay elsewhere.

12. Espagne and Werner maintain: "The separation of the material of the *Passagen*-project from the Baudelaire texts (and from the Theses [on History]) is today difficult to justify" (ibid., p. 597). True enough. But not only could one say the same of all Benjamin's writings in the 1927–40 period. As our discussion of allegory in chapter 6 has just indicated, the *Passagen-Werk* can also not be "separated" from his earlier study on German *Trauerspiel*. Nor can Benjamin's Baudelaire "book" be severed from the even earlier translations that Benjamin made of this poet's "Tableaux Parisiens" and other parts of the *Fleurs du mal* (III, pp. 7–82). Benjamin was compulsively, obsessively loyal to his philosophical ideas, a fact that gives his work as a whole, however fragmentary the parts, its extraordinary intensity of focus.

13. Letter, Benjamin to Pollock, 28 August 1938, I, p. 1086.

14. In their article, Espagne and Werner ignore this letter with its evidence counter to their thesis. They have generally not paid sufficient attention to the already published letters found in the editorial notes to the six-volume *Gesammelte Schriften*.

15. Letter, Benjamin to Horkheimer, 28 September 1938, V, p. 1167. Cf. his wording in a letter to Adorno the following week: "Decisive, as I formulated it [to Horkheimer], is the fact that a Baudelaire essay that did not deny its responsibility to the problematic of the Passages could be written only as part of a Baudelaire *book*" (letter, Benjamin to Adorno, 4 October 1938, V, p. 1168).

16. This is a fully plausible interpretation of the fact (stated by Espagne and Werner in order to prove their opposing position) that in the revised, 1939 exposé, "all new initiatives in conceptualization [. . .] are derived from the theoretical results of work on Baudelaire" (Espagne and Werner, p. 601).

17. This assumption makes it possible to explain certain changes in format in the 1939 exposé. The "chapters" have been reduced to six, with the elimination of the original chapter II, "Daguerre or the Panorama" (see below, note 18). The remaining five chapters are given letters (A–E), while roman numerals reappear as subsections of the chapters, each of which is divided into three parts (a procedure that necessitated the rearrangement of whole paragraphs of the text). This change might be dismissed as insignificant, but for the fact that in the case of chapter "D," "Baudelaire or the Streets of Paris," the material, "radically redesigned" from the 1935 exposé (V, p. 1171), appears in such a way that the three new subsections correspond in tendency if not totally in substance, to the three "parts" of the Baudelaire "book" designated with the same roman numerals. That is, the notes desigted as Parts I, II, and III of the latter that were discovered in the Bataille Archive are, as "moments" of a dialectical presentation, in direct parallel to the the similarly designated parts of the 1939 abstract of the fourth "chapter" of the *Passagen-Werk*: I) the allegorical mode of expression in Baudelaire's poetry; II) the urban phantasmagoria and the socioeconomic context of mass literary productions as these reflect in his works; III) allegory as an expression of social reality, under the Marxian sign of the commodity form.

18. In a sense, this is what already had happened to one of the "chapters," "Daguerre or the Panorama," which was "dropped" in the 1939 exposé "because its essential parts are for the most part covered by considerations that are present in French translation in the Artwork essay" (letter, Benjamin to Horkheimer, 13 March 1939, V, p. 1171).

19. Letter, Benjamin to Horkheimer, 28 September 1939, upon completing the first Baudelaire essay (V, p. 1168). A separate article on Haussmann had been contemplated since 1934 for the French Communist journal *Monde* (V, p. 1098).

20. Benjamin, letter to Horkheimer, 28 September 1939, Walter Benjamin, *Briefe*, eds. Gershom Scholem and Theodor W. Adorno, 2 vols. (Frankfurt am Main: Suhrkamp Verlag, 1978), vol. 2, p. 774.

21. Letter, Benjamin to Adorno, 4 October 1938, *Briefe*, vol. 2, p. 778.

22. All quotations from letter, Benjamin to Horkheimer, 28 September 1938, *Briefe*, vol. 2, pp. 774–75.

23. "Zentralpark" (1938–39), I, p. 677.

24. See above, chapter 6, section 4.

25. Letter, Benjamin to Horkheimer, 28 September 1938, *Briefe*, vol. 2, p. 774.

26. Letter, Benjamin to Adorno, 4 October 1938, V, p. 1168.

27. My decision to discuss these Blanqui texts in chapter 4 in the context of the theme of the Nineteenth Century as Hell which dominates in the early notes, will not please those who see the Blanqui material as an indication that Benjamin had very much changed his own position in the late 1930s. Blanqui's cosmology was not a new orientation, but a confirmation of Benjamin's earlier argument.

28. Letter, Benjamin to Horkheimer, 13 March 1959, V, p. 1171. The historical figure of Louis Philippe—the "bourgeois king"—was never prominent in the *Passagen* Werk. His

name provides no *Konvolut* title; he is not referred to in the entries in any conceptually coherent way. He seems merely to represent the historical era of pre–1848 which was the time of the "blooming of the arcades" (V, p. 1216 [1935 exposé note no. 10]).

29. The "now-time" of the dialectical image was "on the one hand the concluding point" of the *Passagen-Werk* as "a continuous phenomenology of the commodity form, and on the other, a petrified process, the exploding of continuity": "The discontinuity implied by the dialectical image imperils this structure [of the text], even as it is supposed to function as its final building block. The suggested theory of improved nature provides, rather, a halfway utopian alternative to commodity fetishism" (Espagne and Werner, pp. 622–23). The authors claim that in the Baudelaire "book" these two poles are held in "a tentative and temporary state of equilibrium" that "possesses the character of a certain self-negation" (ibid., p. 624).

30. See above, chapter I, section 4.

31. It will be considered at length below in chapter 7.

32. He called it "dialectics at a standstill" (V, p. 577 [N2a, 3]). See below, chapter 7, section 2.

33. V, p. 1011 (G°, 19). In this world, the old (the time of Hell), repeats itself in the new, but this repetition is one of "strict discontinuity": "the always-again-new is not the old that remains, nor the past that returns, but the one and the same crossed by countless intermittences" (ibid.).

34. He wrote to Scholem that the "inner construction" of the *Passagen* "book" was analogous to the *Trauerspiel* study, in that "here as well the unfolding of a traditional concept will stand at the midpoint. If there it was the concept of *Trauerspiel*, here it is the fetish character of the commodity" (letter, 20 May 1935, V, p. 1112).

35. The idea of the "trace," mentioned in the early notes (V, p. 1048 [c°, 1]), is developed in *Konvolut* I ("das Interieur, Spur").

36. The figure of the ragpicker (*chiffonnier*) which appears in the *Passagen-Werk* is treated as a key to Benjamin's method in Irving Wohlfarth, "The Historian as Chiffonnier," *New German Critique*, 39 (fall 1986), pp. 142–68.

37. Gershom Scholem, *Walter Benjamin: The Story of a Friendship* (London: Faber & Faber, 1981), p. 197.

38. "Der Begriff der Kunstkritik in der deutschen Romantik," I, p. 41 (ital. Benjamin's).

39. See, however, the *paralipomena* for the Karl Kraus essay, where keywords are arranged in a rudimentary coordinate schema (II, p. 1090). Benjamin refers to his own work pattern as approaching "the center in concentric circles" in a letter to Adorno, 10 June 1935 (V, p. 1121).

40. I, p. 1177.

41. These included not only concentric circles (see the "further schemata" for the Krauss essay, II, p. 1092) but, as with a series of the Baudelaire "book" notes, isolated, abbreviated idea clusters that are circled without relation to others in the page (see Envelope 5, Benjamin papers, Bataille Archive, Bibliothèque Nationale, Paris).

42. They cite parts of the fourth paragraph of this note. See Espagne and Werner, p. 605.

43. Note, Envelope 5, Benjamin Papers, Bataille Archive, Bibliothèque Nationale, Paris.

7 Is This Philosophy?

1. V, p. 575 (N2, 4).

2. Letter, Adorno to Benjamin, 20 May 1935, Envelope 5, Benjamin Papers, Georges Bataille Archive, Bibliothèque Nationale, Paris.

3. The influence of Brecht, "without meaning thereby to be prejudiced" against him, "must stop here, precisely here" (letter, Adorno to Benjamin, 20 May 1935).

4. The possibility "that the work, just as it is really conceived, would be accepted by the Institute I consider as unlikely as it would please me if I were mistaken" (letter, Adorno to Benjamin, 20 May 1935).

5. The Marxist concepts of both Brecht and the Institute were in Adorno's opinion "too abstract," and functioned "like *dei ex machina*" in their analyses (letter, Adorno to Benjamin, 20 May 1935). Adorno, who himself did not become a full member of the Institute until 1938, cautioned that "for us," thinking must proceed "as a consequence of our own categories"; he urged Benjamin "to write the Passages true to your own "Ur-history," for in that way: "It is my deepest conviction that the work would hold up best precisely as a Marxist one [. . .]" (ibid.).

6. Letter, Karplus to Benjamin, 28 May 1935, V, p. 1115. Karplus, who had been Benjamin's close friend since the twenties in Berlin, had participated with Adorno, Horkheimer, and Lacis in the Königstein conversations of 1929, during which Benjamin had read from his first notes for the *Passagen-Werk*. In 1935 she was spending considerable time with Adorno, whom she married in 1937.

7. See Benjamin's reply to Adorno 31 May 1935, V, pp. 1116–19.

8. Letter, Benjamin to Scholem, 20 May 1935, V, p. 1112.

9. Letter, Benjamin to Adorno, 31 May 1935, V, p. 1118.

10. This *Konvolut* includes notes that were formulated in the project's first stage (see especially the 0° series of the early notes), giving evidence of a continuity within Benjamin's method from the project's inception to his last text, the Theses on History ("Über den Begriff der Geschichte," 1940).

11. V, p. 575 (N2, 6).

12. V, p. 574 (N1a, 8).

13. V, p. 578 (N3, 2).

14. V, p. 579 (N3a, 1; again in the Theses on History).

15. V, p. 578 (N3, 4; again in the Theses on History).

16. V. p. 594 (N10, 4).

17. See V, p. 591 (N9, 4).

18. "Engels says [. . . :] 'It should not be forgotten that law does not have its own history any more than does religion.' What applies to both of these applies first really in a decisive way to

culture" (V, p. 583 [N5, 4]). Again: " 'There is no history of politics, law, knowledge, etc., of art, religion, etc.' " (Marx, cited V, p. 584 [N5a, 3]). See also N6a, 1 (that cites Engels to the same effect, who in turn is cited in the Fuchs essay, II, p. 467) and N7a, 2 (that can be read as a criticism of Marx and Engels): "[. . .] a homogeneous history of, say, economics, exists as little as does one of literature or jurisprudence [. . .] a continuity of historical presentation is unattainable."

19. Following Karl Korsch, Benjamin rejected the reduction of Marxism to a " 'universal theory' "; it provided instead "totally undogmatic guidelines for research and practice' " (Korsch, cited V, p. 607 [N17a and N17]).

20. Letter, Benjamin to Karplus, 16 August 1935, V, p. 1139.

21. This was its "really problematic component: [. . .] to prove the materialist presentation of history imagistic in a higher sense than the presentation that has been handed down to us" (V, p. 578 [N3, 3]).

22. The "theory" of the work was "most tightly linked to that of montage" (V, p. 572 [N1, 10]).

23. Benjamin said that he was in fact bringing Goethe's concept of ur-phenomena "out of the pagan connection with nature and into the Judaic connection with history" (V, p. 577 [N2a 4]). Like Goethe's *Urpflanze*, while these originary phenomena could exist alongside those that came later, they had all the characteristics that develop in the later forms. (See above, chapter 3, section 2).

24. "It can be considered one of the methodological objects of the work to demonstrate a historical materialism that has annihilated from within itself the idea of progress" (V, p. 574 [N2, 2]).

25. V, p. 587 (N7, 7).

26. V, p. 587 (N7, 6).

27. "The destructive or critical moment in the materialist writing of history comes into play in that blasting apart of historical continuity with which, first and foremost, the historical object constitutes itself" (V, p. 594 [N10a, 1]).

28. V, p. 594 (N10, 3).

29. V, p. 578 (N3, 2).

30. "The present determines where within the past object its fore- [*Vor-*] history and its after- [*Nach-*] history separate from one another in order to enframe its nucleus" (V, p. 596 [N11, 5]).

31. V, p. 587 (N7a, 1).

32. V, p. 594 (N10, 3).

33. "Thus we always perceive past events 'too late' and 'politics' needs the 'presence of mind' to 'foresee' the present" (Benjamin, citing Turgot, V, p. 598 [N12a, 1]).

34. V, p. 574 (N2, 2).

35. V, pp. 591–92 (N9, 7; cf. Q°, 21 and Q°, 23).

36. V, p. 577 (N2a, 3).

37. V, p. 570 (N1, 1; also N9, 7).

38. V, p. 587 (N3, 1; cf. P°, 4).

39. V, p. 595 (N10a, 3).

40. V, pp. 595–96 (N11, 4).

41. V, pp. 602–03 (N15, 1).

42. V, p. 571 (N1, 4).

43. V, pp. 570–71 (N1, 4).

44. Adorno, "Zu Benjamins Gedächtnis," *Über Walter Benjamin*, ed. Rolf Tiedemann (Frankfurt am Main: Suhrkamp Verlag, 1970), p. 15.

45. Letter, Benjamin to Adorno, 31 May 1935, V, p. 1117.

46. Cf. the 1935 exposé: "The commodity presents such an image pure and simple: as fetish. Such an image is presented by the arcades, which are both house and street. The prostitute, too, presents such an image, salesgirl and commodity in one" (V, p. 55).

47. V, p. 574 (N1a, 8).

48. This was his argument as early as his dissertation, "Der Begriff der Kunst in der deutschen Romantik," I, pp. 7–122.

49. See his criticism of Benn, Celine, and Jung, V, p. 590 (N8a, 1; cf. K7a, 2).

50. Benjamin "did not respect the boundary between literary writers and philosophers" (Adorno, *Über Walter Benjamin*, p. 16).

51. "In *l'art pour l'art* the poet for the first time confronts language the way the consumer does the commodity on the open market" ("Taste," written for the first Baudelaire essay, I, p. 1167).

52. "Taste," I, p. 1169. We may assume that Benjamin's criticism of the theme of "absence" in certain schools of contemporary thought would be the same.

53. Baudelaire's poem is a vision of "water, steel slate/staircases and arcades" in a frozen landscape in which all of nature's activity has stopped:

And heavy cataracts,
Like crystal curtains,
Hung suspended, dazzling,
On walls of metal.

("Rêve parisien," *Les Fleurs du mal*, trans. mine).

54. Hans Robert Jauss, *Toward an Aesthetic of Reception*, trans. Timothy Bahti, intro. Paul de Man, *Theory and History of Literature* vol 2, eds. Wlad Godzich and Jochen Schulte-Sasse (Minneapolis: University of Minnesota Press, 1982), p. 172.

55. Jauss, p. 173.

56. Jauss, p. 179.

57. Jauss, p. 179.

58. Benjamin's political criticism of every cultural "continuum" is considered at length in chapter 9 below.

59. Paul de Man, *Blindness and Insight: Essays in the Rhetoric of Contemporary Criticism*, second ed., rev., intro. Wlad Godzich, *Theory and History of Literature* vol. 7, eds. Wlad Godzich and Jochen Schulte-Sasse (Minneapolis: University of Minnesota Press, 1983), pp. 182–83.

60. De Man, p. 183. (It does not occur to de Man to point out that this particular allegory of father-to-son transmission expresses the fact that within the university institutions of this society, culture has been inherited traditionally along partriarchal lines of descent.)

61. De Man, p. 174. In contrast, for de Man, there is no literary history outside of literary interpretation. While he insists upon the "materiality" of the object, it is a materiality that is represented, never present. For him "the bases for historical knowledge are not empirical facts but written texts, even if these texts masquerade in the guise of wars or revolutions" (ibid., p. 165). Because there is no cognitive point of reference outside of texts, all knowledge is intratextual. Moreover, the nonidentity between sign and meaning has always been there; allegory, a demystifying literary form, merely brings this nonidentity to conscious expression (ibid., p. 27). Thus, while criticizing Jauss' historical "continuum" as a literary invention, de Man does not criticize literary inventions.

62. Peter Bürger, *Theory of the Avant-Garde*, trans. Michael Shaw, foreword by Jochen Schulte-Sasse, *Theory and History of Literature* vol. 4, eds. Wlad Godzich and Jochen Schulte-Sasse (Minneapolis: University of Minnesota Press, 1984), p. 68.

63. "'In the field of allegorical intention, the image is a fragment, a rune ... The false appearance [*Schein*] of totality is extinguished'" (Benjamin, cited in Bürger, p. 69).

64. Bürger, p. 69.

65. Bürger, p. 72.

66. Bürger, p. 78.

67. Bürger, pp. 90–91.

68. Bürger, p. 90.

69. Bürger, p. 90.

70. "The historical avant-garde movements were unable to destroy art as an institution; but they did destroy the possibility that a given school can present itself with the claim to universal validity" (Bürger, p. 87).

71. Bürger, p. 88.

72. Bürger, p. 92.

73. We are referring to the *Passagen-Werk* here. In contrast, Benjamin's earlier work, *One Way Street*, was clearly an avant-garde, aesthetic work.

74. Bürger, p. 84.

75. Bürger, p. 66.

76. "As I feel generally, then, about our theoretical disagreement, it is not really something going on between us, but, rather, it is my task to hold your arm steady until the sun of Brecht has once more sunk into exotic waters" (letter, Adorno to Benjamin, 18 March 1936, I, p. 1006).

77. I, p. 1096. Adorno's position was that such an "extinction of the subject" was simply the mimetic replication in philosophy of the subject's real powerlessness within modern mass society.

78. V, p. 1250 (exposé note no. 23).

79. See chapter 6 above.

80. I am aware that much is riding on my interpretation of the word "*treulos*" in the *Trauerspiel* study (see the passage: the "intention" of the allegoricists, in their interpretation of the image of Golgatha, "ultimately does not persist faithfully [*treu*] in contemplation of the bones, but instead treacherously [*treulos*] leaps over into Resurrection" [I, p. 406]), and that earlier interpreters have taken Benjamin to be establishing an ironic distance between this word and his own judgment. But I find it inconceivable that Benjamin should actually affirm the Christian idea of bodily crucifixion and spiritual resurrection, as it is so foreign in conception precisely to the "theological" elements of his thinking.

In his letter to Benjamin, 2 August 1935, urging him to "restore theology" to his conception (V, p. 1130), Adorno referred to "the fetish as the faithless [*treulos*] final image for the nineteenth century, comparable only to the death's head." He seems to have understood that commodified nature itself was "faithless." Benjamin commented in the margin: "How does this meaning stand in regard to exchange value?" (see original of this letter in the Bataille Archive, Bibliothèque Nationale, Paris). His answer to this question is his interpretation of Baudelairean allegory (see chapter 6). Criticizing Baudelaire for his inability to transcend the melancholy contemplation of the allegoricist, Benjamin's own notion of transcendence was political (to "smash" the mechanism that endlessly rearranged the fragments of the material world in its given state), not spiritual ("faithlessly" to abandon the material world altogether). Compare in this connection Benjamin's praise of Proust: "With a passion known by no poet before him, he made his concern the faithfulness to things [*die Treue zu den Dingen*] that have crossed our lives. Faithfulness to an afternoon, a tree, a spot of sun on the carpet, faithfulness to robes, furniture, perfumes or landscapes" (V, p. 679 [S2, 3]).

81. Gershom Scholem, *Walter Benjamin: The Story of a Friendship* eds. Karen Ready and Gary Smith (London: Faber & Faber Ltd., 1982), p. 125.

82. Scholem, *Walter Benjamin*, p. 125.

83. Scholem, *Walter Benjamin*, p. 125.

84. Scholem, *Walter Benjamin*, p. 125.

85. *Trauerspiel* study, I, p. 217.

86. I, p. 217.

87. I, p. 217.

88. Letter, Benjamin to Adorno, 31 May 1935, V, p. 1117 (cited above, section 3).

89. Scholem, *Walter Benjamin*, p. 38.

90. "I think one can say without disrespect that hardly ever had there been a Jewish theology of such vacuity and insignificance as existed in the decades before World War I [. . . .'O]rthodox theology has suffered from what might be called Kabbalah-phobia'" (Gershom Scholem, *The Messianic Idea in Judaism, and Other Essays in Jewish Spirituality* [New York: Schocken Books, 1971], p. 321).

91. Scholem, *The Messianic Idea*, p. 1.

92. The Theses on History demonstrate this clearly, as does this note in preparation for their writing: "In the concept of the classless society, Marx secularized the concept of the Messianic Age. And that was as it should be" (I, p. 1231). This quotation is discussed in section 9 below.

93. For an excellent discussion of Benjamin's connection to anticapitalist Messianism as the "new Jewish sensibility" of the generation of 1914, see Anson Rabinbach, "Between Enlightenment and Apocalypse: Benjamin, Bloch and Modern German Jewish Messianism," *New German Critique*, winter 34 (1985): 78–124. See also the laudable work of Michael Löwy.
   Note that within this tradition Messianism had Christian as well as Jewish adherents. Leo Löwenthal writes that in the early 1920s Benjamin shared his own interest in Franz von Baader, a conservative Catholic philosopher, "whose religious philosophy of redemptive mysticism and solidarity with society's lowest classes is evident in Benjamin's Theses on the Philosophy of History (see Leo Löwenthal, "The Integrity of the Intellectual: In Memory of Walter Benjamin," trans. David J. Ward, in *The Philosophical Forum*, special issue on Walter Benjamin, ed. Gary Smith, vol. XV, nos 1–2 (fall-winter 1983–84): 148.

94. "They draw upon everything: not just texts which manifestly deal with the Last Days, but a great deal else, and the more the better. The more colorful and the more complete the picture, the greater the possibility of creating a dramatic montage of the individual stages of the redemption and the plenitude of its content" (Scholem, *The Messianic Idea*, p. 32).

95. Gershom G. Scholem, *Major Trends in Jewish Mysticism* [first published in 1941] (New York: Schocken Books, 1946), p. 10.

96. Scholem, *Major Trends*, p. 8.

97. Scholem, *Major Trends*, p. 13.

98. "'[. . .] there is no sphere of existence including organic and inorganic nature, that is not full of holy sparks which are mixed up with the Kelipoth [lower realms] and need to be separated from them and lifted up'" (Isaac Luria, cited in Scholem, *Major Trends*, p. 280).

99. V, p. 588 (N7a, 7).

100. On the Christian Kabbalah, see Gershom Scholem, *Kabbalah* (New York: Quadrangle, 1974), pp. 196–200.

101. *Trauerspiel* study, I, p. 358.

102. Marxists have attempted to excuse the undeniable theological terminology in certain of Benjamin's writings by dismissing it as metaphor; they blame the editors of Benjamin's work for underemphasizing the significance of the Marxian/Brechtian motifs in comparison (see, e.g., Hildegaard Brenner, "Die Lesbarkeit der Bilder. Skizzen zum Passagenentwurf," *Alternative* 59/60 [1968], pp. 48ff).
   On the other side of the fence, Scholem considered that Benjamin's efforts to fuse theological metaphysics and Marxism made him "not the last, but perhaps the most incomprehensible victim of the confusion between religion and politics [. . .]" (letter, Scholem to

Benjamin, 30 March 1931, Walter Benjamin, *Briefe*, 2 vols., eds. Gershom Scholem and Theodor W. Adorno [Frankfurt am Main: Suhrkamp Verlag, 1978]), vol. 2, p. 529).

103. Gershom Scholem, *From Berlin to Jerusalem: Memories of My Youth*, trans. Harry Zohn (New York: Schocken Books, 1980), pp. 128–29.

104. I am relying *solely* on Scholem here. While aware that his interpretation of the Kabbalah has not gone unchallenged, it was the one that influenced Benjamin most significantly. All spellings of Kabbalist terms are Scholem's.

105. Scholem, *Major Trends*, p. 14.

106. Scholem, *The Messianic Idea*, p. 67.

107. Scholem, *The Messianic Idea*, p. 68.

108. "'The Torah as it now exists (or as it is now observed) will not exist in the Messianic Age'" (Cardozo [1668], cited in Scholem, *The Messianic Idea*, p. 65). Cf.: "'[. . .] everyone who wants to serve God as he does now (i.e., by the traditional way of life) will in those days (of the Messiah) be called a desecrator of the Sabbath and a destroyer of the plantings (i.e., a downright heretic)'" (Iggeret Magen Abraham [1668], cited in ibid., p. 72). Parenthetical comments, Scholem's.

109. See Gershom Scholem, "Redemption through Sin," *The Messianic Idea*, pp. 78–141.

110. Jewish scholars had traced a direct, gradual progression from the rationalist orientation of medieval Rabbinic thought through the Enlightenment to the positivistic rationalism of the present day; at the same time they took the revolutionary sting out of the Messianic idea, bringing it into line with the bourgeois progressive doctrine of history (see Scholem, *The Messianic Idea*, pp. 24–33).

111. Scholem, *Major Trends*, pp. 319–20.

112. "[. . .] the renewal of the world is simply more than its restoration" (Scholem, *The Messianic Idea*, p. 14).

113. Scholem, *The Messianic Idea*, p. 87.

114. "'In that age there will be neither famine nor war, nor envy nor strife, for there will be an abundance of worldly goods'" (Maimonides [twelfth century], cited in Scholem, *Major Trends*, p. 29).

115. Scholem, *The Messianic Idea*, p. 71.

116. Scholem, *The Messianic Idea*, p. 10. Indeed, not progress but catastrophe anticipates redemption, which is "an intrusion in which history itself perishes" (ibid.).

117. "To know the stages of the creative process is also to know the stages of one's own return to the root of all existence" (Scholem, *Major Trends*, p. 20). This knowledge, while esoteric, is not elitist in the sense of being comprehensible only to scholars or philosophers. To cite Scholem: "It must be kept in mind that in the sense in which it is understood by the Kabbalist himself [*sic*.], mystical knowledge is not his private affair which has been revealed to him, and to him only, in his personal experience. On the contrary, the purer and more nearly perfect it is, the nearer it is to the original stock of knowledge common to mankind [*sic*.]" (ibid., p. 21).

448

118. Gershom Scholem, *Kabbalah*, pp. 152–53.

119. Throughout its history, Kabbalism manifests "an almost exaggerated consciousness of God's *otherness*" (Scholem, *Major Trends*, p. 55).

120. Scholem, *Kabbalah*, p. 147.

121. Scholem, *Kabbalah*, p. 88.

122. "The identification of evil with physical matter, though it occurs occasionally in the Zohar and in other kabbalistic books, never became an accepted doctrine of either. [. . . T]he major interest was rather the question of how the Divine was reflected in matter" (Scholem, *Kabbalah*, p. 125).

123. Scholem, *The Messianic Idea*, p. 46.

124. Scholem, *The Messianic Idea*, p. 13.

125. *Kaf ha-Ketoret* (sixteenth century), cited in Scholem, *The Messianic Idea*, p. 42.

126. Scholem, *Major Trends*, p. 26.

127. "The thing which becomes a symbol retains its original form and its original content. It does not become, so to speak, an empty shell into which another content is poured; in itself, through its own existence, it makes another reality transparent which cannot appear in any other form" (Scholem, *Major Trends*, p. 27).

128. Cf. I, p. 340.

129. Scholem, *Major Trends*, pp. 27–28.

130. Scholem, *Major Trends*, p. 28.

131. Scholem, *Major Trends*, p. 28.

132. Letter, Benjamin to Ludwig Strauss, 10 October 1912, cited in Rabinbach, "Between Enlightenment and Apocalypse," p. 96.

133. Benjamin was, of course, a "Marxist heretic" as well (see Rabinbach, "Between Enlightenment and Apocalypse," p. 122).

134. Scholem, *Kabbalah*, p. 266.

135. Letter, Scholem to Benjamin, 30 March 1931, *Briefe*, vol. 2, p. 525.

136. Letter, Benjamin to Scholem, 14 February 1929, *Briefe*, vol. 2, p. 489. Scholem's recollections provide us with some conception as to what specifically Benjamin knew about the Kabbalah. Their talks in the early years of Scholem's scholarship (before he immigrated to Palestine) have already been mentioned. Subsequently, during Scholem's visit to Paris in 1927, Benjamin (who was just beginning the Arcades project) "was the first person I told about a very surprising discovery I had made: Sabbatian theology—that is, a Messianic antinomianism that had developed within Judaism in strictly Jewish concepts" (Scholem, *Walter Benjamin*, p. 136.

In 1932 Benjamin requested and received from Scholem a copy of the latter's lengthy article on the Kabbalah which was published that year in the *Encyclopedia Judaica*, vol. 9, pp. 630–732 (ibid., p. 181). He particularly liked the part on the dialectic of the Kabbalist Isaac Luria (who in turn influenced Sabbatai Zevi) and, sending Scholem in exchange a copy of his own "History of Bolshevism," he wrote the dedication: "From Luria to Lenin!" (ibid., p 192).

137. "If my interest is already totally incompetent and helpless, then it is still an interest in *your* works, not any general one" (letter, Benjamin to Scholem, 29 May 1926, *Briefe*, vol. 1, p. 428).

138. Letter, Benjamin to Scholem, 15 January 1933, *Briefe*, vol. 2, p. 561.

139. See the discussion in Winfried Menninghaus, *Walter Benjamins Theorie der Sprachmagie* (Frankfurt am Main: Suhrkamp Verlag, 1980), pp. 91–92 and *passim*.

140. For the succession of the ten Sefiroth, see Scholem, *Major Trends*, p. 213.

141. See below, chapter 8, section 1.

142. The novel is discussed in "der Sürrealismus" (1929), II, pp. 295–310.

143. *Trauerspiel* study, I, p. 350.

144. Louis Aragon, *Le paysan de Paris* (Paris: Gallimard, 1953), p. 141.

145. "A mistake lying near at hand: to consider Surrealism an aesthetic movement" (notes to the Surrealism essay, II, p. 1035).

146. II, p. 297.

147. II, p. 297. Note that neither drugs nor religion were rejected totally. "The opium of the people, Lenin called religion" (ibid., p. 277); but if both deceived the mind, they also intensely sharpened visionary optics.

148. Letter, Benjamin to Max Rychner, 7 March 1931 [copy sent to Scholem], *Briefe*, vol. 2, p. 523.

149. V, p. 1023 (M°, 14).

150. In light of the full *Passagen-Werk* document, the frequently voiced interpretation that Benjamin returned to theological language only after Stalin's purges of 1936, or the Nazi-Soviet Non-Aggression Pact (1939) is impossible to sustain. If his political pessimism was new at this later time, his theological language was not.

151. Letter, Benjamin to Werner Kraft, 25 May 1935, V, p. 1115.

152. V, p. 579 (N3a, 2; cf. 0°, 79).

153. Cf. V, p. 577 (N3, 1).

154. Note here, in contrast to those who would modernize religion by seeing in AIDS, Chernobyl, or nuclear war a realization of the prophetized Apocalypse, the all-important difference: The text represents the historically transient truth of reality, rather than reality representing the eternal truth of the texts. In short, truth is in the object, not the text, which, incapable of predicting the future, can only apply descriptively after the fact.

155. Quotations from the 1844 manuscripts of Marx (which were first published in 1928) appear frequently in *Passagen-Werk* entries. Benjamin used the Landshut and Mayer edition (1932) of Marx's early writings (see especially *Konvolut* X entitled "Marx," V, pp. 800–02 and passim).

156. Entries X3a, 4—X4a, 1 (V, pp. 806–08) concern themselves with Marx's theory of abstract labor.

157. V, p. 466 (J80, 2/J80a, 1).

158. See above, chapter 4.

159. V, p. 1057 (g° 1).

160. V, p. 580 (N4, 2).

161. V, p. 574 (N2, 1; again, 0°, 9).

162. V, p. 465 (J79a, 1)

163. V, p. 465 (J80, 2)

164. "Theory of the collector; elevation of the commodity to the status of allegory" (V, p. 274 [H2, 6]). The allegoricist and collector are "antithetical poles"; at the same time, "there is in every collector an allegoricist" and vice versa (V, p. 279 [H4a, 1]).

165. V, p. 271 (H1a, 2).

166. See above, note no. 129.

167. See above, note no. 125.

168. Theses on History, I, p. 701.

169. Cf. Benjamin's citing Korsch (on Marx): "'Only for the present bourgeois society, in which [. . .] the workers as citizens are free, with equal rights, does the scientific demonstration of their actual continuous lack of freedom in the economic sphere have the character of a theoretical discovery'" (Karl Korsch, cited V, pp. 605–06 [N16a, 1]).

170. Theses on History, I, p. 704.

171. Theses on History, I, p. 701. Cf.: "Being conscious that they are exploding the continuum of history is a charateristic of the revolutionary classes in the moment of their action" (ibid.).
In a note to the Theses, Benjamin observes that the common understanding of what Marx means by the revolution is not the same as his own, Messianic one: On Marx: "through a series of class struggles humanity achieves a classless society in the course of the historical development. = But the classless society is not to be conceived as the endpoint of a historical development. = Out of this mistaken conception has come, among other things, the idea held by his successors of the "revolutionary situation" which, it is well known, will never come {.} = To the concept of the classless society its authentic Messianic face must be given again, precisely in the interest of the revolutionary politics of the proletariat itself" (notes to the Theses on History, I, p. 1232).

172. Hermann Lotze (1864), cited V, p. 600 (N13a, 2). Cf. an earlier entry, which cites Marx's early writings: "'The critic can . . . begin with any form of theoretical or practical consciousness and develop from the *particular* forms of existing reality the true reality as its norm and final purpose'" (Marx, letter to Arnold Ruge, September 1843). Benjamin comments: "The starting point of which Marx speaks here need not at all connect with the last stage of development. It can be undertaken for epochs long past, the norm and final goal of which, then, must of course not be represented with regard to the developmental stage that

follows it, but instead in its own right as a preformation of the final purpose of history" (V, pp. 582–83 [N5, 3]).

173. V, p. 600 (N13a, 1).

174. V, p. 608 (N18a, 3).

175. V, p. 578 (N3, 1).

176. V, p. 589 (N8, 1).

177. Pierre-Maxime Schuhl (1938), cited V, p. 609 (N18a, 2).

178. "Strength of hatred according to Marx. The desire to fight of the working class. To cross revolutionary destruction with the idea of redemption" (notes to the Theses on History, I, p. 1241).

179. Bertolt Brecht, *Arbeitsjournal*, 2 vols., ed. Werner Hecht (Frankfurt am Main: Suhrkamp Verlag, 1973), vol. 1, p. 16 (journal entry of 25 July 1983). Note, however, Brecht's positive evaluation of the Theses on History, despite the explicitly theological language they contain: "the small work is clear and avoids confusion (despite all metaphors and judaisms)" (ibid., p. 294).

180. Adorno's essay, "Charakteristik Walter Benjamins" (1950), written two years after he had read the *Passagen* manuscript, remains one of the most accurate descriptions of Benjamin's philosophy, one that does justice to both "mystical" and "enlightenment" poles. While Adorno mentions Benjamin's indebtedness to the Kabbalah, he does not attempt, as we have here, to spell out the connection, perhaps because Benjamin himself never explained this indebtedness explicitly. Thus: "It is difficult to say to what extent he was influenced by the neo-platonic and antinomian messianic tradition" (Theodor W. Adorno, "A Portrait of Walter Benjamin," *Prisms*, trans. Samuel and Shierry Weber [London: Neville Spearman, 1967], p. 243).

181. See Susan Buck-Morss, *The Origins of Negative Dialectics: Theodor W. Adorno, Walter Benjamin, and the Frankfurt Institute* (New York: Macmillan Free Press, 1977) pp. 88–90, also pp. 140 ff. for their intellectual friendship. Note that despite Adorno's concern over the Institute's possible influence on the *Passagen-Werk*, he was not alone among its members in his appreciation. Löwenthal recalls: "In this Messianic-Marxist dilemma I am wholly on Benjamin's side—indeed I am his pupil," and he mentions that for Marcuse, too, the Messianic utopian motif played a significant role, whereas Horkheimer "in his later years [. . .] ventured—a bit too far for my taste—into concrete religious symbolism" (Leo Löwenthal, "The Integrity of the Intellectual: In Memory of Walter Benjamin," *The Philosophical Forum*: 150 and 156.

182. Letter, Adorno to Benjamin, 17 December 1934, V, p. 1110.

183. See below, chapter 8.

184. Adorno, "A Portrait of Walter Benjamin," *Prisms*, p. 235.

185. Adorno, "A Portrait of Walter Benjamin," *Prisms*, p. 236.

186. The fact that I am omitting from this discussion one of the most intelligent and capable writers on Benjamin, who, moreover, believes precisely that Benjamin's Messianism and his Marxist politics were one and the same, requires an explanation. I am referring to the essays of Irving Wohlfarth, a brilliant reader of Benjamin's texts. Like de Man, Wohlfarth's method

is textual criticism, not philosophical analysis. Despite recent attempts to disregard the boundary between these fields, I believe there is a difference, one that precisely in interpreting so "literary" a writer as Benjamin must be considered. Philosophy (even a philosophy of images) is conceptual, and concepts point beyond the text to a referential world of objects (even if to their surface attributes) the meaning of which (even if it always only given in a text) maintains a moment of autonomy. As Adorno said, no object is wholly known, and yet the striving for this knowledge is precisely what philosophy cannot relinquish. For this reason, a totally immanent, esoteric interpretation of Benjamin's texts, while adequate as a *literary* reading, is not so as a philosophical reading. The latter stubbornly rivets its attention on *what* is represented, not merely how. That being said, let me add that I have the greatest respect for Wohlfarth's work, and I recognize that in contrast to his nuanced analyses my own may bear the Brechtian stigma of "coarse thinking" (*plumpes Denken*).

187. The essay, "Historischer Materialismus oder politischer Messianismus?" first appeared as "Materialien zu Benjamin's Theses 'Über den Begriff der Geschichte,'" in the anthology of the same name, ed. Peter Bulthaup (Frankfurt am Main: Suhrkamp Verlag, 1975), pp. 77–121. A second version, the introductory section of which is significantly altered, appears under the new title in Rolf Tiedemann, *Dialektik im Stillstand: Versuche zum Spätwerk Walter Benjamins* (Frankfurt am Main: Suhrkamp Verlag, 1983), pp. 99–142. This version has been translated (by Barton Byg) as "Historical Materialism or Political Messianism? An Interpretation of the Theses 'On the Concept of History'" in *The Philosophical Forum*, special issue on Walter Benjamin: 71–104.

188. In the first version of this essay, Tiedemann directs his argument explicitly against Gerhard Kaiser, who claims Benjamin *identifies* theology and politics, and "'thus doesn't secularize theology but theologies Marxism'" (Kaiser, cited in Tiedemann, "Historischer Materialismus..." in Bulthaup, ed., p. 80).

189. Tiedemann, "Historical Materialism...," *The Philosophical Forum*: 90.

190. Tiedemann, "Historical Materialism...," *The Philosophical Forum*: 81.

191. Benjamin [I, p. 1231], cited in Tiedemann, "Historical Materialism...," *The Philosophical Forum*: 83.

192. Tiedemann, "Historical Materialism...," *The Philosophical Forum*: 95.

193. Tiedemann, "Historical Materialism...," *The Philosophical Forum*: 90.

194. Tiedemann, "Historical Materialism...," *The Philosophical Forum*: 96.

195. Tiedemann, "Historical Materialism...," *The Philosophical Forum*: 95. He concludes critically: "Benjamin's theses are no less than a handbook for urban guerillas" (*ibid.*, p. 96). A far more positive evaluation of Benjamin's anarchism, and of Benjamin's attempt to merge theology and reolutionary politics, is provided by Michael Löwy in his excellent essay (which appeared too late to be fully incorporated into my discussion here), "A l'écart de tous les courants et à la croisée des chimens: Walter Benjamin," *Rédemption et utopie; Le Judaïsme libertaire en Europe centrale* (Paris; Presses Universitaires de France, 1988), pp. 121–61.

196. Jürgen Habermas, "Bewusstmachende oder rettende Kritik—die Aktualität Walter Benjamins," *Zur Aktualität Walter Benjamins*, ed. Siegfried Unseld (Frankfurt am Main: Suhrkamp Verlag, 1972), p. 207. "My thesis is that Benjamin did not resolve his intention to unite Enlightenment and mysticism, because the theologist in him was not able to understand how to make the Messianic theory of experience serviceable for historical materialism. So much, I feel, must be granted to Scholem" (ibid.).

197. Habermas, p. 202.

198. Habermas, p. 205.

199. Habermas, p. 211.

200. Habermas, p. 212 and 215.

201. Habermas, p. 206. Habermas disagrees here with Adorno, who "apparently never hesitated to attribute to Benjamin precisely the same ideological-critical intention that ensued from his own work—erroneously" (ibid., p. 209).

202. Richard Wolin, *Walter Benjamin: An Aesthetics of Redemption* (New York: Columbia University Press, 1982), p. 225. The claim that Benjamin possessed a "nostalgic consciousness" was first made by Fredric Jameson in his book, *Marxism and Form: Twentieth-Century Theories of Literature* (Princeton, N.J.: Princeton University Press, 1971), p. 82.

203. Wolin, pp. 264–65.

204. "The Marxist disdain for tradition is also evident in the unreflective employment of the method of ideology-critique [. . .]" (Wolin, p. 265).

205. Speaking of the "failures" of Benjamin's life, Wolin writes: "There is also the admittedly ambivalent resolution of his general philosophical project itself: the attempt to combine the methods of materialism and metaphysics, to force the absolute to step forth from an unmediated constellation of material elements" (Wolin, p. 272). Wolin ultimately rejects Benjamin's self-understanding as a philosopher: "Benjamin, for all his forays into the arcane region of Jewish mysticism remains, first and foremost, a literary critic" (ibid., p. 26); "the aesthetic consciousness as guarantor of historical truth" was Benjamin's "general framework," as it was that of Bloch and Lukács (ibid., p. 27).

206. Cf. V, p. 578 (N3, 4).

207. V, p. 595 (N11, 3).

208. V, p. 592 (N9a, 3).

209. Benjamin was critical of such consciousness, describing the "unambiguously regressive function" of C. G. Jung's theory that archaic images were conjured up by artists in their "'nostalgia,'" due to the "'lack of satisfaction offered by the present,'" causing them to try "'to compensate for the onesidedness of the spirit of the age'" (V, p. 589 [N8, 2]).

210. V, p. 578 (N3, 1).

221. Letter, Adorno to Benjamin, 2 August 1935, V, p. 1128.

212. Especially V, p. 588 (N7a, 7).

213. V, p. 577 (N2a, 3; also N3, 1; N10a, 3).

214. André Monglod (1930), cited V, p. 603 (N15a, 1).

215. The most intelligent analysis of the significance of film for Benjamin's epistemology (and conversely, of Benjamin's epistemology for film) is Miriam Hansen's essay, "Benjamin, Cinema and Experience: 'The Blue Flower in the Land of Technology.'" In her understanding of the "ambivalence" of Benjamin's notion of the object's "looking back at you," and her

explication of the "optical unconscious" generally, Hansen's discussion is clarifying precisely because of its ability to bring Benjamin's mysticism into a fully "actual" discourse (see Miriam Hansen, Harvard University Press, forthcoming).

216. Earliest notes (pp. 27–29) V, 1013–14 (H°, 16).

217. V, p. 572 (N1a, 1).

218. V, p. 578 (N3, 4).

219. V, p. 576 (N2a, 3).

220. V, pp. 598–99 (N13, 1).

221. V, p. 594 (N10, 5).

222. V, p. 599 (N13, 3).

223. V, p. 594 (N10, 5).

224. Lotze, *Mikrokosmos* (1858), cited V, p. 599 (N13, 3).

225. V, p. 1030 (O°, 36).

226. Letter, Benjamin to Karplus [April 1940], I, p. 1227.

227. Theses on History, I, p. 693.

8 Dream World of Mass Culture

1. Certain interpreters of Weber (e.g., Reinhard Bendix), relying particularly on his early works, conflate the process of rationalization with the evolution of history itself. Others (e.g. Wolfgang Mommsen) rightfully point out that particularly in the late-written parts of *Wirtschaft und Gesellschaft* Weber understood the rationalization process as an ideal type, a fundamental form of societal structural dynamics, the appearance of which was neither limited to Western development nor synonymous with it. (See Wolfgang J. Mommsen, "Rationalisierung und Mythos bei Max Weber," in Karl Heinz Bohrer, ed., *Mythos und Moderne: Begriff und Bild einer Rekonstruktion* [Frankfurt am Main: Suhrkamp Verlag, 1983], pp. 382–402.)

2. Benjamin suggests that Piranesi's etchings of ancient Rome were "probably" the source of Baudelaire's self-professed " 'natural predilection' " for this city ("Das Paris des Second Empire bei Baudelaire," I, p. 593).

3. V, p. 494 (K1a, 8). Following Weber, one might argue that the charismatic leader becomes desirable as a way of breaking out of the iron cages of modernity's rationalizations, whereas, according to Benjamin, fascism is an *extension* of the reenchantment of the world and of mass man's illusory dream state (—while for Adorno and Horkheimer in *Dialektik der Aufklärung*, fascism is seen as an extension of modern rationality itself).

4. On this point, in turn, Weber might well have concurred. He describes modernization as a process of "rationalization" only in the formal and instrumental, not the substantive sense of reason. Mommsen cites a passage in Weber's famous lecture, "Wissenschaft als Beruf," that in fact anticipating the Surrealists, recognizes in modernity a return of " 'the old and numerous gods' "; but they are " 'disenchanted and thus [take] the form of impersonal forces,' " who " 'climb out of their graves, strive for power over our lives and begin again their eternal

struggle among each other'" (Weber, cited in Mommsen, "Rationalizierung...," *Mythos und Moderne*, P. 390).

5. V, p. 96 (K2a, 1).

6. *Einbahnstrasse*, IV, p. 132.

7. V, p. 1007 (F°, 13).

8. V, p. 993 (A°, 5).

9. "'All symbolism must arise from nature and go back to it. The things of nature both signify and are. [...] *Only in* mythology *is there a truly symbolic material: but mythology itself is only first possible through the relation of its forms to nature.* [...]. The rebirth of a symbolic view of nature would thus be the first step toward a restitution of a true mythology'" (Schelling, cited in Manfried Frank, *Der kommende Gott: Vorlesungen über die Neue Mythologie, I. Teil* [Frankfurt am Main: Suhrkamp Verlag, 1982], pp. 198–99 [itals. Schelling's]).

10. Wagner viewed the *Volk* as the true wellspring of art, yet the individual artist was to bring the people's spirit to expression (see Frank, *Der kommende Gott*, pp. 226–31).

11. V, p. 1021 (G°, 26).

12. V, p. 1021 (G°, 26).

13. It has been pointed out that the Romantics generally did not subscribe to a nationalist conception of the human "community," and that unlike their twentieth-century followers, their concept of the *Volk* clearly had progressive political implications. "A universal mythology [according to Schelling] indeed united not only a *Volk* in a nation; what was involved, as is stated literally, was a 'reunification of humanity' that is, a supranational community without separation of private from public right, without a gap between society and state—a thought that lives on directly in Marx's idea of a 'universal human class' [...]" (Frank, *Der kommende Gott*, p. 203).

14. Cf. "Aragon: new mythology," noted under: "New meaning of the Arcade," in 1935 exposé note no. 9, V. p. 1215.

15. V, p. 1006 (F°, 4, and a variant, F°, 10; another list includes: "Ballhorn, Lenin, Luna, Freud, Mors, Marlitt, Citroen" [h°, 1]). These muses, found "hidden" in Aragon's 135 pages on the Passage de l'Opera, were so transitory that several of them have faded totally from public recognition. Kate Greenaway, a late nineteenth-century illustrator of children's books, was a name connected with a Victorian style of children's clothes; Baby Cadum was the advertising image for Cadum soap; Hedda Gabler was Ibsen's feminist heroine; "Libido," Freud's life instinct, represented transitoriness itself (cf. II, p. 1033). Benjamin also names the "worldwide traveler Mickey Mouse" as a "figure of the collective dream" (Artwork Essay, I, p. 462).

16. V, p. 1207 (exposé note no. 3).

17. Cf. V, p. 1208 (1935 exposé note no. 3).

18. Louis Aragon, *Le paysan de Paris* [1926] (Paris: Gallimard, 1953), p. 145. Cf. Benjamin: "Powers of the metropolis: gas tanks" (V, p. 1207 [exposé note no. 3 on "the best book about Paris"]).

19. V, p. 583 (N5a, 2).

20. V, p. 583 (N5a, 2).

21. V, p. 584 (N5a, 2).

22. Aragon, *Le paysan de Paris*, p. 142.

23. Aragon, *Le paysan de Paris*, pp. 141–43. It has been observed that "the mythical in Aragon describes an experience in which the usual separation between consciousness and concrete matter, subjectivity and nature, is overcome, and in moments of illumination, it is eliminated" (Hans Freier, "Odyssee eines Pariser Bauern: Aragons 'Mythologie moderne' und der Deutsche Idealismus," *Mythos und Moderne*, pp. 165–66).

24. Aragon, *Le paysan de Paris*, p. 141.

25. Aragon, *Le paysan de Paris*, p. 143. Under threat of demolition, the arcades " 'have become effectively sanctuaries of a cult of the ephemeral' " (ibid., cited V, p. 140 [C2a, 9]). Cf. Benjamin: "Architecture as the most important witness of the latent 'mythology.' And the most important 19th-century architecture is the arcade (V, p.1002 [D°, 7]).

26. For Aragon, "mythology hardly unfolds in the form of a story. The narrative structures of mythological stories, and therewith, the genealogical form of mythical explanations of existing reality, are not the object of his interest" (Freier, "Odyssee eines Pariser Bauern," *Mythos und Moderne,* p. 164).

27. "I have understood nothing but that myth is above all a reality [. . .]" (Aragon, *Le paysan de Paris,* p. 140).

28. Aragon, *Le paysan de Paris*, p. 146.

29. Aragon, *Le paysan de Paris*, p. 146.

30. "We conceive of the dream 1) as an historical 2) as a collective phenomenon" (V, p. 1214 1935 exposé note no. 8).

31. V, pp. 492–93 (K1, 4).

32. The Romantics had anticipated this problem. Schelling, for example, while explicitly rejecting the " 'impotent praise of past eras and powerless chastising of the present,' " recognized "the incapacity of an atomized . . . society to justify itself" (Frank, *Der kommende Gott,* p. 195).

33. Benjamin cites S. Giedion: " 'The 19th century: Remarkable interpenetration of individualistic and collective tendencies. As in scarcely any previous era, all actions were branded as "individualistic" (ego, nation, art). Subalternly, however, in proscribed, everyday areas, it had to, as in ecstasy, create the elements for a collective formation . . . It is with this raw material that we must concern ourselves, with grey buildings, market halls, department stores, exhibitions' " (Giedion, cited V, p. 493 [K1a, 4]).

34. "Because he [Aragon] individualizes the mythic, its point of connection to collective forms of consciousness is still only imaginary [. . . based on] individual experiences through which the universal cannot become concrete" (Freier, "Odyssee eines Pariser Bauern," *Mythos und Moderne,* p. 167).

35. V, p. 580 (N4, 1).

36. V, p. 1014 (H°, 17; again N1, 9).

37. V, p. 1214 (1935 exposé note no. 8).

38. "Whereas with Aragon there remains an impressionistic element—'mythology'—(and this impressionism is to be held responsible for the many empty philosophemes in the book), here we are dealing with dissolving 'mythology' into the space of history" (V, p. 1014 [H°, 17; again N1, 9]).

39. V, p. 1214 (1935 exposé note no. 8).

40. Letter, Benjamin to Scholem, 15 March 1929, V, p. 1091. Cf. his letter to Siegfried Kracauer (25 February 1928): "[. . . P]recisely *this* Paris study [. . . stands] very near to my interest in children's toys—and if you come upon the mention [in it] of dioramas, peep-shows, etc., then you surely know what to expect from it" (V, p. 1084).

41. V, p. 994 (A°, 8).

42. *Einbahnstrasse*, IV, p. 93, trans. by Edmund Jephcott and Kingsley Shorter, in Walter Benjamin, *One Way Street and Other Writings* (London: NLB, 2979), P. 53.

43. Cf "Aussicht ins Kinderbücher" (1926) and "ABC-Bücher vor hundert Jahren" (1928), IV, pp. 609–15 and 619–20. In 1985 Benjamin's book collection was brought to the University of Frankfurt, Institut für Jugendbuchforschung, under the directorship of Klaus Doderer. During his trip to Moscow in 1927, Benjamin noted in his diary a discussion he had with a Russian children's book collector about his "great plan" for a documentary work to be called "Fantasy" (IV, p. 1049).

44. IV, p. 1049.

45. Scholem, "Walter Benjamin," *On Jews and Judaism in Crisis: Selected Essays*, ed. Werner J. Dannhauser (New York: Schocken Books, 1976), p. 175. (The writings to which Scholem refers are "Berliner Chronik" and *Berliner Kindheit um 1900*.)

46. Scholem, "Walter Benjamin," *On Jews and Judaism*, p. 193.

47. Scholem, "Walter Benjamin," *On Jews and Judaism*, p. 185.

48. Scholem, "Walter Benjamin," *On Jews and Judaism*, p. 175.

49. *Einbahnstrasse*, IV, p. 115, trans. Jephcott and Shorter, *One Way Street*, P. 74.

50. Walter Benjamin (with Asja Lacis), "Programm eines proletarischen Kindertheaters," II, p. 766.

51. "Programm eines proletarischen Kindertheaters," II, p. 766.

52. Piaget's entire project, the grounding of a universal, cognitive psychology, remains innocent of this historical specificity of the development of formal rational operations, a deficiency that becomes especially troublesome in the crosscultural application of his tests (see Susan Buck-Morss, "Socio-Economic Bias in the Theory of Piaget and its Implications for the Cross-Culture Controversy," *Jean Piaget: Consensus and Controversy*, eds. Sohan and Celia Modgil (New York: Holt, Rinehart and Winston, 1982).

53. Cf. Benjamin, "Probleme der Sprachsoziologie," (1935), a review of literature in the sociology of linguistics, which acknowledges Piaget's writings, but, predictably, is interested

in what Piaget sees as the more primitive, "egocentric" stage the child's use of language (as opposed to "socialized" language), because this stage is "tied to the situation," that is, to the child's activity: Egocentric language is a form of thought prompted when this activity is interrupted (III, p. 474).

54. "Programm eines proletarischen Kindertheaters," II, P. 768.

55. "Programm eines proletarischen Kindertheaters," II, p. 768. Here was Benjamin's answer to Marx's famous question in the third thesis on Feuerbach: "The materialist doctrine that men are the products of circumstances and upbringing and that, therefore, changed men are products of other circumstances and changed upbringing, forgets that it is men who change circumstances and that it is essential to educate the educator himself" (Karl Marx, "Theses on Feuerbach," *The Marx-Engels Reader*, ed. Robert C. Tucker, 2nd ed., rev. [New York: W. W. Norton & Company, 1978], p. 144).

56. Paul Valéry, *Idée Fixe*, trans. by David Paul, Bollingen Series XLV. 5 (New York: Pantheon Books, 1965), p. 36.

57. Benjamin recalled his own schooling: "References to objects were no more to be found than references to history; nowhere did it offer the eye the slightest refuge, while the ear was helplessly abandoned to the clatter of idiotic harangues." ("Berliner Chronik," VI, p. 474, trans. Jephcott and Shorter, *One Way Street*, p. 303).

58. If in the modern age artistic and political radicalism converged, it might have to do with the fact that artists sustained mimetic cognition and developed it to maturity: The artist "looks more closely with the hand there, where the eye grows weak [. . . and] transposes receptive impulses of the eye muscles into the creative impulses of the hand" ("Programm eines proletarischen Kindertheater," II, p. 766).

59. See Susan Buck-Morss, *The Origin of Negative Dialectics: Theodor W. Adorno. Walter Benjamin and the Frankfurt Institute* (New York: The Free Press, 1977), p. 171 and passim.

60. Notes to Theses on History, I, p. 1243.

61. "If we imagine that a man dies at exactly fifty years old on the birthdate of his son, with whom the same thing occurs, and so forth—the result is: Since Christ's birth, not forty persons have lived. the purpose of this fiction: To apply to historical time a meaningful measure, adequate to human life" (V, p. 1015 [I°, 2]). Cf. Marx's comment in *The German Ideology*: "History is nothing but the succession of separate generations [. . .]" (*Marx-Engels Reader*, p. 172).

62. "Moskau," IV, P. 318, trans. Jephcott and Shorter, *One Way Street*, p. 179.

63. "One comes upon the terrifying, the grotesque, the grim side of the child's life. Even if pedagogues are still hanging onto Rousseauean dreams, writers like Ringelnetz and painters like Klee have grasped the despotic and inhuman side of children" ("Alte Spielzuge," IV, p. 515).

64. "Programm eines proletarischen Kindertheaters," II, p. 768. "It is the task of the theater director to rescue the child's signals out of the dangerous magic realm of mere phantasy, and to bring them to bear on material stuff" (ibid., p. 766).

65. "It is a familiar image, the family gathered under the Christmas tree, the father deep in play with a train set which he just gave as a gift to his child, while the son stands nearby crying. If such a need to play overcomes the adult, that is no unbroken fallback into childishness. Children, surrounded by a giant world, manage play with things their size. But the

man whom reality positions differently, threateningly, with no way out, robs the world of its terror through its reduced size copy. Making a bagatelle out of an unbearable existence has contributed strongly to the interest in children's play and children's books since the close of the war" ("Alte Spielzeuge," IV, p. 514).

66. "Programm eines proletarischen Kindertheaters," II, p. 766.

67. *Einbahnstrasse*, IV, p. 147, trans. Jephcott and Shorter, *One Way Street*, p. 104.

68. See Benjamin's correspondence, II, pp. 951–55.

69. "Über das mimetische Vermögen," II, p. 210.

70. "Über das mimetische Vermögen," II, p. 211.

71. The perception of similarities between two objects was "a late, derivative behavior," following the "activity of making oneself similar to the object" which was basic to magic ("Über das mimetische Vermögen, II, p. 211).

72. This expressive element in objects was a "spiritual essence" (*geistiges Wesen*), yet it emanted from material bodies (including the human body), rather than from the subject's *ratio*. (See "Über Sprache überhaupt und über die Sprache des Menschen," II, pp. 140–157).

73. "Über das mimetische Vermögen," II, p. 211. Astrology concerns "not the influences or powers of the stars, but the archaic human ability to adapt to the position of the stars at a particular moment. It is the hour of birth [. . .]" (II, p. 956).

74. "Graphology has taught us to recognize in handwriting images wherein the unconscious of the writer is hidden. It is to be supposed that the mimetic procedure, which comes to expression in this form, in the writing activity of the person, was of the greatest importance for writing in the very distant times when writing originated. Thus writing is, next to language, an archive of nonsensual correspondences" ("Über das mimetische Vermögen", II, pp. 212–113).

75. "Über das mimetische Vermögen", II, p. 211.

76. "Probleme der Sprachsoziologie,"III, p. 478. This review of current authors in the sociology of language (incuding Piaget, Vygotsky, Saussure,Yerkes, Ernst Cassirer, Lévy Bruhl), was Benjamin's way of informing himself concerning the recent literature.

77. Artwork essay, I, p. 500. Benjamin refers here specifically to Freud's analysis of slips of the tongue, in *The Psychopathology of Everyday Life*.

78. Artwork essay, I, p. 500.

79. Artwork essay, I, p. 496.

80. Artwork essay, I, p. 488.

81. Artwork essay, I, p. 499.

82. V, p. 1026 (O°, 2).

83. Artwork essay, I, p. 495.

84. "Über einige Motive bei Baudelaire," I, p. 614.

85. Artwork essay, I, p. 488.

86. *Einbahnstrasse*, IV, p. 103, trans. Jephcott and Shorter, *One Way Street*, p. 62.

87. "Über einige Motive bei Baudelaire," I, p. 628n.

88. Notes to the Artwork essay, I, p. 1040.

89. "Der Sürrealismus," II, p. 309.

90. "Der Sürrealismus," II, pp. 309–10.

91. See above, chapter 2 and introduction to part II. Irving Wohlfarth has pointed out to me that Benjamin's choice of the word *"Feen,"* rather than fairy tale (*Märchen*), is meaningful. It suggests a "fairy scene," indicating that Benjamin was not intending to *narrate* a fairy tale in a story-telling fashion (a practice which, he tells us in the 1936 essay, "der Erzähler," had grown precarious in modern times), but to portray it, transforming dream images into dialectical images through a montage of historical representations. Yet I believe Benjamin's "fairy scene" was to have the same effect as a fairy tale as a form of instruction, and I have therefore used the term's interchangeably below.

92. V, p. 1002 ([D°, 7])

93. V, p. 494 (K1a, 8), *Konvolut* K is entitled "Dream City and Dream House; Dreams of the Future, Anthropological Materialism, Jung."

94. V, p. 513 (L1a, 1). Their overhead roof lighting created the "underwater atmosphere of dreams" (O°, 46; cf. H°, 4).

95. V, p. 1012 (H°, 1). "It is remarkable that the constructions which the professionals recognize as the precursors of today's way of building effect the awake but architectually unschooled sensibility as particularly old-fashioned and dreamlike (old railroad stations, gas stations, bridges)" (V, p. 493 [K1a, 4]).

96. V, p. 1002 (L1, 1).

97. See *Konvolut* L. Significantly, Benjamin does not mention the movie theater as the penultimate "dreamhouse." On the contrary, in its technological reproduction of collective dream spaces, film provides the opposite effect: "Our taverns and our metropolitan streets, our offices and furnished rooms, our railroad stations and our factories appeared to have locked us up hopelessly. Then came the film and burst this prison-world asunder by the dynamite of the tenth of a second, so that now, in the midst of its far flung ruins and debris, we calmly and adventurously go travelling" (Artwork essay, I, p. 500, trans. Harry Zohn, in Walter Benjamin, *Illuminations*, ed. Hannah Arendt [New York: Schocken Books, 1969], p. 236).

98. V, p. 494 (K1a, 7; cf. O°, 8).

99. One of the last such images was the frontispiece to Hobbes' Leviathan, with its image of the king's body composed of atomistic and equally subservient individuals.

100. V, pp. 492–93 (K1, 4; cf. G°, 14).

101. V, p. 494 (k1a, 9; cf. O°, 69).

102. V, p. 496 (K2, 6).

103. "Der Sürrealismus," II, p. 307.

104. Letter, Benjamin to Scholem, 30 October 1928, V, p. 1089.

105. V, p. 1058 (h°, 3).

106. V, p. 234 (G1, 7; again 1935 exposé note no. 8).

107. In the 1935 exposé, he wrote: "Every epoch . . . carries its ending within it, which it unfolds—as Hegel already recognized—with cunning" (V, p. 59).

108. The goal of Benjamin's "new dialectical method of history writing" was "the art of experiencing the present as the waking world to which in truth that dream which we call the past [*Gewesenes*] relates" (V, p. 491 [K1, 3; cf. F°, 6]).

109. "Franz Kafka," II, p. 415. Similarly, Benjamin wrote that it was "more proper to speak of a trick than a method" when describing the procedure of the Surrealists ("Der Sürrealismus," II, p. 300).

110. "Franz Kafka" (1934), II, p. 415. The passage continues: "And fairy tales for dialecticians are what Kafka wrote when he tackled legends. He placed little tricks into them and then read out of them the proof 'that even inadequate and indeed childish means can serve as rescue'" (ibid). In the *Passagen-Werk*, the parallel with Odysseus is direct: "The coming awakening stands like the wooden horse of the Greeks in the Troy of the dream" (V, p. 495 [K2, 4]).

111. "The condition of consciousness in its multiple patterns of sleep and waking has only to be transferred from the individual to the collective. To the latter, of course, many things are internal that are external to the individual: architecture, fashions, yes, even the weather are in the interior of the collective what organ sensations, feelings of illness or health are in the interior of the individual. And so long as they persist in unconscious and amorphous dream form, they are just as much natural processes as the digestive processes, respiration, etc. They stand in the cycle of the ever-identical until the collective gets its hands on them politically, and history emerges out of them" (V, p. 492 [K1, 5]).

112. V, p. 490 (K1, 1; cf. F°, 7).

113. V, p. 490 (K1, 1 cf. F°, 7).

114. V, p. 1054 (e°, 2; cf. D2a, 1).

115. V, p. 576 (N2a, 1).

116. See above, chapter 5.

117. V, p. 493 (K1a, 3; cf. M°, 20).

118. V, p. 492 (K1a, 2; cf. M°, 16).

119. V, p. 1057 (h°, 1).

120. Theodor W. Adorno, *Über Walter Benjamin*, ed. Rolf Tiedemann (Frankfurt am Main: Subrkamp Verlag, 1970), p. 13.

121. See below, chapter 10, section 3.

122. "Der Erzähler" (1936), II, p. 458.

123. V, pp. 455–456 (J75, 2).

124. V, p. 494 (K2, 2; cf. I°, 8).

125. Cf. V, p. 579 (N3a, 3), and: "What Proust does for individual childhood is here to be done for the collective" (K1, 2). Evoking Proust, Benjamin says that in the dialectical images, "the past draws together into a moment" and thereby "enters into the involuntary memory of humanity" (Notes to the Theses on History, I, p. 1233).

126. "Franz Kafka" (1934), II, p. 416.

127. V, p. 1026 (O°, 5).

128. V, pp. 1052–53 [e°, 1]).

129. V, p. 1032 (O°, 56).

130. V, p. 1054 (e°, 2).

131. Louis Veuillot (1914), cited V, p. 492 (K1a, 1).

132. V, p. 493 (K1a, 6).

133. Bloch (1935), cited V, p. 497 (K2a, 5).

134. Benjamin referred to these chronicles of his childhood as a " 'history of my relationship to Berlin' " in a letter to Scholem, 28 February 1932, cited in Gersholm Scholem, *Walter Benjamin: The Story of a Friendship* (London: Faber & Faber, 1981), p. 180.

135. In the *Passagen-Werk* he included one childhood memory: "Many years ago in a city tram I saw an advertising placard which, if it had entered into the world with proper things, would have found its admirers, historians, exegeticians, and copyists, as much as any great literature or great painting. And in fact it was both at the same time. But as can occur sometimes with very deep, unexpected impressions, the shock was so strong, the impression, if I may say it thus, hit me so powerfully that it broke through the bottom of consciousness and for years lay irretrievable somewhere in the darkness. I knew only that it had to do with '*Bullrichsalz*' [a brand name for salt]. [. . .] Then I succeeded one faded Sunday afternoon [. . . in discovering a sign on which was written] '*Bullrich-Salz*.' It contained nothing but the word, but around this verbal sign there arose suddenly, effortlessly, that desert landscape of the first placard. I had it back again. It looked like this: Moving forward in the foreground of the desert was a freight wagon drawn by horses. It was laden with sacks on which salt had already dribbled for a while onto the ground. In the background of the desert landscape, two posts carried a large sign with the words: 'is the best.' What about the trace of salt on the path through the desert? It constructed letters, and these formed a word, the word 'Bullrich-Salz.' Was the preestablished harmony of Leibniz not childishness compared with this knife-sharp, finely coordinated predestination in the desert? And did there not lie in this placard a likeness for things which in this life on earth no one has yet experienced? A likeness for the every-dayness of utopia?" (V, pp. 235–36 [G1a, 4]). Note that the child's inventive reception of this mass-culture form as a sign of nature reconciled with humanity indicates that childhood cognitive powers are not without an antidote to mass culture's manipulation.

136. In 1936 Benjamin proposed to Horkheimer an essay for the Institut on Klages and Jung: "It was to develop further the methodological considerations of the *Passagen-Werk*, confronting the concept of the dialectical image—the central epistemological category of the

"*Passagen*"—with the archetypes of Jung and the archaic images of Klages. Due to the intervention of Horkheimer this study was never executed" (ed. note, V, p. 1145). Still, the *Passagen-Werk* material makes clear the line that Benjamin's argument would have taken. Where Jung would see, for example, the recurrence of a utopian image as a "successful return" of unconscious contents, Benjamin, far closer to Freud (and Bloch), argued that its repetition was the sign of the continued social repression that prevented realizing utopian desires (K2a, 5). Or, where Jung would see the image of the beggar as an eternal symbol expressing a transhistorical truth about the collective psyche, for Benjamin the beggar was a historical figure, the persistence of which was a sign of the archaic stage, not of the psyche, but of social reality that remained at the mythic level of prehistory despite surface change: "As long as there is still one beggar, there still exists myth" (K6, 4).

137. V, p. 1236 (version of the 1935 exposé).

138. "Berliner Chronik," VI, p. 489, trans. Jephcott and Shorter, *One Way Street*, p. 316.

139. V, p. 576 (N2a, 2).

140. V, p. 576 (N2a, 2).

141. V, p. 490 (K1, 1; again F°, 1).

142. V, p. 118 (B3, 6).

143. Although one can find statements by Benjamin that seem to lament this situation, he was no supporter of the traditional bourgeois family (which he called in *Einbahnstrasse* "a rotten, gloomy edifice" [IV, p. 144]), and whatever positive attitude he had toward theology, it did not include the institution of organized religion (—*Berliner Chronik* recalls his dislike of synagogue services for the "familial no less than divine aspects of the event" [VI, p. 512]). In the *Passagen-Werk* Benjamin mentions as the one positive "social value of marriage" the fact that by *lasting*, it postpones indefinitely any finally decisive quarrel and settlement! (V, p. 438 [J67, 1]).

144. V, p. 1214 (1935 exposé note no. 8).

145. "Traumkitsch" (1925), II, p. 620.

146. For an identification of the various exposé versions, see the editor's note, V, p. 1251.

147. In the first typescript of the exposé (sent to Adorno) the conception of the generation as the inheritor of culture is implicit in statements such as: "[. . .] in these [collective] wish images there emerges an energetic striving to break with that which is outdated—which means, however, the most recent past" (V, p. 1239). An earlier version ("M") is more explicit: "this inexorable confrontation with the most recent past is something historically new. Other neighboring links in the chain of generations stood within collective consciousness, [and] scarcely distinguished themselves from one another within that collective. The present, however, already stands in the same relation to the most recent past as does awakening to the dream" (p. 1236).

148. V, pp. 45–59 and 1223–49; also Benjamin's letter to Karplus, p. 1140. See also preparatory notes for the exposé from 1934–35, especially nos. 5–9, pp. 1209–14, and notes added later, pp. 1249–51.

149. V, p. 1138.

150. V, p. 1139.

151. V, p. 1139.

152. Note, however, that Benjamin continued to work on the manuscript of *Berliner Kindheit um 1900*, reworking the material for possible publication as late as 1938. The most definitive revision is not the one published in IV, but the one more recently discovered Benjamin's papers the in Bataille Archive, Bibliothèque Nationale.

153. Entries of *Konvolut* K, devoted to this dream theory, are listed in the notes to the Baudelaire "book" compiled in the late 1930s (Bataille Archive, Bibliothèque Nationale).

154. See above, chapter 1, section 5.

155. Letter, Adorno to Benjamin, 2 August 1935, V, p. 1129.

156. V, p. 1129.

157. At the end of 1936, Benjamin spent time with Adorno in San Remo, and wrote that he had benefited immensely from their discussions, particularly in regard to "those aspects of my planned book which are most dissatisfying to me in the 1935 exposé: I mean the line of thought that has to do with the collective unconscious and its image fantasy" (letter, Benjamin to Horkheimer, 28 March 1937, V, p. 1157).

158. The original copy of Adorno's letter of 2 August 1935, is among the Benjamin papers in the Bataille Archive. Benjamin gave it a careful reading, making penciled notes and also double red lines in the margin—not always at those points in Adorno's formulation that the latter would himself have considered most eloquent. Benjamin's notations include exclamation marks and question marks, apparently indicating points of disagreement.

159. Shortly before receiving Adorno's reaction to the exposé, Benjamin wrote to him expressing his preference for Freud's theory over the theories of Fromm and Reich, and asking whether Adorno knew if in the writings of Freud or his school there was "at present a psychoanalysis of awakening, or studies on this theme?" The same letter stated that he had begun to "look around" in the first volume of Marx's *Capital* (letter, Benjamin to Adorno, 10 June 1935, V, p. 1121–22). In March 1937 he wrote to Horkheimer that "the definitive and binding plan of the [*Passagen-Werk*], now that the material research for it is finished except in a few small areas, would proceed from two fundamentally methodological analyses. The one would have to do with the criticism of, on the one hand, pragmatic history, and on the other, cultural history as it is presented by the materialists; the other would deal with the meaning of psychoanalysis for the subject of materialist history–writing" (p. 1158).

160. Marx, cited V, p. 583 (N5a, 1).

161. Marx, cited V, p. 570.

162. V, p. 495 (K2, 5; cf. M°, 14).

163. V, p. 495 (K2, 5).

164. It is wrong to emphasize the significance for Benjamin of psychonanalytic theory. In the 1930s, his reception of Freud was still largely mediated, coming from two distinctly unorthodox sources, Surrealism and the Frankfurt Institute. His initial exposure to Freud's writings had been as a student, and it was far from positive. Scholem reports that in Bern in 1918, "Benjamin attended Paul Häberlin's seminar on Freud and produced a detailed paper on Freud's libido theory, arriving at a negative judgment. Among the books he read in connection with this seminar was Daniel Paul Schreber's *Denkwürdigkeiten eines Nervenkranken*, which appealed to him far more than Freud's essay on it [. . .]. From a salient passage in this book Benjamin derived the designation "*flüchtig hingemachte Männer* [hastily put-up men]." Schreber,

who at the height of his paranoia believed for a time that the world had been destroyed by 'rays' hostile to him, gave this answer when it was pointed out to him that the doctors, patients, and employees of the insane asylum obviously existed" (Scholem, *Walter Benjamin*, p. 57). Scholem also reports: "I do not remember his ever contradicting my expression of profound disappointment at Freud's *Interpretation of Dreams*, contained in a letter I wrote to him a few years later" (ibid., p. 61). In 1921 Benjamin wrote that if capitalism was a religion, Freudian theory was part of the "priest-domination of this cult" (VI, p. 101). He commented in his article on Goethe for the Soviet Encyclopedia that Freud describes the bourgeois psyche "perceptively and flatteringly," as did Goethe in *Das Leiden des Jungen Werther*" (II, p. 709).

165. Scholem tells us: "to him Surrealism was something like the first bridge to a more positive assessment of pyschonanalysis, but he had no illusions as to the weaknesses in the procedures of both schools" (Scholem, *Walter Benjamin*, pp. 134–35). It was not until the mid–1930s, in response to Adorno's warnings that his concept of the dreaming collective brought him close to Jung, that Benjamin resolved to begin a more serious study of Freud, specifically, to write an attack on Jung (see V, pp. 1069, 1158, 1162). He took notes on Freud as background for his second essay on Kafka. Even at this time, however, it was not so much the central writings of Freud that interested him as the "similarities" that he was surprised to find betwen his own theory of language (in "*Über das Mimetische Vermögen*") and Freud's essay on "Telepathy and Psychoanalysis" published in 1935 (letter, Benjamin to Werner Kraft, 30 January 1936, *Briefe*, 2 vols., eds. Gersholm Scholem and Theodor W. Adorno Frankfurt am Main: Suhrkamp Verlag. 1978], vol. 2, p. 705)—specifically, the notion that telepathy, a form of understanding already present in insects [!], is phylogenetically a pre-cursor of language (see II, p. 953). Entries relevant to Freudian theory that appear in the post–1935 entries to *Konvolut* K, are largely limited to excerpts from a book by the Freudian analyst, Theodor Reik, on the healing power of memory which derives from the fact that the conscious reconstruction of the past destroys its power over the present (V, pp. 507–08 [K8, 1; K8, 2]).

166. Sigmund Freud, *The Interpretation of Dreams*, trans. and ed. James Strachey (New York: Avon Books, 1965), p. 123.

167. Freud, p. 194.

168. V, p. 1212 (1935 exposé note no. 5).

169. V, p. 1210 (1935 exposé note no. 5).

170. V, p. 506 (K6a, 2).

171. V, p. 261 (G13, 2).

172. V, p. 52 (1935 exposé).

173. V, p. 669 (R2, 2).

174. "Zentralpark," I, p. 677 (cf. V, p. 175 [D9, 3]).

175. V, p. 448 (J71, 7). The phrase is Goethe's.

176. V, p. 1210 (1935 exposé note no. 5).

177. V, p. 1215. The Brecht quotation (from a 1935 article) continued: " 'They [the rulers] would prefer that the moon stand still, and the sun no longer run its course. Then no one would get hungry any more and want supper. When they have shot their guns, their opponents should not be allowed to shoot; theirs should be the last shots' " (cited B4a, 1).

178. V, p. 1209 (1935 exposé note no. 5).

179. V, p. 1000 (D°, 1).

180. V, p. 1035 (P°, 6).

181. *Berliner Chronik*, VI, P. 499.

182. V, p. 1033 (O°, 67).

183. V, p. 1033 (O°, 68).

184. VI, p. 471. trans. Jephcott and Shorter, *One Way Street*, p. 300.

185. VI, p. 488, trans. Jephcott and Shorter, *One Way Street*, p. 316.

186. V, p. 1018 (K°, 28).

187. V, p. 59 (1935 exposé).

188. Letter, Benjamin to Scholem, 9 August 1935, V, p. 1137.

189. V, p. 130 (B9, 1; cf. B1a, 4).

190. V, p. 113 (B1a, 4).

191. V, p. 1018 (K°, 27).

9 Materialist Pedagogy

1. V, p. 603 (N15, 3).

2. V, pp. 1026–27 (0°, 5).

3. "Über den Begriff der Geschichte," I, pp. 693–704. Adorno wrote in 1950 that these Theses on History "sum up the epistemological reflections, the development of which accompanied that of the Arcades project" (Theodor W. Adorno, "Charakteristik Walter Benjamins," *Über Walter Benjamin*, ed. Rolf Tiedemann [Frankfurt am Main: Suhrkamp Verlag, 1970], p. 26). Espagne and Werner argue that this statement "does not correspond literally to Benjamin's statement" in his (22 February 1940) letter to Horkheimer, that the Theses were " 'to serve as a theoretical armature to the second Baudelaire essay' " (Benjamin [V, pp. 1129–30], cited in Espagne and Werner, p. 646). They use this fact to bolster their claim that the Baudelaire study superseded the Arcades project. My criticism of this claim has been stated above (introduction to part III).

4. Theses on History, I, p. 696 (cf. V, p. 584 [N5a, 7]).

5. Theses on History, I, p. 696.

6. Theses on History, I, pp. 696–97.

7. Ed. note, II, p. 1355.

8. "Eduard Fuchs, der Sammler und der Historiker," II, pp. 472–73.

9. Fuchs essay, II, p. 473.

10. His trip to Moscow in 1927 had convinced him that the problem of cultural education was just as acute in a postrevolutionary society, where the Communist Party's attempt to teach the "classics" of European literature popularized bourgeois values "in precisely the distorted, dreary fashion for which, in the end, it has imperialism to thank" ("Moskauer Tagebuch," VI, p. 339; see also chapter 2 above).

11. "Über einige Motive bei Baudelaire," I, p. 608. It had become "also one of the most frequently published books" (ibid.).

12. This was in opposition to the view of Brecht, who believed that Baudelaire " 'in no way brings to expression his epoch, not even a ten year period. He will not be understood for long; already today too many explanatory notes are necessary' " (Brecht, cited in the editorial afterward, Walter Benjamin, *Charles Baudelaire: Ein Lyriker im Zeitalter des Hochkapitalismus*, ed. Rolf Tiedemann [Frankfurt am Main: Suhrkamp Verlag, 1974], P. 193).

13. I, p. 1166. Ellipses in parentheses indicate crossed-out phrases in the notes.

14. Fuchs essay, II, p. 477. Benjamin's interpretation of the Hegelian legacy in Marx's theory speaks precisely to this point: It was not that Marx's theory allowed the proletariat to take possession of the heritage of German idealism. Rather, the real historical situation of the proletariat, its " 'decisive position within the production process itself' " (C. Korn [1908], cited ibid., p. 473) made possible Marx's radical rereading of Hegel. The real and present image of the proletariat at one stroke "rescued" Hegel's philosophy for the present, and levied against that philosophy its most devastating critique.

15. Fuchs essay, II, p. 478.

16. Fuchs essay, II, pp. 467–68.

17. Notes to the Theses on History, I, p. 1236.

18. V, p. 592 (N9a, 5).

19. I, p. 1242.

20. Notes to the Theses on History, I, p. 1231.

21. *Einbahnstrasse*, [IV, pp. 116–17], trans. by Edmund Jephcott and Kingsley Shorter, Walter Benjamin, *One Way Street* (London: New Left Books, 1979), p. 75.

22. "Zum gesellschaftlichen Standort des französichen Schriftstellers" (1934), II, p. 787.

23. "Zum gesellschaftlichen Standort...," II, p. 789.

24. "Surrealism" (1929), II, p. 309.

25. V, p. 588 (N7a, 3).

26. V, p. 576 (N2a, 3; again, N3, 1).

27. J. Joubert (1883), cited V, p. 604 (N15a, 3).

28. V, p. 595 (N11, 3).

29. V, p. 572 (N1, 11).

30. Letter, Benjamin to Adorno, 9 September 1938, I, p. 1103.

31. Rudolf Borchard (1923), cited V, p. 1026 (O°, 2; again, N1, 8). The stereoscope, invented between 1810 and 1820, was the image of Benjamin's theory of historical perspective (cf. letter, Adorno to Benjamin, 2 August 1935, V, p. 1135).

32. At times the entries appear to have a quite simple relationship to the "present." We are told, for example that whereas in the past the aristocracy visited the baths, now they are visited by film stars. The nickname of Bismarck, the "iron chancellor," which marked "the entry of technology into language" (V, p. 231 [F8, 5]) is a fact that resonates with the contemporary nickname of Stalin, "the steely one" (*der Stahlene*). Benjamin notes that the Hyde Park site of the 1851 exposition evoked "a cry of alarm," because "for a fantasy spectacle one ought not to sacrifice the trees" (V, p. 247 [G6; G6a, 1]). In 1937 the same cry was heard from the "Friends of the Esplanade des Invalides": "Let us not destroy the capital under the pretext of the exposition. We must save the trees!" Their protest prompted a reply from Léon Blum himself, who initiated an investigation (see the series of articles in *La Semaine à Paris*, February–August, 1937, [Paris, Bibliothèque de l'Histoire de la Ville de Paris]). If such details had made their way into a finished *Passagen-Werk* they would have had the effect of suggesting to the reader how the work was to be read.

33. "Passagen" (1927), V, p. 1041.

34. V, p. 1045 (a°, 2).

35. V, p. 1038 (Q°, 23).

36. Gropius' model factory exhibited in Cologne in 1914 had walls of glass; and it was for this exhibition that Paul Sheerbart built his "Glass House" (cf. Benjamin's mention of Sheerbart in connection with glass architecture as a utopian expression [1935 exposé, V, p. 46]).

37. V, p. 573 (N1a, 5).

38. V, p. 1035 (P°, 3).

39. See above, chapter 5.

40. V, p. 292 (14, 4).

41. V, p. 528 (M1a, 4).

42. V, p. 1030 (O°, 33).

43. Notes to the Theses on History, I, p. 1244.

44. V, p. 1218 (1935 exposé note no. 15.).

45. Several of the photos of architecture in the previous section are taken from Sigfried Giedion's *Bauen im Frankreich* (1928), which was one of Benjamin's earliest sources. (See also entries from the much cited book by Adolf Behne, *Neues Wohnen—Neues Bauen* [Leipzig: Hesse and Becker Verlag, 1927]).

46. "It is the particular property of *technical* forms of style (in contrast to art forms) that their progress and success are proportional to the *transparency* of their social content. (Thus, glass architecture)" (V, p. 581 [N4, 6]).

47. In a somewhat similar way, Adorno in these years developed a theory of Schönberg's atonal music as anticipatory of a new social order. There was an important difference in their examples, however. Schönberg's transcendence of bourgeois tonality was the inner-musical accomplishment of an individual artist working in isolation, drawing out the consequences of the musical tradition he had inherited. In contrast, the transformations of fashions, architecture, furnishings, and "style" generally were collective projects, accomplished through the collaboration of engineers, commercial designers, factory producers, and others. Moreover, as use-values rather than autonomous art, they entered into people's everyday experience, as part of the contents of the collective unconscious. At least potentially, Benjamin's approach thus avoided the elitism intrinsic to Adorno's cultural criticism. (See Susan Buck-Morss, *The Origins of Negative Dialectics: Theodor W. Adorno, Walter Benjamin and the Frankfurt Institute* (New York: Macmillan Free Press, 1977), chapter 8, pp. 127–31.) The idea of cultural forms as anticipatory can also be found in Ernst Bloch.

48. Cf. V, p. 775 (W5a, 5). Benjamin notes also Ledoux's plan for a residential complex that for the first time proposed "'what we in the present call a common kitchen building'" (Kaufmann [1933], cited V, p. 742 [U17, 3]).

49. V, p. 786 (W11a, 3).

50. "Fourier wants to see the people who are not useful for anything in civilization, who only go about trying to catch up on the news and spread it further, circulate at the dinner tables of the harmonists, in order to spare people the time of reading journals: a divination of radio that is derived from studying the human character" (V, p. 793 [W15, 5]).

51. He imagined an "optical telegraph" (V, p. 793 [W15, 2]).

52. V, p. 783 [W9a, 3]).

53. V, p. 776 (W6, 4; also W6a, 4; W8a, 1).

54. V, p. 1058 (h°, 4). Yet he had always understood these dream images as ambivalent (see above, chapter 8, section 8). If Fourier's phalanstery anticipated public housing, it also privatized the building style of the arcades, a "reactionary transformation" that was "symptomatic" (V, p. 47 [1935 exposé]).

55. Benjamin's correspondence indicates that he was both late to realize the danger of fascism and late to acknowledge the inadequacy of the Soviet-led Communist Party as a force of opposition against it (see Walter Benjamin, *Briefe*, 2 vols., eds. Gershom Scholem and Theodor W. Adorno [Frankfurt am Main: Suhrkamp Verlag, 1978], vol. 2, pp. 536, 646, 722, and passim).

56. This was Benjamin's description in 1934 (see letter, Benjamin to Adorno, 18 March 1935, V, pp. 1102–3).

57. V, p. 994 (A°, 9; again d°, 1, M3a, 4).

58. "Die Wiederkehr des Flaneurs," III, p. 198.

59. "Das Paris des Second Empire bei Baudelaire," I, p. 539.

60. V, p. 554 (M13a, 2).

61. V, p. 964 (m2a, 3).

62. "Das Paris des Second Empire bei Baudelaire," I, pp. 537–39.

63. Benjamin writes that he acts as if he knew Marx's definition that "the value of every commodity is determined [. . .] by the socially necessary labor time of its production [. . .].

In his eyes and frequently also those of his employer, this value [for his labor time] receives some fantastic compensation. Clearly the latter would not be the case if he were not in the privileged position of making the time for the production of his use value observable for public evaluation, in that he spends it on the boulevards and thus at the same time displays it" (V, pp. 559–60 [M16, 4]).

64. V, p. 562 (M17a, 2; cf. M19, 2; both entries are post-1937). For a fuller treatment of this theme, see Susan Buck-Morss, "The Flaneur, the Sandwichman and the Whore: The Politics of Loitering," *New German Critique* 39 (fall 1986): 99–140.

65. V, p. 967 (m4, 2).

66. I, p. 516.

67. Notes to *Charles Baudelaire*, I, p. 1174.

68. V, p. 436 (J66, 1).

69. V, p. 469 (J81a, 1).

70. "Only in the summer-like middle of the nineteenth century, only under the sun, can one think of Fourier's fantasies as realized" (V, p. 785 [W10a, 4, late entry]).

71. "The historical index of [dialectical] images says not only that they belong to a particular time; it says above all that only in a particular time do they come 'to legibility'" (V, p. 577 [N3, 1]).

72. Benjamin records that, ironically, "Napoleon III belonged to a Fourierist group in 1848" (V, p. 789 [W12a, 5]).

73. "Zum Geschichtsphilosophie, Historik und Politik" (1934), VI, p. 104.

74. The first note to the 1935 exposé includes a chronology of the steps in this process, from the 10 December 1848 presidential election of Louis-Napoleon Bonaparte to his dissolution of the Republic three years later, and his subsequent, successful plebiscites (V, pp. 1206–07).

75. De Lignières (1936), cited V, p. 926 (d12a 2).

76. The Benjamin papers in the Bataille Archive include press clippings on Mickey Mouse and Walt Disney from French newspapers (Paris, Bibliothéque Nationale).

77. The first full-color animated cartoon by Walt Disney appeared in 1932, entitled "Flowers and Trees": A crabby tree stump disrupts a romance between two young trees, and starts a fire that threatens the whole forest. Birds puncture clouds, causing rain to fall that drowns the flames. The stump is destroyed, the lovers marry with a glowworm for a wedding ring, while flowers celebrate the nuptials. A *Passagen-Werk* entry notes the difference between the work of Grandville and that of Walt Disney: Disney "'contains not the slightest seed of mortification. In this he distances himself from the humor of Grandville, which always carried within it the presence of death'" (Mac-Orlan [1934], cited V, p. 121 [B4a, 5]).

78. "For an explanation of Fourier's extravagances, one can draw on Mickey Mouse, in whom, precisely in the sense of Fourier's fantasies, the moral mobilization of nature has taken place: In it humor puts politics to the test. It confirms how right Marx was to see in Fourier, above all else, a great humorist" (V, p. 781 [W8a, 5]).

79. Notes to the Artwork essay, I, p. 1045.

80. Eighteenth-century prospectus, cited V, p. 702 (T2, 5).

81. V, p. (E°, 33).

82. V, p. 1207 (1935 exposé note no. 3).

83. V, p. 1207 (1935 exposé note no. 3).

84. V, p. 500 (K3a, 1).

85. V, p. 595 (N11, 1).

86. C. E. Jung, (1932), cited V, pp. 589–90 (N8, 2).

87. V, p. 963 (m1a, 6).

88. "Über einige Motive bei Baudelaire," I, p. 609.

89. "[. . . T]he flames on the sides of the Nuremberg stadium, the huge overwhelming flags, the marches and speaking choruses, present a spectacle to [today's] modern audiences not unlike those American musicals of the 1920s and 1930s which Hitler himself was so fond of watching each evening" (George Mosse, *The Nationalization of the Masses* [New York: Howard Fertig, 1975]), p. 207).

90. Le Corbusier, *Urbanisme*(1927), cited V, p. 184 (E2a, 1; see also E2, 9).

91. "A story has it that Madame Haussmann, at a party, reflected naively: "It is curious, every time that we buy a building a boulevard passes through it" (V, p. 192 [E5, 4]).

92. Washington, D. C., was rebuilt in the depression years according to the tenets of neoclassical design.

93. Cabinet des Estampes, Bibliothèque Nationale, V, pp. 941–42 (g2a, 3).

94. Saint-Simon's ideas "were closer to state capitalism than to socialism'" (Volgin [1928], V, p. 720 [U6, 2]). "Saint-Simon was a predecessor of the technocrats" (U5a, 2); Benjamin notes: "the points of contact between Saint-Simonianism and fascism" (V, p. 1211 [1935 exposé note no. 5]).

95. Robert Moses, cited in Marshall Berman, *The Experience of Modernity: All that is Solid Melts into Air* (New York: Simon and Schuster, 1982), p. 290.

96. Despite the Nazi ideology of *volkish* culture, Hitler favored neoclassicism over the Teutonic tradition, so that the plans by Speer which he commissioned resembled the 1930s building projects in Washington, D.C., far more than the German buildings of the past. Benjamin cites Raphael's attempt to correct "the Marxist conception of the normative character of Greek art": "'the abstract notion [. . .] of a "norm" [. . .] was created only in the Renaissance, that is, by primitive capitalism, and accepted subsequently by that classicism which . . . began to assign it a place within the historical sequence'" (Max Raphael [1933], cited V, p. 580 [N4, 5]).

97. V, p. 1212 (1935 exposé note no. 5). Nazi urban design stressed the monumentality of state buildings, with the goal of "'reawakening'" the soul of the German people (Robert R. Taylor, *The Word in Stone: The Role of Architecture in National Socialist Ideology* [Berkeley: University of California Press, 1974] p. 30). For Hitler, "'community' architecture never meant building to meet the needs of the community," for example, workers' housing or hospitals

(ibid., p. 28). He praised the state architecture of ancient Rome—temples, stadiums, circuses, and aqueducts—in contrast with the architectural emphasis in Weimar, Germany, where "hotels and 'the department stores of a few Jews' " were prominent (ibid., p. 40). On *Reichskristallnacht* 1938, twenty-nine department stores, all owned by Jews, were burned.

98. Benjamin's criticism of the Commune (see *Konvolut* k) is, rather, that it had "illusions" of itself as a continuation of the spirit of the 1793 (see V, p. 952 [k2a, 1]). Note that precisely the same "illusions" were held by the French Communist Party in the 1936 elections: Their slogan was "that Communism was the Jacobinism of the twentieth century" (Joel Colton, "Politics and Economics in the 1930s," *From the Ancien Régime to the Popular Front: Essays in the History of Modern France in Honor of Shepard B. Clough,* ed. Charles K. Warner [New York: Columbia University Press, 1969], p. 186).

99. Cf. Benjamin's reference to Fourier in the Theses on History, in the context of protesting against the Social Democrats' "technocratic" image of utopia (found in fascism as well) that glorifies work and has a conception of nature which "differs ominously from socialist utopias before the 1848 revolution": "Labor as now understood boils down to the exploitation of nature, which with naive complacency is contrasted to the exploitation of the proletariat. Compared with this positivistic conception, the fanatasies of someone like Fourier that have been so much ridiculed prove to be surprisingly sound. According to Fourier, well-conceived social labor should have as its result that four moons illuminate the earth's night, ice recede from its poles, sea water no longer taste salty, and beasts of prey serve human beings. All this illustrates a form of labor which, far from exploiting nature, is capable of releasing from her the creations that lie dormant in her lap" (I, p. 699, cf. v, pp. 775–76 [W6, 4; also W11a, 8; W14a, 6; W15, 8]).

100. "Über einige Motive bei Baudelaire," I, p. 589 (cf. V, p. 152 [C7a, 4]).

101. V, p. 184 (E2, 10).

102. V, p. 203 (E10a, 2).

103. V, p. 198 (E7a, 3).

104. Dubech-D'Espezel (1926), V, p. 854 (a1a, 1).

105. V, p. 208 (E13, 2).

106. V, p. 585 (N6, 5).

107. Louis Aragon (1935), cited V, p. 579 (N3a, 4).

108. His hotel was at the "strategically particularly important" corner of the rue du Four and the Boulevard Saint-Germain, not far from the Palais Bourbon and the Chamber of Deputies. (Letter, Benjamin to Gretel Karplus (beginning of February 1934), V, p. 1099). For an excellent biographical account of Benjamin in the 1930s, see Chryssoula Kambas, *Walter Benjamin im Exil: Zum Verhältnis von Literaturpolitik und Asthetik* (Tübingen: Max Niemeyer Verlag, 1983).

109. The article was planned for the Communist newspaper *Le Monde.*

110. The book was most probably *Histoire de Paris* by Lucien Dubech and Pierre D'Espezel (1926), which is cited heavily in the entries from this period in *Konvolut* E, entitled "Haussmannization; Barricade Fighting." The article on Haussmann drew on material from this *Konvolut* of the *Passagen-Werk.* Benjamin wrote to Karplus in February 1934 that Brecht considered Haussmann an especially important theme, and that by taking up this theme, he had

"again come into the immediate proximity of my Arcades project" on which work had been temporarily interrupted, (V, p. 1098). The article, never completed, would have had striking political relevance for the particular historical moment.

111. The "tactic of civil war" was "underdeveloped" (V, p. 182 [E1a, 6]). Already in the 1848 revolution, Engels noted, barricade fighting had more " 'moral than material significance' " (Engels, cited ibid., E1a, 5).

112. On the abortive Blanquist putsch of August 1870: "Telling for the forms of street fighting was the fact that the workers preferred daggers to guns (V, p. 204 [E10a, 5]). The heyday era of the barricades had been the revolution of 1830, when "6,000 barricades were counted in the city" (1935 exposé note no. 19, V, p. 1219). "In the suppression of the June insurrection [1848] artillery was employed in the street fighting for the first time" (V, p. 202 [E9a, 7]).

113. Letter, Benjamin to Karplus, February 1934, V, p. 1099. That street demonstrators were no match for a state willing to use force was demonstrated that evening, when the police and *gardes mobiles* stopped the crowd, killing fourteen, and wounding over a thousand (see Joel Colton, *Leon Blum: Humanist in Politics* [Cambridge, Mass.: The MIT Press, 1974], p. 94). It was during this period of political instability, 1934–35, that Benjamin composed the *Passagen-Werk* exposé.

114. Benjamin may have been with Fritz Lieb that day, to whom he wrote in 1937: "Do you remember our Bastille Day together? How reasoned now appears that discontent which we then dared to express only half aloud" (letter, Banjamin to Lieb, 9 July 1937, [*Briefe*, vol. 2, p. 732]).

115. "Everywhere the strikes took a common form. The workers remained in the plants day and night, posting security guards, solicitously caring for the machinery. Food and blankets were brought in by their families and sympathizers; entertainment was provided. There was little or no vandalism. Indeed the workers seemed to be treating the factories as if the plants already belonged to them, which was enough to frighten the bourgeoisie. *Le Temps* saw something sinister in the very order that reigned in the factories" (Colton, p. 135).

116. Trotsky, cited in Colton, p. 152.

117. Volume VII of Benjamin's collected works (yet to appear) will consist of his correspondence, and may indicate otherwise.

On the constellation of the *Front Populaire* and the *Passagen-Werk*, see the excellent article by Philippe Ivernel, "Paris—Capital of the Popular Front," trans. Valerie Budig, *New German Critique* 39 (fall 1986): 61–84, or the original French publication (which spells the author's name correctly) in *Walter Benjamin et Paris:* Colloque international 27–29 juin 1983, ed. Heinz Wismann (Paris: Cerf, 1986), pp. 249–272. See also the well-researched essay by Jon Bassewitz "Benjamin's Jewish Identity during his Exile in Paris," (in print), which puts Benjamin's work in the context of the Left-cultural debates in Paris during the 1930s.

118. Indeed, that potential was stifled by the leadership, as Benjamin commented retroactively on the occasion of further strikes in December 1937: "[I]n so far as the strike movement is a continuation of those that preceded it, it seems ill-fated. In two years, the leadership has succeeded in robbing the workers of their elementary sense of instinctive action—their infallible sense for when and under what conditions a legal action must give way to an illegal one, and when an illegal action must become violent. Their current actions instill fears in the bourgeoisie, but they lack the intention, the real power to intimidate" (letter, Benjamin to Fritz Lieb, 31 December 1937, cited in Chryssoula Kambas, "Politische Aktualität: Walter Benjamin's Concept of History and the Failure of the Popular Front," *New German Critique* 39 (fall 1986): 93–94.

119. V, p. 937 (d18, 5; see also d1, 2; d1a, 2; d10a, 1; d12, 2; d18a, 1).

120. Letter, Benjamin to Fritz Lieb, 9 July 1937, *Briefe*, vol. 2, p. 732. His appraisal was no less critical with regard to the Communist Party's opportunism during the Spanish Civil War, where "martyrdom is suffered not for the actual issue, but far more in the name of a compromise proposal [. . .] between the revolutionary ideas in Spain and the Machiavellianism of the Russian leadership, as well as the Mammonism of the indigenous leadership" (letter, Benjamin to Karl Thieme, 27 March 1938, *Briefe*, vol. 2, p. 747).

121. V, p. 798 (W17a, 1).

122. Despite some criticism of consumer novelties because their production ate into national resources, cosmetics and fashions were not eradicated in fascist Germany; instead, these were encouraged as domestic industries, against the dominance of the French in this field. The demand for private homes was encouraged; mass consumption of the automobile was the state goal, achieved with Volkswagen in its "classic" Beetle style. (See *Sex and Society in Nazi Germany*, ed. Heinrich Fraenkel, trans. J. Maxwell Brownjohn [New York: J. B. Lippincott Company, 1973]).

123. As one of his first actions, Hitler founded the "Kraft durch Freude" (Strength through Joy) association to organize leisure time activities such as tourism, sports, and theater and concert attendance. The "Travel and Tourism" bureau organized planned holidays—and later organized the transport of Jews to the death camps.

124. Karl Marx on the February Revolution, 1848, cited V, p. 183 (E1a, 6).

125. There was a difference, in that Blum was fully committed to republican parliamentarianism. In contrast: "The Saint-Simonians had very limited sympathies with democracy" (V, p. 733 [U13, 2]). The radical, romantic Saint-Simonian l'Enfantin "greeted Louis-Napoleon's coup as a work of Providence" (V, p. 741 [U16a, 5]). But his advocacy of class harmony and state capitalism portended the welfare state philosophies of Blum and Franklin D. Roosevelt as well, and it was *this* position that Benjamin considered the central error of the Left; its correction was the aim of materialist education.

126. Voglin (1928), cited V, pp. 717-18 (U5, 2).

127. Cited V, p. 734 (U13, 9).

128. Voglin (1928), cited V, p. 720 [U6,2]).

129. "All social antagonisms dissolve in the fairy tale that *progrés* is the prospect of the very near future" (V, p. 716 [U4a, 1]).

130. See above, chapter 4.

131. See *Le livre des expositions universelles, 1851–1989* (Paris: Union centrale des Arts Décoratifs, 1983), pp. 137 and 310. Benjamin notes the precedent: In the 1867 exposition "the oriental quarter was the central attraction" (V, p. 253 [G8a, 3; also G9a, 6]).

132. *Le livre des expositions*, pp. 145–156.

133. The latter had its own pavilion where one could sit inside, totally engulfed in this material, that has since proven carcinogenic.

134. See Invernel, *New German Critique*, p. 76.

135. As a precursor: "The world exposition of 1889 had a historical panorama [. . . that depicted] Victor Hugo before an allegorical monument of France—a monument that was flanked by allegories of defense of the fatherland and of labor" (V, p. 664 [Q4, 5]).

136. Brochure, Pavillion de Solidarité, (Paris: Bibliothèque de l'Histoire de la Ville de Paris). Cf. Jean Cassou (1936), cited V, p. 953 (k2a, 6) on the "'naive dream'" of the universal expositions, expressed by Gustave Courbet: "'an imperishable order, order by the citizens.'"

137. V, p. 256 (G10a, 2).

138. Paul Lafargue (1904), citing Fourier, cited V, p. 770 (W3a, 2).

139. Notes to the Artwork essay (1935–36), I, p. 1039.

140. I. p. 1039.

141. I, p. 1040.

142. Léon Daudet (1930), cited V, p. 155 (C9a, 1).

143. Hitler, cited by Albert Spier [sic.], *Inside the Third Reich* (New York: Avon Books, 1970), p. 172.

144. Theses on History, cited above, section 1.

145. Letter Benjamin to Karplus, 19 July 1940, V, p. 1182.

Afterword: Revolutionary Inheritance

1. V, p. 591 (N9, 4).

2. Lisa Fitko to Gershom Scholem, telephone conversation, 15 May 1980, cited V, pp. 1191–92.

3. Letter, Henny Gurland to (her cousin) Arkadi Gurland, V, pp. 1195–96, engl. trans, from Gershom Scholem (who says incorrectly that the letter was written to Adorno), *Walter Benjamin: The Story of a Friendship* (New York: Faber and Faber, 1982), pp. 225–26 (italics, mine. Note that the italicized translation has been modified: It reads in the original, "I had to leave all papers (*alle Papiere*)—implying Benjamin's as well—whereas Scholem has translated it, "I had to leave all my papers [. . .].")

4. V, p. 1203.

5. Cited V, p. 1198.

6. Cited V, p. 1198 (italics, mine).

7. These items were sent by the Spanish officials to Figueras. Rolf Tiedemann traveled to Spain in June 1980 to investigate whether a file on Benjamin still exists that might contain the "few other papers." No file could be found. See Tiedemann's protocol of the trip, V, pp. 1199–1202.

8. When Hannah Arendt arrived at Port Bou several months later, she could find no trace of his grave (Scholem, *Walter Benjamin*, p. 226).

9. V, p. 1202.

10. Scholem, cited V, pp. 1203–94.

11. V, p. 1214.

12. V, p. 1119.

13. Benjamin, cited V, p. 1205.

14. Theses on History, I, p. 659, trans. by Harry Zohn in Walter Benjamin, *Illuminations*, ed. Hannah Arendt (New York: Shocken Books, 1969), p. 255.

15. "Über einige Motive bei Baudelaire," I, p. 611.

16. *Einbahnstrasse* (1928), IV, p. 103.

17. "Kafka," II, p. 415.

18. Theses on History, I, p. 695 (thesis VI).

19. I, p. 698 (thesis X).

20. I, p. 699 (thesis XI).

21. I, p. 700 (thesis XII).

22. I, p. 694 (thesis II).

23. V, p. 76 (1939 exposé).

24. I, p. 697 (thesis VIII).

25. The fairy tale has something very specific to do with redemption. Benjamin tells us in "Der Erzähler" that Russian folk belief "interpreted the Resurrection less as a transfiguration than (in a sense related to the fairy tale) as a disenchantment" (II, pp. 458–59).

26. Theses on History, I, p. 702. Note that this criticism was not new in 1904. It rewords one of the earliest *Passagen-Werk* notes, which calls for rejecting the "once upon a time" that lulls one in classical historical narration (V, p. 1033 [O°, 71]).

27. Theses on History, I, p. 693 (thesis I), trans. Zohn, *Illuminations*, p. 253.

28. Theses on History, I, p. 694 (thesis II), trans. (with minor changes) Zohn, *Illuminations*, p. 254.

29. "Der Erzähler," II, p. 458, trans. Zohn, *Illuminations*, p. 102.

30. V, p. 587 (N7, 5).

31. V, pp. 490–91 (K1, 2).

32. V, p. 588 (N7a, 5).

33. V, p. 571 (N1, 2).

34. See e.g., Carol Jacobs' interpretation of Benjamin in *The Dissimulating Harmony* (Baltimore: The Johns Hopkins University Press, 1978); also Irving Wohlfarth's excellent critique of Jacobs in "Walter Benjamin's 'Image of Interpretation,'" *New German Critique* 17 (spring 1979).

35. Deconstruction is a form of postmodernism, the philosophy of which, it could be argued, refers less to a chronological period than an epistemological stance. Whereas modernism in philosophical terms is wedded to the Enlightenment dream of a substantively rational society, postmodernism takes its philosophical lead from Nietzsche, Baudelaire, and Blanqui. If the terms are defined this way, Benjamin must be counted as a modernist.

36. Notes to the Theses on History, I, p. 1231.

37. V, p. 1046 (a°. 4).

38. V, p. 595 (N11, 3).

39. V, p. 592 (N9a, 3).

Bibliography

I Works by Walter Benjamin

Aufklärung für Kinder; Rundfunkvorträge. Ed. Rolf Tiedemann. Frankfurt am Main: Suhrkamp Verlag, 1985.

Benjamin papers, George Bataille Archive. Bibliothèque Nationale, Paris.

Berliner Chronik. Ed. Gershom Scholem. Frankfurt am Main: Suhrkamp Verlag, 1970.

Briefe. 2 vols. Eds. Gershom Scholem and Theodor W. Adorno. Frankfurt am Main: Suhrkamp Verlag, 1978.

Gesammelte Schriften. 7 vols. Eds. Rolf Tiedemann and Hermann Schweppenhauser, with the collaboration of Theodor W. Adorno and Gershom Scholem. Frankfurt am Main: Suhrkamp Verlag, 1972–.

II English Translations of Benjamin's Works

Charles Baudelaire: A Lyric Poet in the Era of High Capitalism. Trans. Harry Zohn. London: NLB, 1973.

"Central Park." Trans. Lloyd Spencer. *New German Critique* 34 (winter 1985): 1–27.

Illuminations. Ed. Hannah Arendt. Trans. Harry Zohn. New York: Schocken Books, 1969.

"N [Theoretics of Knowledge; Theory of Progress]." Trans. Leigh Hafrey and Richard Sieburth. *The Philosophical Forum* (Special Issue on Walter Benjamin. Ed. Gary Smith). XV, nos. 1–2 (fall/winter 1983–84): 1–40.

One Way Street and Other Writings. Intro. Susan Sontag. Trans. Edmund Jephcott and Kingsley Shorter. London: NLB, 1979.

The Origin of German Tragic Drama. Intro. George Steiner. Trans. John Osborne. London: NLB, 1977.

Understanding Brecht. Intro. Stanley Mitchell. Trans. Anna Bostock. London: NLB, 1973.

III Archives

Cabinet des Estampes, Bibliothèque Nationale, Paris.

Caisse Nationale des Monuments Historiques et des Sites, Paris.

Archiv Gerstenberg, Wietze.

Historisches Museum, Frankfurt am Main.

The Jewish National and University Library, Jerusalem.

International Museum of Photography at George Eastman House, Rochester, N.Y.

Musée Carnavalet, Paris.

Museum of Modern Art, New York.

Victoria and Albert Museum, London.

Wide World Photos, New York.

IV Books and Periodicals

Adorno, Theodor W. *Gesammelte Schriften*. Vol. 1: *Philosophische Frühschriften*. Ed. Rolf Tiedemann. Frankfurt am Main: Suhrkamp Verlag, 1973.

Adorno, Theodor W. *Prisms*. Trans. Samuel and Shierry Weber. London: Neville Spearman, 1967.

Adorno, Theodor W. *Über Walter Benjamin*. Ed. Rolf Tiedemann. Frankfurt am Main: Suhrkamp Verlag, 1970.

Agamben, Giorgio. "Un importante ritrovamento di manoscritti di Walter Benjamin," *Aut...Aut...*189/90 (1982): 4–6.

Applebaum, Stanley, Intro. and Commentary. *Bizarreries and Fantasies of Grandville*. New York: Dover Publications, 1974.

Aragon, Louis. *Le paysan de Paris*. Paris: Gallimard, 1953.

Barnicoat, John. *Posters: A Concise History*. New York: Thames & Hudson, 1985.

Barrows, Susanna. *Distorting Mirrors: Visions of the Crowd in Late Nineteenth-Century France*. New Haven: Yale University Press, 1981.

Baudelaire, Charles. *Art in Paris: 1845–1862. Salons and Other Exhibitions*. Trans. Jonathan Mayne. Ithaca: Cornell University Press, 1981.

Baudelaire, Charles. *The Flowers of Evil [Les Fleurs du mal]*. Rev. ed. Eds. Marthiel and Jackson Mathews. New York: New Directions, 1962.

Berman, Marshall. *The Experience of Modernity: All That is Solid Melts into Air*. New York: Simon and Schuster, 1982.

Bleuel, Hans Peter. *Sex and Society in Nazi Germany*. Ed. Heinrich Fraenkel. Trans. J. Maxwell Brownjohn. Philadelphia: J. B. Lippincott Company, 1973.

Bloch, Ernst. *Erbschaft dieser Zeit* [1935]. Vol. 4 of Ernst Bloch, *Gesamtausgabe*. Frankfurt am Main: Suhrkamp Verlag, 1962.

Blossfeldt, Karl. *Urformen der Kunst. Photographische Pflanzenbilder*. Ed. Karl Nierendorf. Berlin: Ernst Wasmuth, 1928.

Bohrer, Karl Heinz, ed. *Mythos und Moderne: Begriff und Bild einer Rekonstruktion*. Frankfurt am Main: Suhrkamp Verlag, 1983.

Brecht, Bertolt. *Arbeitsjournal*. 2 vols. Ed. Werner Hecht. Frankfurt am Main: Suhrkamp Verlag, 1973.

Brenner, Hildegaard. "Die Lesbarkeit der Bilder. Skizzen zum Passagenetwurf," *Alternative* 59/60 (1968): 48–61.

Buck-Morss, Susan. "Benjamin's *Passagenwerk*: Redeeming Mass Culture for the Revolution." *New German Critique* 29 (spring/summer 1983): 211–240.

Buck-Morss, Susan. "The Flâneur, the Sandwichman and the Whore: The Politics of Loitering." *New German Critique* 39 (Fall 1986): 99–140.

Buck-Morss, Susan. *The Origin of Negative Dialectics: Theodor W. Adorno, Walter Benjamin and the Frankfurt Institute*. New York: Macmillan Free Press, 1977.

Buck-Morss, Susan. "Socio-Economic Bias in the Theory of Piaget and its Implications for the Cross-Culture Controversy." *Jean Piaget: Consensus and Controversy*. Eds. Sohar and Celia Modgil. New York: Holt, Rinehart and Winston, 1982.

Buck-Morss, Susan. "Walter Benjamin: Revolutionary Writer." *New Left Review* 128 (1981): 50–75 and 129 (1981): 77–95.

Bulthaupt, Peter, ed. *Materialien zu Benjamins Thesen "Uber den Begriff der Geschichte."* Frankfurt am Main: Suhrkamp Verlag, 1975.

Bürger, Peter. *Theory of the Avant-Garde*. Trans. Michael Shaw, foreword Jochen Schulte-Sasse. *Theory and History of Literature*, vol. 4. Eds. Wlad Godzich and Jochen Schulte-Sasse. Minneapolis: University of Minnesota Press, 1984.

Colton, Joel. *Leon Blum: Humanist in Politics*. Cambridge, Mass.: The MIT Press, 1974.

Colton, Joel. "Politics and Economics in the 1930s," *From the Ancien Régime to the Popular Front: Essays in the History of Modern France in Honor of Shepard B. Clough*. Ed. Charles K. Warner. New York: Columbia University Press, 1969.

Le Corbusier. *Toward a New Architecture*. Trans. Frederick Etchells. New York: Dover Publications, 1986.

Le Corbusier. *Urbanisme*. Paris: G. Grès & Cie, 1925.

Crystal Palace Exposition: Illustrated Catalogue. London, 1851.

De Man, Paul. *Bindness and Insight: Essays in the Rhetoric of Contemporary Criticism*. 2nd ed., rev. Intro. Wlad Godzich. *Theory and History of Literature*, vol. 7. Eds. Wlad Godzich and Jochen Schulte-Sasse. Minneapolis: University of Minnesota Press, 1983.

Doderer, Klaus, ed. *Walter Benjamin und die Kinderliteratur: Aspekte der Kinderkultur in den zwanziger Jahren.* Munich: Juventa Verlag, 1988.

Espagne, Michael, and Michael Werner. "Vom Passagen-Projekt zum 'Baudelaire': Neue Handschriften zum Spätwerk Walter Benjamin." *Deutsche Vierteljahresschrift für Literaturwissenschaften und Geistesgeschichte* 4 (1984): 593–657.

Evenson, Norma. *Paris: A Century of Change, 1878–1978.* New Haven: Yale University Press, 1979.

Fletcher, Angus. *Allegory: The Theory of a Symbolic Mode.* New York: Cornell University Press, 1982.

Frank, Manfried. *Der kommende Gott: Vorlesungen Über die Neue Mythologie, I. Teil.* Frankfurt am Main: Suhrkamp Verlag, 1982.

Fuld, Werner. *Walter Benjamin: Zwischen den Stühlen.* Munich: Hanser Verlag, 1979.

Geist, Johann Friedrich. *Arcades: The History of a Building Type.* Trans. Jane O. Newman and John H. Smith. Cambridge, Mass.: The MIT Press, 1983.

Giedion, Sigfried. *Bauen im Frankreich.* 2nd ed. Leipzig: Klinkhardt & Biermann, 1928.

Habermas, Jürgen. "Bewusstmachende oder rettende Kritik—die Aktualität Walter Benjamins," *Zur Aktualität Walter Benajmins.* Ed. Siegfried Unseld. Frankfurt am Main: Suhrkamp Verlag, 1972.

Heartfield, John. *Photomontages of the Nazi Period.* New York: Universal Books, 1977.

Holsten, Siegmar. *Allegorische Darstellungen des Krieges, 1870–1918.* Vol. 27 of *Studien zur Kunst des neunzehnten Jahrhunderts.* Munich: Prestel-Verlag, 1976.

Ivernel, Philippe. "Paris, Capital of the Popular Front." *New German Critique* 39 (fall 1986): 61–84.

Jauss, Hans Robert. *Toward an Aesthetic of Reception.* Trans. Timothy Bahti. Intro. Paul de Man. *Theory and History of Literature.* vol. 2. Eds. Wlat Godzich and Jochen Schulte-Sasse. Minneapolis: University of Minnesota Press, 1982.

Jennings, Michael W. *Dialectical Images: Walter Benjamin's Theory of Literary Criticism.* Ithaca: Cornell University Press, 1987.

Kambas, Chryssoula. "Politische Aktualität. Walter Benjamin's Concept of History and the Failure of the Popular Front." *New German Critique* 39 (fall 1986): 87–98.

Kambas, Chryssoula. *Walter Benjamin im Exil: Zum Verhältnis von Literaturpolitik und Ästhetik.* Tübingen: Max Niemeyer Verlag, 1983.

Kelly, Alfred H. *The Descent of Darwin: The Popularization of Darwin in Germany, 1860–1914.* Chapel Hill: University of North Carolina Press, 1981.

Kiersch, Gerhard, et al. *Berliner Alltag im dritten Reich.* Düsseldorf: Droste Verlag, 1981.

Kirchner, Gottfried. *Fortuna in der Dichtung und Emblematik des Barok: Tradition und Bedeutungswandel eines Motivs.* Stuttgart: J. B. Metzlerische Verlagsbuchhandlung, 1970.

Lacis, Asja. *Revolutionär im Beruf: Berichte über proletarisches Theater, über Meyerhold, Brecht, Benjamin und Piscator*. Ed. Hildegaard Brenner. Munich: Regner & Bernhard, 1971.

Lindner, Burkhardt. "Habilitationsakte Walter Benjamin: Uber ein 'akademisches Trauerspiel' und über ein Vorkapitel der 'Frankfurter Schule' (Horkheimer, Adorno)." *Zeitschrift für Literaturwissenschaft und Linguistik* 53/54 (1984): 147–65.

Le Livre des expositions universelles, 1851–1989. Paris: Union centrale des Arts Decoratifs, 1983.

Lorant, Stefan. *Sieg Heil! (Hail to Victory): An Illustrated History of Germany from Bismarck to Hitler*. New York: W. W. Norton & Company, 1974.

Lough, John, and Muriel Lough. *An Introduction to Nineteenth Century France*. London: Longman, 1978.

Löwenthal, Leo. "The Integrity of the Intellectual: In Memory of Walter Benjamin." (1982) In *Critical Theory and Frankfurt Theorists*. New Brunswick, NJ: Transaction Publishers, 1989, p. 73ff.

Löwy, Michael. "A l'écart des tous les courants et à la croisée des chimens: Walter Benjamin." *Rédemption et Utopie: Le judaïsme libertaire en europe centrale. Une étude d'affinité electiv*. Paris: Presses Universitaires de France, 1988.

Lough, John, and Muriel Lough. *An Introduction to Nineteenth Century France*. London: Longman, 1978.

Lukács, Georg. *History and Class Consciousness* [1923]. Trans. Rodney Livingstone. Cambridge, Mass.: The MIT Press, 1971.

Marx, Karl. "Der 18te Brumaire des Louis Napoleon," *Die Revolution (1852)*. Karl Marx and Friedrich Engels, *Werke*, vol. 8. Berlin: Dietz Verlag, 1960.

Menninghaus, Winfried. *Walter Benjamins Theorie der Sprachmagie*. Frankfurt am Main: Suhrkamp Verlag, 1980.

Miller, Michael B. *The Bon Marché: Bourgeois Culture and the Department Store, 1869–1920*. Princeton: Princeton University Press, 1981.

Mosse, George. *The Nationalization of the Masses*. New York: Horward Fertig, 1975.

Naylor, Gilian. *The Bauhaus Reassessed: Sources and Design Theory*. New York: E. P. Dutton, 1985.

Passagen. Walter Benjamins Urgeschichte des XIX Jahrhunderts. Munich: Wilhelm Fink Verlag, 1984.

Peterich, Eckart. *Göttinnen im Spiegel der Kunst*. Olten und Breisgau: Walter Verlag, 1954.

Pichois, Claude, and François Ruchon. *Iconographie de Baudelaire*. Geneva: Pierre Cailler, 1960.

Rabinbach, Anson. "Between Enlightenment and Apocalypse: Benjamin, Bloch and Modern German Jewish Messianism," *New German Critique* 34 (winter 1985): 78–124.

Roberts, Julian. *Walter Benjamin*. Atlantic Highlands, N. J.: Humanities Press, 1983.

Bibliography

Russell, John. *Paris*. New York: Harry N. Abrams, 1983.

Schäfer, Hans Dieter. *Das gespaltene Bewusstsein: Deutsche Kultur und Lebenswirklichkeit, 1933–45*. Munich: Carl Hanser Verlag, 1982.

Schiller-Lerg, Sabine. *Walter Benjamin und der Rundfunk: Programarbeit zwischen Theorie und Praxis*. Vol. 1 of *Rundfunkstudien*, ed. Winfried B. Lerg. New York: K. G. Saur, 1984.

Scholem, Gershom. *From Berlin to Jerusalem: Memories of My Youth*. Trans. Harry Zohn. New York: Schocken Books, 1980.

Scholem, Gershom. *Kabbalah*. New York: Quadrangle, 1974.

Scholem, Gershom. *Major Trends in Jewish Mysticism*. New York: Schocken Books, 1946.

Scholem, Gershom. *The Messianic Idea in Judaism, and Other Essays in Jewish Spirituality*. New York: Schocken Books, 1971.

Scholem, Gershom. *On Jews and Judaism in Crisis: Selected Essays*. Ed. Werner J. Dannhauser. New York: Schocken Books, 1976.

Scholem, Gershom. *Walter Benjamin: The Story of a Friendship*. Eds. Karen Ready and Gary Smith. London: Faber and Faber, 1982.

Simmel, Georg. *Goethe* [1913]. 3rd ed. Leipzig: Klinkhardt & Biermann, 1918.

Smith, Gary. "Benjamins Berlin." *Wissenschaft in Berlin*. Eds. Tilmann Buddensieg, et al. Berlin: Gebr. Mann Verlag, 1987, pp. 98–102.

Speer, Albert. *Inside the Third Reich*. New York: Avon Books, 1970.

Stahl, Fritz. *Honoré Daumier*. Berlin: Rudolf Mosse Buchverlag, 1930.

Sternberger, Dolf. *Panorama, oder Ansichten vom 19. Jahrhundert* [1938]. Frankfurt am Main: Suhrkamp Verlag, 1974.

Taylor, Robert R. *The Word in Stone: The Role of Architecture in National Socialist Ideology*. Berkeley: University of California Press, 1974.

Tiedemann, Rolf. "Historical Materialism or Political Messianism? An Interpretation of the Theses 'On the Concept of History.'" *The Philosophical Forum* XV, nos. 1–2 (fall/winter 1983–84): 71–104.

Tiedemann, Rolf. *Studien zur Philosophie Walter Benjamins*. Intro. Theodor W. Adorno. Frankfurt am Main: Suhrkamp Verlag, 1973.

Über Walter Benjamin, mit Beiträgen von Theodor W. Adorno, et al. Frankfurt am Main: Suhrkamp Verlag, 1968.

Valéry, Paul. *Idée Fixe*. Trans. David Paul. New York: Pantheon Books, 1965.

Walter Benjamin zu Ehren: Sonderausgabe aus Anlass des 80. Geburtstages von Walter Benjamin am 15. Juli 1972. Frankfurt am Main; Suhrkamp Verlag, 1972.

Wiesenthal, Liselotte. *Zur Wissenschaftstheorie Walter Benjamins*. Frankfurt am Main: Athenäum, 1973.

Williams, Rosalind H. *Dream Worlds: Mass Consumption in Late Nineteenth-Century France.* Berkeley: University of California Press, 1982.

Wismann, Heinz, ed. *Walter Benjamin et Paris: Colloque international 27–29 juin 1983.* Paris: Cerf, 1986.

Witte, Bernd. *Walter Benjamin.* Reinbek bei Hamburg: Rowohlt, 1985.

Witte, Bernd. *Walter Benjamin: Der Intellektuelle als Kritiker. Untersuchungen zu seinem Frühwerk.* Stuttgart: J. B. Metzlerische Verlagsbuchhandlung, 1976.

Wohlfarth, Irving. "Et Cetera? The Historian as Chiffonnier?" *New German Critique* 39 (Fall 1986): 142–68.

Wohlfarth, Irving. "Walter Benjamin's 'Image of Interpretation.'" *New German Critique* 17 (spring 1979): 70–98.

Wolin, Richard. *Walter Benjamin: An Aesthetics of Redemption.* New York: Columbia University Press, 1982.

v. Zglinicki, Friedrich. *Der Weg des Films: Die Geschichte der Kinematographie und ihrer Vorläufer.* Berlin: Rembrandt Verlag, 1956.

Illustration Credits

Barnicoat, *A Concise History of Posters*: 8.2, 8.7.

Bayer, Herbert: 8.4, 8.5.

Bibliothèque Nationale, Paris: 3.3, 3.6, 5.5, 5.6, 9.30.

Bleuel, Hans Peter, *Sex and Society in Nazi Germany*: 9.23, 9.24.

Blossfeldt, Karl, *Urformen der Kunst*: 5.24, 5.25, 5.26, 5.27.

Courtesy of Theodor Bruggemann, Collection of Children's Literature, University of Cologne: 9.2, 9.3.

Buck-Morss, Susan, private collection, 2.2, 9.4.

Caisse Nationale des Monuments Historiques et des Sites, Paris (Arch. Phot. Paris/ S.P.A.D.E.M.): 9.21, 9.22.

Le Corbusier: 5.14, 5.15, 5.16, 5.17, 9.6, 9.14, 9.18, 9.31.

Catalogue of the Crystal Palace Exposition: 4.2, 5.1, 5.2, 9.5, 9.9, 9.10.

Daumier, Honoré: 5.12, 5.13.

Dürer, Albrecht: 6.6.

Eisenstaedt, Alfred: 8.6.

Evenson, Norma, *Paris: A Century of Change*: 4.4.

Fourier, Charles: 9.17.

Fuld, Werner, *Walter Benjamin: Zwischen den Stühlen*: 5.9 (private collection, Gunther Anders).

Geist, Johann Friedrich, *Arcades: The History of a Building Type*: 2.1, 2.3, 2.4, 3.5 (Meyer-Veden).

Giedion, Sigfried, *Bauen im Frankreich*: 3.7, 5.4, 9.7, 9.8.

Archiv Gerstenberg, Wierze: 9.15.

Grandville, *Un autre monde*. Captions by Stanley Applebaum, *Bizarreries and Fantasies of Grand-ville*: 4.6, 5.3, 5.10, 5.18, 5.19, 5.20, 5.21, 5.22, 5.23.

Guys, Constantin: 9.16.

Heartfield, John, *Photomontages of the Nazi Period*: 3.1, 3.2.

Historisches Museum, Frankfurt am Main: 9.26, 9.27.

Holsten, Siegmar, *Allegorische Darstellungen des Krieges, 1870–1918*: 6.5.

International Museum of Photography at George Eastman House, Rochester, N.Y.: 5.7.

The Jewish National and University Library, Jerusalem: 1.4.

Kiersch, Gerhard, et al., *Berliner Alltag im dritten Reich*: 9.28, 9.34, 9.35, 9.38.

Kirchner, Gottfried, *Fortuna in der Dichtung*: 6.1, 6.2.

Klee, Paul: 4.5.

Lacis, Asja, *Revolutionär im Beruf*: 1.3.

Lewis, Martin (photo by Jon Ries): 9.15.

Le Livre des expositions universelles: 4.3, 9.33.

Lorant, Stefan, *Sieg Heil!*: 6.8, 9.36, 9.37.

Lough, John, and Muriel Lough, *An Introduction to Nineteenth Century France*: 5.11.

Courtesy of Nils Ole Lund, University of Aarhus, Denmark: 8.3.

Miroir du monde, Paris: 9.19.

Museé Carnavalet, Paris: 0.1.

Museum of Modern Art, New York: 6.7.

Naylor, Gilian, *The Bauhaus Reassessed*: 9.11 (Victoria and Albert Museum), 9.12 (Bauhaus Archiv).

Peterich, Eckart, *Gottinnen im Spiegel der Kunst*: 6.3, 6.4.

Pichois, Claude and François Ruchon, *Iconographie de Baudelaire*: 6.9, 6.10, 6.11.

Piranesi, Giovanni Battista: 8.1.

Rohwolt Verlag, Berlin: 1.1, 1.2.

Russell, John, *Paris*: 9.13 (Sirot-Angel)

Schäfer, Hans Dieter, *Das gespaltene Bewusstsein*: 9.20.

Illustration Credits

Sternberger, Dolf, *Panorama, oder Ansichten vom 19. Jahrhundert*: 3.4.

Taylor, Robert R., *The Word in Stone*: 9.29.

Victoria and Albert Museum, London: 5.8.

Wide World Photos: 9.1, 9.32.

v. Zglinicki, *Der Weg des Films*: 4.1.

Index

Index

Index

Index

Studies in Contemporary German Social Thought

Thomas McCarthy, General Editor

Theodor W. Adorno, *Against Epistemology: A Metacritique*

Theodor W. Adorno, *Prisms*

Karl-Otto Apel, *Understanding and Explanation: A Transcendental-Pragmatic Perspective*

Richard J. Bernstein, editor, *Habermas and Modernity*

Ernst Bloch, *Natural Law and Human Dignity*

Ernst Bloch, *The Principle of Hope*

Ernst Bloch, *The Utopian Function of Art and Literature: Selected Essays*

Hans Blumenberg, *The Genesis of the Copernican World*

Hans Blumenberg, *The Legitimacy of the Modern Age*

Hans Blumenberg, *Work on Myth*

Susan Buck-Morss, *The Dialectics of Seeing: Walter Benjamin and the Arcades Project*

Helmut Dubiel, *Theory and Politics: Studies in the Development of Critical Theory*

John Forester, editor, *Critical Theory and Public Life*

David Frisby, *Fragments of Modernity: Theories of Modernity in the Work of Simmel, Kracauer and Benjamin*

Hans-Georg Gadamer, *Philosophical Apprenticeships*

Hans-Georg Gadamer, *Reason in the Age of Science*

Jürgen Habermas, *On the Logic of the Social Sciences*

Jürgen Habermas, *The Philosophical Discourse of Modernity: Twelve Lectures*

Jürgen Habermas, *Philosophical-Political Profiles*

Jürgen Habermas, editor, *Observations on "The Spiritual Situation of the Age"*

Hans Joas, *G. H. Mead: A Contemporary Re-examination of His Thought*

Reinhart Koselleck, *Critique and Crisis: Enlightenment and the Pathogenesis of Modern Society*

Reinhart Koselleck, *Futures Past: On the Semantics of Historical Time*

Harry Liebersohn, *Fate and Utopia in German Sociology, 1887–1923*

Herbert Marcuse, *Hegel's Ontology and the Theory of Historicity*

Guy Oakes, *Weber and Rickert: Concept Formation in the Cultural Sciences*

Claus Offe, *Contradictions of the Welfare State*

Claus Offe, *Disorganized Capitalism: Contemporary Transformations of Work and Politics*

Helmut Peuket, *Science, Action, and Fundamental Theology: Toward a Theology of Communicative Action*

Joachim Ritter, *Hegel and the French Revolution: Essays on the* Philosophy of Right

Alfred Schmidt, *History and Structure: An Essay on Hegelian-Marxist and Structuralist Theories of History*

Dennis Schmidt, *The Ubiquity of the Finite: Hegel, Heidegger, and the Entitlements of Philosophy*